Prince Nikola of Montenegro by Ivan Rendić, 1884.

Princess Milena of Montenegro

For my niece Anna Maia

'Nikola and Milena' is first and foremost a collaboration with the Museum of King Nikola I of Montenegro in Cetinje. This project came about through the shared desire to bring new perspectives to the story of Montenegro and its Royal Family. My aim has been to shed light on the history of a small nation which has played a large role in European history. The research for the project constantly revealed how deeply Montenegro was involved in the major events of the late nineteenth and early twentieth century. Along with the larger themes of the nation's history, I hope I have succeeded in bringing to life the personalities of the members of the Royal Family as well as the simplicity and charm of life in Cetinje during the period. With those thoughts in mind, I gratefully acknowledge the contribution of the director and staff of the Museum of King Nikola I. My special thanks are due to Director Andje Kapičić for her knowledge and expertise and to Tanja Jović and Beba Ivanišević for guiding us through the Museum's voluminous archives and photographic material. Among the many people who have given indispensable help my special thanks go to Nataša Dinulović, Kai Gui and Judy Pederneski-Widmann for research, translation, photographic assistance and, not least, their comments and suggestions which have been a great help throughout this project. Thanks are due to Professor Radoš Ljušić, Jelena Paunović, Brenda Ralph Lewis, Tanja Petrushevski and Danica Vulović.

Marco Houston

FIRST PUBLISHED IN THE UNITED KINGDOM 2003. © Leppi Publications
BRITISH LIBRARY CATALOGUING IN PUBLICATION DATA

Leppi Publications
Nikola & Milena, King & Queen of the Black Mountain
ISBN 095216444-2

Copyright © 2003 Leppi Publications
Savonarola Editoriale Inc.

PRINTED IN ITALY BY EUROPRINT INDUSTRIA GRAFICA
REPRODUCTION BY SENA JULIA PUBLICATUS LTD

CAPTION COMPILATION © LEPPI PUBLICATIONS
PHOTOGRAPHIC CREDITS: PHOTOGRAPHS SUPPLIED BY THE MUSEUM OF KING NIKOLA I & SAVONAROLA EDITORIALE INC.

Leppi Publications: 805 Finchley Road, London NW11 8DP.
Tel +44 (0) 208 458 0167 e-mail: sales@leppi.co.uk Web: www.leppi.co.uk

Leppi PUBLICATIONS

NIKOLA & MILENA

King & Queen of the Black Mountain

Marco Houston

L'EPPI PUBLICATIONS

Nikola and Milena: the last, greatest rulers of Montenegro.

*T*he reign of King Nikola and Queen Milena spanned the latter half of the nineteenth century and the first two decades of the twentieth; in all they occupied the Montenegrin throne for fifty-eight eventful years. The bright boy from Njeguši village and the pretty girl from nearby Čevo started their lives as ordinary Montenegrins. Fate chose to place them at the centre of European affairs and, ultimately, to discard them at a moment of upheaval. Their story forms the core of this book. However, the Petrović-Njegoš dynasty's relation to the nation was so close, organically so, that Nikola and Milena's lives can only be understood through the perspective of Montenegro's extraordinary history.

The rise of the Petrović-Njegoš dynasty was the culmination of a long historical process, during which the ruling dynasty and the nation had grown almost symbiotically, each shaping the other, often through the most brutal shared experience. It was crucial, no doubt the Montenegrins would have not had it otherwise, that the ruling dynasty was not, as was so often the case in dynastic history, imposed on the nation, but grew from its tribal-warrior tradition. The Vladikas of Cetinje were elected rulers whose authority was dependent on the consent of their fellow tribesmen.

This meant that Montenegrin rulers had above all else to be respected as tribal leaders and warriors. That the Petrović-Njegoš clan rose to become princes and kings testifies to both their merit and determination. They needed both qualities in good measure for to rule Montenegro was not a matter of wealth and power, though both eventually played their part, more so the desire to unite the tribes and fulfil the country's historic mission of liberating and unifying the South Slav people.

As a statement of intent it was heroic; as a political decision it was near suicidal. The Ottoman Turks at the height of their power brought the Balkans under their sway, except the Montenegrins who retreated to their mountain stronghold and waged guerrilla warfare on their would be conquerors. The Ottomans nearly succeeded in annihilating that resistance, only the combination of undaunted defiance and a harsh, barren battleground ensured that the last banner of Balkan freedom could not be torn down.

That battleground, namely Montenegro's karstic mountain ranges, was both the blessing and the curse of the nation. The Montenegrins were trapped in the inhospitable hinterlands of the southern Dinaric mountains. It afforded them protection from their enemies but also brought isolation and extreme poverty.

Isolation, however, did not mean that Montenegro was forgotten, left in peace to get by as best it could. The Ottoman Turks and the Venetian Republic both sought to use the mountaineers for their own ends and subsequently, as Europe developed the great imperial nation states of the eighteenth and nineteenth centuries, a veritable cacophony of political and military interests threatened.

Montenegro's existence at the sharp end of history gave the nation a very special place in European affairs. Its diminutive size and strategic importance

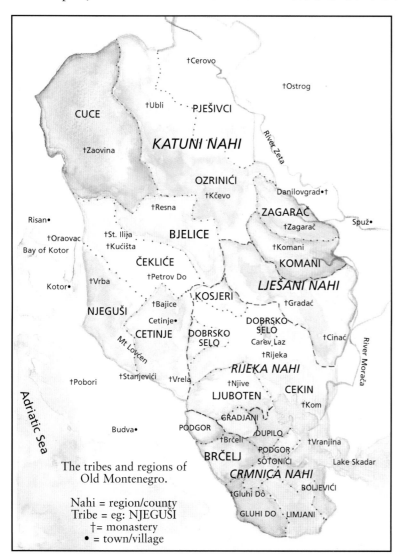

The tribes and regions of
Old Montenegro.

Nahi = region/county
Tribe = eg: NJEGUŠI
† = monastery
• = town/village

meant that great issues were immediate and often highly personal affairs. Its political importance was in direct inverse proportion to its size and inevitably this took its toll on the nation's economic, social and cultural development. A tribal-warrior society continued well into the nineteenth century for there was little opportunity to develop more modern structures.

Nikola I, King of Montenegro.

National survival was dependent on the strength of the tribes and the quality of the nation's leaders. In that regard at least Montenegro was fortunate: the tribesmen were peerless fighters and the Petrović-Njegoš dynasty provided several indisputably great leaders. Vladika Danilo I and Vladika Petar I were exceptional and brave men, Vladika Rade a great poet and philosopher as well as a wise ruler.

The royal era provided two significant as well as controversial rulers. In his brief and violent reign, Prince Danilo I provided a bridge between *de facto* independence and statehood. Danilo's negative characteristics were as striking as his achievements were substantial. The potential for antagonism between princely rule and the nation was evident throughout his reign and culminated with the Prince's murder in 1860.

The last Petrović-Njegoš ruler took the dynasty to unforeseen heights, from which it fell in the upheavals of the Great War. In his long and successful reign, Prince (King from 1910) Nikola I not only gained full recognition for the nation, he also greatly increased its territory. His domestic efforts in education and infrastructure are also praiseworthy; the beginnings of the modern state emerge under his patronage. For those achievements he has every right to be considered the greatest of the Petrović-Njegoš rulers.

He was also an exceptional personality: a patriarchal ruler of his people, a skilled dynast, a statesman, a diplomat and a poet; a man who elicited admiration and exacerbation, praise and condemnation in equal measure. Montenegro's renown was in good part due to the ruler's many talents.

Not the least of those talents was a subtle and acute political ability. In the uncertain and competitive world of nineteenth century Balkan politics, Nikola's adroit populist sensibility enabled him to become the most popular Balkan ruler of his era and a romantic figure on the European stage, while his diplomatic skills and finely honed judgement navigated the dangerous waters of politics and war. Until the very end of his reign, Montenegro was spared the military adventures and upheaval endured by some of its neighbours. At times even the peace of Europe depended on the ruler's decisions; a rasher man on the Montenegrin throne could have plunged not only the Balkans but all Europe into war.

Ultimately, however, Nikola's patriarchal conservatism and the negative aspects of his political talents proved pivotal in the unravelling of his achievements. He was not a man to step aside and let others take charge, nor one to shy away from confrontation. Having been lauded as the worthiest and ablest of rulers, his reign ended deep in the mire of domestic crises, internecine feuds and political controversy. As Yugoslavia, his long held dream, was being forged in the fires of World War One, he was forced to the sidelines and vilified as the greatest of villains.

That the independent state of Montenegro and its ruling dynasty rose and fell together was appropriate, perhaps even inevitable. Although the ruler and the nation were no longer in harmony they were still inextricably bound together. After two hundred and twenty-two years the last Petrović-Njegoš ruler was exiled and Nikola's grandson, Serbia's Aleksandar Karadjordjević, became Yugoslavia's first king as Montenegro became a province of Serbia, itself one of the three constituent parts of the new state.

Montenegro's heroic, tragic history made it a nation unlike any other, one which has provided an array of remarkable characters and inspirational leaders. The final representatives from that select group, Nikola Petrović-Njegoš and his consort, Milena Vukotić, were the last but also the greatest rulers of Montenegro.

Ante Kapičić

Andje Kapičić
Director
The Museum of King Nikola I

Contents

The Rise, Fall and Rebirth of Montenegro.

The Romantic Ruler: Prince Nikola, 1841-1903.

The Royal Marriages.

The Fall of Royal Montenegro: 1903-1923.

The Leading Characters In The Story

The Montenegrin & Serbian Dynasties

Montenegro: Petrović-Njegoš.

Vladika Danilo: *the founder of the Montenegrin dynasty of Petrović-Njegoš, reign 1696-1735.*
Vladika Sava: *reign 1735-1781.*
Vladika Vasilije: *reign 1750-1766 (jointly with Vladika Sava).*
Šćepan Mali (Steven the Small): *reign 1767-1773. The usurper and ruler of Montenegro, of unknown origin.*
Vladika Petar I: *reign 1784-1830.*
Vladika Rade (Petar II): *reign 1830-1851.*
Pero Tomov Petrović: *Vladika Rade's brother, after Rade's death a rival to the throne of Prince Danilo.*
Djordjije Savov Petrović: *Vladika Rade's cousin, refused to become vladika.*
Prince Danilo (also known as Zeko Stankov): *Reign 1851-1860. The first Prince of Montenegro, murdered in Kotor.*
Princess Darinka: *Prince Danilo's wife, born Kvekić.*
Princess Olga: *daughter of Prince Danilo and Princess Darinka.*
Vojvoda Mirko: *brother of Prince Danilo and father of King Nikola I.*
Prince (King from 1910) Nikola I: *reign 1860-1918.*
Princess (Queen from 1910) Milena: *Prince Nikola's wife, born Milena Vukotić of Čevo.*
Princess Ljubica Zorka: *eldest daughter of Nikola I and wife of Petar Karadjordjević, future King of Serbia.*
Princess Milica: *Nikola I's second daughter, wife of Grand Duke Petar Nikolayevich Romanov.*
Princess Anastazija (Stane): *Nikola I's third daughter, wife of Prince Georgi Romanov of Leichtenberg, and subsequently of Grand Duke Nikolai Nikolayevich Romanov.*
Princess Marija: *Nikola I's fourth daughter, died at the age of 16.*
Crown Prince Danilo: *Nikola I's eldest son.*
Princess Milica-Yutta: *Crown Prince Danilo's German born wife, Princess Augusta Charlotte of Mecklenburg-Strelitz.*
Princess Jelena (Queen Elena of Italy): *Nikola I's fifth daughter, wife of King Vittorio Emanuele III of Italy.*
Princess Ana: *Nikola I's sixth daughter, wife of Franz Josef Battenberg.*
Princess Sofija: *Nikola I's seventh daughter, died in infancy.*
Prince Mirko: *Nikola I's second son.*
Princess Natalija: *Prince Mirko's wife, daughter of Colonel Aleksandar Konstantinović.*
Princess Ksenija: *Nikola I's eighth daughter.*
Princess Vjera: *Nikola I's ninth daughter.*
Prince Petar: *Nikola I's third son.*
Prince Mihailo: *Prince Mirko's son, after Crown Prince Danilo's abdication Heir To The Throne.*
Prince Nikola: *Prince Mihailo's son.*

Serbia: Karadjordjević & Obrenović.

Karadjordjević.

Karadjordje (Black George): *leader of the Serbian Uprising of 1804 and founder of the Karadjordjević dynasty. Reign 1804-1813, murdered 1817.*
Prince Aleksandar: *reign 1842-1858.*
King Petar: *pretender to the throne 1858-1903, reign 1903-1921.*
Prince Djordje: *The Heir To The Throne 1903-1909, renounced his rights as heir in 1909.*
King Aleksandar: *Djordje's younger brother and Heir To The Throne 1909-1914, Regent 1914-1921, King of the Serbs, Croats and Slovenes 1921-1929, King of Yugoslavia 1929-1934, murdered.*

Obrenović

Prince Miloš: *reign 1815-1839 and 1858-1860.*
Prince Milan: *reign 1839.*
Prince Mihailo: *reign 1839-1842 and 1860-1868, murdered.*
Prince (King from 1882) Milan: *reign 1868-1889.*
King Aleksandar: *reign 1889-1903, murdered.*

Leading Serbian & Montenegrin Politicians

Božo Petrović-Njegoš: *King Nikola I's cousin and Montenegrin First Minister 1879-1905.*
Gavro Vuković: *Montenegrin Foreign Minister 1889-1905.*
Simo Popović: *Serbian writer and Montenegrin politician, Minister of Education and Nikola I's personal secretary.*

Lazar Mijušković: *Montenegrin Minister of Finance 1903-1905, Prime Minister and Foreign Minister 1905-1906, Prime Minister and Foreign Minister 1915-1916.*
Andrija Radović: *Montenegrin Minister of Finance 1905-1906, Prime Minister and Foreign Minister 1907, Prime Minister and Foreign Minister 1916-1917.*
Lazar Tomanović: *Montenegrin Prime Minister and Foreign Minister, Minister of Justice 1907-1912.*
Niko Hajduković: *Montenegrin Defence Minister, Interior Minister 1917-1919.*
Evgenije Popović: *Montenegrin Prime Minister and Foreign Minister 1917-1919.*
Pero Šoć: *Montenegrin Minister of Justice, Education and Religion 1917-1919, acting Foreign Minister1918-1919, Minister of Justice 1919-1921.*
Jovan Plamenac: *Montenegrin Prime Minister and Foreign Minister 1919-1921*
Nikola Pašić: *The leading Serbian politician from 1904 until 1926.*

A brief note on names, dates, and pronunciation.

Serbo-Croat diacritics have been used for South Slav names and places: 'the Petrović clan from Njeguši village'. Other Slav names, such as Russian, keep as close as possible to the Slav spelling but without diacritic marks: 'Nikolai Nikolayevich'. This is for the reader to more easily differentiate between South Slav and Slav names and places without losing the sense of a general connection between the various Slavic countries and cultures. Other names and titles employ commonly used variants: 'Franz Josef of Austria-Hungary'. For both the Montenegrin 'Knjaz' and the Serbian 'Knez' the title 'Prince' is used.

Dates throughout use the Gregorian Calendar, although for some contemporary quotations the Julian Calendar dates have been adhered to. In such cases the Gregorian Calendar is signified in brackets thus: October 7 [October 19] 1841. For reader reference: the difference between the Julian calendar is twelve days in arrears of the Gregorian throughout the nineteenth century and thirteen days from 1900 onwards.

Diacritics and the pronunciation of Serbo-Croat names and places.
's' as in 'street'.
'š' becomes 'ssh' as in 'sharp'.
'c' is pronounced 'tz'. Therefore 'Cetinje' is pronounced 'Tzetinje', 'Podgorica' is 'Podgoritza'.
'ć' and 'č' are accentuated 'ch'. Therefore 'Petrović' is pronounced 'Petrovich' and 'Morača' is pronounced 'Moracha'.
'z' is soft, as 's' in 'rose'.
'ž' as 'j' in the French *'journal'*.
'dj' as in 'George'.
"nj" as in the French *'campagne'* and also as in 'Cetinje'.

Glossary.

Some words and titles have been kept in the original language. For reader reference an abbreviated glossary.

Aga = Ottoman title approximating to Lord.
Ban = Austro-Hungarian Provincial Governor
Bey = Ottoman Landowner: 'the beys of Bosnia-Herzegovina'.
Grand Vizier = First Minister of the Ottoman Sultan.
Nahi = Montenegrin region/county: 'Katuni Nahi'.
Kmet = Serf.
Pasha = Ottoman Provincial Governor.
Perjanik = Montenegrin policeman and the Royal Family's personal bodyguards.
Raia = flock/peasantry: 'the Sultan's raia'.
Sandžak = A Province or an administrative area within the Ottoman Empire.
Serdar = Lesser Montenegrin title for tribal notables.
Sublime Porte = The Ottoman Government.
Vali = Used interchangeably with Pasha.
Vladika = Orthodox Christian Bishop.
Vojvoda = Montenegrin (and also Serb/South Slav) Chieftain/Duke.
Župan/Grand Župan = Serbian ruler/King.

*The capital of the Ottoman Empire is Istanbul except for chapter one in which Constantinople is used. The Slav variation of Tsarigrad is not used. The Ottoman Empire and its subjects are also referred to as 'Turkey' and 'Turks' as this was common usage during the period. The reader will be aware that this always refers to a supranational empire with subjects drawn from a multi-national and multi-denominational population.

Cetinje's tribute to its founder, Ivan Crnojević (1465-1490), marking the five hundredth anniversary since Cetinje became the capital of Montenegro (1482-1982).

10

The crucible of history and the last outpost of Balkan freedom.

And now a wonder new comes into view: Observest thou ~ if thou thy God dost know! How much is sea and how much is of shore? View Bosnia's plains! Herzegovina see! Albania spreading straight unto the waves! Seest thou how much is Montenegrin soil? One single cloud doth surely cover all![1]

Njegoš: 'The Mountain Wreath'

Since pre-recorded history the Balkans has been the meeting place for peoples and a cradle of cultures. Its geography, the ebb and flow of human migrations, and not least invasion and conquest, have all contributed dramatically to a remarkable history which is characterised by dynamic change and sharp divisions. It is without doubt one of the most diverse and complex developments on the European continent.

The geography of the region has been of particular importance to its cultural and political development. The Balkans, which takes its name from the Turkish word for mountain, is the most easterly of Europe's three southern peninsulas. It is roughly triangular in shape, narrowing at its southernmost point, while to the north it shades gradually into mainland Europe. Its northern boundary is political rather than geographical and has shifted with political changes. The countries generally considered to be definitely Balkan are Albania, Bulgaria, Greece, Romania and the six former republics of Yugoslavia of which Montenegro is the smallest.

Although much of the peninsula is bordered by water, namely the Black, Aegean, Mediterranean and Adriatic seas, it is nonetheless readily open to penetration: to the northeast, where Romania borders the Ukrainian steppe, invasions have been frequent; to the northwest the Danube valley and the Hungarian plain, which extends into Serbia, allow for easy entry; to the east the straits of the Bosphorus and the Dardanelles create a link with Anatolia and Asia; to the west Italy is accessible across the Adriatic; to the south the Aegean and Mediterranean islands provide a connection with the eastern Mediterranean and north Africa.

Similarly, the mountain ranges have not brought protection. Being discontinuous they, too, present only a partial barrier. From the northwest the Dinaric Mountains run from the alpine heights of Slovenia southward down the Adriatic coastline to Albania, then inland and eastward as the Pindus range that stretches into central Greece. From the north, beyond Romania, the Carpathians run southward, then southwest as they cross the Danube and then, as the Balkan range, eastward across Bulgaria. To the south, the Macedonian and Thracian mountains extend into Greece.

The Balkan mountain ranges have exerted another important influence by fragmenting the peninsula into small units and isolating ethnic groups from one another. This has resulted in a lack of cultural and economic integration. It has proved an important development and one that has been accentuated by the region's rivers. The minor rivers often have their source in the coastal mountains and run into the nearest sea, too narrow to carry water traffic they restrict movement along the coastal areas by cutting ravines.

The one major exception to that rule is the massive River Danube which flows from Germany, via Central Europe and the Balkans, to the Black Sea. However, its considerable benefits for trade and communication are offset by low water in the summer, marshlands, the silting up of the Black Sea Delta and the narrow thoroughfare of the Iron Gates between Serbia and Romania. The Danube, like the mountain ranges has, in fact, aided outside influence by connecting the Balkans to Central Europe and the powerful states that have developed there. Furthermore, its Black Sea terminus gave control of movement to two major powers to the east, the Byzantines and their successors the Ottoman Turks, and latterly Russia.

The development and interaction of the various Balkan cultures naturally reflect these enduring influences. Whilst pre-recorded Balkan history is still treated by some in a partisan and contentious way, it is clear that many groups have developed, settled in or passed through the region, interacting and sharing culture with many positive results.

Interestingly, too, for a region that has come to be considered as economically and politically retrograde, the Balkan civilisations of pre-recorded history took first rank amongst European cultures. Along with East Central Europe, the Balkans formed the core of earliest European civilisation which discovered the use of copper and developed a written script.

However, the negative potential of the region's location and fragmented internal structure was a latent danger waiting to be fully realised. At the meeting point of two continents, the Balkans were soon of vital importance in the political and military struggles between Asian and European powers during classical history.

The rise of the Romans marked a crucial turning point for the Balkan peoples. As the Roman Empire expanded into the greatest power of the ancient world, the Balkan tribes were conquered, although colonisation and 'Romanization' was only partial. The Romans mainly settled along the Adriatic coast and the River Danube. The mountainous interior remained more lightly colonised,

(Below and facing page) Two views of the ruins of the Roman town of Duklja, situated just outside Montenegro's present day capital, Podgorica. The early medieval Montenegrin state took its name from the Roman settlement, which was changed to Zeta by the Byzantines and finally became Crna Gora (Black Mountain), of which the most commonly used form is the Italian-Venetian variant, Montenegro.

which facilitated the survival of indigenous cultural characteristics.

The Roman conquest nonetheless encompassed most of the Balkans, whose people in turn made their contribution to the Empire's fortunes. History records numerous examples of emperors being drawn from Balkan stock. Notable among these were Diocletian whose reforms saved the Empire and, who in AD293 chose a fellow Balkan, an exceptional soldier called Galerius, as his co-ruler; and, most famously, Constantine the Great who was born in Naissus, modern day Niš in Serbia. Constantine converted the Empire to Christianity and moved the capital to Constantinople.

It was also during the later Roman period and the Byzantine era that one of the most enduring of Balkan characteristics came to the fore: the struggle for internal integration against powerful centrifugal forces. The decline of the Roman Empire in the third and fourth centuries and its subsequent division between east and west in AD395, brought the advent of Constantinople and Rome as rival political and religious centres. By the sixth century a division between Roman north and west and Hellenic south and east had developed and, over time, an ongoing schism was created between related cultures and peoples, one that would greatly aid future conquerors. In which regard, the Empire's eventual religious split between Orthodox and Catholic Christianity in the eleventh century proved of profound significance.

Incorporated into Byzantium, the eastern half of the divided Empire which bore the task of resisting the barbarian invasions that increased after the fall of Rome in AD476, Balkan soldiers proved amongst its finest defenders. The death in AD565 of another Balkan born emperor, Justinian, whose bold attempt to re-unite Constantinople and Rome as one entity had left the Empire militarily and economically weakened, enabled the barbarian tribes to finally overrun the Balkans. The combined onslaught of two tribes, the Avars and their vassals the Slavs, brought devastation until they were defeated before the walls of Constantinople in AD626.

A new wave of invasions and emigrations followed. The Slavs settled and probably assimilated the Avars, along with many of the indigenous peoples; the Bulgars and Magyars swept down from Asia, the former soon taking up Slav language and culture. New elements and combinations were being added to the Balkan mix as Europe moved into the politically fluid world of the early middle ages.

Slavic societies proved notably successful. Among them two closely related groups, the Serbs

The Balšići dynasty coat of arms. The Balšići family ruled Zeta from the late fourteenth century until 1421.

and Croats, shared language and culture. Both drew strength from social structures that were based around communal families usually known as *zadrugas*. There was, in fact, little if any difference between the two groups, except that the Serbs embraced Orthodox Christianity and the Croats Catholicism, with ultimately divisive results.

The states created by the Balkan Slavs - Bulgars, Serbs and Croats - competed fiercely for hegemony within the medieval Balkan world. Some even grew strong enough to threaten the Byzantine capital, Constantinople; the first to do so being the Bulgarian states of the ninth and tenth centuries.

By the end of the early medieval period the Serbs had founded states on territories that, approximately, they still inhabit to this day. Among these was Duklja. It took its name from the Roman settlement of the first century, the ruins of which can be still be seen today just outside Podgorica. Duklja was renamed Zeta by the Byzantines.

From a Byzantine vassal state, Zeta emerged to become for a period the leading Serb state and a centre of resistance to Byzantium. Its early history is obscure, but the first Zetan state was comprised of a region called Brda (Highlands) and a small portion of the Adriatic coastline. Its northern border ran from Risan on the Adriatic coast to the source of the River Piva, the southern between the lakeside town of Scutari and the port of Kotor. In the eleventh century both Scutari and Kotor became part of the Zetan state. For Zeta and its successor state, Montenegro, both Scutari and Kotor would be of great importance.

Jovan Vladimir (970-1016) was Zeta's first ruler for whom some records remain. His most noteworthy acts were to make Scutari his capital and the refusal to recognise the suzerainty of the Bulgar ruler Samuel of Macedonia. Defeat led to his imprisonment, but he was subsequently released to marry Samuel's daughter Kosara and reinstated as Governor of Zeta. Legend has it that Kosara took pity on Jovan, fell in love with him and persuaded her father to marry them. After Samuel's death his nephew, Vladislav, called the Zetan to Struga where he had him killed.

In the power struggle which followed Jovan Vladimir's death, Vojislav (1034-1050) emerged as Zetan ruler. He renounced Byzantium's suzerainty and won an important military victory at the Battle of Tudjemili in 1042. Vojislav subsequently expanded his territory to include parts of Serbia and Herzegovina. He had set Zeta on the road to full independence from Byzantium.

The intense religious rivalry between Constantinople and Rome was a potent political factor in the Balkans, where their spheres of influence met, and medieval Balkan rulers soon learned to combine war and religious politics to reach their goals. Vojislav's son, Mihailo (1051-1081), initially reconciled with Byzantium but then joined the Macedonian Slav revolt of 1072 against Byzantium. Mihailo's son, Bodin, also enjoyed victory at Prizren, where he was crowned King of the Bulgars, but he was subsequently defeated and captured. The continuing unrest in Byzantium, with its possessions in Asia Minor and Italy threatened by the Seljuk Turks and the Normans respectively, enabled Mihailo to have Bodin released with the help of Norman mediation.

Zeta's importance had grown and Mihailo's appeal to Rome for royal recognition, in 1077, was granted. Zeta was separated from the Archbishopric of Split, a bishopric was established at Bar (although some scholars believe that it was not established until after Bodin's death) and Pope Gregory VII recognised Mihailo as king. Mihailo's death in 1081 ended a thirty year reign of consolidation and growth.

After his father's death, Bodin continued to forward the dynastic interest and made his nephews vassal rulers in neighbouring territories, including Bosnia and Serbia, but was unable to hold onto the latter. Following Bodin's death, which occurred sometime after 1101, a power struggle broke out between his heirs, one made worse by the feudal lords. Civil war in Zeta resulted, giving the Serbian ruler, Grand Župan Stefan Nemanja, his opportunity.

The civil war allowed Byzantium to reconquer much of Zeta, most of the Adriatic coastline and as far inland as Podgorica. Zeta's last ruler to be titled king was Gradinja (1127-46) and his son Radoslav, the last ruler of the semi-independent state, was demoted to prince. Byzantine military success saw much of the Balkans re-taken by 1172. However, regional power really lay with Stefan Nemanja and it was only his personal loyalty to Emperor Manuel Comnenus which delayed Serbia from conquering Zeta before Comnenus' death. By 1186 Zeta had fallen to the Nemanjić state.

With continuing political pressure, externally from Constantinople and Rome, domestically from his feudal lords, Stefan Nemanja aimed to strengthen his rule through improved relations with Rome and good administration. Papal relations were improved with the conversion to Catholicism, in 1199, of Stefan's son Vukan, under whom the Bishopric of Bar was restored.

Another problem for the Nemanjići was Zeta's recent independent era and its still flourishing cultural life, both of which encouraged separatist tendencies. The Nemanjić rulers placated these feelings by allowing for autonomy within the kingdom. In the reign of Uroš I roads were built, mines opened and trade was stimulated. Relations with the coastal towns were carefully nurtured through benefits and the granting of charters, in which Uroš' wife, Jelena of Anjou, was notably active.

The Nemanjić era was a great success which opened up the possibility of a large and independent Balkan state and, in fact, far more than that was nearly achieved. By the start of the fourteenth century the medieval Serbian state was approaching its zenith and a new era for the Balkans, and even the ailing Byzantine Empire, seemed at hand.

That glorious possibility would be followed by catastrophic defeats that not only sealed the fate of the Serbs, but also opened the way for foreign conquest of the Balkans.

Serbia's great empire builder was King Stefan Dušan (1331-1355), a brilliant statesman and military leader. He expanded the kingdom's territories until its borders stretched from the River Danube to the Gulf of Corinth. By 1346 he had crowned himself Emperor of the Serbs and Greeks in Skopje, Macedonia. A major power was being created and Dušan aimed ultimately to be crowned in Constantinople itself.

Relations with Byzantium were inevitably strained by Dušan's ambitions and he sought an alliance with a non-Christian ruler, the Ottoman Turk, Orkan. The Ottomans were as yet only a regional force, their military talents available to the highest bidder. By 1354 Dušan had realised the danger they represented and he proposed an alliance with Rome against the growing Islamic threat, but his focus remained constant: to take Constantinople and reforge the Byzantine Empire in his image.

In 1355 his forces began their advance through Thrace. Adrianople soon fell leaving the route to Constantinople open. As the advance guard reached the outskirts of the city, much of the garrison within its fortified walls were ready to welcome a new ruler to replace the feeble John Paleologus. However, forty miles away in the village of Diavoli, Dušan suddenly fell ill with a severe fever and died. Supposition suggests that the Byzantines had him poisoned: he was only forty-six and had been in good health.

The throne of Ivan Crnojević. The Crnojevići rebelled against Ottoman rule and founded the martial state which became known as Montenegro.

Without its remarkable leader the state he had created declined rapidly. As great as his achievements were the internal cohesion of Dušan's state was weak, and after his death it fragmented back into minor kingdoms, principalities and despotates. It was all the more unfortunate as a new and aggressive power was maturing.

While Christian rulers, amply aided and abetted by their feudal lords, continued their rivalries, nemesis had been steadily building its power in Asia Minor in the form of the Ottoman Turks. From the eighth century onwards, nomadic Turkic tribes had been migrating in Arab territory from Central Asia. The Mongol invasion of the twelfth century forced them westward where they resettled and

"Let us, with a firm will and with persistence fight the Greeks, and, trusting in God and his great Prophet, let us work to win the residence of the Caesars." The inspiring words of Sultan Mohammed II, whose leadership and military prowess brought about the final fall of the Byzantine Empire and its capital, Constantinople, in 1453.

sought out new opportunities. Among the competing tribes overrunning the Byzantine Empire were the Ottoman Turks.

Initially they had been just one of the successor states of the Seljuk Empire destroyed by the Mongols, but from the north-western corner of Asia Minor they were well positioned to seize lands that were Byzantine only in name and ripe for conquest.

Their chieftain Osman, from whom the ruling dynasty took its name, was renowned for his intelligence and wisdom, an inspiring leader whom men willingly served. By the time of his death in 1326, he had calmly, patiently, with, it has been said, the skills of a gardener as much as those of a warrior, laid the foundations from which a great and enduring empire would rise. His successors reaped the harvest in Africa, Asia, the Middle East and Europe, and in so doing recast Balkan history.

For the Serbs, the symbolic date for that historical watershed is St. Vitus' Day, June 28, 1389, when, at the Battle of Kosovo Polje, the Serbian Empire made its last major stand against the rising power of the Ottoman Turks. It was not the overwhelming military defeat it has sometimes been portrayed; in fact the military importance was rather that the alliance, led by Prince Lazar, failed to repulse the Ottomans. It was a close run contest in which Prince and Sultan were both killed, Sultan Murat I, according to folk-legend, by the heroic Miloš Obilić.

A legend grew up around the Battle of Kosovo Polje which became the defining symbol in the history of the Serbs. Folk history remembered it as a momentous defeat and commemorated it in verse and song as a moral victory: the Serb nation had sacrificed itself in the great struggle between Christianity and Islam and would reap its reward in heaven.

Folk history also asserted that after their defeat the surviving Serb nobility fled to Zeta. The actual process was a gradual one, but, as the epic poems rightly recalled, those who rejected Ottoman rule were driven back into the mountainous interior until finally they held onto only a few miles of the hinterlands of the southern Dinaric Mountains.

Through their hard fought struggle against these last remnants of Balkan freedom, the Ottomans were, in effect, the creators of a tiny but enduring foe built on the remains of the Zetan state. It would gain renown as a bastion of Orthodox Slav freedom and culture. Crna Gora, Serbo-Croat for Black Mountain, best known through its Venetian-Italian variant of Montenegro, is first known by that name in the fifteenth century. Its historical roots were in Duklja and Zeta and its spiritual birthplace was at the Battle of Kosovo Polje.

However, the glories of Montenegro were sometime in the future as, in the aftermath of Kosovo Polje, the Ottomans set about consolidating their hold on the Balkans as well as achieving the triumph which had eluded Stefan Dušan. The rise of the Ottomans and the final decline of Byzantium eventually enabled Sultan Mohammed II to capture Constantinople in 1453; his victory made him a legend but it was the culmination of many earlier successes.

Prior to the fall of Constantinople, the Ottomans had already conquered much of the Balkans. The Bulgarians were the first to be defeated and, as the Islamic conquest swept westward, they were followed by the Serbs. The defeat of the Serbs, in 1371, on the River Marica, where the army led by King Vukašin was routed and at Kosovo Polje in 1389, confirmed that the Ottomans would be the dominant power in the Balkans.

Serbian resistance to the invaders had also been weakened as the remains of Stefan Dušan's state crumbled and his feudal lords seized the chance to temporarily reassert independence and enhance their local power.

During this transitional period, Zeta's Balšići family set about trying to secure and expand their own territories. The Balšići were related through marriage to many of the great Serbian families and, according to legend, descended from Serbia's twelfth century hero Vuk Nemanja. They were first noted as rulers of Bar in 1360 and thereafter rose to rule Zeta until 1421. Like the early Zetan rulers they made their capital in Scutari.

Under Djuradj I, Zeta added Prizren to its territory and advances were also made in Herzegovina through an alliance with Prince Lazar of Serbia, Ban Tvrtko I of Bosnia and King Ludovik I of Hungary. Zeta gained the towns of Dragičevce, Konavle and Trebinje. However, these were lost in the war of 1377 with former ally Ban Tvrtko. The Bosnian ruler had benefited from the support of the Hungarians after recognising Magyar suzerainty, which the Balšići had refused.

Djuradj's heir, Balša II, successfully fought back against Ban Tvrtko and also gained territory in Albania. In typical medieval fashion, after his death in 1385 these new territories reverted back to the ownership of his Albanian born wife and were separated from the Zetan state. Balša's heir, Djuradj II, therefore inherited only the region of Lake Skadar and a small portion of the Adriatic coastline around Ulcinj. The Ottoman Turks forced Djuradj II to abandon Scutari in 1392. His policy thereafter was to attempt to forge an alliance with another rising power, the Venetian Republic.

Following Djuradj II's death from injuries sustained during victory over the Ottomans at Gračanica in 1402, his seventeen year-old son, Balša III, radically changed policy. He viewed the Venetians, who had seized Scutari, as the greater threat. With Ottoman assistance he regained his capital. However, the tide soon turned against Balša and, by 1418, Venice had regained the coastal towns of Ulcinj, Bar and Budva. Balša's death came early, in 1421, while seeking an alliance with his uncle, Despot Stefan Lazarević, who ruled Serbia as a vassal of the Hungarians and Ottomans. Balša's military defeats, combined with the lack of an heir, allowed Stefan Lazarević to annex Zeta. Under Stefan's rule the port of Bar was regained from Venice in 1423, and subsequently Ulcinj. The Balšići era ended with the loss of Zetan independence and its annexation to the vassal Despotate of Serbia.

Stefan Lazarević was succeeded by his nephew Djuradj Branković. His overriding need was to pacify his Ottoman masters but this caused the alliance with his feudal lords to break down. Unwilling to share Serbia's vassal status, some of Zeta's lords rebelled under the leadership of Stefan Crnojević and the Crnojevići thereby became Zeta's last dynasty. The facts of the Crnojevići led resistance to the Ottoman Turks confirm once again that folk history has faithfully preserved the essence of events: it was a proud, protracted struggle against ever mounting odds.

By 1435 Stefan Crnojević had established himself as ruler of Zeta. However, he was forced to cede territory to Herzegovina's ruler Stefan Kosača, who took his son, Ivan, hostage to ensure agreements were honoured. The Zetan struck back by negotiating an alliance with Venice and marrying the daughter of the Albanian chieftain Ivan Kastriot. Both acts brought substantive benefits: by 1455 Venice had recognised Stefan Crnojević as ruler, the 'Duke and Captain of Zeta', while his marriage to Mara Kastriot linked the family to the legendary son of Ivan Kastriot, Gjergj, who defied the Ottomans for twenty-four years.

As part of the crusade led by King Vladislav III of Poland, Janoš Hunyadi, military ruler of Transylvania, joined forces with Djuradj Branković, who had fled the Ottomans to Hungary. Their joint efforts drove the Ottomans from the strategic towns of Niš and Sofia.

Djuradj now saw a chance to reclaim his position and accepted Sultan Mohammed II's offer to return to Serbia as vassal ruler, thus ending direct Ottoman rule that had begun in 1439. Djuradj's realism proved timely as King Vladislav's crusade ended abruptly with the destruction of his forces and his own death at the major battle near Varna in 1444.

A nineteenth century depiction of a Montenegrin woman. While they endured notably hard lives in its barren karstic mountains, some of Montenegro's women also took up arms in the struggle against the Ottoman Turks.

The Ottoman armies were freed for other activities, including dealing with the still independent Albanians. The revolt of Gjergj Kastriot, who became known as Skenderbeg, was one of the consequences.

Mohammed II had resolved to crush all rebellion and he brought his forces to the Balkans in July, 1448. The tireless Janoš Hunyadi, seething for revenge, had regrouped his forces and brought as many as seventy-two thousand soldiers, to which Skenderbeg agreed to contribute a further twenty thousand. On October 17, 1448, battle commenced and the Cross and the Crescent clashed once more at Kosovo Polje.

Hunyadi resisted for three days waiting for his ally's reinforcements. However, Skenderbeg had been delayed due to long running disputes with the Venetians. He made haste to join the fray but, within twenty miles of the battlefield, the Albanians were met by fleeing Hungarian soldiers. Deciding to save his army, Skenderbeg retreated to his mountain strongholds. The last chance for the medieval Balkan states to free themselves from the Ottomans was lost at the second Battle of Kosovo Polje.

Skenderbeg's resistance continued but, like that of the Crnojevići, ultimately ended in defeat. As long as it lasted, the Albanian chieftain's resistance was a notable stumbling block to the Ottomans as it also gave vital protection to the Italian city states across the Adriatic. After Skenderbeg's death in 1468 Albania succumbed to the Ottomans.

Zeta was next. The difficult mountainous terrain ensured that the Ottomans struggled every step of the way, but the Zetans were steadily pushed back until the Crnojevići ruled over only the regions of Katuni, Lješane, Crmnica and Rijeka. Scutari had been lost, followed by the Fortress of Žabljak, and Stefan Crnojević's son, Ivan, unable to hold the Morača and Zeta valleys, retreated to defend the little valley between Rijeka and Lake Skadar.

In 1475 Ivan made Obod his temporary capital and, in 1482, he began the construction of his greatest legacy: a new capital on the site of a hitherto obscure village called Cetinje. Ivan considered it no less than his personal homage to God. Forced to take refuge in Italy, in the Church of *Santa De Lorita* he had seen a vision of the Virgin Mary. He prayed that he be allowed to return to his homeland and in return he pledged to build a church to her glory: *"My prayer was answered and I tried with all my heart and soul to fulfil my promise . . . I built a temple in the place called Cetinje to praise and glorify the holy mother . . ."*[2]

It marked the opening of a new chapter in Balkan history. The martial state that arose from the ashes of Zeta would earn comparison with heroic Sparta in Ancient Greece. Ivan's law of male military conscription was an appropriate landmark for its founder: *"Any soldier leaving the battlefield, except at his commander's bidding, or showing signs of fear, should be clothed in the garb of women and driven from the country as a coward and a traitor."*[3]

Ivan's devout and warlike spirit would endure throughout Montenegrin history, enshrined in the last bastions of Serb freedom, the martyr's capital of Cetinje and, above all, the Monastery. Ivan died in 1490. His son Djordje also gained renown by bringing the first printing press to the Balkans on which the first religious books in Old Slavonic were printed. However, time was running out for the Crnojevići.

As the Ottomans consolidated their hold over the Balkans, even mountainous and inhospitable Zeta finally succumbed and was proclaimed an Ottoman *sandžak*. From 1499-1514 Zeta was officially part of the imperial administration, only the area around the new capital held onto its autonomy, though without any form of recognition.

At this historic juncture, Ivan's sons chose opposing paths that mirrored the possible fates for the country. Stefan converted to Islam and became ruler as Pasha of the Sandžak of Montenegro, although his power was never fully consolidated. During Stefan's rule, Djordje retired with his wife to Venice, passing the right of succession to the Orthodox Christian Vladikas (Bishops) of Cetinje. The Crnojevići leave history in 1534. Their legacy contained a blessing in the Vladikas of Cetinje who eventually founded a new dynasty, but also a curse in the Pashas of Scutari from Stefan's family line, reborn and reviled as Bušatlija, who aimed to reclaim their former lands as Ottoman masters.

The foreseeable future clearly belonged to the Ottomans. Their growing presence in Europe had led Pope Urban V to proclaim a crusade as far back as 1366. His fears had proven amply justified as the conquest the Ottomans embarked upon was driven by religious zeal and military prowess. Mohammed II told his war counsel before the final conquest of Constantinople in 1453: *"The Holy War is our basic duty, as it was in the case of our fathers."* Islamic idealism and imperial ambition merged in the Ottoman Empire, its character moulded by its original purpose, that of a military institution fulfilling the holy obligation of expanding the Abode of Islam. It was this clarity of purpose, self-belief and military genius which swept away ancient domains.

The Ottoman military machine was undoubtedly the finest of its day and few, before or since, have conquered so systematically. Crucially, the Ottomans were the first medieval state to maintain a standing army. It was led by two élites. The first were the *Spahi*, exceptional cavalrymen from Central Asia who lived, both figuratively and literally, on horseback. The second were the *Janissaries*, Christian boys taken as slaves in childhood and converted to Islam, superbly trained and absolutely loyal to the Sultan. The assault of an Ottoman army was awe inspiring; indeed the organisation and bravery of these 'holy warriors' was such a marked trait, so reckless of individual life that the Italian historian Paolo Giovio noted: *"Their discipline under arms arises from their justice and severity, which surpasses that of the Romans. They obey their commanders unquestioningly and appear to care nothing at all for their lives in battle . . ."*[4]

With the most fearsome army of the age at their command the Ottomans seemed unstoppable. During the reign of Suleiman the Magnificent (1520-1566) they were able to conquer vast territories, including Syria, Egypt, Mesopotamia, Algeria, Moldavia and Bessarabia. The Battle of Mohacs in 1526, remembered in Hungarian history as the 'tomb of the nation', saw the full might of the Ottoman army decimate the Magyar nobility. Twenty-four thousand men were buried on the battlefield alone, two thousand prisoners massacred and thousands taken back to Constantinople as slaves.

The Ottoman aura of invincibility survived until the siege of Vienna in 1529, where the limitations of their siege strategy necessitated a withdrawal before a harsh winter took its toll. Suleiman, defeated by the weather and staunch resistance, fully expected to return but a crucial moment had passed. The last of the great conquering Osmanli rulers died without capturing Vienna and the Ottomans would not threaten again to overrun central and western Europe.

Although military prowess and the disunity of the Christian powers were vital factors behind the rise of the Ottoman state, they were far from the only ones. The conquerors offered rule that was in several important respects preferable to that of the Christian princes and lords they deposed, and to the downtrodden peasantry it was the aftermath of war that was of greater concern.

In that regard, the Ottomans were in many ways an attractive option. Once the land of the infidel had been ravaged and the rewards of victory taken, the Sultan's new subjects acquired the rights and status due to them under Islamic law. Regardless of race or creed all became *raia* (the flock); the subjects but also the responsibility of the absolute ruler. This centralised power structure removed some of the abuses that had been rampant under the Christian princes and lords, replacing them with provincial governors and creating a relatively uncorrupt and stable environment which provided greater security and economic opportunity.

At its zenith in the fifteenth and sixteenth centuries, voluntary migration to Ottoman lands was not uncommon. Ottoman armies were on occasion even welcomed by Orthodox Christians as liberators from their Latin oppressors. Indeed, the Ottomans, their non-Christian religion notwithstanding, were the true inheritors of the classical tradition, bringing peace to lands left in uncertainty by the decline of Byzantium.

The upper echelons of government inherited much of the good and bad of the Byzantine era and, as in Roman and Byzantine times, the talents of Balkan people were a great asset. Among the ruling élites a meritocracy allowed non-Moslems, often of Balkan stock - Greeks, Slavs, Albanians and Vlachs - to rise to positions of power. Many of the Empire's first ministers, the grand viziers, were Balkan born, and dynastically Balkan and Slav women were also influential.

Suleiman the Magnificent's first child was born to a Montenegrin named Gulbehar. Suleiman also took a Slav wife, the remarkable Russian Roxellana. Her achievement was unique among Ottoman concubines; however, through her intrigues, she probably did more harm than good to the Empire, notably doing away with Suleiman's closest friend, the Greek born Grand Vizier Ibrahim.

In the seventeenth century, by which time the Ottoman dynasty had succumbed to degeneracy and dynastic intrigue, the Albanian Koprulu family provided several grand viziers who were *de facto* rulers of the Empire.

Ottoman rule was a mixed blessing with considerable variations between the regions of the huge Empire. Religious tolerance was an integral and praiseworthy aspect of Ottoman government: freedom of worship was allowed for both Catholic and Orthodox Christians, along with other religions, notably Jews fleeing persecution in Europe. However, religious tolerance was not combined with equality. Likewise, law was not always a guarantee of justice, and legal discrimination along religious lines created a legacy of hatred that would, over time, undermine the cohesion of Ottoman society.

It was at the provincial level that affairs were most problematic. As pragmatic rulers, the Ottomans drew on religious converts from the indigenous populations for governors, administrators and landholders. An effective structure but also one that exacerbated tensions between rulers and *raia*.

The failings of Ottoman government fell heavily on the Balkan peasantry. Socially, economically and legally they were on the lowest rung of society and subject to arbitrary and often brutal local rulers. The benefits of conversion therefore saw many Christians exchange the Bible for the Koran, which brought new problems.

As the new ruling and landowning classes, denounced as renegades by the Christians, accumulated wealth and power, resentment grew. The struggle against the 'Turk' often meant conflict with your neighbour.

However, actual rebellion proved difficult to co-ordinate. Ottoman rule was a more destructive force for the traditional political structures of the Balkans than, for example, Hungary under Habsburg rule, which preserved its nobility and ruling class.

By contrast, during the reign of Mohammed II, all territory south of the River Danube had been placed under the Sultan's direct control. National sentiment and memory lingered, but the majority accepted the new world that had descended upon them and centuries passed before the Balkan peoples began to think in practical terms about

Two of history's implacable enemies, the Montenegrins and the Ottoman Turks, depicted in Novak Radonić's 'Bajo Pivljanin Killing the Turk'. Bajo Pivljanin died in 1685 while fighting the Ottomans and was laid to rest under the Bogomil menhirs near Cetinje's Vlach Church. (Facing page) The Ottoman Turk conquest brought a new ruling culture and new forms of government to the Balkans. This German gravure from 1850 depicts the residence of an Ottoman Pasha (Provincial Governor) in Orsova, Romania.

regaining their independence. Only a few pockets of resistance remained, among them the successors to the Zetan state, the Orthodox Christian Serbs of Montenegro.

"They have little fear of anyone but God, and even for God they don't care much."[5]
Vladika Petar I (1784-1830)

It is seemingly inherent in the relations between conquerors and conquered that there are those who remain defiant despite the superiority of the forces ranged against them. Among these many are assimilated, dispersed or even annihilated, but a few manage to survive if their spiritual resolve is fortified by material factors.

The Ottomans had destroyed the remnants of Byzantium and along with it the emerging states of the Balkans, but the Montenegrins proved to be among their most intransigent opponents, even though they comprised only a few thousand mountaineers who persisted in a lonely, virtually unnoticed resistance. Apart from the Ottomans and their seafaring rivals the Venetians, Europe knew almost nothing of the Montenegrins. Even in the early nineteenth century, Colonel Vialla de Sommièrse, who had been sent by Napoleon Bonaparte to study the tribesmen, recorded that they spoke a Greek dialect!

After the fall of the Crnojevići the Ottomans had embarked on trying to govern this defiant population. To an extent they succeeded and it was only in the small territory that became known as Old Montenegro, a mountainous karst region approximately twenty by forty miles adjacent to the eastern coast of the Adriatic, that freedom and not just local autonomy survived. From the fifteenth to the nineteenth century this land, the expanse of a single cloud, was Montenegro.

Old Montenegro was singular in this but, to a lesser degree, the tribes living under varying degrees of Ottoman rule also clung onto freedom and cultural identity. These refuge area warriors fashioned egalitarian tribal societies that had their roots in the traditional Balkan Slav *zadruga*. These communal families were the basic social unit from which the clans and tribes were formed.

The tribe was a self-governing entity with its own history, traditions and laws. Its affairs were democratically organised through the election of a vojvoda (chieftain) and a tribal skupština (assembly). The skupština decided tribal policy on major issues, such as relations with the regional pashas and inter-tribal relations, which often involved disputes over land, pasture and water rights. Power was also devolved to a large degree down to the clans, as prescribed by customary law.

Social relations were traditional, conservative and sharply defined. All males were equal before the law, but individual and clan status was a competitive affair in which the most prized virtues were honour and bravery. The status of women, while inferior to the males, was also protected by law and honour.

The men were society's defenders and providers: they fought the enemy and raided across the borders to feed their families. The women were society's workhorses: they endured notably hard lives for as well as being wives and mothers, they were also workers and labourers. Many have concluded that Montenegro would not have survived without its remarkable womenfolk; some even became warriors and gained equal status with their male counterparts.

The Montenegrin variant of tribal life inevitably stressed martial qualities and glory in battle was the chief topic for their epic poems, sung to the accompaniment of the national instrument, the

'The Player of the Gusle' by Vlaho Bukovac, 1919. In the Serb lands history was passed on from generation to generation through epic folk poems sung to the doleful monotone of the one stringed gusle.

one stringed gusle. Self-sacrifice in battle was expected, as much an expression of collective obligation as of individual bravery; for a Montenegrin to die peacefully in his bed was considered deeply shameful. Fearlessness in the face of overwhelming odds combined with ferocious guerrilla tactics characterised Montenegrin warfare. A recent historian of the Ottoman Empire has concluded that the mountaineers made the Turks seem clumsy and the Albanians effete.[6]

The struggle for freedom, tribal and individual, lay at the core of the Montenegrin identity. Naturally, those preoccupations influenced its people's mentality: freedom also became an abstract ideal, one intertwined with the very fact of being born Montenegrin.

Whilst that outlook contributed hugely in ensuring survival, it was something of a double-edged sword. It was not only Ottoman rule that was rejected, but any that infringed on hard won freedoms. Although the Vladikas of Cetinje were revered, their attempts to centralise power through new laws and taxation were often resisted, on occasion by open rebellion. Montenegro's internal relations were a complex, volatile balance as freemen could find much to argue about amongst themselves.

> *"I do not have the right to punish Montenegrins for defending their honour. It is our custom that if one does not return an insult in kind that person would become a laughing stock."*[7]
> *Vladika Rade (1830-1851)*

One custom the tribes were determined to retain was the notorious blood feud. It was not the arbitrary revenge it seemed to foreign travellers, but part of an established system of unwritten laws and customs which, in specific circumstances, sanctioned homicidal retaliation. Disputes, sometimes involving blood feuds between whole clans and even tribes, were settled through the arbitration of the tribal elders. They were often successful but their rulings were not binding; the clans and each warrior had both the right and duty to take blood revenge.

As late as 1860, Prince Danilo's (1851-1860) Serbian secretary Milorad Medaković observed: "*Osveta* [to wreak vengeance] *is something born in man. The Montenegrin would rather die than live shamefully.*"[8] With that mindset, conciliation could be difficult and blood feuds were not uncommon. However, a financial penalty, the burning of the perpetrators property or exile was also considered appropriate punishment. The outcome of blood feuds also depended on the character of the men involved and even in such a harsh code of honour there was room for compromise. Disputes could on occasion bring clans closer together and some were resolved by inter-marriage.

Montenegro's inner turmoils were a reflection of its constantly threatened existence and the daily struggle for subsistence its people waged. It could, in fact, be said that Montenegro was a nation born out of conflict which existed in a state of permanent conflict. If the greatest danger of all, the Ottomans, demanded servitude and threatened annihilation, tribal and inter-tribal feuds could also lead to destruction. It is undoubtedly a tribute to the tribes that a balance was maintained between unity for survival and tribal autonomy, but it was a precarious balance nonetheless.

The inhospitable environment which enabled resistance also undermined the ability to co-operate. At most the economy barely provided subsistence and the tribes were forced into competition with one another for scant resources. The meagre yields from livestock or crops and the almost total absence of trade, what existed was little more than local bartering, meant that cross-border and inter-tribal raiding were frequent. In time, raiding became an accepted and even heroic occupation, coming after battlefield glory as the favoured topic for the bards of the gusle. Under such grinding poverty the tribes could on occasion be seduced into betrayal by Ottoman bribes, although they would still join together against a large scale military threat.

The twenty thousand or so tribesmen of Old Montenegro formed the core of resistance. Their military capacity, at most, a few thousand warriors scattered across tiny villages nestling in the mountain valleys. Among them were the Njeguši. Folk history tells how they emigrated from the foot of Mount Njegoš in Herzegovina during the sixteenth century, but their name is recorded in Montenegro as early as 1435 and was reckoned to be four hundred households strong. The Njeguši, who proudly maintained that they had never paid tax tribute to the Ottomans, were known as a chivalrous tribe, if also stern and unyielding.

They were among the first to sustain rebellion to the point of full independence. In large part this was due to fate having been a fraction kinder to the tribes of Old Montenegro: with the Venetian Republic representing a force to counter the Ottomans along the Adriatic coast they had a powerful ally close at hand. During the seventeenth century the Venetians were struggling with the Ottomans for naval dominance of the Mediterranean and the mountaineers were a tiny but constant breach in the fortress of Ottoman dominion. As a result, the Republic offered them support, albeit intermittent and, like so many Venetian policies, self-interested.

However, even the tribes of Old Montenegro were in constant danger and faced devastating attacks which threatened their very existence. They fought a hateful enslavement only to maintain a desolate freedom. It was an existence the Yugoslav political leader and writer Milovan Djilas, a native Montenegrin, described thus: "*The land is one of utter destitution and forlorn silence. Its billowing crags engulf all that is alive and all that human hand has built and cultivated. Every sound is dashed against the jagged rocks, and every ray of light is ground into gravel . . . all is stone. Even all that is human is of stone. Man himself is made of it . . . Every evil assails him, and he uses evil to ward off evil, on a soil where even the wild beast has no lair.*"[9]

In this isolated wilderness, brutal reality, history and legend were fused into the expression of a people's suffering, hardened by long centuries of conflict into a concrete desire: to liberate and reunite the Serb people, to avenge the defeat of Kosovo Polje. Resistance to the Ottoman Empire, the unceasing enmity between the Cross and the Crescent and the desire for freedom found their sharpest expression amongst the Montenegrins. That struggle became the creed and sustenance of the mountain warriors who made their stand amidst the barren heights of Montenegro.

Vladika Danilo I (1696-1735). Danilo was the first of the Petrović-Njegoš rulers, after whom the vladika's chair was hereditary in the Petrović clan.

The founding of a dynasty and the rebirth of a nation.

This land used to be twice as bare, without even a cock crowing, and in those days there was not a Tsar Peter or a Vladika Danilo to be despised for everything and to be blamed for all that went wrong.

Vladika Danilo Petrović-Njegoš I

Sir, Montenegro is a nation of knights with noble characters, fighting as exalted heroes for dear freedom.

Vladika Petar Petrović-Njegoš I

After the demise of the Crnojević dynasty, the rulers of Montenegro were the Vladikas of Cetinje, who were elected through the tribal skupština. It is often asserted that without this shift to theocratic government Montenegro may not have survived, that power struggles between competing tribal vojvodas and alliances with the regional pashas would have led to incorporation into the Ottoman Empire. The vladikas acted as the focal point for Montenegrin identity and resistance and, in their role as religious and moral leaders, they welded the loose tribal confederation into a unique entity, a kind of spiritual brotherhood based on a shared history, culture and religion.

Fortuitously, several vladikas were exceptional men able to confront the challenges of uncertain and violent times. In the sixteenth and seventeenth centuries the Vladikas of Cetinje had been chosen from various clans, but each had to be *an exemplary Montenegrin from one of the best families.*[1] It was under one such leader that the resurgence began in 1688, during the reign of Vladika Vissarion. The tribes united as allies of the Venetians during the prolonged Turco-Venetian Mediterranean wars, and Montenegro emerged as a political and military factor in Islamic-Christian wars.

The tribes of the Katuni Nahi, most notable among them the Njeguši with their unique tradition and status, were the natural source of leadership for the tribal confederation. From within the Njeguši two clans, the Petrovići and the Radonjići, rose to dominate political life. The Petrovići made the seat of the vladikas their own and leaned toward Russia; the Radonjići dominated the governorship and allied themselves with Venice and subsequently with Austria. Both were elected by the tribal skupština and decrees required the seal of both rulers to become law. Although the governors lacked the prestige of the vladikas, they were a rival and, at times, an almost equal source of power. Both played a role in laying the foundations of the Montenegrin state, although it would fall to the great Petrović rulers to forge the nation.

The vladikas were much more than religious leaders, being also warriors, the arbitrators of feuds and aspiring law-makers. From Vladika Danilo's reign (1696-1735) onward, they struggled to bring the freemen of Montenegro under their rule, but even during Vladika Rade's reign (1830-1851) little had changed. Offered a hereditary title by the Ottomans if he would recognise the Sultan's suzerainty, Rade's refusal captured the essence and limit of his authority. *"As long as my people defend me,"* he declared *"I need no Turkish title to my throne; if they desert me such a title would avail me little."*[2] In his reign, Vladika Petar I (1784-1830) laid down a code of law and established a court, both of which were landmark reforms his successors would build upon. The tribes accepted both, but in name only; indeed they could do little else, bound as they were by their own laws and customs. Each tribe was a self-governing, autonomous entity, in many ways a world in itself.

A keen sense of honour and a warrior's definition of freedom fortified the tribesmen in their struggles against their enemies but, by necessity, tribal policy also carefully weighed the Ottoman threat against their allegiance to Cetinje. The highland tribes were some of the most able fighters, but even large tribes, such as the Piperi and Bjelopavlići, negotiated with the pashas while the vladikas laboured ceaselessly to bind them closer to Cetinje.

The first Petrović ruler, Vladika Danilo, was born in Njeguši village to the Herak clan and christened Nikola. Folk history recalls that all the Njeguši were descended from two brothers, Raić and Herak. Along with the other Njeguši clans, the Herak had emigrated from their lands at the foot of Mount Njegoš in Herzegovina and had risen to play a leading role within the tribe. Nikola Herak was sent to Cetinje Monastery to be instructed as a monk and took the name of Danilo.

His reign set precedents for both his successors and for Montenegro itself. The first, and in a way the most telling, was his enduring regret at becoming ruler. On his election he was so reluctant to accept the vladika's staff and gown that, no doubt with a premonition of the troubles which lay ahead, he wept. Montenegrins would never respect a weakling or a coward as ruler, but if strong emotions were a Petrović trait so were courage and determination. Fortunately, Danilo had both in abundance.

In 1700 Danilo went to Secui, Hungary, where Patriarch Arsenije Čarnojević III, a Montenegrin from Baice, invested him. It was a symbolic act of Serb solidarity. As Patriarch of Peć, Arsenije had led the fleeing Serbs from Kosovo Province in the great exodus of 1689-90. A small contingent of Austrian troops had briefly invaded the province and the Serb population welcomed them as liberators. Ottoman forces re-established order with brutal reprisals and, further north, they forced the Austrians to abandon the strategic town of Niš and the fortress of Belgrade. Patriarch Arsenije led more than thirty thousand Serbs into exile under the protection of the Austrian Empire.

Whatever fears Danilo's position held for him, the first Petrović ruler boldly styled himself 'War Lord of the Serbian Land'. There was more bravado than substance in this title, for he was ruler of an undefined and limited territory. The first Montenegrin states, Duklja and Zeta, were medieval fiefdoms but recognised entities; whereas Danilo's territory was barely a state at all, rather an act of defiant will in the face of potential annihilation. Turkish forces had reached Cetinje in 1687 and were followed by a devastating epidemic that swept the country, forcing many to emigrate. In 1690 the forces of Suleiman Pasha Bušatlija attacked again, razing the Monastery to the ground. After such disasters the resources Danilo had at his command to protect his people and rebuild the country were remarkable only by their absence, but his defiance remained. He told the people: *"If we will sell our silver and gold we can gather together an army and wage war . . ."*[3]

While the ebbing tide of the Ottoman conquest could still threaten to overwhelm the Montenegrins, a new power was emerging as a counterbalance. During the Turco-Russian war of 1711, Tsar Peter the Great of Russia (1689-1721) sent envoys to the Balkans to rouse opposition to Ottoman rule. Peter dreamt of reclaiming Istanbul for Christendom and he saw in Montenegro an ally in his holy mission of *"conquering the Turk and glorifying the Slav faith and name."*

Isolated Montenegro had long awaited the day when a great liberator would come. Tsar Peter sent two Serbs, Mihailo Miloradović from Herzegovina and Ivan Lukačević from Podgorica, to deliver his Grammata. An excited Danilo told his people: *"We have heard, dear brothers, that we have, God knows where, in the east a Christian Emperor . . . but being closed in by these mountains we could not understand anything. You thought that he would never know about us, a handful of people surrounded by snakes and scorpions, and that his envoys would never come here, but today, thank God, we can see them among us and read his Grammata. His envoys are not foreigners but our brothers and Serbs, who say that his Empire is bigger and stronger than any other in the world. He is at war with Turkey for no other reason than to protect Christianity and free the monasteries, to raise the holy cross and liberate the Christian subjects of Turkey. We have to pray to God to help him and take our weapons to go to war with him. Russians and Montenegrins are of the same tribe so let us be neighbours. Therefore, go prepare yourselves for war and I will do the same . . ."*[4]

Danilo led his men into battle. The Turks were besieged in their fortresses of Nikšić, Spuž,

An antique map of the Western Balkans, from 1694, of 'Old and New Pannonia and Illyria' by C.J. Bismarci for Cluver's 'Introductio in omnem Geographiam', engraved by Herman Mosting of Luneburg. The territory held by the Montenegrins is unnoted, indeed, the map makers are hardly likely to have been aware of their existence. Cetinje and, rather more surprisingly, the nearby port of Kotor are both ignored, while the coastal cities of Ragusa (Dubrovnik) and Budva, as well as Scodra (Scutari) at the southern shore of Lake Skadar are shown. The Ottoman conquest had recast Balkan history and, until the mid-nineteenth century, the Balkan Slavs would most usually have been referred to as Ottoman or Turkish Christians.

Podgorica and Žabljak. The Montenegrins had high hopes these vital territories would be theirs, but they could not be taken without professionally trained soldiers and the machinery of siege warfare. Another unhappy precedent was set as Russia, pressured into peace after the military debacle on the River Pruth, left the Montenegrins to their fate as the hastily made peace allowed the Tsar to bring his army home intact. Montenegro was not even mentioned in the peace treaty of 1712. The Sublime Porte treated Montenegro as a subdued province and demanded tax tribute be paid to Istanbul. Inevitably hostilities continued.

A major victory was gained on August 9, 1712, on the field that became known as Carev Laz (Tsar's Field). Danilo was wounded when the Montenegrins staged a devastating ambush against the invaders. The size of the forces involved has been disputed, but the army of the brutal Vizier of Bosnia, Numan-Pasha Ćuprilić, suffered by far the greater casualties and was forced to retreat.

The mountaineers had provoked the Sultan's wrath and, in 1714, Pasha Ćuprilić returned with

(Above and facing page) Views of Njeguši valley today. The birthplace of the Petrović-Njegoš vladikas and princes, as well as the heartland of Montenegrin resistance. The tribes of Katuni Nahi were the first to sustain their independence against the Ottoman Empire.

an army made up of janissaries and irregular soldiers, the latter greatly feared due to their indiscipline and bloodlust. A force of thirty thousand overran the four thousand fighters of Cetinje, Čevo and Njeguši, occupying Montenegro right up to the border of Venetian territory. Katuni Nahi was burned to the ground and those who remained were killed or taken as slaves. Cetinje Monastery recently rebuilt, was again destroyed, and even Danilo only survived by taking refuge in a cave above Paštrović. Pasha Ćuprilić's campaign would remain unsurpassed for its savagery, plundering and destruction.

More than two thousand survivors fled to the Bay of Kotor while Danilo made haste to Russia. In the meantime, erstwhile ally Venice obliged the Turks by closing its borders to fleeing Montenegrins. When the Venetians subsequently refused to extradite the refugees who had nonetheless entered their territory, Turco-Venetian war resulted. It was not enough to turn the tide in Montenegro's favour, but bands of fighters took to the mountains and harried the occupying forces until they retreated during the winter.

Despite the fickleness of the Venetians the alliance continued. Montenegro and its Vladika, who had suffered torture at the hands of the pashas, viewed Ottoman rule as an absolute evil to be fought at all costs. To this end, they were prepared to place themselves under Venetian rule. In February, 1717, a delegation of vojvodas proposed to the Venetian Senate that, provided internal self-rule and religious autonomy were respected, Montenegro would agree to become a Venetian protectorate. Thereafter the new allies waged a joint campaign at Bar and Ulcinj, but in the Treaty of Požarevac, concluded on July 21, 1718, Montenegrin efforts again went unrewarded. The Ottomans, relentlessly asserting that Montenegro was an imperial province, even traded off four of its communes to the Venetians. The mountaineers would have many hard lessons in the art of diplomacy.

Danilo's reign marked the beginning of the Petrović-Njegoš dynasty, though it had come to power in difficult circumstances: Danilo had not managed to gain recognition for his country and the

freemen of Montenegro had almost paid the ultimate price for their independence. However, two vital political precedents had been set: relations were opened with Russia and the vladika's chair was made hereditary in the Petrović clan.

Danilo's journey to St. Petersburg had gained the promise of a subsidy from Russia which, Tsar Peter the Great promised, would continue as long as Russia existed: *"We know that you went to war alongside us because we share the same religion and because we called on you. Due to our long war against Sweden, we cannot give you the reward that you deserve, but still, to show our gratitude we are sending through Vladika Danilo . . . one hundred and sixty gold medals engraved with our image to your vojvodas and five thousand roubles. I have ordered that your priests be given garments, church books and every third year five hundred roubles to Cetinje Monastery. And because we are now at peace with Turkey we advice you to make peace with them as well."* The rulers who followed Danilo would have some means at their disposal to build the nucleus of a proper state.

The Petrovići were confirmed as hereditary rulers and the clan's leading role in Montenegro was consolidated. They were still constrained by the theocratic rather than princely nature of their rule, which prevented the vladika from marrying, and it became traditional for a nephew to be nominated as successor. This naturally pleased the Ottomans, who would have gone to war to prevent the creation of a Montenegrin principality, as well as the free tribes, who were still wary of becoming subordinate to Cetinje. Danilo's successors would have a long and arduous battle against these centrifugal forces.

Danilo's achievements were hard won and, he felt, the gratitude of his people insufficient: *"This land used to be twice as bare, without even a cock crowing, and in those days there was not a Tsar Peter or a Vladika Danilo to be despised for everything and to be blamed for all that went wrong."* His dying words tell us why he continued the struggle: *"Tears mingling with these words I write, Vladika Danilo, sorrowful and sad, giving myself to death for the sake of our Lord, for the sake of the people."*[5] Along with Vladika Petar I and Vladika Rade, his reign became part of national legend.

Sima Milutinović-Sarajlija, a Serbian who played a notable role in the nineteenth century history

(Above) The vladika's staff and gown, the symbols of Montenegrin religious faith, military resistance and political independence.
Facing page: (Top) Vladika Sava and (bottom) Vladika Vasilije. Sava was unable to maintain the unity of Montenegro's tribal confederation and eventually handed over the reins of power to his nephew, Vasilije. However, despite Vasilije's considerable efforts, feuding and disunity continued, so much so that both Russia and Austria's envoys advised their governments against supporting Cetinje. Following Vasilije's death on March 21, 1766, the remarkable impostor Šćepan Mali (1767-1773) usurped power. Šćepan managed to restore some degree of order to Montenegrin affairs through draconian punishment. He finally came to a grisly end, his throat cut by a Greek servant who was in the pay of the Pasha of Scutari.

of Montenegro, remembered Danilo's character and achievements: *"Danilo was a man of his word . . . he did not tolerate those, including himself, who cursed, swore and used foul language. The people loved him greatly and if he had only one enemy in his homeland, Asiatics, he would have been much more fortunate in his endeavours for the Serb people. The greatest achievement he should be thanked for was to remove the Turkish spirit from Montenegro once and for all, even the shadow of Turkish or foreign rule over his people."*[6]

Vladika Danilo's successor was Vladika Sava (1735-1781), by unfortunate contrast the weakest of the Petrović rulers. Sava was a spiritual man, inclined toward the quiet contemplation of the monastery rather than the glory of the battlefield. He lacked the strength of character the Montenegrins expected from their leaders.

Sava's greatest failing was his inability to prevent the clans returning to blood feuds as the pressure of warfare continued. Allied to Russia and Austria in their failed campaign of 1736 against the Ottomans, although playing a minor role in the hostilities, Montenegro subsequently endured a seven-year blockade centred on the economically vital Lake Skadar.

The Vladika and his nephew, Vasilije, had been in personal dispute for sometime and Sava reconciled the situation by making Vasilije his assistant. It was a sensible move and the younger man, who had the qualities of initiative and energy that Sava lacked, soon took over the reins of government. In 1750 he went to Vienna and pleaded for protection from Austrian Empress Maria Theresa. Unsuccessful with the Habsburgs, in 1752 he left Austria to try for better results in Russia, where he spent the next two years.

In Russia Vasilije's crusading spirit achieved some results and he returned to Montenegro with five thousand roubles and church books. He then set about galvanising the people against the enemy and the outcome was a spate of raiding. This, in turn, provoked a retaliatory expedition in 1756. Despite staunch resistance led by Governor Stanislav Radonjić, the campaign went badly and only severe weather prevented the Turks from overrunning Cetinje.

Vasilije travelled to Russia again but his credibility was in decline. His unrealistic political proposals and the plots being hatched against him from within his own entourage aroused Russian suspicions. Although the Tsarina still gave five thousand roubles to Vasilije, he left accompanied by a minder, the envoy, Prince Puchkov, whose task was to see that the funds were properly distributed.

On arriving in Cetinje they were greeted by a large and, to Puchkov's eyes, unruly crowd. Sava suggested that the envoy make the transaction in private, but Puchkov wanted it done in public at a tribal assembly. Sava's rather disconcerting reply was that only a few select vojvodas should attend as trouble could break out without warning. Sworn to secrecy, the vojvodas were summoned and the roubles finally handed over.

Prince Puchkov was left with a very dim view of the state of Montenegrin affairs, which he recorded as wild, disorderly and senselessly violent. He distrusted Vasilije, thought little better of Sava and suspected that Cetinje was keeping the aid for itself. He advised St. Petersburg that sending Russian priests might improve matters.

Russian disapproval had some effect on Vasilije who concentrated on spiritual matters until his next and final trip to Russia. In 1765 he departed for St. Petersburg to plead for a renewal of aid, this time to no avail. He died, in March, 1766, while still in Russia.

Though a flawed leader, Vasilije was a man of great energy and his death left a vacuum. His dream of an Orthodox-Christian empire centred on Russia would influence Montenegro's future policy as well as the sentiments of its people. However, with no domestic leader to take his place, the moment was ripe for one of the most charismatic and intriguing, but also one of the most shady characters in Montenegrin history to make his mark.

Šćepan Mali (Steven the Small, 1767-1773), an impostor of uncertain but possibly Dalmatian or Herzegovinian origin, appeared in Montenegro claiming to be Tsar Peter III of Russia, who had been murdered by the lovers of Tsarina Catherine II in 1762. The Venetians recorded: *"A curious, unknown person, claiming to be Peter III of Muscovy, has appeared in Dalmatia and Albania. He has proclaimed himself as lawmaker in religion and politics . . ."*

The Montenegrins fell for the story but Vladika Sava was cautious enough to inform the Russian Ambassador in Istanbul. The Ambassador's reply was that Šćepan was an impostor and Sava, his suspicions confirmed, circulated the letter to the vojvodas. Šćepan was not willing to be shifted and conflict broke out, he even had Sava incarcerated for a few weeks.

As Šćepan gathered support, the Venetians saw trouble ahead and a reward for the impostor's removal was offered. Count Zorzo Cadić Cornetta undertook to poison Šćepan, but he proved unable to deliver his potion.

Russia, too, tried to deal with this unexpected and disturbing phenomenon by dispatching Prince Dolgorukov and a small

(Above and top) The Petrović family house in Njeguši village. Built in 1577, it was a communal dwelling but also the house of government, from where it was decided that Vladika Danilo I would undertake his historic journey to Russia in 1714.

band of soldiers to Montenegro.

Turco-Russian war had broken out again in 1767 and Catherine II, who aimed to use the Montenegrins to disrupt the Ottoman Empire's western provinces, was faced with the awkward prospect of sending her envoy to prepare them for war after the man posing as her dead husband had been proclaimed their leader.

Prince Dolgorukov arrived on the Adriatic coast hoping to maintain secrecy, but both the Venetians and the Turks were well aware of his mission. The Pasha of Bosnia, Silahdar Mehmed, reported that twenty men and an interpreter had arrived in Venetian held Dalmatia with a large shipment of war materials, ammunition, guns, gunpowder and swords. Aided by the Montenegrins, they took the supplies into the mountains and stored them in the capital and in villages near the border.

On arrival in Cetinje, the Russians made ready to deal with Šćepan. They were greeted by Vladika Sava, several monks, *rakia* (local Montenegrin brandy) and rowdy hospitality. The vojvodas arrived firing their weapons, followed by Šćepan and his entourage. Prince Dolgorukov denounced Šćepan in the name of the Tsarina and would have had him shot, but the vojvodas refused to allow it, even though he apparently admitted that he was a fraud and gave his name as Raičević of Dalmatia.

The Russians still managed to arrest and imprison him in a room above their lodgings. Prince Dolgorukov tried to take control of the situation by issuing several proclamations to enforce his authority, but it soon became known that the Turks were delighted by the squabbles in Cetinje and were preparing to attack. Insult was added to injury by a Venetian attempt to poison Dolgorukov and he decided to abort the mission. He had Šćepan freed, as much to save his own skin as for political reasons; during the perilous journey down to the coast he even had to accept Šćepan's help: *"Were it not for Šćepan Mali, who knew well the perils of Montenegro's mountains and virtually carried me in his arms, I would surely have fallen into the chasm."*

Šćepan re-asserted his leadership with draconian punishments which stifled lawlessness and border raiding. However, with the Turks very well prepared by the able Silahdar Mehmed, who had been sent specifically to control the Montenegrin border, there was little hope of success for a major uprising. In September, 1768, military defeat duly came at Ostrog Pass. The Bjelopavlići tribe were plundered, while the Venetians took the opportunity to follow suit along the coast.

Despite these setbacks Šćepan proved an effective ruler. This was confirmation, if any were needed, that he could not have been the ineffectual Tsar Peter III, a character who could never have been so ruthlessly determined. Whoever Šćepan really was and whatever his motives, he became a true leader of the Montenegrins, although he admittedly lacked the vital quality of bravery in battle.

If he had come seeking riches or glory, he found little of either; he was a romantic interlude but Montenegro's cursed history demanded self-sacrifice, even from such a bold impostor. Šćepan was badly maimed, losing an eye, while laying mines during road construction and was ultimately assassinated in September, 1773, at Brčela Monastery on the order of Mahmoud Bušatlija, Pasha of Scutari. A Greek servant in Mahmoud's pay cut Šćepan's throat whilst shaving him.

Vladika Sava returned to power and Montenegrin affairs relapsed into chaos. Relations with Russia had deteriorated and, in 1777, Sava's nephew once removed, Archimandrite Petar Petrović-Njegoš, Governor Jovan Radonjić and Serdar Ivan Petrović spent six fruitless months in St. Petersburg, trying but failing to gain a personal audience with the Tsarina. Montenegrin hopes turned to Austria only to find an equally depressing response.

After Vladika Sava's death on March 11, 1781, power was briefly held by Arsenije Plamenac (1781-1784) of Crmnica, the only vladika after Danilo I not of the Petrović clan. He ruled from Brčela Monastery, but his health was poor and in his short reign he failed to bring about improvements. The Austrian envoy, Colonel Paulić, who was sent to Montenegro in 1782 to see if Habsburg influence could be exercised, described a volatile situation in which the Radonjići, who had also confirmed themselves as hereditary rulers in 1770, had a chance to seize power. Paulić reported: *"Radonjić's father had hoped to gain the highest respect but failed. His son now also tries to do so and would possibly succeed if he were more talented and had more money . . . Vladika Plamenac's inclination is for drink and he has lost the respect of the people, he could be of little hindrance."* Colonel Paulić shared the opinion of Prince Puchkov and advised Vienna against investing in the Montenegrins.

Much therefore depended on Petar Petrović Njegoš. He had gained experience as a member of Vasilije's entourage and his abilities were sufficiently apparent to Vladika Sava that he would have handed over power before his death, if circumstances had been more favourable. Petar would fulfil and even surpass Montenegrin expectations and, after a long and successful reign, be made a saint by his grateful people.

However, his early years proved particularly difficult. Transitions of power in Montenegro were vulnerable times, which often tempted the country's enemies to take advantage. This particularly applied to the neighbouring pasha's in Herzegovina and Scutari. On Petar's accession, Montenegro was particularly vulnerable being internally divided and internationally isolated. Just how far relations with

(Above and facing page) Interior views of the Petrović family house in Njeguši village. Three families lived together, each having one large room. The stone house also acted as a fortress in times of conflict.

Russia had deteriorated was demonstrated by the fact that Petar's investiture took place on Austrian territory. Naturally, the Tsarina's blessing was sought, but, in Vienna, Russia's Prince Golitsyn refused to grant Petar a passport. Instead he turned to Austria's Emperor Joseph II, and on October 24, 1784, Metropolitan Mojsej Putnik invested Petar in Karlovci, Srem.

During Petar's absence, Pasha Mahmoud Bušatlija launched a devastating attack. The Ottoman Empire had long since begun its decline, and provincial rulers such as the Bušatlijas were the Empire's servants in name only, who sought territories and riches for themselves that were kingdoms in all but name. Claiming to be descended from the Crnojevići, they desired not only Montenegro, which they viewed as simply their inheritance stolen in the reign of Vladika Danilo, they also had their eyes on the Morea and Macedonia. The Bušatlijas sought power nominally within the Ottoman system, as did the notorious Ali Pasha Teppelini in Albania, but were actually ambitious warlords. Mahmoud Bušatlija, therefore, had little respect for the Montenegrins who disrupted his borders and rudely asserted their freedom.

His opportunity lay in the tribal disunity within Montenegro. Bribes ensured that tribal feuds increased in intensity, making it that much easier to invade and conquer. Once again, Cetinje and the Monastery were burned to the ground. Fortunately, the inhospitable environment yet again prevented total defeat. The devastated capital boasted only one water-well, and it was almost impossible for an army of occupation to survive in the rocky wasteland. Knowing the Montenegrins would soon retaliate with guerrilla warfare Pasha Bušatlija retreated, but left devastation in his wake.

On his return in the autumn of 1786 Petar found the country in ruins. Two thousand houses had been burned, the Paštrović clan had been massacred and thousands of sheep and cattle had been stolen. The survivors were forced to live in caves with only grass roots and wild plants for food.

Disease and famine inevitably took their toll as the Venetians added to the misery by blocking Montenegro's trade routes with Kotor.

Petar set about rebuilding the tribal confederation, rousing the people to face the continuing threat from Pasha Bušatlija: *"Your great glory is known throughout the world and I was always proud to call myself Montenegrin; now, with a sad and wounded heart, I see that glory has faded, mostly because in your hearts there is the seed of disunity. I will work tirelessly and gladly sacrifice all that I have for the good of my fatherland and the freedom of my people."*

Despite these brave words the people were too demoralised to rebuild the Monastery and even objected to the felling of trees for building material. Petar resorted to his religious powers of reprimand and cursing, which the superstitious people greatly feared: *"If you are such enemies of the holy church that you prevent me from felling the wood that I bought with my money, you have destroyed even what is left of our Monastery. I will, I trust to God, find some place to live, but, instead of helping me to rebuild the church as you as Orthodox Christians should, you are undermining me. God will punish you."*[7]

Even though Montenegro's condition was truly desperate, Pasha Bušatlija knew that his victory was incomplete. The highland tribes were torn between their natural loyalties and the military threat; however, while they could be bribed or subdued, they would never accept status as Ottoman subjects so long as they could look to the free region of Katuni.

Pasha Bušatlija tried threats to separate the borderlands from Cetinje and warned Petar: *"I intend to send my fierce Albanians against them . . . again I say to thee that whosoever comes to their aid, I will strike at them also with all my strength."* This was no idle boast: the Albanians were renowned as the Empire's finest troops and the borderlands between Scutari Province and Montenegro were notoriously dangerous.

Petar gathered the tribes for the inevitable conflict, which commenced at Martinići, the heartland of the Bjelopavlići, on July 23, 1796. Pasha Bušatlija, his forces augmented with French officers sent by Napoleon Bonaparte, made his final assault on October 4, at the Battle of Kruši. The Vladika and the Governor shared command as the Turks were routed. Pasha Bušatlija was killed by Bogdan Vukov of Zalazi, who became a national hero and Bušatlija's head was placed in triumph on Tablja Fort above Cetinje Monastery.

It was an historic victory for Montenegro and there were many benefits: the ambitions of the Pashas of Scutari were destroyed; the highland tribes, the Piperi and Bjelopavlići, united with Montenegro through their skupštinas; the Ottomans were forced to recognise, albeit temporarily, that Montenegro was more than a rebellious province. Where his predecessors had always denied it, Sultan Selim II proclaimed that: *"The Montenegrins have never been subjects of our Sublime Porte."*

Significant though the victory at Kruši had been, it was only a small step along the road to recognition. And, at a time when the Napoleonic wars looked as if they were going to permanently reshape the political map of Europe, international affairs were fluid and far from favourable to Montenegrin aims in general. In 1797 the Venetian Republic ceased to exist when it was ceded to Austria by Napoleon Bonaparte. This enabled Montenegro to briefly reclaim some coastal territory, but it proved a short-lived gain. Also in 1797, France temporarily recognised Austria's right to occupy the formerly Venetian governed Bay of Kotor, an ominous and significant precedent. Continuing poor relations with Russia, including a failed plot to discredit and remove Vladika Petar, also added to Montenegro's precarious position.

In these circumstances, it was vital that Montenegro's claims be asserted: after all, *de facto* independence was not the same as international acceptance of Montenegrin statehood or its territorial ambitions. Efforts to gain these continued through alliances with Austria and Russia as they resisted Napoleon's continental ambitions.

Napoleon's armies, however, were enjoying unblemished success. So far undefeated, they had taken Dubrovnik in 1806 and advanced on Kotor Bay. Under the pressure of these events and after two decades, Montenegro's relations with Russia finally thawed. Their combined forces drove the French back to the walls of Dubrovnik and took territory as far north as the island of Korčula. The French retaliated by joining forces with Turkey and attacking the Russians, who withdrew their Mediterranean fleet. In the Franco-Russian peace treaty of 1807 France gained control of Kotor Bay and, in the

(Below) Vladika Petar I's residence in Rijeka Crnojevića. Later Petrović rulers would also build their own residences in the lakeside village, which eventually became a favoured retreat for the Royal Family in the nineteenth century.
(Inset) Vladika Petar I's *Stega*, the first, albeit largely symbolic, attempt to give Montenegro a general legal code.

same year, the Franco-Turkish alliance went on to inflict defeats on the Montenegrins at Nikšić and Klobuk.

If the French saw themselves as liberators in the revolutionary Napoleonic mould, the Montenegrins were equally certain that they too were fulfilling that heroic role. In 1807 Petar went down to the coast to parley with General Auguste Marmont in his headquarters at Kotor. Petar's loyalty to Russia could not be shaken and, as they lost patience with each other, the two leaders traded insults.

Marmont commented contemptuously: *"Montenegrins are inhuman and savage. They, like barbarian nations, cut off their enemies heads."*

Petar retorted: *"Sir, Montenegro is a nation of knights with noble characters, fighting as exalted heroes for dear freedom. That they take heads is true but one should not be surprised by this; rather that the French people in the middle of a market-place beheaded their own king. The Montenegrins learned from the French, they just use it differently, only taking the heads of their enemies, never having beheaded their own ruler or fellow tribesmen."*

Marmont replied: *"You should know Vladika that until today your land has been known as the Black Mountain, but in the future it will run red with Montenegrin blood. French armies will conquer your proud mountains and show you there is an even braver nation."*

The revered Vladika Petar I (1784-1830). Petar's reign spanned a crucial period in Montenegrin history. His successor, Vladika Rade, made him a saint in 1834.

His threats notwithstanding, Marmont prudently made no attempt to detain Petar whose guards were waiting outside. They had advised the Vladika that if there were any trouble he should throw the Frenchman out of the window for them to deal with! It would not be the last time Montenegrin and South Slav freedom clashed with Europe's revolutionary movements.

Before long the tide of French success began to turn. The Franco-Turkish advance was stopped at Piperi in 1811, while British and Russian co-operation was vital in the defeat of the French at Kotor. In three further attacks in 1812 forces from Herzegovina and Scutari were also defeated, although Petar was badly wounded in one of these confrontations, at the Battle of Ljubotinje.

Now that the Venetian Republic had gone and Napoleon's armies were in retreat, there was a possibility for Montenegro to gain Kotor Bay. However, the opportunity proved difficult to grasp, for the religious question proved a complication. As Petar pleaded with Russia to support his claims, the Catholics of Kotor Bay opted for rule by Austria. It was a worrying reminder of how the divisions between Orthodox and Catholic separated the South Slav populations.

The Montenegrins nonetheless fought on during 1813 with weaponry supplied by Russia and Great Britain. An assembly held in Dobrota resolved to unite Kotor Bay with Montenegro, but the Congress of Vienna, which convened in 1815 after Napoleon's final defeat at Waterloo, had other arrangements in mind. While the primary purpose was to push the French back to their pre-Napoleonic borders, the Austrians were also given control of Kotor Bay. It was a bitter blow after so many bloody battles and from their allies, Russia and Austria, there was no aid to lessen Montenegrin suffering.

The consequence was that, in 1816, over two thousand Montenegrins starved to death. The subsequent exodus led Petar to fear: *"There would be none left to defend these lands from the*

Turks."[8] Petar's hopes had unravelled. He had spent what little money there was in trying to liberate Kotor Bay, and even though Russia had withdrawn its subsidy he had still rejected Napoleon Bonaparte's offer to become Patriarch of Dalmatia. The result was only greater hardship.

In the autumn of 1816 Petar wrote to Serbia's Prince Miloš Obrenović asking him to receive Montenegrin emigrants. Miloš complied: "*His Holiness Petar Petrović, Orthodox Serb Metropolitan and Commander of Montenegro, informed me in his letter of the great hunger in his state, and asked if I would mercifully accept a few hundred Montenegrin families with their cattle into our Serbian land to save them from hunger! My brothers, Serb people, I gave my soul for this nation and for my brothers, and today I want with all my soul to bring them to my bosom. I will help with documents to allow them to travel through Bosnia. I am just fearful that it is not too late, that they do not have bad weather on their journey, and I would receive them as brothers.*"

Prince Miloš' generosity was gladly accepted but relations between Serb rulers would not always be so cordial. A philanthropic gesture towards a few hundred starving Montenegrins was one thing, political considerations often another. Miloš himself was consolidating his rule in Serbia, ousting his rival Karadjordje (Black George). His relations with Petar did not develop further and future co-operation between the Serb states would often prove fraught with difficulty and division.

The Napoleonic wars served as particularly cruel lessons, illustrating Montenegro's parlous place on the chessboard of diplomacy and war. The refusal to fully support its independence was bound up with the fear of the consequences if there were a wider Balkan uprising. Serbia had risen against Turkish rule in 1804, led by the iron willed Karadjordje. Montenegrin volunteers went to their aid as Serbia struggled free from 1807 until 1813 when, while other powers were occupied fighting Napoleon Bonaparte, the Turks were able to crush the rebellion. Turkish armies invaded from three sides, restoring Istanbul's rule with savage brutality and forcing Karadjordje to flee. Although Serbia, now led by the astute Prince Miloš, achieved vassal state autonomy, it was becoming ever clearer that the Balkan peoples were being used by larger powers as their own self-interest dictated. The Greeks were more fortunate than Montenegro or Serbia. With Great Power support they gained independence in 1830.

Within Montenegro Petar's authority had grown steadily and he began to build the nucleus of a state. In 1798 a series of laws were promulgated, which were updated at the tribal assembly held at Stanjevići in 1803; it was the first step to introducing a general legal code. Central institutions were also founded, including a court of law and arrangements for the levying of taxes. Problematically, the attempt to tax the tribes provoked rebellions. Taxation had been a powerful reason for rejecting Ottoman rule and the tribes resented its imposition from Cetinje. The symbol of their freedom, which they defended with their lives, was attempting to impose one of the most hated of feudal bonds; why resist oppression from Istanbul merely to accept it from Cetinje? This put Petar in an unenviable position: how could Montenegro become a proper state without the institutions of government and the material means to run them?

Petar was well aware that he lacked the means necessary for building a state and, worse than that, even lacked the means to keep the peace. He commented mournfully: "*I have no stake, no rope and no bayonets, nothing with which I can do anything save for what tongue I may have, and were it not for this, there would be bloodshed everywhere.*"[9]

Actually, this was not entirely true. Petar was not quite as high-minded as he claimed. It was true that he was a moral and self-sacrificing leader, but there was another, less noble, way of forging a nation: by acts of ruthlessness and these he did not eschew. In 1821 he founded the perjaniks, his personal guard of twenty-five men drawn from the most prestigious tribes. Faced with rebellion he had to assert his authority, and to do so he sent the perjaniks to kill two prominent tribal leaders.

However regrettable, this was a normal move in a society bidding to become an integrated state, but at the same time Montenegro was not like other European societies: it was not bound together by feudal ties or the relations developed through trade and commerce, but by something much more ephemeral and emotional, blood and honour. However much he was revered, even the life of the Vladika was put at risk by taking measures which were an affront to blood and honour. In this context, harsh policies were not the answer to the realities of poverty and the desire for tribal autonomy. Petar's state building attempts could never have been substantial, only symbolic.

The Montenegrins would cherish his memory but Petar's struggles on their behalf had worn him out. Like the first great Petrović ruler, Vladika Danilo, Petar, too, might well have concluded: *"That I have lived among this bad and ungovernable people is enough."* Indeed, Petar's own lament was a variation on this gloomy theme: *"If I had done this for any other nation on earth, they would have thanked me and I would have lived among them in happiness and joy, my name honoured by them with eternal love, but among you, my heart has withered from your sins and my old age has become embittered so that I am unable to find rest or joy . . ."*[10]

Nonetheless, Vladika Petar's reign was an era of great victories for Montenegro and he is remembered as a leader of vision and wisdom. His letters to the tribes, such as this remonstrance to the Bjelopavlići, were eloquent and enduring justifications of both his policies and of the mission of the Petrović-Njegoš vladikas: *"It has been forty years since you, with God's help and your brother Montenegrins, as well as with my great efforts and sacrifice, lifted from your necks the heavy burden and slavery of the Turks. Ever since I have been teaching you, pleading and cursing for you to live in peace and harmony, to work for your own welfare and good name, to love and fortify your freedom so that you never forget the suffering of your fathers and forefathers under Turkish tyranny and oppression. So today, praise be to God, you are no longer Turkish slaves . . . and behold, the fortified towers and Turkish domains of Spuž are in your hands, and behold your own precious will and freedom."*[11]

(Below) On Orlov Krš (Eagle's Rock), the hill that rises up behind Cetinje Monastery, there is a monument to Vladika Danilo I. Danilo was originally buried in Podostrog Monastery, near Budva on the Adriatic coast. In 1893, during the preparations for the bicentennial anniversary of the Petrović-Njegoš dynasty, it was decided to build a monument to Danilo in Cetinje where his remains could be laid to rest as he would have wished. The monument was completed in time for the celebrations in 1896. (Left) A Turkish banner captured in the Battle of Kruši of October 4, 1796, at which the Pashas of Scutari's dreams of conquering Montenegro met with their final defeat.

Vladika Rade Tomov Petrović-Njegoš by Johann Boss, 1853. The most remarkable and talented of the Petrović-Njegoš rulers.

The noble genius of Montenegro's bare, bloody rocks.

Above all things on earth I would like to see concord among brethren in whom the same blood courses, whom the same milk has nourished, and the same cradle lulled . . .[1]

We have a custom that became a law: to return in kind whatsoever is given to us. If we did not punish evil with evil, long ago mosques would have appeared in these mountains and this handful of Slavs would have lost their name.[2]

Vladika Rade

Chapter III

Vladika Rade: 1830-1851

It is not certain that Vladika Petar I formally designated Rade Tomov Petrović-Njegoš (Vladika Petar II 1830-51) as his successor before his death in the autumn of 1830. Although Petar had called an assembly of the vojvodas, there were other urgent reasons to do so. Trouble was brewing in the Turkish border provinces and there was also bad blood amongst the tribes. While the old man's death was anticipated, the end came quickly with little warning, taking all, including the Petrovići, by surprise. Petar had been feeling unwell for a few days but he did not feel it to be anything serious. On the evening of October 30, 1830, he went to the Monastery kitchen to warm himself but felt tired and returned to his room to rest. He died in his sleep. It was, enigmatically enough, the night before the assembly was due to be held on St. Luke's Day.

The uncertainty regarding the succession became a highly contentious issue. Petar had originally nominated his nephew, Mitar Stijepov, Archimandrite of the Monastery of Stanjevići, and sent him to Russia to be educated; tragically Mitar sickened in the unhealthy climate and died. In 1823, the vojvodas had chosen Djordje Savov Petrović as Petar's successor and he, too, was sent to Russia to be prepared for his future. Djordje decided he was not suited to a religious career and, in 1829, he transferred to a military school. Petar had said of Djordje's cousin, Rade, that he was a wise and brave young man, even that he regretted not having sent him to Russia instead of Djordje. That said, Rade had not considered entering the church and had actually asked that he be allowed to go into business. Therefore, although tradition demanded that Petar's successor be both a monk and literate, in the end it was clan politics which decided the issue.

The day after Petar's death his 'Last Will and Testament' was read to the vojvodas and, to their astonishment, Rade, who was only seventeen, was named as his successor. It was immediately suspected, and with good reason, that Rade's friend and tutor, the poet Simo Milutinović-Sarajlija, who had been Petar's personal secretary, was the real author. Rade did not hear of his succession until the day it was announced. His relatives called him to the Monastery, dressed him in his late uncle's cassock and thrust the vladika's staff and cross into his hand. His younger cousin, Stanko Stijepov, pushed him outside, shouting at him to go and meet the vojvodas and the people. A shocked and bemused Rade stumbled forward as his relatives came forward to kiss his hand, which greatly embarrassed him.

The appointment was not valid until the vojvodas had given their approval, and Governor Vuko

Radonjić was minded to overturn this sudden accession: *"Let Djordje come himself and refuse at the assembly and then we can choose another."* However, Djordje's father supported Rade saying: *"I know that Djordje renounced his right, as his father I recognise Rade as master."*[3]

An assembly was hastily convened at Velje Guvno where the Archimandrite of Ostrog, Josif Pavićević, again asked that Rade's election be confirmed. An ominous silence ensued, until two vojvodas stepped forward and shouted their acceptance, challenging anyone who disagreed. The assembly signalled its assent with the firing of guns into the air.

Behind the theatre and ritual lay the political rivalry between the Petrovići and their most closely related clan, the Radonjići. One of the vojvodas supporting Rade was Serdar Filip, an ally of the late Vladika Petar I and a hero in his own right. There were many heroic songs about Serdar Filip and Rade later glorified him as the greatest living Montenegrin in his poem 'The Tower of Djurišići'. Serdar Filip was a fearsome warrior and to cross his path could have been a fatal mistake. He placed his honour and his sword behind young Rade at Velje Guvno declaring: *"Is there any Montenegrin who does not accept this? If there is let him speak out and deal with me."*[4] His support was crucial, bringing undecided vojvodas over to the new ruler's side.

Josif Pavićević signed the document of ratification first and, reluctantly, Governor Vuko signed last. However, the Radonjići had not accepted the appointment and were contemptuous of Rade, whom Governor Vuko dismissed as *"that little sniveller."* In this tense atmosphere the Petrovići moved with haste to fully establish the new ruler and in January 1831, with the assent of the Pasha of Scutari, Vladika Hadži Zaharija of Raška and Prizren installed Rade as Archimandrite. The end was nearing for both the Radonjići and the Governorship, an office that had existed since 1717 and had been held by the clan since 1750.

Encouraged by Austria, which still refused to recognise Rade, Governor Vuko continued his campaign. Vuko, however, was either careless or unlucky. Secret correspondence was intercepted and he was accused of treason. Although the evidence was circumstantial he was found guilty and stripped of his office. A clan war seemed imminent and a truce was agreed between the two clans. It did not last: the Petrovići struck first, at Vuko's brother, the influential and wealthy Djuzo, the primary focus for the clan's fears and of Rade's intense hatred. Djuzo was murdered on May 5, 1831, St. George's Day, the patron saint of both clans. An act of political ruthlessness which outraged and shocked the clans, historians cite it as the moment when the Petrovići set themselves apart from their fellow clans.

The remaining Radonjići were treated harshly: Vuko and his brother Marko were thrown into an improvised dungeon in the Monastery fruit cellar and a punitive raid was made against the clan, wherein several were killed. Few believed Vuko actually guilty of treason and the sentence was commuted to exile. However, the contest was over. The Radonjići's long running rivalry with the Petrovići had sealed their fate, and the last Governor died exactly as an enraged Vladika Petar I had once predicted: *"Your money is in Kotor and that is where you will leave your bones."* The way was now clear for Rade to remake Montenegro's government in his own image.

In August 1831, Ivan Ivanović Vukotić, originally from the village of Golubovci in the Ottoman ruled Plain of Zeta which bordered Montenegro, returned from Russia. He had risen to be a non-commissioned officer in the Russian army and had subsequently become wealthy through an inheritance. He now thought to place his wealth behind the Montenegrin cause. In particular, he dreamed of liberating Zeta's urban centre, Podgorica, from the Turkish yoke. He made a bold entrance by claiming he had been sent on a mission by the Russians and quickly became an ally of the Petrovići.

Rade realised that Vukotić's romantic grandeur was an illusion, but when the rumour spread that he had been no less than a General in the Russian army, Rade seized upon the opportunity. Using the seal from Tsar Peter the Great's Grammata of 1711 they forged an imperial decree that instructed Montenegrins to obey the new ruler.

The Vladika and the 'General' now set about constructing a new government. Vukotić installed himself as President of the newly formed Senate of Montenegro, made his nephew Vice-President and gave seats to the leading vojvodas. The new state needed new laws, so Ivan composed a statute with thirty clauses, the most important of which prohibited the state from interfering in religious matters. Even though it was all government on the hoof, it was also a further step in state building that consolidated the power of the Petrovići and helped keep the peace.

Vladika Rade was elected by the tribal assembly on October 31, 1830. However, Rade Tomov Petrović-Njegoš was as surprised as the Montenegrin tribal vojvodas to find himself proclaimed the nation's leader. In the aftermath of his election the political struggle between the Petrovići and their rivals, the Radonjići, turned violent. The Radonjići, who had shared power through the Governorship, were accused of treason and of being in league with Austria. Their leaders were either killed or exiled.

Rade's accession had come about through the machination of clan politics and although he had soon shown that his political skills were not lacking, his personal qualities were largely unknown. The Montenegrins could not yet know it but chance had provided them with a remarkable leader; the imposing, handsome and exceptionally gifted young ruler would prove to be a defining personality in the country's history.

Standing at some six-foot-six inches, tall even for a Montenegrin, Rade was described by the Italian botanist Bartolomeo Biasoletto as *"of magnificent appearance, kind, courteous and cultured."* Other observers noted his intelligence and charm, as well as a brooding nature marked by outbursts of temper. Most significantly, Rade had an unquenchable thirst for knowledge and eagerly educated himself in European literature and languages. He would mature to become a poet and a philosopher of stature, one who gave eloquent expression to Montenegrin beliefs and aspirations.

Certainly a surprising man to find among those bare, bloody rocks, a lonely genius about to bloom, he was, less surprisingly, popular with and enjoyed the companionship of the fair sex. Rade, however, had received a warning about getting involved with women, a warning he was not inclined to heed. *"Some,"* he said, *"gave me the advice not to turn my eyes towards the female sex, but one cannot, even from his death bed, avoid to look at a beautiful creature."*[5] Although he was forbidden to marry by his religious position, it did not prevent Rade from having several love affairs.

Rade was many things, but he was not by inclination a monk. He rarely wore the long black robes of the Orthodox priests, preferring instead the national costume, and hated wearing a beard which he pointedly kept neatly trimmed in preference to the more traditional long, but untidy and usually uncut variety.

An unconventional churchman, Rade was also conspicuously lax in his official duties: he preferred to invest priests by the dozen rather than repeat the tedious ceremonies and cared little for preaching. He liked best to be among the people who revered him all the more for it. He had a habit of offering cigarettes to the people he met who would find an unusual use for them: *"As was his custom he would offer cigarettes made from Montenegrin tobacco in Lješane. However, those who received cigarettes from Vladika Rade would not smoke them but cut them into small pieces and save them as saintly relics."*[6]

Although he was rather casual in his approach to religious form, religion as moral philosophy was an absolute truth for Rade. He was also a profoundly spiritual man, but this was a personal rather than a narrowly religious philosophy, one influenced by the many religious currents that met in the Balkans which he combined with his own remarkable perceptions. He accepted his earthly task as part of those lofty obligations: the Montenegrins, their well-being, their protection and, above all, the liberation of the Serb people throughout the Balkans were the inspiration of his life and duties he never neglected as long as he lived.

He realised the need for the nation to be governed by agencies imbued with genuine authority. The prestige of the Petrovići, he believed, could be a most useful tool to that end and Rade pronounced his late uncle a saint in 1834. None doubted that Vladika Petar I deserved every accolade and honour, but his sainthood was also something more: the glorification of the Petrović dynasty and a further strengthening of their authority. It also gave notice that Rade would continue the work begun by his predecessor, and he set about building upon the basic institutions of central government, establishing the Senate and the Guardia.

The Senate, the executive and judicial body that Rade had founded with Ivan Ivanović Vukotić, was at the heart of the fledgling state. The senators were chosen from among the most respected vojvodas, thereby giving the tribal leaders incentive to support the centralisation of government. The Guardia formed the next tier of government. Rade asserted, with some exaggeration, that it was one hundred and sixty-four men strong. The reality was that its thirty-two men, salaried at twenty thalers a year, acted as the executors of Senate decisions. Established in each district, with its headquarters at Rijeka Crnojevića, the Guardia was a kind of regional police force and court, while the Senate remained the higher authority. The Vladika's personal guard, the perjaniks, was increased, and the first prison was established.

These reforms were important steps in Montenegrin governance, but their dignity was somewhat reduced by some embarrassing revelations. Rade was certainly embarrassed when his friend, Serbia's leading cultural figure, Vuk Stefanović Karadžić, recorded that all Montenegrins, even the senators, went without underwear, and that the building housing the Senate was separated to allow the senators to enter on one side and cattle on the other.

Vuk's public airing of these unfortunate facts angered another member of Rade's family: his cousin Djordje, who objected to Vuk's candid portrayal of Montenegrin poverty. When the two met in Trieste, Vuk's welcoming embrace was met with hostility: *"You and I are not going to do that"* Djordje told Vuk. *"No one knew about the Vladika's donkey but now, because of you, the whole of Europe does. Did you not have anything more pleasant and interesting to write about than his donkey? I can see that you have a crippled leg* [Vuk's left leg was withered due to a life-long problem with rheumatism], *but you clearly have a crippled mind as well. Next time you come to Montenegro I will break the other leg so you will not be able to walk at all."*

Fortunately, Vuk survived Djordje's wrath, although on a visit to Cetinje in 1852 he confessed

Vladika Rade built the first rulers residence in Cetinje, the Biljarda, that took its name from Rade's favourite pastime of playing billiards. The future ruler of Montenegro, Nikola Mirkov Petrović-Njegoš, remembered his childhood encounters with the great Vladika: *"I was a frail young boy playing in the Biljarda. The Vladika had forbidden anyone to touch the billiard table, balls and cue, but I had never seen a billiard table before. Where could I? So, my biggest pleasure was to go into the salon of the Biljarda and play with the white balls on the stretched silk of the billiard table. Those balls were very beautiful to me! I was only so high that my head reached to just over the side of the billiard table, so I was able to aim the balls left and right with both hands. One time the Vladika came unexpectedly and quietly. I did not notice him. What to do now? I felt guilty and, being afraid, hid under the billiard table."* Rade did not notice young Nikola hiding under his beloved billiard table, but on another occasion Nikola found himself in trouble: *"He had forbade me to go outside in the rain or snow, but I disobeyed him. He saw me from the window and called to me to come to the fire-place room. I was all wet from the snow and rain and I did not dare to approach him. I stood by the door like a culprit. I remember a tall man coming to me, taking me under my arms and lifting me up very easily, to look me in the eye. He placed me on top of a high cabinet, which was so high that everybody else had to step on a chair to be able to put something on top of it, but the Vladika was so tall that he could reach it easily. My punishment was to stay up there until my clothes had dried."*

to the new ruler Prince Danilo: *"Your Highness, I am afraid because Djordje wants to break this healthy leg!"* Danilo was an even fiercer personality than Djordje and regarded this as overly emotional and unmanly. He told Vuk: *"Do not be afraid, man. You behave as if your mother was a Latin!"* Vuk replied diplomatically: *"Your Highness, I am placing my faith in you."*[7]

Rade knew that Vuk's observations wounded Montenegrin pride, but only because they were true. The country was certainly poor and undeveloped, even by Balkan standards. As one of a handful of literate men, Rade saw clearly that education was of paramount importance. Even the capital lacked a school and, in 1833, he asked Tsar Nikolai I to educate five Montenegrin boys in Russian schools, while four more were sent to Kotor.

By the mid 1830's the first elementary schools were founded in Cetinje and Dobrsko Selo. The students were given state grants, in real terms funds from the Vladika, that afforded them room and board. It was a start, but Montenegrin students had to be clansmen and warriors too and were often obliged to excuse themselves to defend their homes and land from attack. In 1834, with the help of Venetian money, a Russian printing press was brought to Montenegro.

Progress was slow, but Rade's determination unwavering. He wrote to Serbian statesman Ilija

Vladika Rade's staff and gown. The ruler, however, preferred to wear his Montenegrin national costume and was rarely seen in the glory of his priestly regalia.

Garašanin: *"I have been doing my best, as I still do, to expand education and therefore I have founded primary schools, while I plan to found secondary schools as well, because I am certain that is how the nation becomes educated and achieves happiness."*[8]

As for infrastructure, only the smallest steps could be taken. The first road, a horse trail for the Katuni Nahi was laid, running from Cetinje to the River Crnojevići, and the first hostel was built at Krstac *en route* to Kotor Bay. The road workers were paid well and each man given a medal with the inscription 'Courage, for faith and freedom'. Rade knew what was needed and how little could be done, yet he did what he could.

He found much the same problem in his foreign policy. Although the near constant state of rebellion that passed for peace in the Turkish provinces continued, the moment was not yet ripe for the wars of liberation. That would have to wait until the reigns of Prince Danilo and Prince Nikola. All the same, some progress was made to dignify the nation. The battles and conflicts fought in Rade's reign enabled Montenegro to maintain its traditional claims to Herzegovina Province, territory around the basin of Lake Skadar and parts of the Adriatic coastline.

Initially Rade's hopes had been raised by Turkey's troubles. Sultan Abdul Mejid's 'Tanzimat Reforms' were a major attempt to revitalise the Ottoman Empire, but this provoked a rebellion from the powerful Moslem landowners, the *beys* of Bosnia-Herzegovina. The *beys* were defeated but, with Istanbul's authority in the Balkans apparently ready to crumble, Rade searched for opportunities to add to Turkish difficulties.

He found an unlikely ally in a Serb renegade, Ali Pasha Rizvanbegović, Vizier of Mostar in Herzegovina. Ali Pasha had come to prominence by helping Istanbul defeat the *beys*, after which he was rewarded with the Pashalik of Mostar. Naturally, to begin with, he was Rade and Montenegro's sworn enemy and the clans of Grahovo and the Uskoks were the *casus belli* between them.

The clans of Grahovo, on Montenegro's western border with Herzegovina, were waging a protracted struggle to free themselves from the grip of the *beys*. Unification with Montenegro would bring freedom and their leader, Vojvoda Jakov Daković, defied Ali Pasha's warnings: *"We are not the Sultan's raia, nor do we recognise the Sultan's authority, we are the men of the Vladika of Montenegro, who is our sovereign."* Punishment soon followed this defiant statement: Ali Pasha brought an army of twenty thousand to Grahovo and razed it to the ground. Rade and a few hundred angry Montenegrins responded with an impetuous attack on August 23, 1836, but they were, predictably, defeated. Thirty-two of the best Montenegrins and ten men of Grahovo died, among them two Petrovići: Rade's younger brother Joko and Stevo Stankov. Bloodied but defiant, the Montenegrin army stood its ground until Ali Pasha left the field.

Rade justified his actions to the Russian Consul in Dubrovnik, Jeremija Gagić: *"Grahovo is ours, and what is ours we do not relinquish easily, just as no one else gives up what is his, for if we gave in our small tribe would disappear among our many enemies."*[9]

The belligerents agreed a peace treaty which defined the tribute the clans of Grahovo would pay to the Sublime Porte, but the border remained disputed and lawless and it was only a matter of time before tensions resurfaced. It was Ali Pasha who raised the stakes by imprisoning Jakov Daković, a priest, and several clansmen. They were released in the spring of 1839, but not before a band of Grahovo men, who had tried to rescue Daković, were captured and beheaded.

The Uskoks, who lived on the upper reaches of the Morača River, were constant raiders into Turkish territory. Rade, like Vladika Petar I before him, saw the Uskoks as Montenegrins for, like the Njeguši, they were Herzegovinian refugees. However, neither Petar nor Rade had even visited them. Despite that failing, the Uskoks still looked to Cetinje and Rade to protect them from Ali Pasha, who wanted to drive them from their homes. Skirmishes and acts of treachery abounded but, so long as they could survive, Rade felt the Uskoks would eventually unite with Montenegro.

If the tribes of Grahovo and the Uskoks were a bone of contention between Rade and Ali Pasha, necessity often makes for strange bedfellows and the activities of a feared Turkish commander, Smail Aga Čengić, brought the Vladika and the Pasha together. Smail Aga, reputedly a true Turk but most likely a renegade Slav, had distinguished himself in the imperial army, most notably at the Battle of Grahovo in 1836. He specialised in the subjugation of the peasantry and was hated by the Serb *raia*.

Smail Aga controlled extensive territories, greater in extent than the whole of Montenegro, and both Rade and Ali Pasha had good reason to fear his ambitions. And, as much as Rade despised a renegade, he also knew that Ali Pasha was at heart a Serb, whose aristocratic loyalty was to himself and the Herzegovinian *beys* rather than the Sublime Porte. In the meantime, Serbia's Prince Miloš Obrenović had informed Ali Pasha that Smail Aga had asked the Sublime Porte for an order to move against him. Once armed with the news of this imminent threat, Ali Pasha had little difficulty realising that turning the Montenegrin's desire for vengeance toward the Lord of Gacko served his own interests very well. In fact they needed little encouragement. Humiliated at the disastrous encounter at Grahovo, they were thirsting for revenge against the Turks, while the Petrovići's goal was the head of Smail Aga: honour and prestige would be restored with a single blow.

Both Ali Pasha and Rade were complicitly, if not overtly, involved in the plot to get rid of Smail Aga, which culminated with his ambush and murder in the woods near the village of Mijetičak. Spies in his retinue had hobbled the horses and the misty morning lent surprise to the attack. A single bullet sufficed, after which the feared warlord was beheaded as his retinue were hunted down.

Rade had no doubt it was a justified killing, as he informed Jeremija Gagić: *"The well-known criminal Smail Aga Čengić, Lord of Gacko, Pljevlja, Kolašin, and Drobnjaci, used to attack our borders every year with several thousand men. A few days ago he pitched his tent on our borders once more and began gathering men to attack Morača. Our people found out about it and, on September 23 [October 5, 1840], three to four hundred of them attacked him in his tent and killed him along with fourteen other evildoers . . ."*[10]

The actual killers were a band from the Drobnjaci clan and Rade hurried out from Cetinje to congratulate them. Their leader, Novica Cerović, presented him with a gruesome trophy: the severed head of Smail Aga. Despite his part in the murder plot, Ali Pasha sought to keep up appearances for his masters in Istanbul and sent an army to punish the Drobnjaci. Several villages were put to the torch and around seventy were killed. This pacification of rebellious *raia* was the least he could be seen to do. The fact that only the Drobnjaci suffered for Smail Aga's death made it something of a token strike rather than a serious reprisal, which served to screen Ali Pasha's pact with Rade from the Sublime Porte.

The other local Ottoman governors were genuinely outraged and inevitably more brutal. One of them, Smail Aga's brother, Ali Aga, killed a Serb traveller and a band of Drobnjaci; the monk who had brought the news to Rade was hacked to pieces on his way back from Cetinje. Neither side shrank from horrific acts and neither could see a resolution except in the other's destruction. Rade had risked a full scale invasion with the assassination and the Drobnjaci their own destruction, but both had gambled successfully.

Nonetheless, both enemies and allies alike were infuriated by the audacious act. From the

Turkish viewpoint, Smail Aga's murder had not robbed them of a 'well known criminal', but of an effective operative whose death was all the more grievous because it had been brought about by infidel rebels. The Turks also blamed the Russians for being unable to control their Montenegrin ally, but both powers, fearing each other, declined to take military action. Conversely, among the tribes and the restless *raia* of Herzegovina the assassination restored the prestige of Cetinje and its ruler.

Furthermore, the plot to kill Smail Aga was not just a temporary measure, designed to serve one aspect of mutual self-interest. A political friendship arose out of it, which was sealed in the autumn of 1842 when Rade and Ali Pasha met on neutral territory, in the Austrian ruled port of Dubrovnik.

The meeting was also the occasion for a clash of two fair sized rival egos, which saw the two rulers doing their utmost to outdo the other in prestige. Rade, accompanied by several vojvodas as a guard of honour, was at his most handsome as, dressed in national costume, he made his entrance. However, Ali Pasha outmanoeuvred him: pleading ill health and stormy weather he arrived a full eight days late to ensure that he could make his arrival as the senior figure.

Despite the competition for prestige, the talks went well. So well in fact that an emotional and drunken Ali Pasha arm-twisted Rade into becoming his blood brother. It was a slight embarrassment for Rade but also a further indication of Ali Pasha's weakening allegiance to the Sublime Porte. Both Ali Pasha, the old realist, and Rade, the young idealist, represented a potential threat of South Slav unity to an already weakened Empire desperately trying to reform itself and survive. To be sure, the Sublime Porte would respond.

The liberal minded Sultan Abdul Mejid had confided to Britain's Lord Stratford de Canning that he only needed to find ten pashas to co-operate with his reform programme to be certain of success. Ali Pasha was certainly not among the ten, but Osman Pasha Skopljak of Scutari, son-in-law to the late Smail Aga, proved to be a man the Sultan could rely on.

On September 21, 1843, Osman attacked Montenegro from Lake Skadar, taking the island of Vranjina, the rock of Lesandro and gaining control of the exits at Rijeka Crnojevića and the River Crmnica. The Montenegrins, anticipating further incursions, responded by blocking the exits at Vranjina and Žabljak. However, Osman did not plan to take Cetinje, since he knew how often this had proved a futile exercise.

Instead, he sought to exploit economic vulnerability. By cutting off Montenegro from the Plain of Zeta he waged another kind of war: a blockade which threatened the slow strangulation of the local economy. Osman could even claim that the islands were already his possessions, neatly reversing the argument the Montenegrins liked to use over the disputed border territories. Trade between Montenegro, Scutari Province and Podgorica was choked off and, without access to livestock, fish and salt, starvation became an immediate threat. Fortified with troops and cannon, Osman could repulse any attempt to lift the blockade; whereas Rade's two ageing cannon had such short range that they could not even reach the Turkish positions.

Osman then set about trying to divide the Montenegrins. He offered the border tribes bribes and offered Rade the same status as the Prince of Serbia if he accepted Turkish suzerainty. Rade refused outright. Politically it was a reasonable offer but acceptance would have negated the national struggle, the fundamental reason for Montenegro's resistance and, above all, it would have been a betrayal of the ideal that sustained the Vladika.

Unable to break the stranglehold all Rade could do was to turn to the Great Powers. He hastened to Vienna to meet with Austria's Prince Metternich and sent pleas to Russia. Help was promised by all but nothing of substance materialised. Rade journeyed to Trieste and Venice in the hope of acquiring munitions, and finally onto Dubrovnik to hire shipbuilders, but even the commercially minded port that Rade considered everyone's flunky refused to take his money.

Rade's relations with Ali Pasha hinted at the potential for South Slavs of different faiths to join forces, but his relations with Osman Pasha emphasised the opposite: the division the Ottoman conquest had created between them. There was an ideological and deeply personal hatred between the two men for Osman Pasha was a Serb from Bosnia whose father, Suleiman Pasha, had put down the Serbian uprising in 1813.

Rade wrote to the renegade striving to rekindle the bond between Serbs: *"Above all things on earth I would like to see concord among brethren in whom the same blood courses, whom the same*

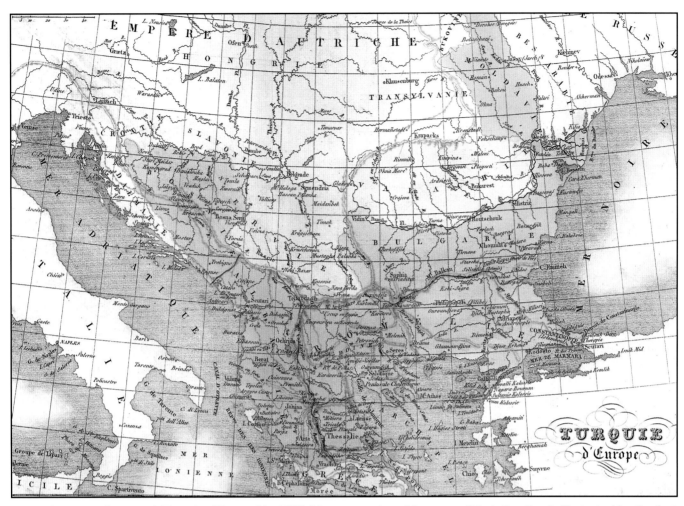

An antique French map of 'Turquie d'Europe' in 1836. Montenegro's ambiguous political situation is illustrated by the fact that, while the capital Cetinje is shown, the existence of an independent state or its borders are unmarked. The Ottoman Empire steadfastly refused to recognise Montenegrin statehood, and the other European powers offered intermittent support if and when it served their interests.

milk has nourished, and the same cradle lulled . . ." Osman knew the truth of it: *"You write that we are birds of the same nest, and I know that we are of one blood . . ."* but he cared little for those bonds so sacred to Rade.

Rade's hatred engulfed him: *"Firstly, you said we should purify our hearts and in a cordial way make peace over our borders. The heart that is with the people is ever pure and clean, but with those who are inhuman one must deal inhumanly, for even if he so wished there is no other way . . .When you talk to me like my brother Bosnian, I am your brother, your friend, but when you talk as a Turk, an Asiatic, as an enemy of our tribe and name I am opposing it as would any right thinking man."* Such insolence was too much for Osman: *"I am a Turk and thou art an unbeliever and we cannot agree."*

Osman's contempt brought out the vengeful clansman in Rade and vice versa. Each resolved to do away with the other. Rade sent out an assassin who made it all the way to Osman Pasha's capital, Scutari, but lost his nerve at the vital moment, while an agent in Osman's employ blew up Rade's quarters and another tried to poison him.

Osman shattered Rade's hopes of concord between estranged brothers and anger, cynicism and fatalism colour his subsequent letters, which were clearly written with pen dipped in the ink of bitterness: *"Brutality was always at the base of the Turkish soul, they cover a wolf's heart with sheep's clothing[11] . . . The Turks present themselves to Europe as good people, but towards us they are the same as they were in the seventeenth century[12] . . . Until one of our paths disappears from Europe relations between us will remain the same."[13]*

Though disillusion is often the fate of idealists, in Rade's case his spirit and his sense of mission drew strength from the ugly and seemingly endless struggle the Montenegrins were trapped in. If the issue could not be resolved on the battlefield then the poet and the philosopher, the pen and not the sword, would finally see justice triumph.

In a brief, brilliant burst of creative energy that lasted three years, Rade, writing under the literary name of 'Njegoš', produced his three great poems: 'The Ray of Microcosm', 'The Mountain Wreath' and 'The False Tsar Šćepan Mali'.

Vojvoda Novica Cerović by Ivan Rendić. Vojvoda Cerović is remembered as the leader of the armed band which killed the hated Turkish warlord Smail Aga Čengić in 1840, avenging Montenegro's defeat at the Battle of Grahovo in 1836.

He possessed a remarkable literary talent which he had nourished through studies of the Greek classics and the many Russian books that filled his library. However, poetry was his greatest love, particularly the works of Byron, Dante, Lamartine and Petrarch.

Rade's talent was placed at the service of the nation. It led to the creation of great and distinctive poetic masterpieces. Immersed in the rich oral traditions and folk history that sustained the Montenegrins, his poetry was an expression of his religious philosophy, his love for the people and their culture, and a call to arms in the struggle against their oppressors.

His unfailing ear and feeling for the Montenegrin dialect would result in its greatest poetic expression, while his remarkable perception provided a wealth of insights and sayings that enrich South Slav culture to this day. It was undoubtedly a personal crusade and a labour of love for Rade. The publication of his poems were not acclaimed by, or even known to many, during his lifetime. Despite his originality and genius recognition would only come posthumously.

His greatest work 'The Mountain Wreath' remains controversial, concerning itself with the massacre of Moslems in Montenegro in the reign of Vladika Danilo. Although this event, known as the Montenegrin Vespers, is said to have taken place at the start of the eighteenth century, it is uncertain whether it is fact or legend. The actual event from which folk history takes its cue was highly localised within one clan, the Djeklić. Folk history may also have dramatised processes which took place over much longer periods of time. It has been verified that Moslems settled in the Katuni Nahi and, given the periodic hostility between the Montenegrin tribes and their Moslem neighbours, they may have been forced out over time or assimilated.

Nevertheless, Montenegrin folk history vividly remembered the Vespers and Rade's friend and tutor, Simo Milutinović-Sarajlija, included it in his history of Montenegro. According to Sarajlija, it was the dishonesty and brutality of the Turkish governor, Demir Pasha, which precipitated the event. He had been sent to establish Turkish rule in Albania and on the Plain of Zeta. One of his schemes was to capture Vladika Danilo through a deceit and have him tortured in an attempt to gain his conversion to Islam. Danilo only escaped crucifixion after the people of Zeta gathered a sufficient ransom.

In 'The Mountain Wreath' Rade considers the enduring themes of Serb national history: the Battle of Kosovo Polje, the sacrifice of Miloš Obilić, the treachery of Vuk Branković and, above all, the enmity between brethren divided by hostile religions. Portraying events leading up to the massacre, the breadth and depth of Rade's vision is revealed. He agonises over and fights against each step leading to the brutal climax, but his absolute adherence to and belief in the rightness of the Serb struggle is never in doubt. Rade and Njegoš, the ruler and the poet, believed literature to be man's highest calling, and the single most important contribution he could make to the Montenegrin and Serb cause. That conviction compelled him to create powerful and profound literature of continuing relevance.

Just the same, heroism in battle meant as much to Rade as any Montenegrin, and his literary calling did little to ease his frustration at his political and military impotence. He deeply regretted having won no great battles, although he had willingly risked his life and nearly lost it through reckless bravery in the face of Osman Pasha's cannon. While Rade was visiting the frontlines at Lesandro, the enemy noticed his red coat and took aim at him. He was only saved by the misfortune of a Crmnica man who came to kiss his hand just as the cannonball arrived, literally taking his head off instead of killing Rade. The vojvodas tried to get him away from danger but he refused to budge. *"What the hell!,"* Rade exclaimed, *"I am not moving from here, and I will remain here as long as you. My life is no more dear to me than yours is to you."*[14]

Rade's forthright reaction to danger revealed his personal courage, but also his sense of failure. Throughout his reign he had pushed and prodded at the border territories looking for a weakness, hoping and waiting for the moment when he could add to Montenegro's territory or, better still, set off an avalanche to sweep away Ottoman rule once and for all.

Events outside of Montenegro finally seemed to suggest that the time was right. The hopes of the South Slavs across the Balkans were raised by the liberal revolutions of 1848, which erupted across Europe and confronted the autocratic rulers of the continent with demands for new constitutions. However, the South Slavs found themselves on the side of counter-revolution, just as they had been during the Napoleonic wars. While dreaming of liberation, they found themselves potential victims of other national movements in Hungary and Italy. In particular, the intolerance of Hungarian rule in the Habsburg Empire's Croatian provinces and toward the Serbs of the Banat, Vojvodina, had encouraged South Slav co-operation. They therefore hoped loyalty to Vienna would further their cause. The Habsburgs certainly needed their South Slavs subjects who were the mainstay of the Empire's armies, in Italy under General Radetsky and in Hungary under the Croat General Joseph Jelačić.

The Croats were at the forefront of events and, in defiance of Hungarian rule, the Kingdom of Croatia, Slavonia and Dalmatia was proclaimed on March 25, 1848. Of especial importance was the National Assembly's appointment of General Jelačić as Ban. At the opening of the Croatian Diet, in June 1848, which was attended by seventy Serb delegates and the Serbian Patriarch, High Mass was celebrated in the Old Slavonic language.

Rade was forced to watch all this from the sidelines. He even had the problem of Montenegrin raids on the village of Dobrota led by his uncle, Lazo Proroković of Crmnica, and later another similar attack on Kotor. In response, Rade mounted his white horse and rode down to the coast to patch things up. The Governor of Kotor had prepared a room for him, but Rade went straight onto Dobrota to reassure the frightened people. The following day a meeting was held in Kotor. Lazo was unrepentant telling the Austrians: *"If it were not for the Vladika, we would have burned it all, right up to Dubrovnik, and then you could have asked your Emperor for help."*

Rade tried to reassert his authority but the delimitation of the Austro-Montenegrin border he had agreed to involved pasture, water and rights of way and Lazo's region had suffered in that regard. *"Do not tell me to shut up Master!"* an infuriated Lazo told Rade. *"If you want to make such a peace contract for Montenegro that is your right, but for my region I will not."* Lazo also chastised Rade for having sold the monasteries of Majine and Stanjevići to Austria.

Lazo's raids were a protest against Austria's control of the coastline. A fierce Montenegrin patriot, he detested Austrian rule and wrote anonymously to the people of Kotor Bay: *"We are all dying because of Austria, let us defend ourselves like brothers from that devil . . ."*[15] At the least he hoped to ensure that they did not impose passport controls on Montenegrins travelling down to the coast and, in this much, he succeeded.

Still, the Austrians were mistaken in fearing an organised Montenegrin attempt to annex the bay. The reality was that both attacks had been unauthorised raids, which Rade deplored in private but excused publicly as a provocation on the part of the Austrians.

Lazo and the clans of Crmnica were typically wilful, independent Montenegrins and, even though he was wholly devoted to the people, Rade's dealings with them inevitably took its toll. Like his predecessors he too cried out against his compatriots: *"For God's sake do you know these Montenegrins? . . I was born and raised amongst them and I still do not know them . . . I am tired of everything and I would like to go anywhere else, to some deserted island where there is no one so I can live there in peace."*[16] His sense of duty would never allow him that escape and Lazo was firmly instructed to make amends to the people of Dobrota.

The nuances of Rade's foreign policy can be understood only by recalling that not only did he have to consider Montenegro's aspirations and shortcomings, but also the support amongst the people of Kotor Bay for Croatia, as well as the newly formed Venetian Republic led by Daniele Manin. Liberation could be pursued through many means and it was not the right moment to advance Montenegrin claims to Austrian territory. As a pioneering advocate and enthusiastic supporter of South Slav unity Rade could, however, welcome the declaration from the leaders of Kotor Bay that they would gladly join a united South Slav state, even though it would still be under Habsburg rule.

As revolution continued to threaten the Habsburg throne, Rade searched for ways to further the South Slav cause. He offered General Jelačić two thousand Montenegrin fighters and five thousand to the Russians in their campaign against the Hungarians. Both declined, since the nature of the military campaign and political considerations made the Montenegrins problematic allies.

More direct possibilities lay in assisting Serbia in an uprising against Turkey in the provinces of Kosovo and Bosnia-Herzegovina. To this end, Rade expressed his willingness for Montenegro to unite with Serbia under Prince Aleksandar Karadjordjević. In the proposed unified state Rade was to be patriarch. However, Serbia had other more immediate concerns: namely, assisting the Serbs of the Banat, Vojvodina. The joint campaign against Turkey was never realised, which Rade considered a missed opportunity and a grave mistake.

South Slavs still took hope when the Austrians, freed from Italian concerns by the victories of General Radetsky's forces, turned their attention to Hungary and General Jelačić swept all before him. The Serbs of the Banat, Vojvodina, whose requests for cultural and language rights had been summarily dismissed, were already fighting the Hungarians and General Jelačić went to their aid. He almost reached Budapest but had to turn back to put down a renewed rebellion in Vienna. The Hungarians now marched on Vienna, but were finally defeated at the Battle of Schwechat and Vienna.

The struggle had been a close one and the Habsburg dynasty could have been overthrown had the Hungarians and Italians won a victory. Nonetheless, saving the Habsburgs their throne earned the South Slavs nothing for their efforts.

As in the rest of Europe, the revolutions of 1848 had given the Austrians a severe fright. They believed the only way to restore order was through repression. In this context, the Habsburgs concluded they could not afford to grant concessions, even to their loyal Slav subjects. In an effort to expunge all notions of freedom, which is after all the antithesis of autocracy, they reduced South Slav rights to less than their traditional level. The socialist revolutionary Karl Marx, whose Communist Manifesto was published in 1848,

The Russian Consul in Dubrovnik, Jeremija Gagić. One of his official duties was to report to St. Petersburg on the Montenegrins, but he was also a Serb patriot who became a friend and admirer of Vladika Rade. The correspondence between the two men is regarded as having both a diplomatic and a literary value.

Alongside the Ottoman Empire, Montenegro's western neighbour Venice was one of the few states that had first hand knowledge of the mountaineers. By the time of Vladika Rade's reign the Venetian Republic had fallen under Austrian rule, but Rade hoped history could bolster Montenegro's case for international recognition. On February 25, 1847, the Vladika arrived in Venice to search the Venetian state archives for records of relations between the two states; one of his hopes was to find documents proving Montenegro's right to the Plain of Zeta. Archive Director, Signor Giovanni Antonio Ninfa-Priuli, reported to Governor Palfi of Venice that he had offered full assistance to Rade and asked if he should continue to do so. Ninfa-Priuli received no reply and Rade continued his searches. After Rade's departure in April, the Viennese authorities learned from the Venetians of his activities and official suspicions were aroused. A minor crisis followed as the authorities tried to uncover which documents Rade had seen and copied. Ninfa-Priuli was severely reprimanded and the Venetians were forbidden from allowing Rade a similar opportunity again.

noted that the South Slavs could not have been treated worse had they fought on the losing side.

General Jelačić had been betrayed and had thereby, unwittingly, betrayed his people. *"A more wholesale act of injustice, ingratitude and bad faith, a display on a larger scale of a mean and paltry spirit, grosser fraud, more clumsily veiled, it would be more difficult to meet with in all the pages of history"* was his bitter appraisal.

Vladika Rade had realised earlier than most that the moment of destiny had not arrived, regardless of how promising the upheavals of 1848 may have made it seem for the South Slav cause. He remarked: *"I see great mistakes . . . that a departure has been made from the main goal."* He also lambasted the South Slavs for their own submissiveness. In November 1848, with General Jelačić's armies triumphant, he wrote: *"Oh wretched Slavs! What would Europe do without such slaves? The Austrian Master would have to take off his gloves and the Turkish Lord put aside his pipe . . . It never ceases to surprise me how much our people need their slavery. They are like dogs, for a dog struggles to gain his freedom but once he is free runs back to the leash to be tied."*[17]

The disappointment of the revolutionary year was the last great crisis of Rade's reign; his death,

(Facing page) Vladika Rade (1830-1851). Rade was originally buried in Cetinje but, in accordance with his wishes, in September 1855, his remains were taken to the peak of Mount Lovćen. Since then his mausoleum has become a place of pilgrimage and homage.
(Left) The poet's notebook and

gusle. Amongst Rade's achievements his literary legacy is the most enduring: his two greatest works, 'The Mountain Wreath' and 'The Ray Of Microcosm', remain powerful and provocative works of art.

from that scourge of the nineteenth century, tuberculosis, would be an untimely one.

Although he was an exceptionally tall man, he was not well muscled but rather shallow chested and had shown possible symptoms of the disease as early as 1847. In the winter of 1850 he was laid low by cold and cough and in the belief that it would facilitate a cure he gave up smoking.

It appeared to have worked and from Risan nearby to Kotor, Vuk Popović, a colleague of Vuk Stefanović Karadžić, was full of optimism as he recorded: *"Montenegro's Vladika is fully recovered. He has given up smoking and does not allow anyone to smoke near him."* However, Rade's apparent recovery was only short lived.

One evening, while enjoying his favourite pastime of billiards, his condition worsened. He retired to his room and started to cough up blood. In March he went down to Kotor to take advantage of the sea air and to receive medical treatment, Cetinje not yet having its own doctor. The steep path to the coast, the famous 'ladder' to Kotor Bay, was still covered in snow and the sickly, weak ruler of Montenegro was forced to walk. *"The trip down to Kotor was very hard for me, but a drowning man does not choose boats"*[18] he wrote laconically.

Montenegrins believed that they were particularly susceptible to tuberculosis and word soon spread that the Vladika had contracted the consumptive disease. The people were told it was just a severe cold left untreated, but rumours then spread that Rade had fled a rebellion. He chose to stay unobtrusively in the village of Prčanj, but the people soon found out where he was and brought him gifts from their own homes. He gave them away to the poor.

Rade grew weaker still and, because there was a lack of specialist treatment in Kotor, he left for Italy. However, the hot summer and the stress of travelling only made him worse. Fearing to die on foreign soil he rushed back to Montenegro, his condition worsening all the way. Vuk Popović described his appearance on his return: *"When he set foot on dry land, you should have seen him struggling for life, you would really have thought that he had not long left to live. His doctor made the sign of the cross to him."*[19]

The people of Kotor Bay were by now well aware that the Vladika was dying, and they greeted him by mourning in traditional fashion: wailing, tearing their hair and gouging their skin. They succeeded only in distressing Rade even more. He retreated to Njeguši and the simple folk remedies of his self-taught brother: a healthy peasant diet of honey, fat, milk and cream, aided by the clean, invigorating mountain air. Remarkably, by August, Rade seemed to be recovering, but he sensed that it was only temporary. To avoid the ravages of winter in Montenegro, he departed once more for Italy. It would be a final respite, a last Grand Tour for Montenegro's greatest Vladika, who had become in spirit and deed, if not by title, its first prince.

Between December 1850 and May 1851 Rade visited the great Italian cities; a brief spiritual recuperation, notably in Naples where an American admiral took him aboard ship and received him as the ruler of an independent state. It was the only respite he would receive.

On his return to Montenegro, even with death approaching, Rade was fighting off troubles as a resurgence of Turkish power seemed to be at hand.

Fate had also caught up with his old ally Ali Pasha, whose fall was humiliatingly demonstrated to the *raia*. Ali Pasha had been willing to ally with Montenegro and Serbia during the 1848 crisis. In response, the Sublime Porte sent a formidable new vizier to Bosnia, Omer Pasha Latas, to put an end to his schemes. He had the ageing Ali Pasha ride seated backwards on a donkey, led by his own son, through his capital Mostar, and on toward the Krajina where rebellious *beys* also awaited Omer's retribution. *En route* at Dobrun near Banja Luka, on March 30, 1851, Ali Pasha was strangled in traditional Ottoman style.

The prospects of a Herzegovinian uprising had faded and, as Omer Pasha tightened his grip, Rade rushed to Vienna looking for support in anticipation of an attack. Tsar Nikolai I, who was resting nearby at Olmutz Spa, refused to see him. Counter-revolution was the order of the day for Europe's monarchs and rebels and insurgents, even those of the same race and religion, were an unwelcome reminder of the terrors of 1848.

The few futile weeks he spent in Vienna saw Rade's condition worsen quickly and, against his doctor's advice, he returned to Montenegro. His last days were spent in Cetinje surrounded by his family and the vojvodas. Despite his unremitting struggles he felt that he had failed them: *"I am dying Montenegrins, but I do not regret to die, only not to live for at least two more years and then you would see the legacy I would leave you. I have lived among you, but you did not know me; the time will come when you will remember me and say: 'The Vladika was good in comparison to these other bitter experiences'."*

Death took Rade on October 31, 1851, shortly after a final, tearful meeting with his father. His last hours were fevered and pain stricken. His last words were reported by Vuk Popović: *" 'God and the Holy Trinity help me please! God and Holy Madonna, I entrust to you poor Montenegro! Holy Archangel Michael take my sinful soul.' Then, as he lay on his uncle St. Petar's mattress, death came."*[20]

As both ruler and national poet Rade came to occupy a special place in Montenegrin, Serb and South Slav history, but contemporary opinion about him was mixed. An Italian visitor to Dalmatia wrote in 1852: *"Petar Petrović II . . . was, like his country, known but undiscovered. Some thought that he was in religion and word Orthodox, others that he was sincere and generous, some a genius, some a barbarian and some were glorifying his library . . . he was seen as a poet, a diplomat, a progressive man and even a bandit."*[21]

Rade's different roles, national leader, politician, poet and philosopher, had displayed a multi-faceted talent, but his true stature would only be revealed over time. In the immediate aftermath of his passing, the Montenegrins, naturally, felt the loss most keenly, but South Slavs throughout the Balkans mourned him. In Dubrovnik, Jeremija Gagić, whose job had initially been to keep a close eye on the Montenegrin but who had become his friend, remembered Rade with succinct simplicity: as a noble genius.

Prince Danilo Petrović-Njegoš, Lord of Montenegro and the Highlands, by Johann Boss.

Thunderbolt: the first Petrović prince, absolute ruler and state maker.

Chapter IV

Prince Danilo: 1851-1860

One day a group of us were with Vladika Rade, who was sitting in his chair with his eyes shut and we thought that he was sleeping. Doctor Radišić asked me 'Who will be the Vladika's heir?' I replied simply 'Danilo'. Branko said that he had never heard the name before and the Vladika, without opening his eyes, said with a smile 'If his character stays the way it is now, the whole of Europe will hear about him!'

Dr. Lazar Tomanović

Vladika Rade's chosen successor was his twenty-five year-old nephew Zeko Stankov (Prince Danilo, 1851-1860). He provided a contrast to his uncle in both character and physical stature, but also proved to be a significant ruler. As Vladika Rade had before him, Zeko faced a power struggle before he could assume his position as national leader. The other leading clan members sought to restrict him to a religious role while they dominated political affairs. During Rade's terminal illness they had wielded power through the Senate and saw no reason to now subordinate themselves to the young and inexperienced Zeko.

President of the Senate, Pero Tomov, was acclaimed as leader by the war party which was demanding a stronger policy against the Turks. Meanwhile, Zeko, who was in Vienna when Rade died, decided to delay his return until he had Russia's recognition of his rights as the legitimate successor. By late 1851 he had succeeded and he made his way home, but only to an ominous greeting in Kotor from the two relatives who came to forewarn him of the tense mood in the capital.

In Cetinje he was given an icy reception and found his uncle Pero installed in the ruler's official residence, the Biljarda. Zeko's nephew, ten-year-old Nikola Mirkov, was witness to his return and the power struggle that ensued: *"I met uncle and his escort in the field. They did not walk in mourning but were singing and firing their guns and calling loudly to one another as they strode through town. My uncle saluted everyone, some responded and some did not. Some took off their caps and some responded with 'Good luck to you,' but only one man, a flag bearer named Markiša Ilin Ivanović, shouted loudly 'Good luck to you Master'."*

Evening was falling and Zeko knew he had no time to lose. He continued on, past the Biljarda to the Monastery where he kissed his late uncle's gravestone and wept bitter tears: *"He knelt . . . for a long time, then he went over to St. Petar's coffin, where he prayed and prayed but did not cry . . . When he left the Monastery a servant went to him and said: 'It has been ordered to prepare the upper rooms in the Monastery for you, do you wish to go up?' Zeko declined and asked where Pero was. He was told: 'At the Biljarda'."*[2]

As it unfolded the drama almost turned violent. Young Nikola recalled the scene: *" . . . As a small boy I went with those wonderful men, as a little foal amongst a dense forest of fir and pine trees. I wanted to go with them. At the door of the main hall in the Biljarda stood Marko Šutinov, a perjanik and one of Pero's most loyal followers. Uncle [Zeko] was there, father [Mirko, Zeko's elder brother], Vojvoda Petar and Vojvoda Ivo. Someone said: 'Close the door', then perjanik Marko tried to close the*

(Above) Prince Danilo's elder brother, Vojvoda Mirko Petrović-Njegoš, by Jaroslav Čermak, 1862. Mirko was Montenegro's finest military commander and considered by many to be the strength behind the throne.
(Facing page) Pero Tomov Petrović-Njegoš by Johann Boss, 1853. Vladika Rade's brother and President of the Senate, Pero was opposed to his nephew, Danilo, becoming prince rather than vladika. Pero lost out in the power struggle which ensued and Danilo, as Montenegro's first prince, sent the vanquished Pero into exile, where he died in 1854.

door and said to Milo Novakov, 'Stop!' Milo responded, 'Do not stop, for God's sake.' Those two knights started pushing each other toward the door. 'Not here!' shouted Marko. 'Where else but here?' Milo responded . . . looking at him through bloodshot eyes. It was a hair's breadth from an unprecedented spilling of blood, one brave man killing another . . ."

Zeko's uncles and the other senators were waiting in the Biljarda. Terse greetings were exchanged: "*When uncle said 'Good evening' they responded slowly, 'Good fortune to you.' And Pero, Djordje [Pero's cousin], Stevan [Perkov] and Novica [Cerović] stood up and kissed him. Uncle said 'How are you all?' They responded 'All in good health!' Uncle saw grandfather, went toward him and kissed his hand and asked 'How are you father?' 'I am healthy' he replied.

"Then everyone took their seats but there was no chair for Zeko. He strode around the room two or three times, until he noticed the late Vladika's chair that was covered with a black veil. He quickly went over to it, tore off the veil and sat down: 'Now this chair is no longer empty. Senators and other brothers, I am grieving and I will never get over my great uncle's death, my master and my predecessor, and I will always be sorry that I was not here when he passed away. If I had been here the many imprudences that followed his death could have been avoided. But there is a saying: snow does not fall to cover* people but to show each beast's tracks.' 'Uncle Pero,' Zeko said as he stood up, 'come here to another room.' They went toward the rooms of the late Vladika that Pero had already prepared for himself. Zeko slammed the door. Everybody knew Zeko's violent temper and they could predict what would happen. They were trying to listen and judge from the tone of their voices about the situation. At that moment they heard shouting in the Biljarda hall. Stevan Perkov could no longer contain himself. He decided to go to them. I heard that patriot crying, with tears in his eyes, begging them for love and unity. Stevan talked for a long time, after which he left them to continue their conversation. Stevan's slightly calmer expression predicted success to Zeko's party, and Djordje, my grandfather, and Novica had faith that uncle and nephew would reach an agreement. After a full hour they appeared, much more peaceful, and Zeko said 'I will go to the Monastery this night, and tomorrow I will come here to these rooms of my late uncle.' To this Pero shrugged his shoulders, 'As you like' he replied. Afterward, uncle went to the Monastery with his escort. My God! What breed of men! That same evening, that *same moment, a few men from Pero's party put on their arms and joined Zeko's escort. The whole night long one could hear people singing in the Monastery, and from the windows the sound of gunshots. The Biljarda was silent, not a living soul could be heard."*[3]

Zeko called a tribal assembly for New Year's Day. The vojvodas had unanimously acclaimed Pero two months earlier but now switched their allegiance to Zeko: he was now free to consolidate his rule. Behind the power struggle was the fact that both Zeko and Pero had set their sights on becoming the first Petrović prince. Zeko, however, kept his ambitions secret until he left for Russia in March 1852. From Vienna he sent word to Cetinje ordering the vojvodas to send a memorandum to St. Petersburg requesting he be recognised as prince by Tsar Nikolai I. They gave their assent but only grudgingly as many preferred theocratic rule which they saw as less of a threat to tribal autonomy. It was also rumoured that some of their signatures were forged and the Russians, sceptical of the document and of the forceful young Montenegrin, delayed their decision.

The Tsar had Zeko stay in the Alexander Nevski Monastery, but he made it plain to the monks that he had no interest in religious orders or monastic life. He refused to pray, fast or dress as a monk, preferring his Montenegrin cap and national costume. He even set bird traps in the Monastery to the astonishment of the monks. Finally, by the end of June 1852, his determination had gained him the Tsar's Grammata agreeing that Montenegro become a principality. Having received this recognition he changed his name to Danilo, feeling that his own name, as his nickname of Zeko Mali (Little Rabbit) confirmed, lacked the necessary dignity. This time, Danilo's return fully confirmed his victory: the vojvodas, even Pero, came to greet him.

It was not in the young ruler's nature to forgive and Pero, who had badly misread his strength of character, was now exiled, finding refuge in Kotor. Danilo had shown courage and decisiveness, but also gained more enemies by threatening to punish the vojvodas who had supported Pero.

In his struggle, Danilo had an important ally in his elder brother Mirko, a less volatile personality and a tough, talented military commander. Many soon saw Mirko as the real power in the land but, at times, even he would not be able to restrain his brother.

For good and ill, Danilo's character was fully formed. Although he was a more limited man than his illustrious predecessor, he was equally determined and had his own strengths. Vuk Stefanović Karadžić had introduced Montenegro's first prince to the Serbian public: *"Prince Danilo is not more than twenty-four years old, very short, but passionate and active. Once in the fields he said to the Montenegrins: 'You can see how short I am, but if you do not obey me I will be higher than Lovćen to you. If you do not allow me to become famous for doing good things, I will gain fame by doing bad'."*[4] If he lacked Vladika Rade's spiritual dimension, he was no less a man of his word.

The start of the royal era was marked by the Prince taking a bride: Darinka Kvekić, the daughter of Marko Kvekić, a wealthy Serb merchant from the coastal town of Herceg Novi. Born in Trieste, Dalmatia, in 1838, she was an intelligent, accomplished young woman who spoke four languages (Serbo-Croat, Italian, French and German) and brought a respectable dowry of one hundred and fifty thousand florins. The Prince, however, did not marry for riches. He had met Darinka while dining with her father and fell in love at first sight. Certainly, there were other potential brides of royal descent: the daughter of Prince Aleksandar Karadjordjević of Serbia had been a favoured candidate. Greater dowries than Darinka's were also available: the daughter of the Viennese banker Baron Sina would have come with a dowry of one million florins. Danilo's mind was characteristically clear and unambiguous: *"It is always better to marry a bride who has been seen rather than known by reputation. Treasure is neither of silver nor of gold, but it is here in what to one's heart is dear."*[5]

The engagement was officially announced in October 1854 and, in its inimitable way, Cetinje prepared for its first royal wedding. Vuk Popović reported: *"The wedding table will be set in the field alongside, with no covering and around it seats will be placed for all in the wedding, one clean stone each . . . while the meal is served, boys and girls will sing and dance in rounds, cannons and guns will be fired."*[6] Danilo declined the offer that every vojvoda bring a gift of a young ram prepared on a spit. Instead, he ordered them to dress their best, carry their finest weapons and threatened to shoot anyone who disobeyed him! The wedding date was set for January 24, 1855, when the Vladika of Zadar would marry the couple and Baron Mamula of Austria would be the bridegroom's witness.

An escort of the leading vojvodas was sent to Trieste to fetch sixteen year-old Darinka. They returned to Kotor with the betrothed on January 23 and were greeted by Austrian officials and a large, enthusiastic crowd. Darinka spent the night as the guest of Senator Bjeladinović and the next day they departed for the Montenegrin capital. The Prince's adjutant led the way followed by the vojvodas, all dressed in national costume, with Darinka seated on a brilliantly decorated white horse, her dark hair unfettered and flowing freely in the sea breeze. A more striking sight could hardly have been imagined by the cheering crowds, which was completed by the young lady's gold scarf embroidered with the Montenegrin flag.

As they neared Cetinje, their progress was announced by continuous gunfire. The villagers eagerly joined the celebration and Darinka's escort had grown considerably by the time the Prince greeted them outside the capital. She was suffering badly in the cold weather and Danilo told her to be stout hearted, but there were further trials ahead.

On greeting Darinka, Danilo had kissed his betrothed's hand and broken with Montenegrin custom. It was considered inappropriate for a man to kiss a woman's hand, even more so a young woman of Darinka's comparatively lowly status. Stevan Perkov Vukotić told Danilo, *"I would never kiss the hand of a woman or a Turk."* Mirko supported his brother and also greeted Darinka, by removing his cap and kissing her hand. The vojvodas were outraged: it was she, the soon to be princess, who should have kissed Mirko's hand and that of every man assembled!

Despite these tensions the wedding party arrived in Cetinje by mid-afternoon and the wedding ceremony took place a few hours later, followed by celebrations that continued throughout the night and on into the next day, accompanied by the much enjoyed excitement of gunfire and fireworks.

For the refined young lady, once the excitement and bustle of the wedding and settling in had passed, the capital's two-dozen modest stone houses, the Monastery and the Biljarda were all that remained; Cetinje must have seemed like another world after her cosmopolitan bourgeois upbringing. However, she was an energetic young woman who soon transformed the Biljarda from a bare, simple, even gloomy building, into something more in keeping with the dazzling trappings of European society. Fine furnishings, servants, evening parties and a most elegant and refined young mistress to oversee it all were Cetinje's reward.

The people had mixed feelings toward the Princess: they were proud that the Prince had found such a beautiful and accomplished consort, but they also felt that she was vain and ambitious, and that she was spending too much money. Marriage, however, did little to mellow their fearsome Prince, in fact rather the opposite; the royal couple were known to argue violently, all the more so as Darinka sought to play an active part in her husband's controversial political decisions. Their shared ambitions ensured that there was much to argue about, as did a series of domestic conflicts within Montenegro, war with Turkey and the outbreak of war in Europe.

Danilo had the misfortune to become ruler in a decade of conflict for both the Turkish Empire and Europe. His first experience of war, in 1852, had been provoked by Turkish hostility to Montenegro's new status as a principality. The Piperi tribe were offered privileged status if they accepted Turkish suzerainty and the Montenegrins retaliated by seizing Žabljak, Ivan Crnojević's medieval capital. Danilo prudently evacuated the historic fortress, but the Turks now had a justification for an attack.

Assaulted by five separate armies, the desperate Montenegrin forces held them at bay as Danilo pleaded for Russia and Austria to intervene. Vienna was more than willing.

In the first place, Austria had been incensed by the hospitality the Turks had given to Polish and Hungarian refugees from the revolutions of 1848. Secondly, it was a prize chance to extend their influence in the Balkans. The Sublime Porte was warned that Vienna felt duty bound to intervene on behalf of its Christian neighbours.

The threat worked and, by March 1853, peace was made. To Danilo's great satisfaction, in wording the peace treaty the Austrians referred to the Imperial Firman of 1799, in which the Sublime Porte had accepted that Montenegro was not a vassal state.

Austria's intervention also marked a significant shift in political alignments. Although he was going against national sentiment, Danilo, seduced by French and Austrian promises, remained neutral when the Crimean War - in which Britain, France, Turkey and Sardinia ranged themselves against Russia - broke out in 1854.

The Prince's uncle, Djordje Savov Petrović, led the opposition to what was seen as a

Prince Danilo's bride Darinka Kvekić in a portrait by Jaroslav Čermak, 1862. Danilo fell in love with Darinka at their first meeting. Born in Trieste, Dalmatia, on December 31, 1838, she was the daughter of Marko Kvekić, a wealthy Serb merchant from the coastal town of Herceg Novi. An intelligent, accomplished young woman who spoke four languages, she also brought a respectable dowry of one hundred and fifty thousand florins.

threat to Montenegro's unity and future: these, many felt, were at risk if the nation stood aside as Russia fought against Turkey and its European allies.

In the midst of this turmoil, but with a fine instinct for *realpolitik* and spurred on by his wife, Danilo continued to explore the political opportunities to hand. His aim was to enlarge the principality to include Bosnia-Herzegovina and the port of Bar by accepting Turkish suzerainty. This provoked Djordje Petrović to tell France's energetic agent, the Consul to Scutari M Hecquard: *"Sir, can you see*

Prince Danilo by Johann Boss. Both feared and admired by his subjects, Danilo's controversial personality gave rise to several nicknames. Few would have dared to use the mischievous 'Little Rabbit', given to the ruler because of his short stature and large green eyes, as another nickname, 'The Thunderbolt', was equally appropriate given his notoriously violent temper.

those rocks? There is not one which has not seen Montenegrin or Turkish blood. My great-grandfather, grandfather, father and I all fought and bled . . . to not become our mortal enemy's subjects . . ." Danilo was angered by this outburst and subsequently dismissed Djordje. Mirko took over his position in the Senate.

Although the current of opinion which Djordje represented was a strong one, Danilo had been persuaded by the promises of the Frenchman that the Sublime Porte would welcome his proposal. The new policy was at least justified in one important respect: Montenegro would not, as was feared by his opponents, have been reduced from an independent to a vassal state but, instead, transformed from a tiny principality into a regional power. Danilo negotiated not only for a great enlargement of territory but also the right to mint his own currency; moneys for public buildings, schools, churches and roads; the right to raise his own army and the right to declare war. In short, nothing less than to rule wholly independently without foreign interference. The Sublime Porte's reward would be nominal suzerainty over Montenegro. It was a bold scheme that could not ultimately be realised.

In the meantime, on the domestic front Danilo was equally active, asserting himself as an absolute ruler with harsh determination. Effective taxation was finally imposed and refusal to pay was ruled an act of treason. The new legal code, the Code Danilo of 1855, also further centralised the power of the state by reducing the autonomy of the tribes, notably by outlawing blood feuds and raiding. Resistance was inevitable and three of the great tribes - the Piperi in 1852, the Bjelopavlići in 1854 and the Kuči in 1855 and 1856 - revolted against the Prince's policies and proclaimed their independence. The response was brutally effective, as the treatment of the Kuči demonstrated.

The Kuči, who lived on the Turco-Montenegrin borderlands, were traditionally self-ruling and Vladika Rade had spent a good deal of money trying to woo them, as had the Pashas of Scutari: it was an ongoing imperative that Montenegro assimilate the Kuči. The Prince's secretary, Milorad Medaković, had advocated a gradual policy to win them over rather than bluntly demanding obedience. Danilo acquiesced to the Serbian's advice, but, by 1856, his patience had run out when the Kuči refused to accept a new tax. Mirko was sent to subdue the rebels and carried out his task with merciless force, massacring men, women and children. Over two hundred were killed, thirteen villages were burned, eight hundred homes plundered and four thousand head of livestock taken. The terrified survivors fled as Turkish forces took advantage of the conflict and moved into the Kuči capital, Medun.

Danilo's policies had done much harm to Montenegro: firstly, by causing a civil war and, secondly, Montenegrin neutrality counted for less than nought when the time came for the Allies to punish Russia. Under the terms of the Treaty of Paris (1856) which ended the Crimean War, Russia's protectorate over Montenegro was nullified, making the Montenegrins ancillary victims, as it were, of Russia's defeat. The only bond to be allowed between St. Petersburg and Cetinje was 'mutual sympathy'. The dissolution of the protectorate enabled Turkey's representative to the peace conference to assert that Montenegro was, despite the Imperial Firman of 1799, an integral part of the Ottoman Empire. Danilo angrily repudiated this saying he had greater justification to claim half of Albania and all Herzegovina, lands once held by Montenegro's medieval rulers.

However, the bold plan to forge an absolutist state, change foreign policy, gain territory and international recognition had proven to be flawed. Far from strengthening the bonds between Cetinje and the border tribes, it had precipitated a series of crises and lost the chance to gain an Adriatic port. The intrigues with France and Turkey, the struggle with the tribes and the break with Montenegro's traditional ally Russia had all torn at the fabric of the tribal confederation.

At the centre of the growing storm, Danilo remained nonetheless resolute and defiant. If his greatest flaws were personal ambition and a violent temper, his considerable strengths were a strong will combined with the desire to achieve viable independence. Given these characteristics, it was hardly surprising that the tension with Russia deteriorated into an open split.

After the Crimean War and mindful of Montenegro's neutrality during the conflict, Russia feared the Prince was becoming too independent minded, an unacceptable attitude for a man in local charge of a protectorate. In addition, it was suspected that the Montenegrins in general were angered by Russian acquiescence to Turkey's restated claims on Montenegro, and that the Prince in particular *"was suspected by the Tsar's agents as being . . . angry with Russia for its indifferent behaviour at the*

The Montenegrin law of succession was of male primogeniture, but Prince Danilo's only child was a daughter, Olga (above), born on March 19, 1859. This meant that the line of succession fell to the ruler's nephew, Nikola Mirkov.

Paris Peace Conference . . ."[7]

These worries were sufficiently pressing for a Russian envoy, Consul Stremouhov, to be dispatched to assess the situation. Stremouhov travelled to Cetinje via Dubrovnik, where he heard rumours of the Prince's hostile attitude toward Russia: that in church services mention of the Tsar and the Imperial Family had been banned, and that Russia was being ignored and slighted as if it were a small country of no significance, rather than a far-flung empire and a mighty power.

The Prince's nephew was told of his uncle's reaction to Stremouhov's mission and how the Consul's behaviour made matters worse rather than better. Danilo felt that Stremouhov treated the Montenegrins with disdain and he was, in turn, treated with scorn "*. . . but not because of the Tsar and his Government's instructions, but simply from his own unruliness.*"

The day after Stremouhov's arrival, the two met to discuss state relations. Danilo was prepared to grant him a sympathetic hearing but not to have his dignity slighted: "*The Tsar's greetings to the Prince were warm and cordial, after which uncle was in a good mood and ready to listen very carefully to the Russian and take his advice with the utmost attention . . .*"

However, what lay behind the outward good manners was the fear that Russia's influence in Montenegro was waning. Stremouhov had not been sent to bolster fraternal relations but to criticise and accuse: "*I am authorised to tell you . . . that His Majesty the Tsar objected that you invited Baron Rodić, Governor of Dalmatia, to your marriage; that you sacked from the state administration Djordje Petrović, Russia's leading supporter; that you have stopped mentioning the Tsar and Tsarina's name in your church services; that you have sent your nephew* [Nikola Mirkov] *to Paris to school; that you have received eight cannons as a gift from Austria; that you keep the door open to orientalism and that Montenegrins are day by day losing their famed toughness . . . That, generally speaking, Montenegro has gone astray and pays little attention to Russia. My Sovereign and my Government views with a broken heart the destruction of a Slav province for which Russia paid with its blood and money. You, Prince, in a moment of anger, tore up the Tsar's portrait given to you and trampled it under your feet. In short, for the reasons I have stated, I will be forced to suggest to my Government that the subvention to Montenegro is stopped.*"[8]

St. Petersburg rightly feared that its long term ambition to replace the Ottomans in the Balkans would be undermined by Danilo's parleying with Paris and Istanbul; however, insults and bullying were not an advisable tactic with any Montenegrin, least of all its hot tempered master. Still, Danilo realised that this was no ordinary envoy and, for once, held his temper in check. In fact, he was so taken aback by the outburst he even doubted the Consul's state of mind: "*During Stremouhov's long speech my uncle thought to himself, 'Poor man! Would this state of madness continue for long? Did he have any signs of this illness in Russia or did he catch it on his journey, or here in Cetinje?' In a word, uncle thought that the Russian was completely mad!*"

Stremouhov continued undeterred: "*We will never allow Austrian advice to become authoritative. Montenegro should not look anywhere but to Russia. The Tsar is patron of this state and you are the executors of his will, otherwise you will not get a rouble.*" A bemused Danilo ended the meeting sarcastically: "*Please, would you like some water. You, I would suggest, are not feeling well. Would you like to go and lie down so we can continue this conversation some other time?*"

Having failed to get the better of Danilo, Stremouhov pleaded with Mirko: "*Dear Sir, you and* your brother are two noble souls, two brave men, two honoured persons that I respect and love. The two of you, with our help, could lead this state successfully, if only two people did not have a malign influence. They are the French Consul and, forgive me, Princess Darinka." Mirko loyally defended the Prince and Princess, but these were views that he shared.

Mirko decided he had to reason with his brother and desperately tried to persuade him to at least maintain friendly relations: *"What can you do? The man heard these things in Dubrovnik and Kotor, and there are mean people and liars here as well, and he looks like an idler who might be better employed. It would be best if you are not angry at him, not to scorn him but let him leave in a cordial way, and little by little he will find out that he was wrongly informed."*

Danilo would have none of it: *"No, I do not want that. I will have a few words with him, and after that he can go wherever he likes. I hope I never set eyes on him again."*

Mirko felt it too important an issue to give way on: *"Pardon me, but just do not go mad, tell him whatever you want in a calm way. Do not forget that he is Russia's envoy, the Tsar's man . . . Please, I beg you not to get so angry. This anger and these extremes are not appropriate for you, just receive him normally and tell him politely that he was misinformed and that you hope that time will show that."*

"And now even you are telling me what to do?!"

"I just beg you to be moderate, not to feel sorry and regret it later, and do not ask him to come today but leave it for tomorrow."

Mirko also tried, without success, to enlist Princess Darinka's help, and the following day Consul Stremouhov was sent away by Danilo with dismissive contempt: *"Sir, yesterday, among other falsehoods, you claimed that I had torn up the Tsar's portrait . . . now I ask you to turn around and tell me if you know what is the painting hanging on the wall? . . . Now, Sir, you will leave Cetinje today, but feel free to put in your report that, if you were authorised to say what you have said yesterday, I no longer want to have any dealings with your Government, nor do I need your books, clothes or subventions. Only what God gives us and a hero's fortune. Goodbye!"*[9]

Danilo's confrontational nature had brought matters to a head. Personal ambition had overshadowed the national cause and he had achieved little except to drag Montenegro ever deeper into a mire of unstable diplomacy. Mirko, unable to wean his brother away from French influence and realising his impotence in the matter, pleaded to Danilo's secretary: *"Protect us and do not give in because there is no more that I can do."*[10]

Finally, even Danilo accepted that he had reached an impasse. He

Princess Darinka with her family and daughter, Olga, in the 1860's. After Prince Danilo's assassination in 1860 Darinka left the country, only to return again in 1862 with the hope of reclaiming her prominent role in Montenegro. After a period of good and, reportedly, intimate relations with the new ruler, Prince NIkola, the two came into conflict and she left the country for the last time in 1867. Darinka went to live in Venice, having pensions from both the French and Russian governments as well as receiving some financial help from Nikola. However, with the help of the Russian court, he blocked all of Darinka's subsequent attempts to return to Cetinje. As Princess of Montenegro, Darinka's legacy was twofold: bringing the refinements of European society to Cetinje and building a new residence which, after her departure, became Prince Nikola's residence. Darinka died in Venice on February 14, 1892. She was taken back to Cetinje to be buried next to her husband.

planned to call an assembly of the vojvodas in 1857 to discuss future relations with Turkey, but it had become clear that the tribes were strongly opposed to his policy of rapprochement and the meeting was called off. Given the failure of the new alliances to deliver tangible gains, a return to Montenegro's traditional anti-Ottoman foreign policy was inevitable.

The occasion was provided by an old dispute: the Plain of Grahovo that had been declared neutral in the reign of Vladika Rade. Following the customary border provocations, among them the temporary seizure of the Fortress of Spič and a declaration of union with Montenegro by several villages on the Adriatic coastline, Turkish forces attacked from Herzegovina in May 1858, swiftly advancing toward Grahovo. The Turks encamped on the plain and the Montenegrins took up positions in the surrounding hills. Eight thousand five hundred Turkish soldiers, armed with ten cannon and modern rifles, confronted five thousand five hundred Montenegrins, with one cannon and flintlock rifles supplied with only one or two bullets for each man.

The Turks expected to enjoy a rout, but they were overconfident and made two fatal errors: they underestimated Mirko's military skill and they failed to secure their line of retreat. The battle lasted for three bloody days. The arrogance of General Hussein Pasha cost him his life and that of most of his army. Turkish casualties were over four thousand in the main battle and almost two thousand during the retreat. By comparison Montenegrin losses were light, around two thousand, and the war booty Mirko's soldiers carried away was impressive: eight cannons, twenty flags, six thousand rifles, two hundred tents, two thousand horses, one thousand boxes of munitions and twenty sables. It was a significant victory, of which Prince Danilo declared: *"We could have taken half of Herzegovina without bullets . . . but I placed my faith in the Tsar's Government."*[10] Danilo was angered that Montenegrin calls for international recognition were still going unheeded and he remained sceptical of Russia's worth as an ally. However, he had in fact taken a major step toward that historic goal.

Dynastic affairs were proving no less controversial than foreign policy, but not progressing as well. The royal couple had only one child, not the longed for male heir but a daughter, Olga, born in 1859. At the same time Princess

(Below) Prince Danilo's residence in Rijeka Crnojevića. (Right) A Montenegrin banner from the Battle of Grahovo of May 13, 1858. Danilo's brother, Mirko, led the Montenegrin army in a famous victory over Turkish forces. However, the European powers still refused to recognise Montenegrin statehood and would not do so until the Treaty of Berlin in 1878.
(Facing page) A daguerreotype of Prince Danilo by Anastas Jovanović.

Darinka's desire for a truly royal lifestyle and her free spending was placing previously unknown strains on the national budget.

Vladika Rade had wisely saved money from the annual Russian subsidy of nine thousand ducats per year. In his Will he had left some to family members, of which Danilo had inherited twelve thousand ducats, and the remainder, eighty thousand ducats, was deposited with Russian banks. Rade had regarded it as the people's money which could be used to buy grain in times of famine, or weapons in times of war, but his successor saw little difference between the nation and its master.

Between 1853 and 1856, from a further fifty-four thousand ducats of Russian aid, the royal couple personally disposed of some forty-five thousand ducats. The Prince held the nation accountable to his absolutist rule, but he never rendered a financial account to the people. It was a significant precedent for the future, and also caused Danilo problems during his reign. When the Russian Consul was asked for more money his reply was curt and to the point: *"The Tsar determined this money as aid for the people, not for debts, particularly ones incurred outside of Montenegro."*[11]

Despite these setbacks to his ambitions, Danilo's reign was not short on achievement. There had been the secularisation of government, an increase in territory and the delimitation of the Turco-Montenegrin border after the victory at Grahovo, which gave the country internationally recognised borders for the first time. Not least, in the midst of a decade of frenzied politicking, the aforementioned Code Danilo was established. The first general legal code designed to supersede tribal law, it remains one of Montenegro's most significant landmarks in state building.

His achievements notwithstanding, Danilo's turbulent reign was due as much to his character as to circumstance. He was not a leader who could build consensus such as Vladika Petar I. His strength was rather that of the natural autocrat. *"I will proclaim myself emperor, even if it is for only twenty-four hours"* he once declared. Living fiercely for the moment and motivated by the desire to achieve greatness, he tolerated no opposition, and if he made a threat it was never an idle one. Indeed, his violent temper almost changed the course of dynastic history. Stevan Perkov of the Vukotić clan, one of Vladika Rade's closest friends, fell from favour and Danilo ordered the execution of his son Petar, whose daughter Milena would marry the next Montenegrin ruler. It was only the pleading of the vojvodas that saved Petar.

The Montenegrins rightly both admired and feared Danilo. In contrast to his namesake, Vladika Danilo I, who with considerable bravado had styled himself 'Warlord of the Serbian Land', he could justifiably claim to be 'The Prince of Montenegro and Lord of the Highlands'. Undoubtedly, many were cowed by their arbitrary and impassive master who they nicknamed *"The Thunderbolt"*. However, in Montenegro even an absolutist was bound by blood and honour and Danilo would fall victim to that harsh code of retribution: the blood feud.

Danilo's reign ended abruptly and violently on August 12, 1860, during a holiday in the Bay of Kotor. Never a passive man, he played an unfortunate part in his own demise. Prior to the fateful day

ГОСПОДАР ЦРНЕ ГОРЕ
КЊАЗ ДАНИЛО ПЕТРОВИЋ
1826 - 1860

(Main picture) A view of the Bay of Kotor. Prince Danilo was assassinated at the end of a holiday in the bay. (Inset) Danilo was subsequently laid to rest in Cetinje Monastery.

Prince Danilo's jacket showing the bullet holes made by the gun of Todor Kadić of the Bjelopavlići tribe. The assassins motives were both personal and political, his only regret was *"that there is no man brave enough in Montenegro to kill Mirko."* Danilo, one of Montenegro's strongest leaders, had forcibly suppressed the traditionally autonomous tribes and the regicide was an act of blood revenge: the code of honour and vengeance that Danilo had outlawed only five years previously.
(Facing page) Prince Danilo's funeral procession by Anton Karinger, 1862.

he had been warned that a Montenegrin fugitive had been boasting in Scutari town that he would kill the Prince. Danilo dismissed the warning: *"There is no Montenegrin gun that could bring me down."*[12] Some of his arrogance seems to have rubbed off on his perjaniks, including his most trusted men, Petar Stevanov, who had gone to Dubrovnik on business, and Ivo Rakov, who had left for Njeguši the previous day. Many of the others were simply enjoying their time socialising in Kotor. The holiday had certainly been a particularly happy one for the royal couple: relations with the people of Kotor Bay were excellent and they had decided to buy a house in Dobrota.

On the afternoon of August 12 there seemed little reason to worry as the Prince and Princess enjoyed the delights of Kotor's seaboard promenade. Vuk Popović recorded Danilo's last hours: *"That evening he arrived* [to Kotor] *from Prčanj earlier than usual and left later than usual. During his walk he was so preoccupied talking to the Adjutant from the Consulate of Scutari, that he did not notice the music that was playing, nor the fact that the night was falling quickly, or that the Princess was out of sight . . . The Princess, however, came to him saying 'Dano, it's late.' At eight o'clock that evening, as he was about to board ship, a rifle shot rang out from somewhere in the crowd. He fell to the ground and cried out 'Ah, I have been murdered!' . . . in the uproar there were a few Montenegrins who drew their knives and fired their guns into the air. 'Master, shall we avenge you?' they asked. Danilo replied 'Stay in peace, for God's sake'."*[13]

The angry crowd ran to the town gates, shouting for them to be closed. As yet unnoticed, the assassin was amongst them, but as the cry to shut the gates went up he broke cover and made a run for the mountains. It was only by chance that two policemen were there to halt and arrest Todor Kadić of the Bjelopavlići tribe.

Kadić's motives have been the subject of much speculation, but a personal grudge was certainly included: Danilo had ordered that Kadić's already married sister be remarried to one of Mirko's in-laws. Kadić, who had been living as a fugitive in Turkish territory, had sworn revenge and had already killed his sister's new brother-in-law, Mišan Stevanov Martinović, who, as Montenegro's representative in Istanbul, was an accessible target. However, the only retribution Kadić considered sufficient was to kill the Prince.

Danilo's response was fatalistic and grimly appropriate for a victim of the blood feud he had himself outlawed: *"The Prince was carried to Bjeladinović's house in town, blood gushing from the wound . . . rubbing his sweat stained forehead he said, 'Whoever killed me is a brave man!'."*

Danilo's wounds were clearly fatal but he did not die quickly and his agony continued until the following evening. Darinka was at his side until the very end: *"The Prince told everyone to stay in peace and ordered that Nikola, Mirko's son, be his successor. However, Nikola must not leave home or come down to see him . . . Danilo was lucid until four o'clock in the afternoon of the following day, after which he became delirious . . . Danilo died on August 1 [August 13], at half-past seven in the evening."*

The assassin was condemned to the gallows and hung outside town on October 13, 1860. Before the death sentence was carried out Kadić confessed his motives: *"I did kill the Prince and I do not regret it for a moment, because after exiling me he spent money to find me throughout Turkey and*

Austria. God helped me and I killed him first, and I am glad that he did not die before hearing who killed him. My only regret is that there is no man brave enough in Montenegro to kill Mirko, but he should not count on still being alive next Christmas."[14] The surviving members of the Kadić clan were exiled by Mirko, they took refuge in Scutari.

The regicide was a violent illustration of the still existing conflict between tribal autonomy and the state, between the individual clansman and the absolute ruler. The loss was of a controversial ruler, but one who had great potential as a state builder. Vuk Popović noted that the people of Kotor Bay had warmed to his strong personality and regretted his death: *"Everyone here feels sadness for Danilo, both Catholic and Orthodox, because while he was alive they could leave their front doors open overnight."*[15]

The assassination reopened rifts within the ruling family. Mirko, whose relations with Darinka had been poor due to her influence over Danilo, openly blamed her for his death. At the least, she now put aside her own grievances and helped ensure a peaceful transition of power. Danilo's death meant that the line of succession fell to Mirko's only son, it was a fragile moment in the family's fortunes. As the Prince's final hours were passing, Nikola Mirkov Petrović-Njegoš had been in Cetinje anxiously awaiting news. Overcome by grief and worry, the eighteen year-old had barely conceived that he was about to become the next Prince of Montenegro.

House of Petrović-Njegoš

Stjepan Monk

Petar Njegošević

Stjepan
m. Andjelina

Radul (Monk Petar, born 1620)

Ivan

Śćepac
m. Slava

Ivan

Vladika Sava
(1700-1781)
1735-1781

Vojvoda Radul
m. Vladica

Vladika Danilo
(circa 1670-1735)
1696-1735

Petar

Vladika Vasilije
(1709-1766)
1750-1766

Djuro
m. Kojača Vuković

Savo
m. Mare Milić

Djordje
(died 1868)

Mašan
m. Jovana Radonjić

Vuko
m. Joka Subotić

Ivana
m. Filip Radonjić

Stane
m. Ivo Bojković

Jovana
m. Djuro Doljanica

Gordana
m. Joko
Rucović

Joko
(died 1836)
Battle of Grahovo

Vladika Rade
(1813-1851)
1830-1851

Pero
(died in exile 1854)
(1) m. Gorde Vrbica
(2) m. Jovana Djurašković
(3) m. Gospara Bulajić

Piljo
(d. 1836)

Marija
m. Andrija
Perović

Stane (Ćane)
m P. Djurašković

Nikola (1841-1921)
P. of Montenegro 1860-1910
K. of Montenegro 1910-1918
m.1860 Milena Vukotić (1847-1923)
d. of Vojvoda Petar Vukotić

Anastazija (Gorde)
(1843-1879)
m. Savo Plamenac

Ljubica-Zorka
(1865-1890)
m. **Petar Karadjordjević**
(1844-1921)
K. of Serbia 1903-1918
K. of Serbs, Croats and Slovenes
1918-1921

Milica (1866-1951)
m. 1889 Petar Nikolayevich GD. of Russia (1865-1931)

Anastazija (Stane) (1868-1935)
m.(1) P. Georgi Romanov D. of Leichtenberg (1852-1912)
Div. 1906 m. (2) GD Nikolai Nikolayevich GD. of Russia
(1856-1929)

Marina
(1892-1981)
m Alexander Nikolayevich
Golitsyn (1886-1974)

Roman
(1896-1928)
m Paraskeva Dimitrievna
Chérémeteff (1901-1980)

Sofija
(1898)

Nadezhda
(1898-1988)
m. Nikolai Vladimirovich
Orloff (1891-1961)

Jelena
(1884-1962)
m. Ioann Konstantinovich
Romanov (1886 murd. 1918)

Milena
(1886-1887)

Djordje
(1887-1972)
Cr. P. of Serbia until 1909
m. Radmila Radonjić
(1907-1993)

Aleksandar (1888 murd. 1934)
P. Reg. of Serbia 1914-1918
Reg. of Kingdom of the Serbs, Croats and
Slovenes 1918-1921
K. of the Serbs, Croats and Slovenes 1921-1929
K. of Yugoslavia 1929-1934
m. **Maria** (1900-1961)
d. of Ferdinand I, K. of Romania

Andrija
(1890)

**Sergei, 8th D. of
Leichtenberg,
P. Romanovsky**
(1890-1974)

Jelena
(1892-1971)
m. C. Stephan Tyszkiewicz
(1894-1976)

Petar II (1923-1970)
K. of Yugoslavia 1934-1945
m. 1944 **Alexandra** (1921-1993) d. of Alexander K. of Hellenes

Tomislav
(1928-2000)

Andrej
(1929-1990)

Jelena
(1920-1998)
(illegitimate)
d. of Charlotte Cotier

Aleksandar (1945)   m. (2) 1985 **Catherine** (1949)
Cr. P. of Serbia and Yugoslavia   d. of Robert Batis
m. (1) **Maria de Gloria** (1946)
d. of P. Peter of Orléans-Braganza (div)

Peter (1980)   Alexander (1982)   Philip (1982)

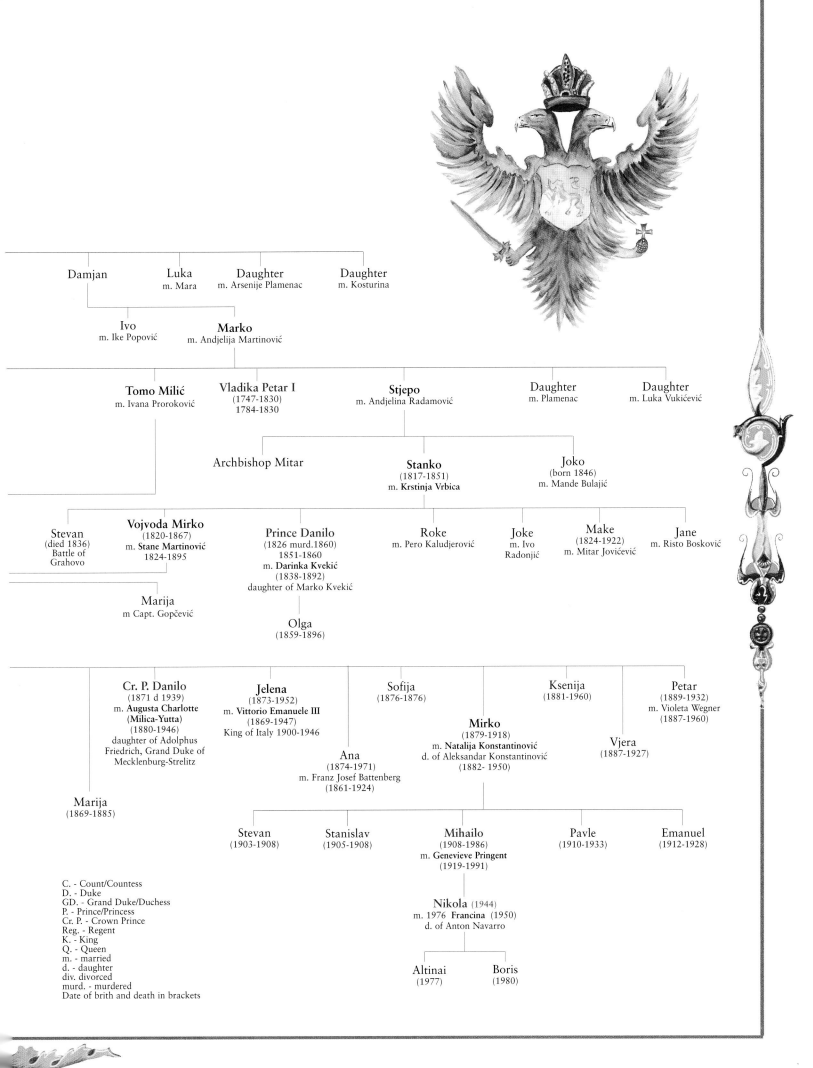

Damjan

Luka
m. Mara

Daughter
m. Arsenije Plamenac

Daughter
m. Kosturina

Ivo
m. Ike Popović

Marko
m. Andjelija Martinović

Tomo Milić
m. Ivana Proroković

Vladika Petar I
(1747-1830)
1784-1830

Stjepo
m. Andjelina Radamović

Daughter
m. Plamenac

Daughter
m. Luka Vukićević

Archbishop Mitar

Stanko
(1817-1851)
m. **Krstinja Vrbica**

Joko
(born 1846)
m. Mande Bulajić

Stevan
(died 1836)
Battle of
Grahovo

Vojvoda Mirko
(1820-1867)
m. **Stane Martinović**
1824-1895

Prince Danilo
(1826 murd.1860)
1851-1860
m. **Darinka Kvekić**
(1838-1892)
daughter of Marko Kvekić

Roke
m. Pero Kaludjerović

Joke
m. Ivo
Radonjić

Make
(1824-1922)
m. Mitar Jovićević

Jane
m. Risto Bosković

Marija
m Capt. Gopčević

Olga
(1859-1896)

Cr. P. Danilo
(1871 d 1939)
m. **Augusta Charlotte**
(Milica-Yutta)
(1880-1946)
daughter of Adolphus
Friedrich, Grand Duke of
Mecklenburg-Strelitz

Jelena
(1873-1952)
m. **Vittorio Emanuele III**
(1869-1947)
King of Italy 1900-1946

Sofija
(1876-1876)

Ksenija
(1881-1960)

Petar
(1889-1932)
m. Violeta Wegner
(1887-1960)

Ana
(1874-1971)
m. Franz Josef Battenberg
(1861-1924)

Mirko
(1879-1918)
m. **Natalija Konstantinović**
d. of Aleksandar Konstantinović
(1882- 1950)

Vjera
(1887-1927)

Marija
(1869-1885)

Stevan
(1903-1908)

Stanislav
(1905-1908)

Mihailo
(1908-1986)
m. **Genevieve Pringent**
(1919-1991)

Pavle
(1910-1933)

Emanuel
(1912-1928)

Nikola (1944)
m. 1976 **Francina** (1950)
d. of Anton Navarro

Altinai
(1977)

Boris
(1980)

C. - Count/Countess
D. - Duke
GD. - Grand Duke/Duchess
P. - Prince/Princess
Cr. P. - Crown Prince
Reg. - Regent
K. - King
Q. - Queen
m. - married
d. - daughter
div. divorced
murd. - murdered
Date of brith and death in brackets

The young Nikola Mirkov during his student days at St. Spiridion's Serbian Orthodox School in Trieste.

Mr. Nikica prepares to make his mark on the world.

It is easier for a coward and a milksop to live anywhere else than in Montenegro, and cowardly Petrović would surprise them all.[1]

Nikola Mirkov Petrović-Njegoš

Nikola Mirkov Petrović-Njegoš was born in Njeguši village on October 19, 1841, the only son of Mirko Petrović and Anastazija (Stane) Martinović. Father Mirko was of medium height, muscular and sinewy, his expression determined and alert, his glance fierce. His voice was described as unusually high pitched for a Montenegrin, but it was powerful and something of a roar when he chose to use it that way. Mirko was noted for being very much his own man, independent in both thought and deed, a respected if not always sympathetic character. Mother Stane was a typical Montenegrin woman, hard working, motherly and loyal. Besides her nickname of Stane, she was also known as Nana, a term of affection given her by the infant Nikola.

Nikola grew up under the defiant and unyielding eye of his father, who imbibed in his son a keen sense of family honour. Nikola's childhood memories were of a poor but proud and stubborn family: *"Stanko, my grandfather, used to smoke his pipe as he walked by the front of the Governor's house, who would tell him to go away with his smoke. One day the Governor went to the window and shot my grandfather's pipe out of his hands . . . We were poor, but we had many friends and we would always be hospitable to passers by. My father was working like any other poor Njeguši man. His modest income improved after meeting the rich and honest merchant Šbutig in Prčanj, who gave my father wheat to sell to the people of Njeguši. My father would collect the money, but sometimes not all of it. Then he would send me to those who had not paid . . . I remember once in winter running in my broken shoes. I met Stevan Radonjić who asked me to show him what I had. When he saw the coins he hit me and I dropped them into the snow. I tried, futilely, to pick them up. Crying, I went home. My father told me not to worry, to leave the coins where they were, for Stevan would pay for his misdeeds one day."*[2]

The family's horizons were, naturally enough, as localised and as limited as any other Montenegrin family. The immediate aim of Nikola's parents were simply to do the best for their son so that he would grow up to take an honourable place amongst the Njeguši. However, Mirko and his younger brother Zeko had the prestige of being Petrovići, which was a source of respect and power in itself, and Nikola's status was greatly raised when, in 1843, Vladika Rade chose Zeko to be his successor. As the nephew of the future ruler, Nikola was placed in the line of succession. It was, therefore, only natural that after Zeko, as Prince Danilo, became Montenegro's first prince in 1852, he should prepare Nikola to be his successor in case he died without a male heir.

The new plans for Nikola's future necessitated that he receive a good education and, in 1852, Prince Danilo sent him to stay with the family of Aleksandar Marinović, a wealthy Serb merchant from Trieste on the Adriatic coast. Trieste had a flourishing Serb community and Nikola was sent to study at St. Spiridion's Serbian Orthodox School. As a late starter he was given a crash course, with private tutors assisting his studies in German, Italian and dance.

Nikola felt very much the provincial in his new surroundings " . . . *without education, a real son of the woods and mountains*", and he found it hard to adjust to the discipline of school life. He remembered his initial misery: "*A real hell, school everyday, Italian teacher, tutor, drawing teacher, dancing teacher and all kinds of misery . . .*" The key to his enthusiasm needed to be found: "*They were punishing me without success until they uncovered the right way to deal with me. When they realised that I was ambitious, they used that to lead me: 'Ha! Niko is a good pupil, no one can study better than he, the way he understands things, the way he reads and writes, the way he pays attention, and geography and cosmology no other pupil knows better than he, and no one else can learn fifty Italian and German words in one day, how well he will read the Apostles for the Transfiguration.' All of this was encouraging me so I really studied hard and my progress was quick.*"[3]

The highly competitive atmosphere brought out the best in the Montenegrin but, moderation being less prevalent than enthusiasm in young Nikola's character, he drove himself to the point of illness: "*I was studying ten or eleven hours a day, even on holidays. Good Mr. Marinović and his wife had no kids of their own; they did not know that this great effort could be bad for me. When uncle visited, he found me very pale and thin and he remarked to Mr. Marinović, 'Niko has been studying well and I can see that it has taken care of his learning, but has it not been too much for him? I would like to gradually reduce his efforts, otherwise it would be better he spends his time running around Cetinje'.*"[4]

Nikola's time spent at St. Spiridion's ensured that his Italian was excellent, his German good, and he completed his elementary school course in time to start at the German Protestant School in 1853. If anything, this school was more competitive, with the students ranked and seated in class accordingly. Once again, Nikola studied day and night to gain a place in the front row of the class, but ambition was no longer his inspiration: "*Was it my desire for knowledge or competitiveness leading me to jump from row to row? I know only that I was pulled by something else, by a desire, by a new feeling, dear and unknown, a sweet allure, some little one, some angel . . .*"

It was a case of *cherchez la femme*: seek out the girl. Nikola had been captivated by a fellow student, a Serbian girl who is remembered only as M.T. "*We made our first acquaintance in school and we would always greet each other in Serbian. I was sitting just behind her, I was taking care of her and she did the same for me. I would gently caress her long hair that fell on her shoulders. She used to smile at me and I was kissing her as a sister, as an icon, as God's angel. In my days abroad, I was always feeling homesick, but after I met her it was much easier. It seemed that she understood me and that she was yearning with me for my Montenegro, which made her even more attractive to me . . .*"

Their youthful affection soon became known around town: "*Our innocent love was no secret for almost the whole Serbian population in Trieste. While I was reading the Epistles, Misses and Madams were looking at my little friend and smiling at her reactions, but not laughing at her because our relations were of the most innocent nature. When we wanted to take a walk we could hear people whispering 'Ecco gli amorosi.' 'What is that amorosi?' I asked her once because she spoke Italian better than I, and was a year older. 'Amorosi?, that means you and I are dear friends.' This was the occasion for our first kiss.*"[5]

Each day Nikola would find M.T. waiting for him on the stairs of St. Anthony's, waiting to walk with him to school: "*After school I would walk her home, not the shortest way, but the longest to stay with her as long as possible. After walking to her door, I would slowly and with melancholy return home thinking about her and about tomorrow's meeting in front of St. Anthony's. That year I started reading the Apostles in the Serbian Church. It felt good to dress myself in the white and red church robes, go to the middle of the church to and read the Apostle's Epistles. Knowing that she could hear and see me, I would read clearly and loudly, and she would tremble for me not to make a mistake.*"[6]

Sadly, they would only enjoy a year together. In 1854 Nikola was called back to Cetinje: "*I had to tell her. She became silent and white as a sheet and she said: 'Is Montenegro far, why do they call you back home? Do not leave! Are you going to return soon? Write to me please!'*" Despite his homesickness, Nikola was almost persuaded to stay and his young love filled his thoughts on the journey home: "*While returning by sea I was thinking of my friend all the time, and when I saw Mount Lovćen from the sea my thoughts were with her. My joy would have been complete if she had been with me. When I arrived home I was very happy but I was still thinking about her. One day Gorde asked me how was Miss M.T. I was so glad to hear my sister's interest I started talking about her with delight.*"[7]

Tragedy lay ahead. Less than a year after Nikola's return home, news of M.T's death reached Cetinje. Nikola was stunned and almost became ill with grief. It was only Montenegro's turbulent and perennially threatened existence that distracted from his loss and brought out his resilience: "*Frequent battles on the border and the bringing back of severed Turkish heads to Cetinje turned my attention, but her memory was indelibly in my soul.*" His recovery was helped by being allowed to recuperate at his own pace: "*I did not work at anything, just hunting and entertaining myself, making excursions to nearby tribes on foot or on horseback . . .*"[8]

His deeply felt loss, and his revulsion

Nikola's parents, Vojvoda Mirko Petrović and Stane Martinović. Mirko was a fierce and fearless man who expected his son to follow his example. Nikola recalled that his uncle, Prince Danilo, was open with his affections but that his father took a very different attitude: "*My father did not take such care of me as uncle, no matter that I was his only son. He would simply say, 'Leave it for God's sake! Our mountains adhere to no rules. He has to be a knight or not to live at all. Whatever can we do with a weakling? Let him be taught the way we were, or he is not of our flock'.*"

at the sight of the severed heads decorating Tablja Fort, turned Nikola's thoughts toward a religious career. Though the gruesome spectacle was a source of pride to many war-hardened veterans, for Nikola it only served to emphasise the cruelty and transience of life. The impressionable and sensitive young man, deeply touched by the teachings of the Orthodox Church, resolved to join the priesthood.

Nikola had been aware of his strong religious feeling from an early age: "*I used to be very eager during church processions in St. Spiridion's. Singing church services and rituals affected me in the same way. Many times I cried in church from delight and pleasure. I would go to church often and being a great admirer of flowers, I would put some in front of the icons of the Virgin Mary and St. Spiridion. What drew me to the church I do not know. Was it love of God and the desire for a peaceful, happy, eternal life, or was it the fear of hell, sin, the devil and eternal torment? Which was prevailing I do not know, but I had a passionate love for the church and service to God, especially evening services. Time spent in God's temple passed quickly. Until my late childhood I desired to become a priest.*"[9]

For a Montenegrin of that era, Nikola's motivations were unusually tender: "*In Cetinje at that time the main topic of conversation was the Turks and war. Would I be a traitor to my country if I were sorry for the Turks? Often those raids and battles led to the severing of heads which, with joy, would be taken in front of my eyes up to the Tablja Fort above the Monastery. I really do not know if*

I felt pity for the Turk or the man, but more for the man I think. When we would go up to the fort to look at those heads, my pulse would taunt me . . . I could not stand it, I was sorry for that Turk, or should I say human head, warmed by the hot sun or cooled by the rain, or pecked by the black raven. I was thinking of mothers, fathers and their offspring and I felt sorry. I hated evil, blood and anyone's misfortune."[10]

However, religion was not the path his father had mapped out for him, and his return to Montenegro also reminded Nikola of what it meant to be a member of that hardy race: "*As the saying goes - you are the company that you keep. My nerves were toughening by the day. Stories of rebels, brave men and poems, little by little began to captivate me, so much so I started to dream of a battle in which I could bring my sword down on a Turk and sever his head.*"[11]

The warriors of Montenegro lived and breathed a cult of heroism and a return to those ways, hunting, horse riding and listening to the epic Serb poems accompanied by the one stringed gusle, restored Nikola's zest for life: "*Because of this I was practising my combat skills and my riding. I can say openly that, by the age of fourteen, I was the best archer and the best rider in Cetinje and its surroundings. I was sharpening my sword, I was getting flint rock from the dirtiest water in Lake Skadar for my gun, and I would take my horse and train him. How many crazy things I did in that time!*" The monastic life, Nikola finally concluded, was not for him. He would be a warrior and a hero: "*It is easier for a coward and a milksop to live anywhere else than in Montenegro.*"[12] His religious feelings lingered but without their former intensity, while the sadness for his beloved M.T. slowly faded.

Under his uncle's watchful gaze, Nikola was now introduced to the adult world: "*I was almost a grown man and the people would not hesitate to talk in front of me. Being in the company of adults I was allowed to smoke and drink, but I was under the strict supervision of my uncle who would teach and reprimand me.*"[13] Danilo was quite a stern guardian and, even though he was the ruler's nephew, Nikola's teenage years were not cosseted ones.

In their tightly knit society young Montenegrin men were encouraged to compete with each other, which, predictably, often involved rivalry for the affections of women. Inevitably this created a good deal of tension and dispute. Nikola had his fair share of arguments and confrontations, and one particularly painful episode would not to be forgotten: "*One priest made uncle angry toward me. And why? This is why! A Turk from Foča* [Bosnia-Herzegovina] *crossed the border with a Serb girl, the daughter of a prince. He wanted to convert* [to Orthodox Christianity] *and to marry her in Cetinje. The girl was beautiful and some of us around her started talking her out of marrying the Turk, but in vain. He went to my uncle and asked that I be the godbrother at his baptism and wedding. The devil be cursed, forgive me God! I was told to be a godbrother!*

"*First of all, of course, the baptism was held secretly by Priest Joko Špadijer, who was a priest only in name. I did not feel good about this, which Špadijer knew and he teased and taunted me . . . he shouted at me, 'Take off his shirt Mr. Nikica.' I said I would not. 'Quick or I will tell the Master.' I was afraid and I did not want to make uncle angry so I told the Turk, 'Take your shirt off.' The Turk removed his shirt and the Priest began to pour a full pot of water over his head, and then, smiling, said to me, 'Now rub his chest.' At that, I angrily left Priest Joko and the converter in the church. Špadijer called me back saying the ceremony could not be finished without me and I should return to the church. He was asking people around to persuade me to go back but I did not want to, until uncle passed by and brought me back to the church himself.*

"*After this I went to uncle and told him what had happened between Joko Špadijer and myself. He became quite angry with the Priest and was waiting for an opportunity to show him that. Špadijer heard about this and told uncle: 'The conversion and wedding of that Foča man is complete, but I beg you Master, do not make me convert or marry anyone else with Mr. Nikica. Yesterday he said to that Turk, 'Spit to Mohammed you swine.' And this morning he was smiling at the girl. I do not want to baptise or marry anyone else with him.' I swear that none of this is true, Priest Joko made it up to show he was not to blame.*

"*Around the same time Mr. Metropolitan Nikanor, a real schismatic and law-breaker, went to uncle to complain about me as well. He wanted to have a very beautiful girl for his mistress, but she was scared of him and kept running away. As well as that, we used to scare her even more, so the*

A gravure of Trieste from the 1860's. The wealthy Adriatic port, then under Austrian rule, was where Nikola began his education in the early 1850's, and where he had his first experience of young love with a fellow student at St. Spiridions, the Serbian Orthodox School in Trieste.

gallant behaviour of Mr. Nikanor was in vain. He blamed me for his failure while he pretended to be saintly and devoted, telling my uncle he had best keep an eye on his nephew and his morality.

"The falsehoods of the Metropolitan and his friend, Špadijer, led, the following morning, to one of the Prince's adjutants being sent to me, 'Sir, by the Master's order, please come with me as you are, without your weapons.' I immediately knew I was accused by those priests and went with the adjutant. When we turned toward the Monastery I said to myself, 'This one is taking me toward the prison, am I that horrible convict?' But I did not go to the prison, I was taken instead to two rooms adjacent to the late Vladika's quarters, which they had prepared for me. 'You will sleep in this room Sir,' said the adjutant, 'and in the next one you will study, but you will not be allowed to go out or talk to anyone, not even with the boy who waits in front of the door.' 'This is bad!' I said to myself, as the adjutant locked me in and gave the key to the servant.

"I languished in there for twenty-five very long days, I was all alone, except in the morning when a priest would come to teach me God's law and Russian language. I did not see a living soul. After I was freed, my uncle reprimanded me harshly, and my father did not want to talk to me for two months. In vain I was trying to excuse myself, I was angry, most of all because Nikanor and Špadijer were mocking me. I hope that God does not allow such holy people to exist anywhere in Christendom, and I cannot believe that there were such priests in the past. I got into the habit of smoking very young, and because I was not allowed to smoke while I was confined, that was the hardest thing for me."[14]

Danilo and Mirko decided that a change of environment was needed to complete Nikola's preparation as the potential future ruler of Montenegro. Prince Danilo had asked the French Government if they would educate four Montenegrins at their expense, and it was decided to send

(Above) Milena Vukotić, daughter of Vojvoda Petar Vukotić and the future Princess of Montenegro. The Vukotić family were from the village of Čevo, a short distance from the capital, Cetinje. Milena came from a highly respected family, her father (facing page) was one of Montenegro's greatest landowners, but she was still a typical peasant girl: uneducated, illiterate and wholly unprepared for the role clan politics had assigned her of consort to the ruler of Montenegro.

Nikola and his relatives Božo Petrović, Stanko Radonjić and Niko Matanović to study at the renowned 'Louis the Great Lycée' in Paris.

They began their studies in January 1856. Nikola's studies went well: his aptitude for languages meant that his French progressed excellently, while he also excelled in philosophy, literature and history. French literature would remain a lifelong passion but not so mathematics, a subject which Prince Danilo was keen for Nikola to excel in: *"I could not master mathematics, no matter that I studied it so much that I made some progress. If anyone asked if I enjoyed it . . . I would reply 'Not at all.' No matter that mathematics is an undeniable truth I still did not like it."* Nikola's scholastic endeavours reflected his developing character, which would always lean toward the artistic rather than the disciplined. However, when his enthusiasm was excited he could work with prodigious energy.

He was also conservative in nature and life in Europe's greatest and liveliest capital city proved to be a difficult adjustment. The entertainments offered to young men did not appeal to Nikola and he spent most of his time studying and reading. His routine was broken by visits to the *Café de Droit*, which was also popular with the Serbian students in Paris. Nikola, however, found them noisy and uncouth: *"To distract me from my problems, I would occasionally go to the Café de Droit to read some Serbian newspaper, but it was so loud there, where the Serbians did not spare even their mothers and fathers . . . Talking about the Serbians in Paris, I recall that there were many of them . . . The café was also frequented by some Serbian politicians. I used to see many Serbians on these occasions, but I did not make acquaintance with them. I did not like their behaviour, a lot of shouting and swearing, so I avoided them."*[15]

More reserved than some of his South Slav brethren, Nikola was a solitary student to whom religion still offered comfort: *"The Pantheon, with its symbols and its organ music, was close to the café. It was wonderful to listen to the music there under those magnificent arches after sunset as it became dark. I could see there were not so many listeners there, perhaps two or three hundred mainly elderly people. I liked to go there as well and take a seat among them. They would look at me as if I were an exotic fish, as if to say, 'What can he be doing here?'."*

If the cosmopolitan aspect of Parisian life made Nikola uncomfortable, he found no antagonism in spiritual diversity: *"I was always very tolerant toward other religions. I could have prayed to God in an Orthodox, Roman or Protestant church equally, and sometimes I would pray even more passionately in the small church of a village than in some magnificent temple."*[16] That tolerance would serve Nikola well later on in life, when his children began marrying into Europe's royal families.

Yet, studying and religion could not cure Nikola's longing for home, so he created his own haven in which to find peace of mind: *"I was even more homesick in Paris. I would fall into those moods every fifteen days and my sadness would heal only after much crying. I was looking at my friends on Sundays and on holidays having fun in and around Paris, and I found my own way to have a good time. I would leave the Lycée, go to the market where the carriages were, take the best one and go to the bakery, buy a big loaf of bread, cold meat, smoked ham and pig tongue, two glasses and a small bottle of brandy. I would put all of that in the carriage, then find an organist and seat him, along with his organ and his dog, next to the driver and me, and we would all go far away to the fortification in the fields where we could be alone.*

"*After dismissing the carriage, we would open the organist's big umbrella on the grass and the three of us, the organist, his dog and I, would sit and have some lunch and talk as brothers . . . That kind organist had a lot of understanding for me. He would gather a bundle of grass for me to lie on, and then he would start playing his organ, trying to send me to sleep. He could not manage it, the poor fellow. I used to lie down, with my head resting upon my arms, looking far, far away, to the high clouds, in the direction where I thought Montenegro might be and cry, moan and sigh. 'Vous n'etes pas gai, mon bon Monsieur?' [You are not happy, my dear young Sir?] 'Jouez, toujours jouez!' [Play, go on, play!] After sunset we would return to town together and as we parted he would say to me, 'A Dimanche prochaine, mon bon Monsieur?' [Until next Sunday, my dear young Sir?].*"[17]

Lonely and homesick though he was, one aspect of France in the era of Emperor Louis Napoleon that appealed to Nikola was its support for the *risorgimento*, the burgeoning movement for Italian national liberation. As a Montenegrin it was a cause that struck a chord, and Nikola became caught up in the wave of popular support for Italy, so much so that he almost abandoned his studies: "*In May 1859, I nearly ran away from school to join Garibaldi's troops. When I heard those military trumpets preparing for battle I cried with misery for not being able to go myself. At that time I made an agreement with a cattle merchant who had a contract with the army, to take me with him as his assistant and transport me to Italy. But, somehow, that failed and I was stopped from going to Magenta or Solferino.*"[18] Some Montenegrin volunteers did in fact join Garibaldi's 'Red Shirts', a favour the Garibaldians would return during the wars of the 1870's.

Fate had decided against Nikola joining the *risorgimento*, but the nearly four years he had spent in Paris had been more than worthwhile. As his uncle and father hoped, Nikola had matured and gained experience of the wider world beyond Montenegro. This "*son of the woods and mountains*" had grown into a young man with a distinct cast of mind.

The romantic in Nikola regretted that he had not been able to join in the fight to liberate Italy but events in Montenegro were soon to bring even greater and more daunting challenges. Firstly, however, there was the unexpected joy of an early homecoming.

Prince Danilo was a difficult, short-tempered character, but he doted on his nephew and worried for his health as if he were his own son. A letter from Nikola's relative, Stevan Radonjić, set off Danilo's fears and prompted him to order his return to Montenegro.

Nikola recalled how this, as it proved fateful, return home came about: "*One week at the beginning of March 1860, at 10am, I was walking in Luxembourg Garden with Stevan Radonjić. We met a Serb that he knew, he stopped to talk with him while I waited a short distance away. While Stevan was talking, I began to feel unwell and sat on the bench that was behind me. Stevan, after parting from his acquaintance, came over to me and saw how pale I was and asked me how I felt. I told him that I was probably feeling poorly because of a strong black cigar I had smoked, and that I felt faint but was fine . . . That same evening Stevan sat down and wrote a long letter about me to my uncle: that I was so thin and ill that it was painful to look at me, that he was afraid I would not recover, and even that he was*

1860: Italy's Giuseppe Garibaldi photographed during the Italian wars of liberation. The South Slavs were inspired by the romantic nationalism which freed Italy from the Habsburg Empire. Nikola, nearing the end of his student days in Paris, became caught up in the emotion and he tried to enlist with Giuseppe Garibaldi's forces as a volunteer: *"In May 1859, I nearly ran away from school to join Garibaldi's troops . . . I made an agreement with a cattle merchant who had a contract with the army, to take me with him as his assistant and transport me to Italy. But, somehow, that failed and I was stopped from going to Magenta or Solferino."*

afraid for my life. Uncle went mad with worry and sent a telegram the same day ordering me to return to Montenegro immediately . . ."[19]

Although his health was not seriously threatened Nikola was glad to finally be going home. An incident on the return journey demonstrated how much his four years in Paris had changed him: *"I was sleeping in my cabin when the servant who knew me came in and said, 'Two boats filled with Montenegrins are coming.' I jumped up quickly to see who they were, not suspecting that my father was among them . . . I went over to greet him and kiss his hand, waiting for him to hug me, but he only said, 'Buon giorno!' [Good day!] He did not recognise me. I had changed very much in the past four years . . . As we were passing by the island of Lokrum I shouted, 'There is Lovćen!' My father then asked Senator Savo Luketin, 'Savo, is that Nikica?' 'Do you not recognise me Miko?' I said. 'No, but come here to your soldier who could not be more happy to see you,' and he started hugging me, his eyes filling with tears."*[20]

Nikola's emotions overwhelmed him: *"I was so happy to see my Montenegrins, my father and Lovćen that I wanted to jump into the sea to arrive sooner. Finally, on April 23 [May 5], the day of our family's patron, St. George, I arrived in Cetinje. My God, what joy! Uncle, aunt, my sister, family, friends, people, everyone was embracing me and talking to me. That evening we had a dinner at the court to celebrate. All of the most important people were invited to the feast. I was behaving so kindly and worthily, and uncle was so pleased to see me in good health instead of the condition Stevan had written to him about from Paris. During dinner I was looking at my uncle with admiration, with those first knights of ours seated around him. What a flock that was, and what a falcon for a leader! There will never be born again, I fear, that breed of men.*

"Was it because of my years abroad, the influence of civilisation, or who knows what, but I was an amazed observer of everything around me, much more than I used to be watching the same society in the same

circumstances. I was imagining that even Jupiter's dinner with the gods was not as magnificent as this one under Orlov Krš [Eagle's Rock]. During that evening and subsequently I realised that my understanding had, indeed, changed.

"What gave me most joy was my uncle's love for me. He no longer saw me as a mischievous child, but as a man he could talk to and exchange opinion with. He was asking me, testing me, teaching me. Oh God, with such love! He was protecting me from everything: sun, draft, practice and any great effort. He was taking care of my food, my sleep, demanding that I was always nicely and richly dressed . . . My father did not take such care of me as uncle, no matter that I was his only son. He would simply say, 'Leave it, for God's sake, our mountains adhere to no rules. He has to be a knight or not to live at all. Whatever can we do with a weakling? Let him be taught the way we were, or he is not of our flock'."

Love and honour were pulling in different directions but honour finally gained the upper hand: *"In spite of uncle's great concern, I was always among the first of the young people in competitions, in*

(Right) Emperor Louis Napoleon III and Empress Eugenie of France. In 1856, at the invitation of Louis Napoleon, Prince Danilo sent his nephew, Nikola, to Paris to complete his education. Nikola's years in the French capital were rather lonely and isolated ones. He found solace in religion and spent much of his spare time at the Pantheon (above) listening to the church services.

The Vlach Church, the oldest surviving building in Lovćen Valley, where Nikola and Milena were married in November, 1860. The original church, dating from around 1450, was a simple construction of wood and mud built by the Vlach shepherds who were employed to guard the cattle of the Zetan nobility. The Church was destroyed several times and today's building dates from the mid-nineteenth century. The outer walls were built using the nearby menhirs left by adherents of the Bogomil religious sect. The Church also boasts one of the most original fences in the world. After Russia gave Montenegro thirty thousand rifles in 1896, the antiquated Turkish rifles, war booty from the wars of 1858 and 1876/77, were utilised by the resourceful builders to make the church fence. (Facing page) An early photograph of Milena Vukotić. Nikola's father, Mirko, and Milena's father, Petar, had hoped to join their houses since becoming blood brothers on the battlefield. Nikola and Milena were betrothed in 1853, when Nikola was aged twelve and Milena aged only six.

target practice, running, jumping and stone throwing. He was worried but proud, as if I was his only child. However, both uncle and father wanted me to excel and they did not want to protect me any longer . . . And I had the same thought: to be proud of myself, no matter alive or dead.

"*From St. George's Day onward I lived in Cetinje, no longer as a child but as a grown man . . . I was present at the council meetings, at the court of law. At all of the gatherings I was next to my uncle, they even brought me a pipe as they did to him. In a word, everyone considered me as a man and even I felt the same way.*"[21]

These idyllic days lasted a little over three months: ninety-nine days filled with the joy of homecoming were shattered, in August 1860, by the murder of Prince Danilo in Kotor at the hands of a vengeful assassin from the Bjelopavlići tribe.

Nikola was grief stricken and horrified by his uncle's death: "*Then I saw that I was not a grown man, but only a foolish and weak child, without knowledge or experience, a small bird in the nest of an eagle that had broken its wings on Kotor's promenade.*"

The assassin struck on August 12 but Danilo clung onto life, and in Cetinje they anxiously waited for news: "*This sudden blow of fate was made worse by many other circumstances. Melancholy, sad and depressed since dawn we were waiting in the Biljarda for hourly news about our wounded master in Kotor. Some gave us slight hope but some horrified us . . . tired and miserable, sleep fooled me for a moment, but then the news arrived that uncle had died. A kind and aged priest came to the chair where I had reclined and fallen asleep, gently took my hand and said, 'Joy be with you, my Master.' I awoke, stood up and said, 'It cannot be true!' But the crying and wailing of the vojvodas confirmed my darkest forebodings. As still as a statue I stood among them, my hair dishevelled, looking at all of them, but seeing no one. They all came forward to kiss my hand but I refused, I could not bear it. Then in a loud voice father said, 'Hold a while, people!' He came to me, 'Nikola, Nikola, poor you, your uncle is dead, now you are the ruler of this land! Do you understand?' 'Oh wretched me!' They say I said this as if it were a premonition of the terrible torment, worry and responsibility that lay behind that word - Master.*

"*On August 1 [August 13], I was proclaimed Master of Montenegro. I still remember that moment, I remember . . . when I was first called Master! I remember how I became numb hearing that word. I remember how bad I felt . . . I almost shouted angrily at anyone who addressed me by that title. For anyone else it might have been tolerable, but for me it was horrible. It reminded me that, He who used to be the whole world to me was no longer alive, He who was the strength of Montenegro; that our mountain realm had fallen, that no one was alive, that I was left alone, alone under the celestial sphere.”*[22]

Immediately after Prince Danilo's funeral the investiture of the new ruler was performed. Vuk Popović reported a solemn mood: *“Princess Darinka pronounced before the people the words of her late husband: that they recognise Nikola, the son of Mirko, as their Prince and Master of all; that they live in peace and love as true brothers; that they preserve and protect their honour and freedom. She then took the prince's calpac and placed it on young Nikola's head, pinned on his chest the order of Montenegro, led him to the ruler's chair and, through her tears, declared, ‘Behold, brothers and countrymen, your Prince and Lord, Nikola!’ Then, after first kissing his hand, she took her seat.*

“Then all exclaimed, ‘Long live our Prince and Master, Nikola.’ With that there began the firing of rifles and cannons, and Prince Nikola thanked them all and wished peace, unity, brotherhood and love, adding, ‘I will endeavour not to fail my ancestors, and I command you to do the same.’ After that he knelt before Princess Darinka, kissed her hand and sat next to her on her left. Mirko walked over to them and first kissed Darinka's hand, then his son's as the new Prince, upon which all in order did the same, and all was at peace.”[23]

Nikola Mirkov Petrović-Njegoš, at the age of eighteen, had become Master of Montenegro. Emotionally and psychologically unprepared for his sudden accession to power, he would, in time, prove to have great strength of character and many other qualities besides. However, for the time being he was caught up in a whirlwind of events.

During this critical period Nikola's guiding light was his father. A man of the war party, Vojvoda Mirko was uneducated, illiterate but intelligent, worldly-wise and fearless. He was the hero of many battles and his exploits as a warrior were Montenegrin legend: most famously the great victory at Grahovo in 1858. Mirko's views were marked by ardent patriotism and an equally firm suspicion of Montenegro's erstwhile allies.

He had held out hopes to become prince himself but had stood aside for his son. Nikola could only guess his father's reasons: *“I could not understand why my father did not want to be master, but he might have told himself, ‘God knows how long that would last; it is better that he [Nikola] is master and I will do all the work until he is ready.’ That is almost exactly how it was, he was working, I was behaving the way I should have, taking on from the start the master's tone and manner, and I looked impressive.”*[24]

As he had been for his late brother, Mirko was the strength behind the throne, but the burden for young Nikola still proved too great: *“Forty days after becoming master I fell ill with pneumonia, my life hung by a thread. My poor father and mother were worried sick for me . . . At this time my father lived in his house near town, I lived alone in the Biljarda . . . the whole family moved in with me: my father, mother, sister, even my fiancée Milena . . . I was very ill.”*[25]

Nikola and Milena Vukotić, a local girl from the nearby village of Čevo, had been betrothed as children, but there had been little opportunity for Nikola to familiarise himself with his prospective bride. However, her gentle, caring nature and her sense of duty were demonstrated to Nikola during his illness: *“After I began to recover I was strictly forbidden fresh water and I wanted it so badly, just to look at it even . . . One day the family were having*

A portrait of Prince Nikola by Ferdo Kikerec, 1875/76.
(Facing page) Princess Milena by Jaroslav Čermak,1862.

lunch and it was Milena's turn to stay with me. 'Ha, God help me,' I told myself, 'she will give me a drink.' So I began talking nicely and sweetly to her. 'Are you sorry that I am ill?' - 'Yes!' - 'Am I going to recover?' - 'You will if God wills it.' - 'I think I am going to die.' - 'You will not.' - 'I will, I can see, from thirst.' - 'You will not man.' - 'I will certainly, but please pass that jug of water.' - 'I cannot!' - 'Why not?' - 'Doctor forbade you being given water.' - 'Ah, what do doctors know. Just pass that jug.' - 'I will not.' - 'You will not?' - 'No!' - 'And you know that I am not going to marry you.' - 'That is your choice.' - 'I will die.' - 'If you die no one can say I murdered the Prince of Montenegro by giving him water.' - 'If you do not want to give it to me, I will take it myself, and you will see one cannot die from water.' And so I went to take the jug but she took it first and said sweetly, 'Oh please do not. I would kill myself if you have even one drop!' I took the jug in my hands but she would not let me drink from it, and started shouting 'Miko [Mirko], Nikola wants to drink!' Then father and everyone from the dining room rushed in. He took the jug and put me back to bed. 'Did he drink?' father asked. 'No Miko, I swear to God.' My mother took Milena's place and Milena went to my sister who asked, 'Ah, my child, how thirsty he is. Did you give him any water?' - 'No, but if I could die instead of him I would give him the jug to drink it all'."[26]

Mirko was doubly impatient for his son's recovery: for political reasons he felt that it was vital Nikola marry as soon as possible. Prince Danilo's murder meant that Mirko and Nikola were the only remaining heirs. If one or both were to be killed the family line of succession would be broken, leaving the country without a leader. Nikola's illness, the unrest in Herzegovina and his many enemies acted as warning to Mirko that the throne was far from secure.

However, if events decided the timing, the union of the clans Petrović and Vukotić had been long planned. The two clans' relations stretched back to the reign of Vladika Rade, who had made an agreement with his close friend and personal secretary Stevan Perkov, that if an opportunity arose they would bring their clans together through marriage. It was purely a clan issue at the time, no one could have anticipated that the two as yet unborn children would one day be rulers of Montenegro.

Mirko and Petar Vukotić, who was one of the greatest landowners in Montenegro, had hoped to join their houses ever since they had become blood brothers on the battlefield during the wars of the early 1850's. Nikola and Milena's betrothal had been agreed in 1853: he was only twelve years old, and she a mere six.

After the death of her mother, in 1856, it was decided to send Milena to Cetinje. Having grown up as a simple, uneducated peasant girl she was given a modest education and instructed in the customs of the royal court. The shy and unassuming girl spent nearly four years under the guidance of Mirko and his family while Nikola studied in Paris. In that time the family developed a great affection for her: "My father and mother loved her as their own daughter. My late uncle also loved her greatly and treated her as his own child, and she showed him her love and respect. In every way she was very beautiful, sweet, kind, gentle and devout."[27]

Montenegrin women were expected to behave demurely and discreetly, so Milena could only express her feelings for Nikola through gestures. He knew of their strength through his sister Gorde:

"She did not talk to me much at that time, it seemed as if she was ignoring me. I understood that and did not want to shame her. Did she love me a lot? That I knew from my good and kind sister who told me, 'Oh brother, she loves you. She prays for you. When I ask her, 'Who do you pray to God for?', she replies, 'For Master [Prince Danilo], then for Miko [Mirko], then for Petar [Vukotić], then for Nana [Anastazija], for Aunt [Darinka], then brother Marko [Vukotić].' When I ask her, 'Do you pray for someone else?', she replies only with a smile on her lips and a blush on her cheek'."[28]

Mirko set about preparing the ground for the forthcoming marriage. Envoys were sent to France and Russia. The vital mission to St. Petersburg was entrusted to Petar Vukotić, who informed Tsar Alexander II of the political situation in Montenegro and of the necessity for the new ruler to take a bride. The controversies that had surrounded Prince Danilo and Princess Darinka, the financial accusations against them as well as their political relations with France and Turkey, suggested to the the Tsar that a Montenegrin bride from one of the leading families would prevent French or Austrian influence being furthered. He concurred that the marriage should go ahead with all haste, and in Cetinje Mirko readied his son to marry.

Nikola, however, had not prepared himself for such an early wedding: *"By the end of September I had recovered from my illness and by St. Petka's Day I had made a complete recovery. A little after St. Petka's Day I noticed that my father was intent on telling me something, making remarks such as 'one cannot go on like this', 'that one should think of the future', 'that a single tree is but a bare log.' Eventually he said to me, 'Niko, you should get married, married as soon as possible.' - 'God be with you Miko! Married! And to whom?' - 'How can you ask? To your fiancée Milena. Who else? She is still a child but a healthy and advanced one. I thought that it could not be done sooner than two or three years from now, but it can and should be, as soon as possible. So is she dear to*

you?' - 'Yes, very much. There is a saying Miko: he who has an early lunch and marries early has no regrets.' - 'So, with God's permission, tomorrow?' - 'Tomorrow is Friday, then it is Saturday, it is not done on these days.' - 'So when is it good?' - 'The first day after Sunday.' - 'Well then, shall I send for our neighbour vojvodas? For in this period of mourning we cannot have a wedding in the way I would prefer.' - 'Indeed, do so'.[29]

Five days later, on November 8, 1860, Nikola and Milena were married. The wedding itself was a modest, family orientated event. Coming so soon after Prince Danilo's murder, with the country still in shock and mourning, it could hardly have been otherwise. In Danilo's memory the Monastery had been designated a place of mourning for two years and, therefore, the ceremony was performed in the little Vlach Church, the oldest building in Lovćen Valley. The witnesses were Nikola's cousin, Vojvoda Krco Petrović, and Princess Darinka's brother, Nikola Kvekić. In the evening the leading vojvodas were invited to the wedding dinner; it was a subdued celebration, signifying the unhappy events that had brought Nikola to the throne.

Prince Nikola Petrović-Njegoš, the artist is thought to be Novak Radonić.

A baptism of fire survived and the Prince's star in the ascendance.

Chapter VI

The Young Ruler: 1860-1874

For myself I can only say this: that I sacrificed more at the altar of the state, that in free will I even gave up my young life to the crown, that is dedicated to the happiness and greatness of Serbs, with conviction and joy.[1]

Prince Nikola Petrović-Njegoš

The young Prince was a striking figure. Viscountess Strangford, a British visitor to Cetinje in 1863, found the young ruler to be, *"An extraordinarily handsome man, looking much older than his real age, very tall and well made. His forehead is wide and open, his hair and eyes nearly black, and the naturally soft, somewhat sad expression of his southern face is animated by a very sweet and frequent smile."* The Prince's national costume struck Strangford as rather exotic, *"His dark blue pantaloons cut in the Syrian style, very full and wide, gathered in at the knees with scarlet garters, a Damascus silk scarf around the loins, and at his waist a huge crimson leathern band, in which the arms are placed . . . The scarlet waistcoat, embroidered in gold, is half concealed by a closely fitting tunic of white cloth, also richly embroidered in gold . . ."* She also noted that the still teenage Milena was, *"A very sweet looking, gentle young creature, slenderly made and of a dark complexion, she is much out of health, and has a delicate and almost sad face."*[2]

The return to a more homespun family lifestyle was apparent and the atmosphere in the capital generally was rather downbeat. Things had not gone well since Prince Danilo's death, particularly the near disastrous war of 1862. A mixed blessing was the return of Princess Darinka, whom, it was rumoured, was having an affair with Nikola. Naturally, her return unsettled Nikola and Milena's still developing relations. More generally, Darinka's ambitious nature suggested trouble, although her intelligence and experience could be useful and she had acted in exemplary fashion during Nikola's inauguration.

Despite the relative personal opulence of Danilo's and Darinka's reign, Cetinje itself had changed little. The royal residence, the Biljarda, was much the same as when Vladika Rade had lived there. It was two hundred and thirty-seven feet long, forty feet wide and consisted of two stories, divided by a long narrow passage, comprising twenty-five rooms in all. At one end was the Prince's study, and at the other the billiard room. The rear of the Biljarda looked onto the court garden and the front looked out over the valley of Lovćen. Solidly built, slated and whitewashed, it was a simple, pleasant dwelling.

Nikola lived with members of his family: Milena, his mother Stane, sister Gorde, and his cousin Božo, while his father Mirko had taken a house nearby. Opposite the Biljarda, construction of a new house for Princess Darinka had begun, while to the rear stood the Montenegrin capital's most imposing building, the Monastery. Cetinje was completed in the immediate vicinity by a few dozen

Milena's early years as the Princess of Montenegro were difficult ones. The young and inexperienced girl, still in her teens, was overshadowed by Prince Danilo's widow, Darinka. Milena's status would rise steadily after the birth of her first child and the departure of Darinka in 1867.

modest stone houses.

Court life under the young ruler had also reverted to a more simple mode. The court etiquette that Darinka had introduced was largely forgotten and there were no lavish parties. Dinner was usually an informal affair.

The occasional guests could be entertained in the reception room, where portraits of the Emperor and Empress of France, which had been given to Nikola during his student days in Paris, of the Tsar and Tsarina of Russia and of Princess Darinka and the late Prince Danilo looked down upon them.

The other remaining trappings of European society were Darinka's legacy. She had turned the ruler's residence into something slightly more suited for a princely ruler than a monk by acquiring fine furnishings.

She had also introduced servants to the court, young men selected from the best families. They were usually family relations who would attend table dressed in full national costume. At the least they added a dash of picturesque colour for foreign visitors to enjoy.

While Nikola enjoyed French cuisine and proudly offered guests the locally produced red wine, which Viscountess Strangford considered excellent and worthy of export, his own tastes were quite plain and he drank in moderation. His favourite dish was boiled potatoes with greens and dried pork or mutton, ideally prepared to his mother's recipe. He ate well and snacked between the two daily meals. He would often take a piece of cooked beef from the kitchen knowing it would not spoil his appetite: "*Like all young and healthy people I was eating heartily and I enjoyed all of our national dishes. I was always satisfied with what was given to me.*" There was little need for a full time chef and Ivo Martinović, who had been Prince Danilo's chef, would only be called for on special occasions; usually meals were prepared by local men such as Marko from Stane's village of Bajice and Lazo from Njeguši.

Nikola's idiosyncrasies were also apparent in his working habits, which Stane found exasperating, understandably so with the Government literally next door to her kitchen: "*Forgive me God! I was making my mother angry very often, usually because I would invite five or six people without telling her or the court manager . . . on one occasion, with the knowledge of my father and Milena, and with their agreement to keep it a secret from my mother, I was working in my study with a senator and two adjutants. When it was time for dinner, the servants told me they were waiting for me in the salon. I told them to start without me and I would come shortly. I called the gentlemen I was working with to follow me . . .*"[3]

Government was a domestic affair and, without as yet the many burdens of state which would accumulate over the years, Nikola still had ample time to enjoy himself: to visit the vojvodas in their houses, walk to market, or just sit in the shade with friends. Playing cards was one of his favourite pastimes and the telling of stories another. Visitors to the Prince would arrive unannounced to share a drink, talk and listen to the gusle.

In summer Nikola would visit Lovćen and Njeguši. As he did not yet have a residence of his own in Lovćen he would sleep outdoors or in a tent. In Njeguši village he would stay with his relative Djuro Petrović, until he built a new house on the site of the old family residence. In winter he would spend time in Rijeka Crnojevića in his late uncle's house.

Along with the energy of youth, Nikola also had the constitution to indulge some unhealthy habits: "*I was smoking . . . terribly much, from sixty to eighty cigarettes a day. I was sleeping erratically. I could fall asleep whenever I wanted, and I could stay awake without tiredness as well.*"

A view of the Biljarda, Nikola and Milena's residence until 1867, and, to the rear left, Cetinje Monastery. (Inset) An early photograph of Milena.

Once, while returning from Paris, he caught up sleep in Turin: for thirty hours! Usually going to bed around midnight or later, he would wake at dawn, sip coffee until around 8am and sometimes write poetry, which he would read to his perjaniks. An early morning hunting expedition, invariably with a good catch, would be followed by a mid-morning nap until midday and another in the afternoon. In both winter and summer, Nikola lived by his own idiosyncratic routines.

However, the responsibilities of his position were already beginning to encroach on his personal freedom: *"After becoming ruler, I used to play sport and exercise amongst a small circle, not to offend in the eyes of my good citizens the dignity of the crown. Later I limited myself in public to modest riding and sharp shooting."*[4]

That dignity was in fact a subtle distinction as there was very little to distinguish the Royal Family from their subjects. Nikola's national costume, that important symbol of national pride and social status, was the same as his countrymen's, except that his overcoat was light rather than dark blue and its decoration more ornate. Mirko was hardly a man to be impressed or seduced by foreign ways, while Stane continued to live as she had always done. She liked to socialise with the people of Cetinje and could often be seen walking through town, always with some work in her hands, such as the socks she knitted which relatives and friends would sell at the market in Kotor.

Cetinje remained as tightly knit, self-contained and parochial as ever, but Nikola was not in the least embarrassed by it, in fact rather the opposite. Overlooking those modest scenes, he would proudly tell visitors about his poor but honest Montenegrins: of the time a visitor had left a tent on a hillside for three years and returned to find everything as he had left it, and that if a visitor were to lose anything, even in the remotest corner of the country, it would be brought to the Prince within three days.

Nikola's pride in the national character was also expressed in a desire to protect his people from foreign influence. He always wore national dress and demanded everyone follow suit. The mixing of dress styles was forbidden and flaunting of the dress code was sternly dealt with. Meeting a young schoolteacher in Cetinje, Nikola saw that he had a walking stick as an accessory, although it was known that only the Prince and those with disabilities were allowed to carry them. The transgressor,

(Left) Omer Pasha Latas. A Serb born in the Habsburg Empire's Croatian provinces, he served as a cadet in the Austrian army until 1828 when he deserted and fled to Turkey. He went on to become one of the Sublime Porte's most formidable military governors. Having quelled the major Bosnian revolt of the early 1830's and executed the disloyal Ali Pasha Rizvanbegović of Herzegovina in 1851, he reasserted Istanbul's authority in the two provinces. In 1862 he led an army fifty-five thousand strong against Montenegro. His campaign nearly overran the capital, Cetinje, but resistance had taken its toll on Omer's soldiers and he later admitted that, if the Montenegrins had not been deprived of munitions by an arms embargo, his exhausted army would have lost the vital battle at Rijeka Crnojevića. This letter (insets below) pre-dates the conflict which began in March 1862.

February 1862
To Cattaro [Kotor], Montenegro

To His Royal Highness the Prince of Montenegro.

I am quite dismayed as to why Your Royal Highness finds reason to construct a small fortification on the De Tanke Hills, heights that join Montengro to Albania. You have placed me in an impossible situation and I cannot reply immediately to your request. Because of this act, if I agreed to your request, I would justify your unfounded claims of attacks by the Albanians; whereas, as a matter of fact, it is the contrary. It is not the Montenegrins who have been attacked by the Albanians, but we who have suffered hostility from your country. It is for this reason that, before I could accept your demands, it is vital to establish and clarify from which side the attacks come from. Therefore I beg Your Royal Highness to produce proof of the Albanian attacks against Montenegro.

Omer Pasha Latas

who had tried to hide his fashion accessory in his trouser leg, was firmly warned: *"If I see you with it again, I will break it over your head."* Foreign customs and manners were not deemed suitable or beneficial for the Montenegrin character.

However, the young ruler's own views were actually a combination of Montenegrin conservatism and more liberal European influences. Although he had received a western European education, Nikola's cultural tastes remained decidedly Montenegrin. He, too, was steeped in the heroic Serb ballads and liked to play and compose music for the gusle. Conversely, his cosmopolitan upbringing and his essentially gentle nature made some attitudes harder to accept unconditionally: he certainly found his father's overt pride in war trophies taken from the Turks rather embarrassing.

And while Nikola's patriotism was as deep as his father's he was nowhere near as fierce. He would weep when recalling the heroes of the recent wars, such as his friend old Petar Stevanov who had attacked a three thousand strong Turkish force with only one thousand men and suffered terrible injuries. He also had sympathy for his enemies, which was demonstrated when he pardoned Turkish soldiers, even giving them money and an escort back to their homes.

On the whole, Nikola's views tended toward the conservative. His experience of Europe had made him appreciative of more developed societies, but he did not consider native ways inferior, even those traditional and sometimes harsh laws that stamped Montenegrin society as belonging to the 'Orient'. He unhesitatingly believed, albeit with a nod to more tolerant methods, that an unfaithful wife should be punished severely: *"In former days, they would have been put to death. I should imprison them for life."*[5]

Nikola certainly believed in the national mission but he was not inclined to turn Montenegrin society on its head as his firebrand predecessor had. Therefore, any divergence of outlook between father and son in no way threatened discord. Nikola gladly let Mirko wield effective power. After his inauguration he reconfirmed Mirko as President of the Senate and allowed him to preside over much of the general administration of state business and adjudicate disputes in the name of the Prince.

Regarding the older generation of vojvodas and serdars, Nikola was not quite so enthusiastic. He greatly admired their bravery, feelings which he expressed with a romantic flourish: *"They were real cavaliers, incarnations of the musketeers of Alexander Dumas. They were Athos and Porthos, Aramis and D'Artagnan, all from the best Montenegrin houses, all respected and wise, and all as brave as their sables . . . They were those rare kind of people who would never ask for anything, and would receive every little present from me with gratitude."*[6] It was a nice tribute to their chivalric spirit, and Montenegrins could certainly be just as famously proud and comically reckless as Dumas' creations, as was exampled by the two competing warriors who, fully armed and disregarding the fact they could not swim, jumped off a bridge into Lake Skadar to prove their fearlessness. Nikola's perjaniks were obliged to jump in and rescue them!

Nikola, however, realised that an efficient state could not be run by heroes. When he attended debates in the Senate it was sometimes to read documents for the illiterate senators. It showed how far Montenegro lagged behind other states in education and training, even among the ruling elite. The older generation had earned splendid, legendary laurels, but the Prince hardly needed to be a radical to feel that it was time for them to step aside.

Ambitious, eager and filled with the optimism of youth he aimed to raise the nation out of its poverty. Building an infrastructure was the most immediate obstacle to overcome. Roads, bridges and schools were a priority, but the state's finances were grossly insufficient to pay for their construction. There were, however, forests, valleys filled with grapevines, olives and figs, fresh-water rivers bursting with trout, all waiting to be exploited. The crux of the matter was exports: *"Had I a port from which to ship them, I have rivers to bring down my timber, my wine and my fish, by the sale of which I could pay for the roads and build my schools. I have built ten already, but as yet I can do but a mere nothing for the real improvement or encouragement of my people. My neighbours complain that my mountaineers do nothing but fight. They have nothing else to do. If they could gain anything by their flocks and crops they would work hard enough to do so."*[7]

Nikola's hopes had to be tempered by the harsh realities of survival in his karstic mountains, particularly the difficulties of eking out a living in such terrain. For many emigration was the only answer, even though it robbed their country of their skills and effort. In 1861 Nikola was forced to plead to Serbia's Prince Mihailo Obrenović and the Russian Consul in Dubrovnik to allow Montenegrins to emigrate to their territories: *"Our poverty reached a new height this year because the little that the Montenegrins counted on was destroyed by the great heat. There are thousands of families which have to*

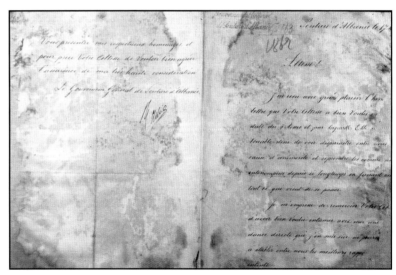

1862. Diplomatic correspondence between Omer Pasha Latas and Prince Nikola while Turco-Montenegrin conflict raged. Hostilities continued until September when the combination of Great Power intervention and war weariness saw peace signed and a return to the territorial status quo.

Governor General of Scutari, Albania, May 17 [May 29]
Your Royal Highness!
I have received with great pleasure the letter of March 6 [March 18], in which Your Royal Highness expresses his wish to remove any cause of animosity between our countries and re-establish the good relations we had in the past. I am here to thank Your Royal Highness to have taken this action and begin talking to me directly, and I am certain that we can progress from here to establish our best relationship.
Proud of our mutual interest.
Please accept my tribute and the assurance of my greatest consideration.

The Governor General of Scutari, Albania

93

A portrait of Prince Nikola by the Viennese photographer Ludwig Angerer. The handsome young ruler was a romantic and rather exotic addition to the ranks of European royalty.
(Facing page) Princess Milena in national costume.

emigrate to escape starvation . . . "[8]

An additional cause of emigration were clan and inter-tribal conflicts. Poor and embroiled in their own local disputes, which often involved the officially outlawed but still prevalent blood feud, on occasion whole families had fled rather than run the gauntlet of eye for an eye retribution.

The blood feud was an issue which affected all levels of society, and that included the ruling class which had seen its share of conflict. Vladika Rade and Prince Danilo had not flinched from eliminating enemies, and Nikola was heir to that cruel legacy which had helped bring the Petrovići to power. He longed to rid Montenegro of the blood feud, but he also knew that some of his subjects would not hesitate to enact it, even if it were directed against their ruler.

Nikola had some frightening personal experience in this respect. Prince Danilo's agent, Joko Kusovac, had carried out the assassination in Istanbul of the then pretender to the throne, Stefan Perović-Cuco. Kusovac had also been employed by Danilo to kill an assassin from the Dobrljani clan, which led to the clan making an attempt on Nikola's life in 1862. Fortunately, all the assassin managed to do was to shoot Nikola's horse from under him.

It was clear that even the ruler could not always suppress or avoid involvement in the blood feud. Indeed, such bravery had to be rewarded. For his efforts in defence of the Petrovići, Joko Kusovac and his family were allowed to live in Prince Danilo's house in Rijeka-Crnojevića and his children were brought into the Royal Family's service.

Montenegro's powerful neighbours, Austria and Turkey, were, at least officially, distressed by the country's inner turmoil, which often spilled over into their territory in the form of emigration and border raiding. Both, however, suppressed and stifled its economy and Nikola regarded them as the real reason for the *"banditry over our battlefields and graves."*[9]

An exchange between Habsburg Emperor Franz Josef and Nikola in Kotor, Montenegro's natural port which the Austrians had ruled since the Congress of Vienna in 1815, encapsulated the country's relations with the Great Powers. *"My brother, the Prince, lives high,"* Franz Josef remarked, to which Nikola replied, *"My brother, the Emperor, has taken all the sea, the Turks have taken all the land, so there is nothing left for me but the sky."*[10]

Without exports trade could only be minimal and the Austrians, who controlled the coastline, made matters worse by placing a quarantine and customs duty on the Montenegrins either importing or exporting. Although he knew hoping for benevolence was pie in the sky, even the fiercely independent Mirko, who tried to introduce rice and coffee to the rocky Rijeka region, swallowed his pride and pleaded for his people be allowed to *"grow rich and happy."*[11]

The stark fact facing any Montenegrin ruler was a country engaged in a long term struggle for survival and independence. It usually made for a painful introduction to the realities of power and an early taste of war was Nikola's baptism of fire.

The immediate causes of the 1862 war, which cast a shadow across the early years of Nikola's reign, predated his accession. Prince Danilo had placed Montenegro on a permanent war footing and, shortly before his death, had been preparing the ground for an uprising against Turkish rule in Herzegovina.

As ever, Danilo's ambitions risked disaster: despite a burning desire to gain their freedom, the Herzegovinians were neither equipped nor organised for a successful rebellion. On one occasion

Danilo took Nikola along to meet the rebel leaders, but he was disappointed by their behaviour: *"On St. Trojica's Day, May 22, [June 3] 1860, I went to Ostrog with uncle. I saw how the uprising in Herzegovina was being organised, heard the people's wishes and lessons for their leaders. My uncle trusted those men and believed that the uprising in Herzegovina would be welcomed but . . . each leader only wanted his own voice to be heard, for only his word to count. That sad Serb 'I' distracted from the work and spoilt our plans. My uncle had chosen fifty good Montenegrins to help the initial uprising, but in vain. Who responded? Only the late Petko Kovačević along with a few Uskoks who were living on the borders since long ago."*

After Prince Danilo's death, Mirko and Nikola still resolved to support the Herzegovinians, although it was in a spirit of fatalism rather than optimism, as Nikola recorded: *"Serbs and Turks became enemies from Tara to Sutorina, battles . . . with heads falling in the lands of Krstac, Korita and Pilatovica . . . From their heartlands the Turks are preparing. In Cetinje we ask ourselves what are we going to do and how? . . . Young and inexperienced, in spite of my good intentions, what could I say? My father told me, 'The Master should work hard for the intervention of the Great Powers, persuade Serbia to help and we will fill the battlefields with Montenegrins and leave the rest to God.'*

"By the end of 1860 and the beginning of 1861 Montenegrin and Herzegovinian guns were firing all the way from Tara to Sutorina; the towers in Korita and Krstac were burned and destroyed; the town of Nikšić was besieged. Šćepan Radojević and Vojvoda Ilija Djukanović, leaders of the uprising, were killing Turks everywhere. Those Herzegovinians, all brave men, were dying like wheat at harvest time. But who can resist Turkish might!"[12]

Turco-Montenegrin hostilities reached their climax in 1862. In April, Omer Pasha Latas launched his campaign based on the traditional three-pronged attack. The skill of their commander and the numerical odds of fifty-five thousand Turkish troops confronting twenty thousand Montenegrins, prefigured a dire outcome.

Battle commenced with Montenegrin forces defending, for the first time, the long borderline from Scutari Province to Herzegovina. Nikšić Fortress was besieged and, in May, Nikola went to Ostrog Monastery with his perjaniks to close off the gorge. The morale and bravery of Montenegrin troops notwithstanding, the border could not be held. The northern and southern armies were forced to combine and, from mid-July, heavier fighting brought greater casualties.

The lack of munitions and food supplies was badly undermining the defence effort. Both were obtainable only on the Austrian black market, but, in this instance, the Viennese authorities would have none of it. Prince Mihailo Obrenović of Serbia had thought to supply Montenegro with weapons and munitions via Austria; that route was now blocked and Nikola instead sent two hundred men through Turkish territory to the Serbian border to collect the arms.

Istanbul was now able to tighten the noose further: threatened with military action by the Sublime Porte if he assisted Nikola, Prince Mihailo could not afford to risk giving the supplies even clandestinely. To make matters even worse, the Montenegrin messengers, who had refused sanctuary in Serbia or Austria, were killed as they tried to return home. Ultimately the only aid received was a shipload of bread from Corfu, frumetin grain from Turin and wheat from Brazil.

As both sides prepared for the final battle disaster loomed: the Austrians imposed a complete blockade of aid and,

with Serbia too wary to act and the Herzegovinians overwhelmed, the poorly armed Montenegrin forces were left virtually defenceless against rifled muskets and artillery.

The battle at Rijeka Crnojevića saw Montenegrin soldiers entirely out of munitions and they were forced to fight with knives, stones, even pieces of wood. By August 14 Turkish victory had been secured. Retreating to Cetinje, the order to evacuate and take the body of Saint Petar I to Mount Lovćen was given. Only a sudden change in the weather, a severe summer storm on August 27, allowed the Montenegrins to push the enemy back a few kilometres.

Nikola had already sued for peace, but a vainglorious commander such as Omer Pasha Latas would have relished occupying Cetinje and, in premature anticipation of that triumph, he had already reported to Istanbul that the capital had fallen. The reality was that his own troops were exhausted and, as he would later admit, if the Montenegrins had brought five thousand fresh and equipped men to Rijeka Crnojevića, he could have offered only weak resistance and would have been forced to withdraw.

Even on the verge of total defeat, Nikola had hoped to carry on fighting and make the price of victory too high: *"This contingent, far from their base and supplies in Scutari, would have come to our rocky region without any water, to find Cetinje burnt out and destroyed by us as the Muscovites did in 1812 . . . the army could have been destroyed with our efforts and by nature itself, especially because the warm summer days were turning to autumn with winter closing in."*[13] However, in his desperation to end the conflict, Nikola accepted the proposed peace terms immediately.

It was a much criticised decision made under extreme pressure. Among the unfavourable terms, which included restrictions on the free movement of Montenegrins and the monitoring of arms shipments, the clause relating to Vojvoda Mirko was noteworthy. His presence had become so provocative to the Sublime Porte that it was stipulated he leave the country. Nikola had been persuaded by the advice that the treaty would be reduced to minimal obligations and, in real terms, that is how it was: Mirko had no intention of going into exile and the border commission set about its work of delimitation knowing full well it was a futile effort.

Although Montenegro's military honour had been salvaged it was at a high price: sixty villages, two monasteries and twenty-three churches had been destroyed; three thousand five hundred soldiers had died and another four thousand had been wounded. Turkish losses were greater still with twenty-one thousand dead and wounded.

Serbo-Montenegrin relations had also suffered. Nikola had been bitterly disappointed when Prince Mihailo Obrenović had been unable to come to his aid during the conflict. Out of sorrow and anger he erected a monument near the Vlach Church to the unfortunate men killed trying to bring arms through Bosnia-Herzegovina.

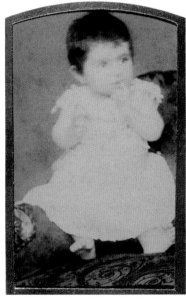

It was not a promising start, but the tension between the two rulers proved short lived. The driving force behind the rapprochement was Mihailo. One of Serbia's most talented leaders as well one of the most ambitious, he had the political skills to realise his vision of a Balkan alliance.

Prince Aleksandar Karadjordjević (1842-1858) had been deposed recently, and in the war of 1862 Prince Mihailo, although he aspired to unify the Serbs, had feared for his own position in the event of an unsuccessful intervention so early in his reign. Mihailo's confidence grew thereafter as Russia favoured Serbia amongst its regional allies. A Serbo-Montenegrin military and financial agreement was made and, in the event of national unification, Mihailo's future position as ruler of the unified Serb state confirmed. Mihailo also concluded agreements with Romania, Greece, Bulgaria and Croatia, laying the foundation for a war of liberation against their oppressors.

However, the rivalry between the Montenegrin and Serbian dynasties, which went back as far as the time of Vladika Rade, was an ongoing complication in the plans for national unification. Rade had offered to dedicate his greatest poetic work 'The Mountain Wreath' to Prince Miloš Obrenović, but when the two rulers met in Vienna they fell out. As they conversed, Rade soon realised that the shrewd and cautious Serbian ruler lacked zeal for a war of liberation. Rade's disappointment meant that there was no dedication to Miloš, and it was instead given posthumously to 'Karadjordje', the founder of the rival dynasty and leader of the Serbian insurrection of 1804, who had been assassinated in 1817 on Miloš' order.

In the 1850's Prince Danilo had offered to act as Prince Aleksandar Karadjordjević's personal guard if he attempted to unite the Serb people. However, it was little more than a symbolic offer aimed at winning popular support for Danilo, who knew full well the offer would be declined.

In the case of Prince Mihailo and Prince Nikola things went more smoothly and a contract was drawn up. Nikola enthusiastically grasped the opportunity: *"For the unity and welfare of Serbdom, I suggested to Serbia's envoy we make a secret contract between our two states towards the liberation and unification of all Serbs. The young and delighted envoy responded to my wish, and we began writing the secret contract, article by article . . . now or never, I thought to myself, all must be sacrificed to make up for the centuries of misery of the Serb nation."[14]*

Nikola's critics would later cite the secret clause, stipulating that he would ascend the united throne in the event of Mihailo dying without an heir, as evidence of his *"machiavellian politicking."[15]* It was an unfairly harsh judgement, even as a retrospective criticism. It was certainly a shrewd move in that few expected Mihailo to have an heir, but also a legitimate and legal way to combine national and dynastic ambitions.

If the two rulers were dynastic rivals both also embodied the Serb national aspiration and were allies in that cause. To strengthen their ties, Mihailo had acted as godfather to two of Nikola's daughters, Milica and Stane, and sent his Foreign Minister, Jovan Ristić, to the christening of his fourth daughter, Marija.

Ristić used the occasion to discuss the operation of the military contract. The Serbians were concerned about previous Montenegrin breaches, such as the territorial negotiations with the Sublime Porte that led to the sale of land around Velje and Malo Brdo for forty thousand ducats, and a gift from the Sultan of a yacht. Belgrade was irked, but had to accept that these transactions of 'Asiatic hypocrisy' were the stock in trade of Turco-Montenegrin relations.

By 1866 relations had improved sufficiently for Nikola to inform Belgrade that he was *"resolutely with Serbia"[16]*, and, by January 1867, that Montenegro was ready for war: *"I received everything in good condition [military equipment] . . . When the time comes, Your Highness, and when you ask, I will give you seven to eight thousand hungry and naked, but good soldiers, who will, I hope, serve you well, especially in your rocky places."[17]*

These plans were brought to a sudden and premature end by Mihailo's assassination on June 10, 1868, in Belgrade's

Six of the royal couple's first seven children were daughters and Nikola was greatly troubled by the apparent lack of suitable husbands. In fact, nearly all made excellent marriages, except for the unfortunate Marija who died aged sixteen from tuberculosis. All benefited greatly from their Russian education at the prestigious Smolny Girls Institute in St. Petersburg, an ideal preparation for aspiring royal brides. Zorka went onto marry the pretender to the Serbian throne, Petar Karadjordjević, while her younger sisters, Milica and Stane, married into the Russian nobility, Ana a German prince and Jelena to Crown Prince Vittorio Emanuele of Italy.
(Above) Prince Nikola's second and third born daughters, Milica, seated, and Stane.
Facing page: (Top) Jelena, left, Marija, centre, and Stane, seated, at the Smolny Institute and (bottom) the infant Jelena.

Košutnjak Park. Rumours soon spread that the assassin was an agent of the rival Karadjordjević dynasty and that Russia supported Nikola's election as Prince of Serbia. Neither rumour was right but there was an element of truth in both.

For his alleged role in the plot, Prince Aleksandar Karadjordjević was sentenced to twenty years in his absence by the Serbian courts. He was subsequently placed on trial in Budapest at the request of the Serbian Government. There he was exonerated, convicted by a court of appeal and, after three years of legal wrangling, exonerated again by the Hungarian Supreme Court. The ageing Prince was involved to a degree, but as the instrument of any plot rather than its instigator.

More relevantly, Prince Mihailo's murderer had openly boasted in a Belgrade coffee house of his plan and it was common knowledge that plots to kill the Prince existed. A more likely accomplice to the plot was the Sublime Porte, whose servant, Omer Pasha Latas of Bosnia, had contacts with the conspirators. Istanbul seems to have tacitly admitted some involvement as Omer was subsequently dismissed from his post and demoted. As for the Serbian authorities, they did not want the messy details of all this emerging as the obvious point of their negligence could be raised. It was expedient to pin as much of the blame as possible on Aleksandar Karadjordjević.

Prince Nikola was not accused of involvement but some thought he might be placed on the throne. Soon after Mihailo's death Nikola made his first trip to St. Petersburg, during which Tsar Alexander II gave him the gift of the sable which had belonged to Serbia's medieval ruler King Milutin. It was a gesture which the Serbian press interpreted as a sign of Russian favour. It was certainly an important moment for Nikola, but the political reality, although important, was less momentous, namely the restoring of ties damaged in his predecessor's reign.

There was even a rumour that Nikola had the support of Serbia's leading socialist figure, Svetozar Marković. However, the pioneering young socialist had little real influence and Serbia's ruling politicians were not inclined to consider Nikola as Mihailo's replacement.

Instead, they acted quickly to promote their own choice. Parliament was convened and Prince Mihailo's cousin once removed, fourteen year-old Milan, was elected. Three regents were appointed, the politicians Milivoje Blaznavac, who had the army behind him, Jovan Gavrilović and Jovan Ristić. Parliament was more concerned with redrafting the constitution after Prince Mihailo's reign and in prosecuting his supposed murderers than changing dynasty.

Nikola, therefore, had good reason to regret Prince Mihailo's death: it was a body blow to their shared aspirations and his dynastic hopes. The Balkan alliance Mihailo had been building quickly faded without its instigator, while the secret contract between the two rulers would only have come into force if the two states were united and the regents saw no reason to continue it. They even claimed that Montenegro had already received more aid from Serbia than agreed. Mihailo's death also marked the end of Obrenović-Petrović friendship: Prince Milan, who would become a controversial and difficult ruler, came to loath his Montenegrin counterpart.

During the same period there had been other hard political lessons for Nikola: that even the most trusted members of his inner circle were not always loyal. In addition to his father, Nikola relied in the early years of his rule on Princess Darinka and a

(Above) Habsburg Emperor Franz Josef and (right) Empress Elizabeth in 1860. Franz Josef had come to the throne at a young age, during the revolutionary upheavals of 1848 that shook the Habsburg Empire to its foundations. Although the South Slavs had played a vital role in saving his throne they received no reward for their loyalty. With Montenegro relations were often tense as Austria's control of the eastern Adriatic coastline, parts of which in earlier times had been Montenegrin territory, was greatly resented. However, when Franz Josef met Prince Nikola in one of those coastal towns, Kotor, he found the Montenegrin ruler to be *"An excellent fellow . . . very friendly toward Austria."* Undoubtedly, Nikola was being tactful as he considered the Habsburg Empire to be one of Europe's *"greedy Great Powers."*

Herzegovinian, Archimandrite Dučić, who had fled to Montenegro after the 1862 uprising. It was Dučić who encouraged better relations between Belgrade and Cetinje, who had shuttled back and forth as the military contract with Mihailo had been negotiated and had been entrusted to bring the sorely needed financial aid from Belgrade. Nikola came to rely on the young, intelligent monk but, in 1867, both Dučić and Darinka abruptly left Cetinje after their conspiratorial activities had been uncovered.

After Prince Danilo's death, Darinka had enjoyed close relations with Nikola and was said have become his lover. Nikola was, the rumours had it, so infatuated with Darinka he was thinking of divorcing Milena.

Their good relations came to an end after Nikola found out that she was conspiring with Archimandrite Dučić on behalf of her daughter Olga. Nikola maintained a discreet silence over the whole affair, but Darinka was known to speak about it with close friends. She was forced to exit Cetinje for a comfortable retirement in Venice.

Nikola may have been sorry to see Darinka go, but he had no such qualms over the departure of Dučić whom he suspected had been working against him for sometime. The extent of the Herzegovinian's scheming had been revealed during a family holiday at Bijela in the Bay of Kotor in 1867.

A proclamation was delivered to Nikola from the Austrian ruled port of Herceg Novi, in which the Montenegrin people expressed the wish that he renounce the throne to facilitate the unification of the Serb people. Nikola believed it was a plot conceived by Archimandrite Dučić in Belgrade and wanted to return immediately to Cetinje but, with an outbreak of cholera in the capital, Mirko refused to let him go and, instead, went himself.

Dučić's plot came to nought but the consequences for the family were still tragic. Mirko contracted cholera and died, although it was subsequently suggested that he was poisoned by his enemies. In either case, his premature death, aged forty-six, deprived the Royal Family of its strongest personality and the country of its finest military commander.

The sudden loss of his father left Nikola at his most vulnerable since becoming ruler. Whether or not his enemies were responsible for Mirko's death, they were rid of a formidable opponent and now hoped that the young Prince, still learning the arts of political intrigue, would prove more malleable.

Once again misfortune had thrown Nikola into the eye of the storm: after the deaths of Mirko and Prince Mihailo he was isolated both personally and politically.

In that context, it was fortunate that for the time being the unification of Serbia and Montenegro was off the political agenda, giving Nikola the opportunity to

(Above) Zorka (sitting), Milica and Stane at the Smolny Institute. Left: (top) Marija and (below) Jelena.

concentrate on domestic matters.

Economic problems posed as much of a threat to the nation as military invasion. Internally the economy was fragmented and weak; the regions were isolated from one another by the lack of communications, both man made and natural, and there were no urban centres to speak of, even Cetinje had a population of less than eight hundred.

Without foreign assistance development would be impossible, which made stable relations with the Great Powers a priority. Foremost in Nikola's mind was renewing ties with Russia. Prince Danilo's reign had seen Montenegro breaking away from its traditional policy of friendship with Russia and a move toward Austria and France, he had even considered accepting Turkish suzerainty for an enlargement of territory.

Nikola was convinced that a policy based on Russia's political and financial support was in Montenegro's long-term interest. A sign of lingering Russian anger could be seen in the activities of the Russian Consul in Dubrovnik, who was actively encouraging Montenegrin emigration. Nikola's plan to request an audience with Tsar Alexander II had to wait until the winter of 1868 when a new consul was appointed. Permission gained, he left for St. Petersburg accompanied by a small retinue comprising of Ilija Plamenac, Stanko Radonjić and Djuro Petrović.

To his dismay Nikola was not made welcome and he was kept waiting for several days before Alexander II granted an audience. When it finally took place it was not a congenial experience as the Montenegrins found themselves accused of ingratitude and disloyalty towards their ally. Nikola pleaded that his predecessor's policy was to blame, that Montenegro's love for Russia was undying, even that he had only come to beg for mercy and forgiveness. It was a gamble, but it paid off. The Tsar agreed to an annual subsidy of eight thousand roubles, Nikola was given an honourary medal and the famed sable of King Milutin (which caused such a stir in Belgrade) and Tsarina Maria Feodorovna donated funds for the founding of a girls school in Cetinje.

Reform being dependent upon finance, Nikola had to accept help wherever he could find it and, on the return journey, he stopped in Vienna to plead with Russia's rival. Austria-Hungary (the new appellation for the Habsburg Empire following the 1867 political compromise between Vienna and Budapest) offered tangible assistance, but demanded a tough *quid pro quo*. Without considering territorial concessions along the coastline, it was demanded that Montenegro hand over 'criminals and deserters'. That often meant those who had found refuge from unhappy circumstances in Austro-Hungarian and Turkish territory. However, in practice it only amounted to a statement of intent. The benefit was an agreement to connect Cetinje with Kotor via a telegraph wire and, by the mid 1870's, the founding of telegraph offices in Rijeka Crnojevića, Vir, Orja Luka and Ostrog.

Postal services were equally in need of improvement. In Vladika Rade's reign Montenegro had only a single postman, who earned seventy thalers a year, covering Cetinje and Kotor weekly. That system had continued up until Nikola's reign. In 1871 a postal convention was agreed with Austria-Hungary, enabling a regular service to commence in 1873. Postal offices were built for Cetinje, Rijeka Crnojevića and Vir and, in 1874, Montenegro joined the Universal Postal Union.

Another important, indeed vital, step toward modernisation was road construction. Vladika Rade had made some pioneering efforts, but these had barely been improved upon and further development was sorely needed.

At the time of Nikola's accession, Montenegro's roads were little more than paths carved through the mountains and forests. Difficult to use for pedestrians let alone for horses or carriages, the state of the nation's roads was so poor that Nikola remarked: *"The whole world is throwing stones off its roads while we are putting them on!"*[18] To make the rudimentary transportation system even worse, Montenegro's rivers and streams would often flood their banks and wash away the dirt tracks.

Progress was made with the help of a Viennese loan for the building of a road from Rijeka Crnojevića through Cetinje to the Austro-Hungarian border. Vienna completed the remainder to Kotor; a feat of engineering much praised and appreciated by foreign visitors.

There had been opposition to the road link between Cetinje and Kotor from traditionalists who maintained, just as the Prince's father always had, that it would leave the country vulnerable to invasion.

Even so, for a tiny landlocked nation of just four thousand four hundred square kilometres, the road was a vital link to the outside world. More generally, without the infrastructure of roads and bridges the country would remain economically uncoordinated and many villages totally isolated.

Several of the equally needed bridges were built, one of which had a particular significance for Nikola. Many people had died trying to cross the River Zeta in Bjelopavlići territory and, in 1869, Nikola had a bridge built at his personal expense. It was dedicated to his late father who had long hoped to build a bridge across the River Zeta.

Assistance from Vienna was gladly accepted, although Nikola was at pains to reassure St. Petersburg that this had no effect on his loyalty or, indeed, his dependency on Russia.

Nikola wrote to Tsar Alexander II expressing his gratitude: *"Due to the great improvements, we are now able to welcome many more visitors than before and we can offer them hospitality at the expense of the state. I*

(Below) Ostrog Monastery. A profoundly symbolic place of pilgrimage for Orthodox Serbs. Founded by St. Vasilije of Herzegovina in the seventeenth century, it was built on a summit between Nikšić and Danilovgrad. During the war of 1852-53 Vojvoda Mirko and a band of not more than thirty men took refuge in the Monastery. Their bravery against a Turkish force several thousand strong was made possible by the Upper Monastery's site: built into the caves of the mountain with a huge precipice overhanging, it was accessible only by a frontal assault. As the enemy tried to smoke the Montenegrins out by throwing flaming straw upon the Monastery roof, a messenger escaped and went for help. When reinforcements arrived the Turks were routed. One of the heroes of the siege, Savo Martinović,

recalled the intensity of the fighting: *"In the Monastery courtyard we were up to our knees in blood."* Some fifty years later, in 1904, an old priest of Ostrog told English traveller Reginald Wyon how many Turkish casualties there had been: *"In one pit alone we put eight hundred and there were many such. Today thou canst still find their bones on these heights, and thou needst not seek for long."*

(Bottom) Many had died trying to cross the River Zeta and Vojvoda Mirko had long hoped to be able to construct a much needed bridge. It was only after Mirko's death that Nikola was able to build the bridge, which he dedicated to the memory of his late father.

(Facing page) A photographic portrait of Prince Nikola.

would not be able to do this without the help of Tsar Alexander II and I thank him again. In this period it is very difficult to do more, in fact, even these efforts will eventually fail because of the lack of money."[19]

With that rather dismal thought in mind reforms of the state were undertaken. While maintaining some aspects of the traditional social and legal structure of the country, Nikola aimed to continue the process of centralisation and modernisation of government which Vladika Rade and Prince Danilo had begun.

The regional division of seven counties was increased to eight in 1867, and these were sub-divided into forty-four administrative regions which corresponded to the tribal and clan territorial divisions. Complications arose with shared pasturelands, roads and water rights. As it would have been a retrograde step to simply confirm the existing division of lands, the reforms aimed to unite neighbouring tribes within single administrative units.

The Senate remained the highest court in the land but its role was diminished and, by 1874, its responsibilities for foreign and military policy, finance, education and home affairs were removed to executive officers appointed by the Prince. To ensure that state finances were not overstretched each executive was charged with two portfolios. Nikola had thereby reduced the power of the tribal vojvodas. That process was furthered by also taking away their right of automatic military office. Whether or not this particular method of centralisation, of power in the ruler's own hands, was in keeping with Montenegro's political tradition was questionable, but it was a more effective way to carry on government business.

Another important step forward was made in education. Cetinje had only one primary school complimented by another six temporary schools for the rest of the country. In 1869 two special schools were founded in the capital, 'The Seminary and Teachers School' and the Russian sponsored 'Girls Institute'. In 1874 an agricultural school was established which, however, had to be shut down shortly after. By 1875 seventy-two schools had been opened for over three thousand pupils. Construction of the schools and payment of the teachers were the state's responsibility with much of the needed finance being drawn from the relatively wealthy monasteries.

Nikola proudly informed St. Petersburg: *"Every fourth year Montenegro will have about two thousand boys who can read and write. It is a great thing, not only for the people but even the clergy who, until now, were illiterate . . ."*[20]

One further change, less perceptible but nonetheless important, was Milena's growing maturity.

The simple, pious village girl, married when she was just thirteen, had found herself eclipsed by the sophisticated Princess Darinka. She had received some help: from Archimandrite Dučić who tutored her in the Serbian language and religious instruction, while Stanko Radonjić, Nikola's cousin, taught her French, but with little success. Miss Noikom, the Swiss governess to Darinka's daughter Olga, later taught Milena serviceable French.

So long as Darinka remained in Cetinje, Milena was at a disadvantage. Understandably she became a solitary figure who would spend her time sitting in the court garden or in her personal salon, often alone or occasionally talking with a girlfriend.

After the royal couple had their first children Milena's position at court changed for the better. After a wait of four years Milena gave birth to four daughters in close succession: Ljubica Zorka on January 4, 1865; Milica on July 26, 1866; Anastazija (Stane) on January 4, 1867 and Marija on March 26, 1869. Their joy was tempered by the worrying lack of a male heir, but this was soon remedied. On June 29, 1871, a son, Danilo, was born. More children followed: Jelena on January 8, 1873 and Ana on August 18, 1874. They were not the further sons longed for, as was evidenced by the subdued response to their births, but, in recompense, Milena was young enough to have more children.

(Above) Vojvoda Mirko's tomb which lies in Cetinje Monastery. (Below) Mirko's widow, Stane, with her grandchildren. From left to right: Milica, Danilo, Zorka and Stane.
(Facing page) Ostrog Monastery today and (inset) a portrait, by Aksentije Marodić, 1863, of one of its most famed defenders, Vojvoda Mirko. Mirko's death in 1867, aged only forty-six, left Prince Nikola at his most vulnerable since he had come to the throne in 1860. The family's loss was made worse by the suspicion that Mirko had not, in fact, been a victim of the cholera epidemic of that year, but that he had been poisoned by his enemies.

The importance of a child bearing wife could hardly be overestimated, but Milena, quietly and without ostentation, was also developing into a real consort, taking on the role the ambitious Darinka had so jealously coveted. Milena's qualities of good sense and steadfastness were solid supports for Nikola and she was placed in charge of court affairs during his vital visits to Austria-Hungary and Russia in the winter of 1868/69. *All my affairs I entrust to Milena, please deal with her as you would with me*[21] Nikola confidently informed Serbia's Foreign Ministry.

Nikola had survived the torrid early years of war and personal loss and had subsequently set about the great tasks at hand with energy and boldness. The rejuvenated relations with Russia would continue to be the basis of his policies, both national and dynastic, and prove to be a shrewd decision financially, politically and, not least, personally. However, if he could be pleased with the fruits of his labours, he also knew that the fate of the Serb people was largely dependent on developments in the unhappy Ottoman ruled provinces. In 1875 the restless Herzegovina erupted into violent rebellion once more, this time with consequences that were far reaching and of historic importance.

(Left) The Battle of Vučji Do by Perović. One of the crucial Montenegrin victories in the 1876-77 wars. (Inset) A Montenegrin war banner from the battle. (Below) The ruins of Nikšić Fortress. One of the significant advances in Montenegrin warfare was the successful besieging of fortified towns which enabled the Herzegovinian town of Nikšić and, to the south-east, Podgorica to be gained. At Nikšić, Turkish resistance was worn down by casualties and the ever difficult terrain, which hampered Turkish efforts to lift the siege. Nikšić finally fell to the Montenegrins on September 8, 1877.

The fate of the Balkans and the future of Europe in the balance.

Everything in our country is burned and laid waste. With what spirit can we return to this unhappy country of ours? . . . We can only become tranquil under the happiness of the liberty of which Montenegro shows us the example.

Herzegovinian rebel leaders

The territorial aspirations of Serbia and Montenegro awaited developments in the Ottoman ruled Balkan provinces, but local ambitions were not the cause of the next major convulsion in the Ottoman Empire. Nor, initially, were the Great Powers involved. There was a general desire to keep the peace, evident in the caution of both the Serb princes and in the *Draikersbund*, the arrangement for co-operation between the Russian, German and Austro-Hungarian monarchs. These, however, were not enough to offset the Sublime Porte's failure to successfully rule and reform its troubled province of Bosnia-Herzegovina.

After the Crimean War (1853-1856) the optimists had hoped the Ottoman Empire would make good its shortcomings. There had, at least, been a period of relative calm, even though there had also been the Lebanese massacres of 1860, a rebellion on the island of Crete, and war had twice broken out with Montenegro in 1858 and 1862. Reform was still urgently needed if the 'sick man' of Europe were to survive and peace be maintained.

Economically the Empire lagged behind the other European powers and was increasingly indebted to and dependent upon them: the loans given to implement reforms had been guaranteed by France and Britain and underpinned by the Egyptian tribute. Even that dubious method of support collapsed when the Sublime Porte defaulted on interest payments in October 1875. It was tantamount to a declaration of bankruptcy and badly shook the confidence of Istanbul's financial backers. The clandestine negotiations of Khedive Ismail of Egypt to sell his shares in the Suez Canal to a French syndicate only added to the uncertainty and tension.

At the provincial level this meant that officials went unpaid and, to recompense themselves, they set about exploiting the provinces. Administration was corrupt and the state of the peasantry pitiful. The forecast of 1856 by Lord Stratford De Redcliffe, a remarkable British diplomat who had done much to promote reform in the Ottoman Empire, had been all too amply fulfilled: *"If the integrity of the Sultan's dominions be formally secured, there is but too much reason to fear that the Sublime Porte will give way to its natural indolence and leave the edict of reform a lifeless paper, valuable only as a record of sound principles."*

In Bosnia the Moslem landowners had been resistant to the changes proposed by reformers and a major revolt, which endangered Istanbul's rule and threatened to spread further afield, had broken out in 1831. Omer Pasha Latas reasserted control over the troubled province by successfully breaking the power of the *beys* in the 1850's, but in his wake extortion and violence ruled. W.J. Stillman, correspondent for The London Times during the Cretan uprising of 1866, witnessed the condition of the Herzegovinians as *"the most intolerable of all the subjects of Turkey."*[2] His views held good for Bosnia too. As Austria-Hungary's Foreign Minister, Count Julius Andrassy, described it Bosnia had become *"an unproductive and ruined country, where everything has to be created anew."*[3] Naturally, the Herzegovinian peasantry looked to Montenegro, a country which had in recent memory shown the courage to stand alone against the might of the Ottoman Empire.

When rebellion finally broke out again in the summer of 1875, the tangled nature of Balkan politics threatened to ignite a European war. Serbia's Prince Milan Obrenović had forewarned the Russians of the uprising and asked for their support in case of war with Turkey; St. Petersburg not only replied in the negative but also informed Vienna with a suggestion of co-operation. Though suspicious, Britain preferred to leave the Ottoman Empire's internal problems to the Sublime Porte for the time being, while Germany closely monitored events for signs of a wider European conflict. It was in this complex environment that events unfolded only to spiral out of control.

Austria-Hungary immediately warned Serbia that any military action to aid the rebellion would force it to occupy Belgrade. Count Andrassy's fear of Serbia becoming an *"Oriental Piedmont"* on his border (Habsburg politicians had painful memories of the role Piedmont-Sardinia had played in uniting the Italians in the 1860's) concisely described both the danger for the recently reformed and renamed Empire with its large Slav population and the well publicised hopes of Serbia. British Prime Minister Benjamin Disraeli high-handedly dismissed the hopes of the Herzegovinian rebels: autonomy for Ireland, he contended, would be less absurd. Russia did not want to get dragged into another conflict after faring badly in the Crimean War, although public opinion was forcing Tsar Alexander II to be seen to do something. Finally, the Sublime Porte, in no way inclined to allow a rebellious province to upset its precarious internal balance, tried to pin the blame for the trouble on Montenegro.

Despite his sympathy for the Herzegovinians and the fact that public opinion blamed Turkish despotism for the unrest, Prince Nikola had called for caution from the Herzegovinian leaders in 1874. His initial response to the 1875 rebellion was the same, *"to abstain from the uprising since the time has not yet come."*[4] Faced with an influx of refugees, Nikola's first thought was: *"To restrain my people in Herzegovina. I would not stop in these efforts that gain me the friendship of the Tsar's cabinet, as I am convinced that the Austro-Hungarian cabinet, with their great influence, would help to relieve the plight of these people."*[5]

The unrest was soon causing problems in Montenegro. Within a short while, by August, 1875, Nikola was pleading with the Russian Consul in Dubrovnik: *"Sir, the uprising in Herzegovina has filled my country with many Herzegovinians and their livestock who have come to find refuge from the war. It worries me how I am going to find the resources that they need for their poor lives, as is my duty . . . Although Montenegrins are prepared for any sacrifice for their unfortunate brothers, sharing with them their food from the first moment they arrived, one can see that very shortly our supplies will be exhausted, especially as everyday more and more people are coming. That is why I write to you to inform the Tsar and ask him urgently for help. In this respect I also wrote to Andrassy for help."*[6]

Complaints to the Turkish authorities in Sarajevo resulted in an agreement whereby the rebels could return under guarantees for their safety and have their complaints heard by the relevant officials. However, *en route* to Sarajevo, local police attempted to arrest the rebels and a fight broke out. This inevitably prompted more Herzegovinians to flee into Montenegro.

Field hospitals were hurriedly set up in Cetinje, Grahovo, Župa, and Andrijevica. In the first three months of war two hundred and fifty casualties were treated in field hospitals, with the same number cared for by the Montenegrin people in their own homes. The growing crisis led to the creation of the 'Cetinje Committee for Help', set up with the support of Princess Milena, who donated three hundred ducats, and other family members. Further assistance was later provided by the Russian and Swiss Red Cross agencies.

Prince Nikola greatly feared the dangers of beginning war prematurely, but he was under growing pressure to change policy or, at least, allow volunteers to cross the border. Even the Serbs of the Austro-Hungarian ruled Vojvodina region joined in the criticism of the pacific policies of Belgrade and Cetinje. The Prince used his semi-official journal, *Glas Crnogorca* (The Voice of Montenegro), to

(Right) Sultan Abdul Aziz. Another addition to the list of Ottoman rulers who lacked both political judgement and psychological stability. After his deposition in May 1876, he is thought to have committed suicide by slashing his wrists with a pair of scissors, but murder has also been suggested. Sixteen Turkish doctors all concurred on a suicide verdict, only the British physician had his doubts. Abdul Aziz was succeeded by his nephew who reigned briefly as Sultan Murad V. (Below right) William Ewart Gladstone with his grandson. The leader of Britain's Liberal Party was a staunch supporter of independence for the Balkan states.

try to calm public opinion. The nation would not be bound to neutrality: *"The very thought contradicts the past of Montenegro and the patriotism of Prince Nikola,"* Glas Crnogorca proclaimed. It was also an accurate forecast of events to come.

While none among the Great Powers dared risk a general war in a Europe aptly described by Disraeli as *"armed to the teeth"*, nor could they find a solution and the actions of Turkish forces heightened tension. A meeting in Sarajevo between international consuls representing the Great Powers was used as a cover to send two battalions in to massacre rebels; the credibility of the increasingly derided 'Concert of Europe' was further undermined. The Sublime Porte was not yet prepared to negotiate with the rebels, who continued in the hope of bringing Europe in on their side.

With Turkish forces intensifying their efforts, Prince Nikola knew that neutrality had become morally and politically unsustainable. The Herzegovinian leaders were told at a meeting, symbolically held at Vladika Rade's mausoleum on Mount Lovćen, that Montenegro would sustain them until an appropriate moment, or if possible strengthen and accelerate the movement for liberation. W.J. Stillman described Nikola's dilemma: *"The personal tendencies of the Prince, unlike his predecessors, were to attain his ends by patience and peaceful appliances if possible, but his people have a very different way . . . and the most that could be done was the least possible to the national feeling, but without losing sight of the national aspiration."*[7]

As they struggled with their political and military predicament, the thunder of the Serbian and Montenegrin princes was briefly stolen by the pretender to the Serbian throne, Prince Petar Karadjordjević. He had joined up with a Bosnian band in the north-west of the province. His experience in the French Foreign Legion, fighting as a volunteer against Prussia in 1870, and the much needed finance he brought to the cause made him a leading figure within the uprising. He had hoped to be made commander of the rebel forces, but, predictably, Prince Milan in Belgrade opposed this plan. Petar continued to fight as an ordinary soldier under the pseudonym Petar Mrkonjić, creating a legend for himself.

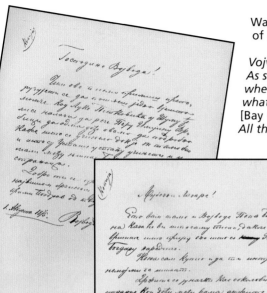

War correspondence in the distinctive Montenegrin style of Commander Mašo Vrbica.

Vojvoda,
As soon as you receive this letter we suggest that you send a handy boy to Luka Petrović, wherever he is in the woods, to tell Pero Ilijin Vrbica to come to us and give us details of what has happened and what the rebels have been able to do, and if there are any Boka [Bay of Kotor] people or other foreigners with them.
All the best.

Sincerely yours, Vojvoda Mašo Vrbica

Amiable Lazar,
You have with you Vojvoda Bogdan. He will tell you what I wrote to him about. Therefore, carry out as soon as you are able the orders given to Pop [Priest] Bogdan. I have bought the horse so do not send one. Be as brave as falcons and treat foreigners well. Carry out these instructions and stay in good health.
1 [13] August, 1875

Vojvoda Mašo Vrbica

(Facing page) War Allegory by Segebard, 1876.

By August 1875 the revolt had spread to Bosnia and both Serbia and Montenegro were inexorably moving towards war with Turkey. Prince Milan's caution did not blind him to the obvious: if Serbia genuinely wanted to be a Balkan Piedmont the hour seemed at hand and failure to seize the opportunity could result in the loss of his throne. The continuing success of Turkish forces heightened the growing political crisis in Serbia, while Prince Nikola realised that his men would finally go to war regardless of his orders. A secret agreement was finally made for both states to be ready for war by March 1876, Serbia raising one hundred and twenty thousand troops and Montenegro fifteen thousand.

The momentum of events, and with it the crisis, scaled fresh heights. In May the German and French consuls were murdered by a mob in Salonika, in Ottoman ruled Macedonia, and riots in Istanbul led to the dismissal of the Grand Vizier and subsequently the deposition of the unstable Sultan Abdul Aziz, who was considered by many to be half mad. He was replaced by his nephew who assumed power as Sultan Murad V.

Events in the hitherto passive province of Bulgaria, where rebellion had been building throughout the year despite a severe lack of resources, added further fuel to the fire. The Sublime Porte saw the danger of an uprising on several fronts and determined to extinguish the Bulgarian problem at any cost. The consequence was appalling.

As news filtered out of the atrocities committed by the notorious *Bashi-Bazouks*, the Turkish irregulars who, it was claimed, killed upwards of twenty thousand in the most brutal and humiliating manner, opinion throughout Europe turned against Turkey. The graphic reports of the massacre at Batak, sent by the American journalist J.A. MacGahan for The Daily News, provoked a wave of revulsion in Britain: "*The church was still worse. The floor was covered with rotting bodies quite uncovered. I never imagined anything so fearful. There were three thousand bodies in the churchyard and church . . . All over the town were the same scenes. The man who did all this, Achmed Aga, has been promoted and is still the Governor of the district. No crime invented by Turkish ferocity was left uncommitted.*"[8] The plight of the Sublime Porte's Christian subjects had become a moral crusade, and public opinion a significant factor from Moscow to London.

In response to the upsurge of public outrage, Austria, Germany and Russia, hastily combined their peace efforts. The result was the 'Berlin Memorandum' of May 12, 1876. It called for a ceasefire between the warring parties, while humanitarian relief and reconstruction were to begin immediately, and if the Sublime Porte was unable to fulfil its obligations, the *Draikersbund* would take "*effacious action in the interests of peace.*"

The French and Italian governments accepted the 'Berlin Memorandum' without delay, but in

Britain imperial considerations and national prestige brought objections both considered and facetious. Was it right that Istanbul be made to pay for damage caused by a war it had not started? Could the Sublime Porte afford the two months fulfilment period which would only encourage the rebels to continue until Europe intervened? However, Prime Minister Disraeli's flippant comment that *"They are beginning to treat England as if we were Montenegro or Bosnia"* revealed more about his own views and those of Queen Victoria than any measured statesmanship. It also exposed a Europe-wide potential for disaster if the interests and prestige of the Great Powers were threatened.

Disraeli's relations with Queen Victoria during the crisis deserve attention. The flamboyant statesman and the monarch, whom he assiduously flattered and was about to elevate to the position of Empress of India, were hostile to allowing a Russian led alliance decide Turkey's fate. Disraeli would have preferred a continuation of the Crimean War policy of upholding Ottoman integrity, but continued making ill-considered statements which confused and dismayed the European diplomats. If London offered little that was constructive, Queen Victoria's divided cabinet could, at the least, agree with her basically pacific stance: *"We have no intention of making the state of the Ottoman Empire a cause of quarrel with Russia . . ."* The Russian Ambassador noted Britain's policy to be indecisive and torturous but not warlike. *"England feels isolated and dares not admit her solidarity with Turkey"* he informed St. Petersburg.

One negative consequence of the rejection of the 'Berlin Memorandum' by *"Her Majesty and her Vizier"* (as the satirists labelled Queen Victoria and Disraeli) was to convince Prince Nikola that diplomacy was futile. He drew on the lessons of history to condemn Britain's imperial disregard for the fate of fellow Christians: *"England surrounded by sea, now surrounds itself with a sea of sad indifference toward the destiny of Christians. They can perish in thousands, only English interests must live. Those sins cannot go unpunished forever. Venice, her predecessor at sea, is remembered only by history now."*[9]

Nikola's lambasting of British policy was understandable. Montenegro had become the makeshift home for *"refugee families, whose dwellings have been destroyed, and whose means of living have been annihilated. Such a state of misery must be seen to be believed . . . This nation, small and poor shares what it has with the exiles, whose number already nearly equal half its own and seems to increase every day. What it does it does heartily and without regret, but the moment approaches when it will be materially incapable of doing anything, it will have nothing left to share."*[10]

Given international inaction and the *de facto* state of war which existed between Montenegro and Turkey the outlook was bleak, but formal declarations had not yet been made, leaving a glimmer of hope for diplomacy.

The Slavic rulers were not yet set on war. Prince Milan, unsure of Russian support, was still hesitant about entering into conflict, while Tsar Alexander II viewed war warily; he saw the spectre of revolution in the Balkan unrest.

However, neither ruler was in control of public opinion anymore. Pan-Slav feelings were reaching fever pitch in Russia and the momentum for war was building: both the Tsarina and the Tsarevich were known to

(Left) Sultan Murad V, who succeeded his uncle Sultan Abdul Aziz. Murad had lived a secluded life imposed on him by his suspicious uncle. This meant that although he was intelligent and open to ideas of liberal reform, he was politically inexperienced and emotionally fragile. The strain of seeing Abdul Aziz's deposition and subsequent death, as well as the assassination of several government ministers by a Circassian infantry captain, led to Murad's total breakdown, and he was returned to private life and descended into alcoholism. (Below left) Murad's younger brother, Abdul Hamid. On September 7, 1876, Abdul Hamid was girded with the 'Sword of Osman'. The new ruler had also been deliberately kept away from public life, but Abdul Hamid proved to be a stronger character than his brother and ruled the Ottoman Empire for over three decades.

support Russian intervention; Russia's General Cherniayev joined Prince Milan's army, despite the Tsar's personal disapproval; donations were collected for the Serbs in the streets of St. Petersburg and the Metropolitan of Moscow offered prayers for a Serbian victory.

Without decisive measures to end the conflict in Bosnia-Herzegovina war was unavoidable and both Serb rulers were finally dragged into war. Montenegro declared officially on June 28, 1876, closely followed by Serbia on June 30.

Although outnumbered and outgunned by their enemies, Montenegrins rejoiced that rebellion had turned into a war of liberation. Prince Nikola's mood was quite different. His apprehensions for the campaign ahead were expressed in a letter to Vojvoda Ilija Plamenac: *"For God's sake! It is time to start taking out the munitions. Within four days we will not be able to take out anything. I have to declare war on Turkey today, political circumstances demand it, and Austria can forbid our exports at anytime . . . Hurry up for God's sake . . ."*[11] In the event, though, it would not be the Montenegrin campaign that faltered due to lack of preparation but Serbia's.

Pitchforked into war by its politicians and intelligentsia, Serbia was not ready for a major campaign with an army that was badly equipped and poorly led. The peasant soldiers fought gallantly but were unable to join up with the Montenegrins through the Sandžak and, within three weeks, Serbian forces were driven out of Turkish territory. By August, the Turks had captured Knjaževac and Zaječar and concentrated their efforts on the vital Morava Valley. The Serbian army managed to resist at Aleksinac, but only for six days and, although the Montenegrins had continued their campaign in Herzegovina, Prince Milan was reluctantly forced to look for a settlement.

Montenegro commenced hostilities when Turkish forces attacked the staunchly independent Kuči tribe. Prince Nikola's army advanced into Herzegovina, capturing the Fortress of Gacko and besieging Nikšić. Although the battle for Podgorica brought heavy losses, after two months the campaign had been a string of successes, and October's victory at Medun led to the Kuči tribe joining Montenegro. Nikola had every right to consider himself a liberator and recorded in his diary that the Moslems of the village of Medaniće had told him: *"If God gives you Herzegovina we are yours."*[12]

The one outstanding failure of the campaign had been the inability to link up with Serbian forces. Some laid the blame on Nikola's excessive caution, others on his self-interested calculation. Neither accusation was fair.

Nikola knew how limited his resources were and wisely involved himself fully in the minutiae of the campaign. He told his cousin Božo Petrović: *"Božo, do not expose my army like that day in Maljat,"* and demanded of Commander Vojvoda Mašo Vrbica: *"Do not keep me in uncertainty tomorrow as you did today, write to me every half an hour, and if you do not have time to write send a messenger . . ."*[13]

Undoubtedly, the constant threats from Austria-Hungary also restrained Nikola's campaign strategy, so much so that Vienna's envoy in Cetinje, Colonel Thommel, felt able to report: *"Any intention of direct co-operation with Serbia . . . has almost certainly been abandoned."*[14]

However, Serbia's troubles were to make matters more rather than less complicated. The frustrated war party sought to bring Russia into the conflict and, on September 17, proclaimed Prince Milan as king. He refused outright, having been informed by the increasingly influential Count Andrassy that international recognition was out of the question.

As the danger of Turkish forces overwhelming all of Serbia and reinstalling its garrisons loomed large, in the Ottoman capital a palace revolution replaced Sultan Murad, who had suffered a mental breakdown, with his brother Abdul Hamid. The position of the hardliners was strengthened and they saw no reason to negotiate unless Serbia's autonomy was severely limited.

Without concerted action by the other Powers, Russo-Turkish war had become unavoidable. Yet there was still no consensus on what should be done: Russia and Austria-Hungary secretly discussed the partition of Turkey's European provinces; Great Britain was engaged in a fierce internal debate on foreign policy; France and Italy were looking for opportunities to raise their respective status as Great Powers. Only Germany, under the formidable guidance of Prince Otto von Bismarck, was a more pacific player, but he had little sympathy for the suffering Balkan peoples.

For Serbia the military situation continued to deteriorate with further defeats and, by October, the

Prince Milan Obrenović of Serbia by Felix Tournachon Nadar, 1874. Although reluctant to go to war against the Ottoman Empire, Milan realised that failure to do so risked the loss of his throne. He gave in to public opinion, but the military campaign went badly and, by the end of 1876, Turkish forces were victorious and ready to reoccupy Belgrade. Only Russia's diplomatic intervention and the subsequent Russo-Turkish war of 1877 saved Serbia.

Sublime Porte was, despite Russian threats, dictating terms to Belgrade. These comprised a six months armistice; personal homage to the Sultan by Prince Milan; restoration of four permanent Turkish garrisons in Serbia and the reduction of the country's standing army to ten thousand men. St. Petersburg responded by issuing an ultimatum to the Sublime Porte restricting the armistice to two months, while Prince Nikola saw no reason to grant Turkish forces respite and refused to halt Montenegro's campaign.

In Herzegovina, the anger of the frontline victims of the whole tangle had led to their leaders rejecting the renewed, and genuinely well intentioned, diplomatic efforts of Count Andrassy: it was too little and much too late. The Herzegovinians could not be convinced that the Sublime Porte would, or even could if it wished, fulfil any undertakings of reform. This feeling, as well as their solidarity with the Montenegrins, was expressed in the manifesto drawn up by the rebellion's leaders: *"We can only become tranquil under the happiness of the liberty of which Montenegro shows us the example."*

The conflict had reached a turning point and a small chance for peace existed. Turkey was bloodily triumphant in Bulgaria and Serbia but unable to reap the benefit; Serbia, although defeated, was still hoping for Russian assistance and Montenegro awaited reward for its efforts.

However, little had changed politically and the peace talks, which began in December 1876, dragged on into the New Year. Mistrust and intransigence dominated and the St. Petersburg-London impasse could not be overcome.

Russia on the brink of war still hoped for peace, but the Sublime Porte overplayed its hand, due to the mistaken expectation of British support. Beyond the Balkans, Britain's policy makers were

motivated by the fear of Russia controlling the Dardanelle Straits and its further expansion into Asia, but they, too, had no desire for a major war.

The Russians concentrated on their secret negotiations with Austria-Hungary, which resulted in an agreement that would have given Bosnia-Herzegovina to Vienna and swept Turkey out of Romania and Serbia. Vagueness on the part of Russia regarding the exact portion of Bosnia-Herzegovina to be allocated to Austria-Hungary reflected the Tsar's desire to compensate Montenegro in Herzegovina.

A last ditch effort to avert war came with the six-power protocol of March 31, 1877. This was, in effect, a final ultimatum to the Sublime Porte for the *"amelioration of the lot of the Christians of Turkey"*, but it also included the ceding of Nikšić to Montenegro. Against British advice and in the mistaken hope that Russia would back down at the last minute, it was rejected by the Ottoman parliament in Istanbul. All efforts had been in vain: diplomacy had run its course and war between Russia and Turkey was now inevitable.

The declaration of war finally came on April 24, 1877, quickly followed by a series of striking Russian victories. By mid-June, its forces had crossed the Danube at Galatz and Sistova and occupied the northern section of the Shipka Pass in central Bulgaria.

(Above) Osman Nuri Pasha, hero of the 'Siege of Plevna'. Plevna Fortress was the last line of defence for the Ottoman capital, Istanbul. The three month siege, mounting casualties and disease brought the Russian advance to a halt.
(Left) British Prime Minister Benjamin Disraeli. His pro-Turkish policies were based on the conviction that British imperial interests in Asia were threatened by Russian expansion. The close relations between Disraeli and Queen Victoria proved strong enough to ride out a wave of sympathy for the Balkan states, but were condemned by Montenegro's Prince Nikola who wrote:
"England surrounded by sea, surrounded itself now with a sea of sad indifference toward the destiny of Christians. They can perish in thousands only English interests must live. Those sins cannot go unpunished forever. Venice, her predecessor at sea, is remembered only by history now."
(Facing page) Tsar Alexander II of Russia. His peaceful inclinations, in particular his memories of the horrors of the Crimean War, saw him weep as he watched his armed forces leave for the military front. However, Russia's campaign against the Ottoman Empire was a military triumph, and it was only the intervention of the other European powers which prevented Russia from imposing a harsh settlement on the defeated Turks.

The triumphant advance continued unchecked until Plevna Fortress, the last line of defence protecting the Ottoman capital. Russian forces launched two major attacks during July but were thrown back by strong resistance. Plevna's commander, Osman Nuri Pasha, inspired his men to an unexpected, dogged, heroism which significantly slowed the Russian advance.

With some thirty thousand dying in the next attempt to take the fortress in September, it had become clear that Russia would only be successful if it called upon the help of its Balkan allies.

Romanian assistance would prove vital but Serbian participation had been barred at the Tsar's personal insistence. Prince Milan's military failures had lost him Russia's favour and he realised that if the country did not benefit after its sacrifices, the loss of his throne was imminent.

Milan was, therefore, desperate to rejoin the war, but Austria-Hungary again threatened action in Belgrade and Bosnia-Herzegovina if Serbian forces were mobilised. Further difficulty arose when

Britain's Turcophile Ambassador in Istanbul suggested sponsoring a *coup d'état*: "*The only thing to be done is to get up a revolution in the principality and put Karadjordjević against Milan . . . This the Grand Vizier is ready to do but he wants some money.*"

For Prince Nikola events were unfolding much more promisingly. Taking advantage of the transfer of Turkish troops to the Bulgarian front, the Montenegrins succeeded in liberating towns along the Herzegovinian and Albanian borders. In September, Nikšić finally fell, then the isles on Lake Skadar and, by early 1878, the coastal towns of Bar and Ulcinj. However, the brutality of these battles convinced Nikola to revert to the old methods of warfare. Vojvoda Mašo Vrbica was instructed: "*The Turks beheaded one Zajarčanin and, if they started it, I give the order for our army to start taking Turkish heads and show them to me. I give this order because it will raise army morale.*"[15]

No quarter could be given in battle, but where possible Nikola aimed to avoid bloodshed. He instructed Vojvoda Ilija Plamenac: "*Inform the people that, if they surrender before the shooting starts, you have been ordered to halt the army before Ulcinj, so that they can give up their weapons, after which you will take no further military action. The people should stay in their homes without fear. If some want to leave they can but they will not be allowed to return. We will leave some soldiers in town to maintain order and we will approve the leader the townspeople elect . . .*"[16]

Hostilities were finally drawing to a close with a militarily triumphant Russia having obliterated earlier Turkish victories and now, seemingly, free to dictate terms to its old enemy. The final fall of Plevna Fortress, on December 10, 1877, signalled the end of resistance, and three days later Britain requested guarantees that Russia would not occupy Istanbul or the Dardanelle Straits. Although Russia refused, claiming that giving such a guarantee would only encourage further resistance and thereby force an occupation, the army was exhausted and the generals feared a second campaign with Britain possibly entering the conflict.

War and disease had taken a high toll on both sides and, by January 31, 1878, the armistice was signed and fresh peace talks begun. In the first instance Russia dictated terms as military victor, and in the second a conference of the Great Powers agreed on the revised map of the Balkans. Both treaties were to have lasting consequences.

The Treaty of San Stefano was imposed by Russia on a defeated Turkey. The Sublime Porte was willing to placate its conqueror. One of the Sultan's ministers bluntly acknowledged the reality: "*Your arms are victorious, your ambition is satisfied, but Turkey is lost. We accept everything that you desire.*" However, force of arms alone was not sufficient for the equable settlement of the Balkan question, and Russia's self interest in the fate of the South Slavs was already all too apparent.

In the final few weeks of war Serbia had belatedly rejoined the fray, proving a useful ally, but Russo-Serbian relations remained strained. The shift in Russian policy to favouring Bulgaria as a satellite state over Serbia remained. Therefore, Serbia was allowed only minor territorial gains comprising of the Bosnian villages of Mali Zvornik and Zakar, and four counties in Kosovo Province. The other territories claimed by Belgrade, although largely occupied by its forces, were assigned to Bulgaria.

Montenegro fared far better. Its independent statehood was finally recognised, along with a large territorial increase. The Herzegovinian towns of Gacko, Bilek and Nikšić were gained; to the north-east a portion of the Sandžak; to the south-east Podgorica, Spuž and Žabljak and access to the Adriatic Sea through the ports of Bar and Ulcinj. A threefold increase in territory, strategic access points into Bosnia-Herzegovina and opportunities for foreign trade were ample reward for a successful campaign.

The Sublime Porte accepted the terms, but short of another

Germany's Otto Von Bismarck, who famously considered the Turkish question *"not worth the bones of a single Pomeranian grenadier"*, chaired the Congress of Berlin. Bismarck had little interest in and much disdain for the Ottoman Empire; he would have gladly accepted its partition among the Great Powers if that had been a practical option. However, he also feared that its collapse could drag not only Germany but all Europe into war. The Treaty of Berlin managed to forestall that calamity but it also paved the way for future conflicts. (Facing page) An antique map from 1882 illustrates the results of the treaty. Diplomacy based on imperial priorities it was imposed on the Balkans by the European powers: the independent Balkan states were set in rivalry with one another; Austria-Hungary was given control in Bosnia-Herzegovina and Turkey's remaining European provinces, Macedonia and Albania, were left at the mercy of corrupt and often brutal misrule.

military campaign Russia could not enforce the treaty in the teeth of Austro-Hungarian and British opposition. However, the injustices of San Stefano were not the concern of the Great Powers. It was the increase in Russian influence which made the treaty unacceptable to Vienna, London and Berlin. Reluctantly, Russia's statesmen accepted that, without another war, San Stefano could not become reality. Germany now came forward to play the role of honest broker and a congress was convened in Berlin.

The eventual final settlement, enshrined in The Treaty of Berlin of July 13, 1878, would influence the future course of Balkan and European politics until the outbreak of World War One. The vital question of Bosnia-Herzegovina was left entirely unresolved, although Austro-Hungarian troops were allowed to occupy the province and bring it under Vienna's administration. Predictably a new revolt broke out and it took one hundred and fifty thousand Austro-Hungarian troops three months and five thousand casualties before they could take control. For the future of the independent Balkan states the treaty was as bad as San Stefano: encouraging regional rivalry and, in particular, disappointing both Serbia and Bulgaria while at the same time exacerbating tensions between them.

Ultimately Serbia fared better than had seemed likely but, as Russia had promoted 'Big Bulgaria' at San Stefano, Prince Milan now turned to Austria-Hungary. Within a few years Serbia's foreign policy was placed under Vienna's control in a secret treaty. Having lost Russian favour, the benefits of rapprochement with Vienna also offered tempting prospects for economic development and political stability. Meanwhile, Bulgaria was traumatised at the loss of the vast gains of San Stefano, above all Macedonia, and future Serbo-Bulgarian relations would be poisoned by their rival claims to the blighted province.

Montenegro was also deeply disappointed by the Treaty of Berlin. Along the Adriatic coastline Austria-Hungary took the fortress of Spič and the coastline as far south as Bar, with only the mainly Albanian populated districts of Plav and Gusinje offered as meagre compensation. Although the vital towns of Podgorica and Nikšić were kept, the denial of a port, a link to Serbia through the Sandžak and the stifling of Montenegro's Herzegovinian ambitions were victories for Austria-Hungary. Prince Nikola instructed his representatives at the congress: *"Once our affairs are completed . . . tell each of the Great Power representatives that Montenegro has not been properly rewarded and that her new frontiers in many places are completely unnatural . . . the Montenegrin people feels fear and sorrow that, because of these unnatural frontiers, they will be agitated and hindered in their pursuit of peaceful development."*[17]

In actual fact, Montenegro had not been treated harshly: its territory was nearly doubled and, within a couple of years, the ports of Bar and Ulcinj would be regained in a trade off for Plav and Gusinje. Still, Prince Nikola was right: Montenegro's gains at the Berlin Congress were not enough to create a viable economic state, and the small stretch of coastline subsequently granted was only for commercial purposes, lest it become by proxy a Russian naval base in the Mediterranean.

Disraeli's comment that *"Montenegro only needs a garden to grow some cabbages and some potatoes"* amply demonstrated how little regard the Great Powers paid to the viability and stability of the smaller states. As for the defeated Turks, Otto von Bismarck, who had remarked that there was no reason to hold a conference unless everything had already been decided beforehand, bluntly informed the Sublime Porte's representatives that they were to accept amendments to the Treaty of San Stefano as dictated.

The powerbrokers succeeded in their main objective of preventing war on the grand scale, but in doing so they casually sacrificed the aspirations of the Balkan peoples, whose people saw their hopes horse-traded away. The independent Balkan states, and even the provinces still under Ottoman rule, were treated as little more than spheres of Great Power interest, in this instance falling within the orbit of either Russia or Austria-Hungary.

The diplomatic outcome was also historic in that Russia was not the beneficiary of the war it had won: St. Petersburg's long cherished plans to replace the Ottoman Empire in the Balkans had been dealt a body blow and it was Germany and Britain that gained most from the final peace settlement.

German prestige and power, particularly through its rising influence over Austria-Hungary, was enhanced. However, the young nation, that had been unified through war as recently as 1870, showed a disappointing lack of sympathy for the national aspirations of others.

Otto von Bismarck was far more concerned with keeping the peace in Europe; the partition of Turkey was acceptable, or its propping up, so long as the Great Powers were agreed amongst themselves. Germany's rise to the first rank of that select group had been confirmed and Bismarck was now the pre-eminent figure of European diplomacy.

Britain gained a protectorate over the Mediterranean island of Cyprus, which was felt to be a further bulwark against Russian ambitions, and could also consider its possessions in Asia better secured. Disraeli's far-sighted imperialism had triumphed. A policy wittily satirised by the French representative to the conference St Vallier: *"England with the Turk is like a surgeon who, to help someone who has had both legs broken by a wicked neighbour, should break his arms also."*

If peace between the Great Powers was the achievement, to many it seemed that the future had been sacrificed for the present. For Disraeli it was *"peace with honour"* and Bismarck could share in the glory and proclaim *"Turkey in Europe is once more"*, but, with embittered foresight, Russia's Prince Gorchakov predicted that Bosnia-Herzegovina *"would be the tomb of Austria-Hungary."*

The inequities and contradictions of the Treaty of Berlin would prove combustible material; however, for the immediate future, the Balkan question had been resolved.

ILLUSTRATING THE BERLIN CONGRESS TREATY, JULY 1878.

The Patriarchal Ruler

Like his predecessor, he belongs to the class of royal and noble authors. And his songs circulate from the northern extremity of Herzegovina to Skodra. Over this tract of country he rules, if not by right of territory, yet by the gifts of personal influence, over hearts, if not over minds.

R Denton

A portrait of the Royal Family commemorating the proclamation of the Montenegrin Kingdom on August 28,1910.
Back Row: (From left to right) Princess Vjera, Grand Duke Peter Nikolayevich, Prince Franz Josef of Battenberg, Princess Ksenija, Crown Prince Danilo, Prince Mirko, Princess Natalija and Prince Petar. Seated: (From left to right) King Vittorio Emanuele III, Crown Princess Milica-Yutta, Queen Elena of Italy, Queen Milena, King Nikola I, Grand Duchess Milica Nikolayevna and Princess Ana of Battenberg. Front row: (From left to right) Crown Prince Aleksandar Karadjordjević of Serbia, Princess Marina Petrovna Romanov (daughter of Grand Duchess Milica, who in 1927 married Prince Alexander Nikolayevich Golitsyn) and Princess Jelena Karadjordjević.

À SON ALTESSE

NICOLAS Ier PETROVITCH NIEGOCH

PRINCE DE MONTÉNÉGRO

The three decades of peace which followed the Treaty of Berlin saw the Montenegrin Royal Family find a noteworthy niche for itself within European dynastic affairs: the royal couple's eldest daughter, Zorka, married the pretender to the Serbian throne Prince Petar Karadjordjević, reopening possibilities for a dynastic union between the two Serb states; Milica and Stane consolidated the Russian connection with marriages to Romanov grand dukes and Jelena's marriage would be the most brilliant of all, to Vittorio Emanuele, Crown Prince of Italy.

The younger royal children grew up in the relaxed and loving environment of the Montenegrin court. Eldest son Danilo was the focus of the nation's hopes. His progress was eagerly watched and his education and well being carefully supervised.

Danilo's rather belated choice of bride, the German born Princess Augusta Charlotte of Mecklenburg-Strelitz, added another link in the dynastic chain, as did Princess Ana's marriage to Franz Josef Battenberg from the House of Hesse.

Second son Mirko's marriage to Natalija Konstantinović, the daughter of an exiled Serbian colonel, was promising but controversial. Mirko and Natalija hoped to gain a Balkan throne and, as Natalija's family was related to Serbia's ruling dynasty, the unloved Obrenovići, foremost in their thoughts was the Serbian crown. Further grist to that mill were the ambitions of Prince Nikola's son-in-law, Petar Karardjordjević, who hoped to reclaim his grandfather Karadjordje's throne for himself and his children.

Prince Nikola's family certainly had excellent chances of eventually displacing the Obrenovići, but there was plenty of scope for rivalry and dispute as to whom it would be: one of his sons or his son-in-law.

The Prince's youngest children were less fortunate: daughters Ksenija and Vjera were noted for their intelligence and good looks but circumstances worked against either finding a suitable husband.

Princess Milena and (facing page) Prince Nikola, *circa* 1880. The family continued to grow and a further three children were born in the 1880's: two daughters, Ksenija and Vjera, and a son Petar.

Both, nonetheless, contributed to the family's rising fortunes through their charitable work and creative talents, Ksenija as an accomplished photographer and Vjera an excellent artist. Nikola and Milena's last child, a third son named Petar, would struggle to find a role for himself within the family.

The Royal Family's attractive characteristics and the relatively benign international situation proved a fortuitous combination. Prince Nikola showed himself to be an excellent ambassador for the nation and a romantic ruling figure. The prejudice some had shown to the little nation was usually dispelled by the personality and wit of the ruler and the charm of his family.

From St. Petersburg to London, even in the eyes of the old enemy Turkey, Nikola raised Montenegro's standing. The patriarchal ruler undoubtedly had something of a golden touch and, as was often noted, good luck. It was a new era and a new experience for the nation which, under the Prince's astute guidance, enjoyed an era of peace and progress.

118

"Opposite our house, but larger and more imposing, is the court, the official residence of the Prince's family. The windows of our houses face each other and in these two buildings live all the people that I love, and all the events that I remember happened there . . . My grandfather . . . Prince of Montenegro, master of this land and its people . . . middle aged, dressed in a white jacket embroidered with gold . . . On his head grandfather wears the traditional Montenegrin cap from which he is never parted. He takes it off only during lunch and when he goes to church. He probably takes it off when he goes to bed but I never saw that . . . His face is plump and broad. Behind his serious but rarely gloomy expression are two still youthful and piercing eyes. His greying moustache is slightly trimmed and two deep creases are simply cutting his cheeks."[1]
Prince Djordje Karadjordjević

Prince Djordje Karadjordjević's childhood memories of Cetinje in the late 1880's and early 1890's capture the intimacy and the family atmosphere of the Montenegrin court under Prince Nikola and Princess Milena. A family affair it most certainly was, with the capital home to two royal families, a crowd of children and the Prince's many relatives. Opposite the Royal Family's residence was the home of Prince Petar Karadjordjević and his two brothers, Arsen and Djordje, from where Prince Petar organised his campaign to reclaim the Serbian throne. However, the heart and soul for both families was the Palace, where Nikola's kindly persona and Milena's warmth attracted the Karadjordjević children who played with the Petrović children in the court garden.

By this time Nikola was in his forties, he had put on weight but was still a commanding, handsome figure, and, unusually for a Montenegrin woman in those hard times, Milena was still youthful. Her influence had grown steadily over the years but she would never embarrass her husband in public or contradict him. "As the Prince likes it" she would always say, her traditional upbringing and her sense of duty coexisting easily within her nature. To listen and to obey were maxims she lived by, although as a respected wife and mother her influence, always exercised behind the scenes, was considerable in political as well as family affairs.

Prince Nikola continued his efforts to modernise Montenegro and his proudest achievement was the improvement of the country's roads (right). However, the average Montenegrin household did not benefit greatly and life continued to be a matter of subsistence for most, as shown (below right) by a house in Katuni Nahi.
(Facing page) 1885: Cetinje welcomes Crown Prince Rudolf of Austria-Hungary.

After the death of her eldest daughter Zorka, Petar Karadjordjević's wife, in 1890, Milena became a mother figure to their children, although Petar still oversaw their education and development. Milena's mission was to protect her charges, only leaving them to the care of nannies when she was ill or too busy with official duties. Milena was equally protective toward her own children. Milica and Stane through marriage had left to live in Russia and Milena hoped she would not have to send her other children to be educated abroad; she preferred to raise them as Montenegrins. However, Jelena and Ana were keen to leave Cetinje for the excitement and sophistication of Europe, and in an age when arranged marriages for royalty were the norm, both had told their parents they would only marry for love. In the meantime the young princesses bided their time with sport and play, horse riding, hunting, and spoiling the younger children with cuddles and kisses.

The younger children, Mirko, Ksenija, Vjera and Petar, along with Prince Petar's sons Djordje and Aleksandar and daughter Jelena would play together, often joined by the children of foreign ambassadors and others from the leading Cetinje families. The leader of the gang was the oldest, Mirko. If they played soldiers he was their commander giving the orders and when they sneaked into neighbours' gardens it was he who would decide the plan of attack.

One day the children were caught stealing apples and, in fear of the Prince's anger, they begged the owner not to give them away. Fortunately their victim seems to have looked kindly on this mischief and the Prince never heard of the incident. Still, any admonishment would have been purely nominal. Nikola's fondness for children made him something of an easy touch for their wiles.

Both the Petrović and the Karadjordjević offspring would remember their childhood days in Cetinje as idyllic, but some thought it was not an ideal upbringing for those born to become rulers in the turbulent Balkans. Most significantly, Prince Petar objected to the protected upbringing given to the Montenegrin princes.

Nikola and Petar's characters and attitude to life were very different, a fact which was evident in their

relations with the children.

Nikola would greet the little ones, his pockets stuffed with sweets, and the atmosphere in the Palace was always enlivened by his good natured presence.

The Karadjordjević children found a stark contrast between the relaxed atmosphere of the Petrović house and their father's. Petar, preoccupied with his political ambitions, would spend hours alone in his study, which his children would carefully avoid, afraid of disturbing their father's work and incurring his wrath.

The children were given a small horse for riding lessons. When Nikola's youngest son took his turn he would be chaperoned by at least three perjaniks to protect him from a fall. Petar was outraged by such molly-coddling. His two sons took a more robust and adventurous attitude. One of them once jumped straight onto the horse and hit it with his riding crop. As it galloped away and the perjaniks chased after him, Petar shouted: *"Stop! You can run and protect your princes, but let my children fall down and even hurt themselves."* Milena, who was watching, cried out: *"For Gods sake no! They can fall down and break an arm or leg!"* Petar stood firm: *"Let them break their arm, leg or even skull. If you raised your sons this way they would not be as incapable as they are."*[2] These were harsh words spoken in anger, but they reflected an opinion which was also held by several members of Nikola's inner circle of friends and advisors.

For the moment though, the loving environment the Montenegrin royal children enjoyed ensured that they were an appealing and lively bunch which invariably charmed. In 1887, Grand Duchess Maria Alexandrovna of Russia, wife of Alfred, Duke of Edinburgh, met the Royal Family in Kotor. She described the meeting in a letter to her daughter Marie, later Queen of Romania: *"Before we reached the town of Cetinje, we were met by the Prince's eldest son, a very pretty boy aged sixteen, very tall and dark, with most excellent manners and such a bright clever look . . . At the house we were met by the Princess and her daughters, all in national dress. I used to know the two young ladies when they were in Russia, but now they are quite grown up and such nice, lively girls. They amuse George [Prince George of Wales, later King George V 1910-1936] very much and he is great friends with them. They laugh and talk and he gets on in French and does not mind it. There is also a dear little boy of eight years, dressed in lovely costumes; he comes in making beautiful bows, and kisses one's hand. He is called Mirko and his father simply adores him but he does not spoil any of them. In fact he is very strict and everyone obeys him in a wonderful way and is devoted to him . . ."*[3]

A good deal of this childhood promise would be fulfilled and the Serbian politician and writer Count Čedo Mijatović could comment some twenty years later: *"It is well known that all the sons and daughters of Prince Nikola are highly gifted in one way or another . . . Jelena who is no mean painter or poet . . . her sister Ana and her brother Prince Mirko are known for their musical compositions."*[4]

"Like his predecessor, he belongs to the class of royal and noble authors. And his songs circulate from the northern extremity of Herzegovina to Skodra [Scutari]. Over this tract of country he rules, if not by right of territory, yet by the gifts of personal influence, over hearts, if not over minds."[5]
R Denton

Creative talent was common among the Petrovići and Nikola possessed the poetic gift which was so prevalent within the clan. Vladika Rade was the greatest South Slav poet of the nineteenth century and Nikola's father, Mirko, had contributed some twenty-nine ballads commemorating his experience of the battles with the Turks between 1852 and 1862. Nikola had been writing poetry since his youth, glorifying the memories of his forefathers but also expressing his religious feelings and his love of family life.

He had also composed songs for each of the Montenegrin tribes as well as the words for the national anthem, which had been set to music. Naturally, it recalled the medieval glories of the Serbs:

"There, over there . . . beyond those hills,
Ruined lies, they say,
My Emperor's Palace; there they say,
Once heroes had gathered.
There, over there . . . I see Prizren!
It is all mine - home I shall come!
Beloved antiquity calls me there,
Armed I must come there one day."

The political purposes of their poems and songs were largely taken for granted by Montenegrins, who regarded them as a natural expression of national identity and collective sentiment. In that vein, Nikola's patriotism and love of literature, as well as his ambitions, saw him eager to make his mark as a poet.

He began his most famous work 'The Empress of the Balkans', a verse drama in three acts, in the winter of 1880. He dedicated himself entirely to its completion and was even criticised for not paying enough attention to political issues, most importantly trouble on the Albanian border over

(Below left) Princess Ana aged eight, (below right) Prince Mirko and (facing page) Crown Prince Danilo.

(Above) Crown Prince Danilo aged ten and (facing page) younger brother Mirko. The two boys had very different characters. Mirko was attention seeking, creative and impulsive; Danilo was more reticent and less extrovert, characteristics it was felt came from his mother's side of the family. (Right) Grand Duchess Maria Alexandrovna, daughter of Tsar Alexander II, with her husband Alfred, Duke of Edinburgh, son of Queen Victoria. In 1887 Maria greatly enjoyed meeting Prince Nikola and his children in Kotor.

unfulfilled territorial clauses of the Treaty of Berlin. But Nikola was undeterred and each day would read his efforts to a few friends, tirelessly editing the work and asking for their opinions.

It soon became something of a *cause célèbre* within the capital as the people enthusiastically followed suit. Soon all, from the vojvodas and serdars to the workers in the publishing house and the students, were composing their own rhymes.

Nikola liked to invite a select group to hear his latest draft. While all were understandably keen to please the Prince, some tried a little too hard, with comic results. "*What do you think about this work of mine?*" Nikola asked the new adjutant, Beara. "*My Master, I understand it the same way the donkey understands the measurement system but, speaking from my soul, I am pleased, very pleased . . . We all say that your drama is nice, My Master, it really is! But its real quality one can only see on the stage.*" "*That's right*" the Prince agreed, "*so we will have to wait until summer for some travelling theatre to come!*" Tomaš Vukotić saw his opportunity: "*It is a long time to wait until the summer and who knows what can happen! If only I could see it before! And those travellers cannot speak Montenegrin properly, the way it is written! God save us! We would not understand every third word, they would ruin your nice rhymes, My Master!*" Everyone agreed and Lipovac joined in: "*Even the best actors in Belgrade cannot speak our dialect . . .*" "*And what can I do? I cannot create others!*" exclaimed the exasperated Prince. Finally, Lipovac tried to outdo the others: "*Why could we not try? Me, for example, I can play Stanko! By God! I have never been an actor before but I will try. Here goes!*"[6]

The flattery of Nikola's courtiers often struck visitors as being rather excessive, but the vanity of the Balkan mountaineer, royal or otherwise, was legendary.

The finished work was a worthy effort which was well received and subsequently performed in Cetinje, Belgrade and Novi Sad. It was also published in many languages including Russian, English, German, French, Italian, Hungarian and Dutch.

A tale of heroism, betrayal and redemption from medieval Montenegrin history, 'The Empress of the Balkans' remains a charming and lyrical work, though it lacks the depth of great poetry. That Nikola's poetry nonetheless came from the heart was shown by his reaction to Čedo Mijatović's critique: "*Your drama is not drama at all; it has much lyrical poetry of great beauty, and it has many interesting political discussions and even political programmes. Your Balkan Empress tells me what I already know, that you are a good lyrical poet, but a better and greater Serb patriot.*" Nikola could not conceal his feelings: "*With equal frankness I will tell you that you have disappointed me. But, as you gave me some consolation, I thank you."*[7]

Mijatović had hit upon the underlying flaw in the work: the subordination of art to politics, the muse of the poet stifled by the aims of the ruler. Still, if Nikola was not a creative genius such as Vladika Rade, he was a talented poet. If he failed to reach the loftiest heights, his poems and songs certainly added to the romantic aura surrounding the nation and its ruler.

"Prince Nikola, the lord of this warrior nation, is a man of imposing stature, so broad-shouldered that his height seems far less than it really is, walking with head erect and firm tread and clad in the rich national costume. The stranger involuntarily doffs his cap and receives in return a short military salute, but accompanied by such a piercing glance from a pair of cold grey eyes that he wonders if he is not an intruder in the land. This is, however, far from the case. Under that austere exterior beats a warm heart and an affability of manner to which the lowliest of his peasants will testify."[8]
Reginald Wyon and Gerald Prance

There were few, if any, more romantic rulers in late nineteenth and early twentieth century Europe, a fact confirmed by the observations of the growing number of foreign visitors. One thought Nikola: *"A democrat, the friend and confidant of his people. I remember a big tree under which he used to hold his cabinet meetings, and afterwards smoke a pipe with the peasants."*[9] Another noted: *"Montenegro is entirely unlike any other country in the world . . . on every hand the beneficent rule of Prince Nikola is apparent. Every man in Montenegro swears by his Prince, whom he almost worships. They call him their father . . . The Prince is accessible to all his people, more so to them indeed, than to the diplomats. Sometimes, early in the morning, he will sit in an armchair on the steps leading to the entrance of his Palace, and there hear the complaints or petitions of his people."*[10]

It was, as the future would reveal, a unique nation living through a unique era, in many ways an idyllic historical moment filled with the charm of the ruler and the nation coexisting in symbiotic harmony.

Montenegrins proudly guarded their freedoms, but they were also keenly aware of social standing and prestige. The Prince, as head of the country's leading family, was bound up in those relations which found expression in and were reinforced by the rituals of daily life.

Only the Prince and Princess would walk together through town as it was considered presumptuous, even for a vojvoda and his wife, to copy the royal prerogative. Milena's position was a privileged one as female social display was frowned upon. Most wives stayed at home, only going out on family business.

Such conservatism meant that for a Balkan town, let alone a European one, Cetinje's social life was tranquil. Many found it outright dull. However, it conformed to the sensibilities and feelings of its people.

In that context, the Prince's

daily walk was an important event for both the ruler and his subjects, bringing confirmation, cohesion and pleasure to the community.

When the Prince was seen leaving the Palace and heading for the nearby market, the people closest to the market quickly took off their caps and stopped their conversations; others, seeing the sign, followed suit and then all fell silent. The Prince continued on accompanied by only a few perjaniks until he reached the market, where the senators met him. They, too, took off their caps and joined him.

On reaching the nearby mulberry tree, all paused as the people nearest to the Prince formed a circle around him. Then, as the escort continued on its way, the people they passed by also removed their caps and joined them. From the end of the street, the Prince went onto the elm tree, or down to the meadow and the Vlach Church, with the whole escort in tow.

Where he chose to stop, a perjanik would place his overcoat on the ground for the Prince to sit. The senators sat to his left and right, while the people remained standing until the Prince respectfully commanded the eldest to sit. Then he would begin speaking, his favourite topic being the bravery and honesty of Montenegrins.

Afterward the Prince and his escort returned to the Palace, where he would wave to the people as a sign for them to go to their homes, as they did so discussing the Prince's words amongst themselves. All were pleased and even those at the rear of the escort could proudly tell their wives that they had walked with the Prince.

Other social pleasures were provided by state visits and official receptions. Like every Montenegrin household the Royal Family observed the festivals and religious rites of the Orthodox tradition, but a few new additions were made. One example was the adoption of that very nineteenth

(Above) Prince Nikola's eldest daughter, Zorka, was the first to wed. Her marriage to the pretender to the Serbian throne, Prince Petar Karadjordjević, produced five children: two daughters, Jelena and Milena, and three sons Djordje, Aleksandar and Andrija. Milena died in infancy and Zorka's premature death came shortly after Andrija's birth, the child only outliving his mother by a few short weeks.
(Right) The Prince's study. An historic room for Montenegro in which Nikola not only wrote much of his literary work, but also his political and diplomatic correspondence.
Facing page: (Top) A portrait by Vlaho Bukovac from 1883 of Prince Nikola's seventh daughter, Ksenija, and (bottom) Prince Nikola's national costume. Although he travelled widely and mixed with the élite of European society, Nikola disliked modern sartorial habits and felt most comfortable wearing traditional clothes.

century innovation, centennial commemorations.

For the Petrović-Njegoš dynasty the most important event of this kind was the celebration of its bicentennial in 1896. Other significant dates were also marked: the turn of the century enabled Nikola and Milena to mark forty years of their rule and marriage and, in 1908, the fiftieth anniversary of the Battle of Grahovo. The weddings of the royal couple's numerous children also provided occasions for further ceremony.

On official occasions the little Palace became a beehive of activity and a rather informal court style developed. Nikola entertained visiting royalty, politicians and dignitaries in the 'big fireplace' salon, in Milena's salon the diplomats and their wives gathered, while the young Crown Prince scurried between the two. In the upper salons guests could dance and play games, in the Prince's salon they talked politics and matters of state.

Nikola's idiosyncratic nature also made a contribution to the court style. While enjoying the grand occasion, Nikola cared little for the minutiae of ceremony. His double standard exasperated the Foreign Minister, Gavro Vuković, who remarked: *"Regardless how small and patriarchal, our court tried be like the great courts. For every official occasion, I made a court protocol but the Prince liked to make a mess of that strict order. He would take congratulations without order, as he used to do in the past, because he disliked ceremony. He liked order, for other people!"*[11]

"It is difficult to rule a people known for their cleverness and courage, but grandfather is doing it easily and everybody loves him. He is strict, and his whole appearance demands respect, projects authority and encourages submissiveness."[12]
Prince Djordje Karadjordjević

If the Prince was a patriarch, it was a predictable development considering the way royalty had grown out of the tribal system. In fact he could just as easily be described as the nation's vojvoda and a good example of this aspect of Nikola's rule could be seen in the legal system.

The Prince acted both as a judge and the last court of appeal. Although an updated legal code was placed on the statutes in the 1870s, many Montenegrins still chose to petition the

127

Prince Nikola continued the tradition of national poetry both Vladika Rade and his own father, Vojvoda Mirko, had contributed to. Nikola had been composing poetry since his youth and as ruler had written songs for each of the Montenegrin tribes, as well as the national anthem which had been set to music.

Nikola's major poetic work was 'The Empress of the Balkans' which he began writing in the winter of 1880. It was well received and subsequently translated into several European languages (an English edition was eventually published in 1913) and was also performed as a drama and set to music.

'The Empress of the Balkans' was also clearly an attempt to further the Prince's dynastic ambitions. While this was to be expected, indeed, Montenegrin poetry usually dealt with national themes, Nikola was rather disappointed that its literary value was given less credit. Serbia's Count Čedo Mijatović told the Prince: *"Your drama is not drama at all; it has much lyrical poetry of great beauty, and it has many interesting political discussions and even political programmes. Your Balkan Empress tells me what I already know, that you are a good lyrical poet, but a better and greater Serb patriot."* Mijatović had a point: Nikola's poetry obviously lacks the depth and breadth of Vladika Rade's masterpieces. Unsurprisingly, Nikola's repute as a poet rose and fell with his political fortunes, although his efforts are noteworthy contributions to South Slav literature.

ruler personally. In this context, although he was still acting within the constitution, he was also taking on the role traditionally played by the tribal elders.

The pleas brought before him were diverse and required a thorough knowledge of not only statute law, but also traditional law. Nikola knew many of the litigants personally, or at least of their families, and this helped him to adjudicate with a feeling for their dignity, which he balanced with an awareness for the shrewdness of his countrymen and women.

There were many cases of hardship arising from the wars of the 1870's. Srdan Mirkov from Mikulić, an officer who had lost an arm in the wars, was no longer able to work. He had paid off his debts, but was destitute and had young children to provide for. He asked for a small house in Nikšić and a piece of land so his family would not starve. Nikola judged in Srdan's favour, ruling that he also be given rations of flour until he was able to start to work the land.

Another former soldier, Rade Vukičević from Zagreda, asked for help because he had been badly wounded in the war and his four brothers had been killed. Though incapacitated, he still had the entire family to support, consisting of three elderly men, his youngest brother of seven and two nephews. Nikola asked for a letter of confirmation from Vukičević's captain before he made a decision. In the case of Stane Stevova, a war widow with two children, Nikola agreed she be helped but did not

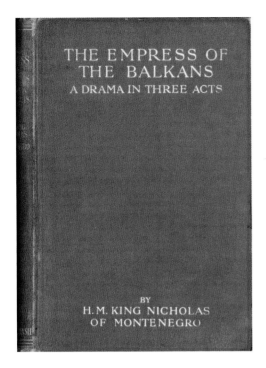

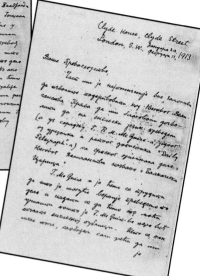

The letter (translation below) from Vojislav M Petrović requesting permission to produce an English language edition of 'The Empress of the Balkans'. The edition (left) was published in the same year, although the translator later wrote that its English theatre performance was prevented by political jealousies.

Clyde House, Clyde Street, London
January 29/February 11, 1913
To His Excellency Marshall Of The Kings Court, Cetinje

Your Excellency,
It is my honour to humbly beg you to request, that His Highness the King allow me to translate into the English language (with the co-operation of G.R.M. McGuire, one of the editors and war correspondent of the Daily Telegraph) from the Serbian original the work of His Highness, 'The Empress Of The Balkans'. Mr McGuire and I would zealously endeavour to produce a true translation, hoping that we would be successful in that as Mr McGuire's pen is already well known to the English audience. For myself, I am at liberty to say that my mother tongue is Serbian, and that I graduated in philosophy-science at Belgrade University and political science at Washington University. I am a Principal Professor at the International Correspondence School, London, Kingsway WC. In addition, I am a member of the Royal British Commission for exams in the civil service. Among other grammars, I have written an English grammar for Serbs and Serbian grammar for English, published by Julius Groos of Heidelberg. With regard to my character, I am at liberty to ask you to speak with Mr Čed. [Čedo] Mijatović (Clyde House, Clyde Street, London) who was kind enough to introduce me to Prince Vojinović at the Hyde Park Hotel. His Highness the King could perhaps be kind enough to recall that he saw me in his villa in Old Bar, when he was gracious enough to grant an audience to General Voicek, Director of the English Red Cross, Captain Bradford and myself as adjutant and secretary to General Voicek. Mr McGuire was also in Old Bar on that occasion. Even at that time we agreed to try to obtain permission to translate 'The Empress Of The Balkans'; even more so as we were aware that a translation from the German version was being prepared. But, if your Excellency endeavours, we would be able to make eventual corrections to the German translation by publishing our translation from the Serbian original first.

Thanking you in advance, I ask for permission to remain Your Excellency's most sincere:

Vojislav M Petrović

want it to be made public: "*Give her a letter for Ilija Gavrov instructing him to give her some food, but she should not tell anyone.*"[13]

Family and marital disputes were not uncommon. Krstinja Sava Vasova asked to be allowed to return to her home after her husband had driven her away and she had fled to her mother across the border. Nikola deferred to rule on the matter and referred her plea back to the law courts.

Although remarriage was possible in Montenegro it was allowed only for the innocent party. Even then permission to take a new wife or husband was not necessarily straightforward. Mitar Milov had been the innocent party in his divorce twelve years earlier and he petitioned Nikola, claiming that the Prince had promised he would be allowed to remarry. Nikola, however, did not think much of Mitar's suitability as a husband and remarked: "*Even if he remarries it will be in vain because that is his nature.*"[14]

(Left) Princess Milica and (facing page) Princess Stane. Both married Russian grand dukes. Stane married twice, firstly to Prince Georgi of Leichtenberg Romanovsky and, after her divorce in 1906, to Grand Duke Nikolai Nikolayevich Romanov. Milica married Grand Duke Peter Nikolayevich Romanov. Stane and Milica gained a degree of influence at the Russian court and earned some notoriety by introducing the Siberian monk, Grigory Rasputin, to the Tsar and Tsarina's inner circle. (Below) Princess Marija, Prince Nikola's fourth daughter who died aged only sixteen. Marija's character can only be surmised but, from the few references there are, she has been described as shy, thoughtful and melancholy.

Petitioning the Prince was certainly not a guarantee of success. Plana P. had burned her house down while her mother-in-law, Radosava, was inside. She had been given a twelve-year prison sentence. Plana's husband, his brothers and Radosava's relatives all signed a petition for a pardon, but Nikola confirmed the court's ruling.

Nikola would often refer a case back to the courts, but the nature of some of the cases attracted his attention.

In one such instance two men asked for help with a letter from their captain, Janko Bošković, confirming that they were in need. Nikola, however, surmised that there was more to this request than first met the eye. His reply illustrates how well he knew the scheming nature of some of his subjects: *"Oh God! What a strange thing! I think that those two poor men owe something to Janko, and he thinks if I give them something he can take it for himself. Give them some wheat!"*[15] Nikola's comments might also have been coloured by the long standing tension between the Njeguši and the Bjelopavlići, Janko's tribe, but he still wanted to offer the men some help.

Some petitioners were hoping for financial gain. Radovan Filipović had a straightforward claim: that the Prince still owed him twenty-five thalers for expenses incurred in Bileća while on state business. Nikola accepted that the money was owed but came to a most patriarchal conclusion: *"I am not going to give it to him now but later, when he will appreciate it more."*[16]

Nikola gave short thrift to less justified claims. Marija Kujova had spent money celebrating the birth of Prince Mirko and wanted to claim it back from the Ministry of Finance, which, of course, had refused her. Nikola's reply was laconic: *"Let the litigant take Mr. Minister to court!"*[17] Petar Vulov, from Lower Morača, brought a similar plea to the Prince. He asked for *"help as he was faithful"* and was summarily dismissed, *"I am faithful to him as well, tell him to go home!"*[18]

Nikola knew how to navigate the intricacies of Montenegrin reasoning, but it was often puzzling to foreigners who saw economic and developmental opportunities being wasted. There were genuine reasons nonetheless, although they very much belonged to the world of ruritania. In these instances, Nikola's knowledge of what was practicable and his sensibility for social propriety were his guides.

Niko Novakov had planted a row of Black Locust trees in his town and asked for them to be protected. He suggested that warning signs be put up and a guard appointed for two years. Nikola refused: *"It would be good to have a guard, but it is not possible to find one. Regarding signs, those who can read*

would not damage the trees anyway and for those who cannot read they would serve no purpose."[19]

A foreigner from a literate society was unlikely to anticipate that train of thought. In the same way, foreigners from countries where prison inmates were regarded simply as criminals, would not have responded as Nikola did when Minister Simo Popović suggested that they could be used as labourers to plant trees in Cetinje. Nikola told him: *"That is what other countries do, but it cannot work with us. There are people from good houses in prison only because of bad luck, and it would be difficult and shameful for them."*[20] Although crimes of honour, such as blood feuds, were prosecuted in the law courts, the perpetrators were regarded as unfortunate to have been forced, by the codes of honour, to commit murder. Forced labour would be considered a grave insult to their good characters.

In another sensitive area, Nikola needed to show both a light touch and a firm hand, always remembering that for Montenegrins personal honour was of paramount importance. There were, for example, instances of soldiers who had emigrated but spent their savings to return home; they pleaded with the Prince to save their honour on the grounds that they had not received medals recognising their service in the wars of liberation.

Equally, a soldier's conduct on the battlefield could not be besmirched. Vučeta Milošev's contribution during the war had been criticised by his captain and, since he felt his military honour had been injured, he asked that an official be sent to witness his bravery. Nikola replied that he would have a chance to show the Prince himself on his next visit to Milošev's battalion.

Blood revenge remained another aspect of honour Nikola had to contend with. Even though retaliatory homicide had become less frequent over time, it was still considered a matter of pride and bravery. The majestic lawlessness of the blood feud demanded that the Prince maintain a balance between law and tradition.

Such cases particularly intrigued two visitors, Reginald Wyon and Gerald Prance, who explored the country in 1902. One of Cetinje's prison wardens explained to them the Montenegrin perspective on the blood feud: *"We have no murderers. Our land is as safe from murder as any other in the world. No one kills to rob or steal in Montenegro. But we just quarrel amongst ourselves. We are hot blooded and shoot quickly, that is all."*[21] Nikola's handling of such delicate cases amply demonstrated the Prince's command of his role.

Each Easter Cetinje's prison was the setting for the Prince to display his mercy to his subjects. In both the male and the female prisons, the majority of the inmates were there because of crimes relating to blood feuds and Nikola would come to the prison to hear their pleas. Wyon and Prance observed: *"In the centre of the little ring sits the massive figure of the Prince, clothed in the long pale blue coat of the upper classes, over which again he is wearing a sleeveless jacket, stiff with gold silk and embroidery. The chair looks ridiculously small under him as he leans slightly to the right, listening to the statement of a blind judge . . . Opposite the Prince are a dozen women with folded hands and*

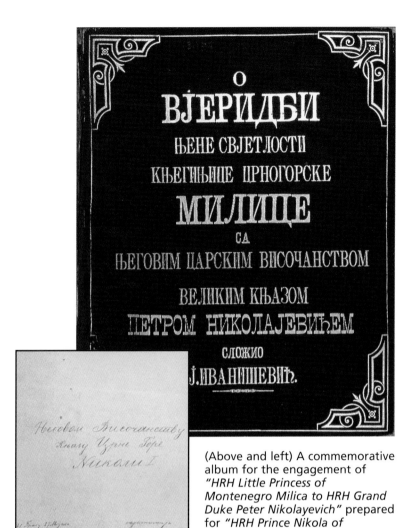

(Above and left) A commemorative album for the engagement of *"HRH Little Princess of Montenegro Milica to HRH Grand Duke Peter Nikolayevich"* prepared for *"HRH Prince Nikola of Montenegro, in Prague on August 27 [September 8], 1889, by the Humble J Ivanišević."*

downcast eyes, and one by one they step forward while a clerk reads from a paper their names, crime and sentences. Some are dismissed at once . . . But now a young woman is before the Prince, wearing the cap, which tells one she is unmarried. The Prince turns to his advisers and puts a few short and pertinent questions. Then he turns again to the girl, 'I pardon thee' he says."[22]

Where harshness was displayed it was in political cases. One of these involved 'Janko' who had insulted the Prince at his own table and been given a year in prison. Another inmate had gone insane and believed himself to be the Prince of Wales, but he had originally been imprisoned for attempting to *"stir up strife against the Prince, and this is the worst crime in Montenegro, for such men are seldom tried."*[23]

If political agitators and thieves had something to fear from patriarchal justice, by and large the prison system itself was tolerant. Considering the arduous nature of Montenegrin life generally, prison conditions were not exceptionally hard. The prison in Cetinje was a plain building without any surrounding walls to prevent escape. Inside the wardens had their own living quarters where the property of the prisoners, including their weapons, were stored.

The cells were in the main courtyard. About twelve men lived in each cell, but each was allowed a bed and personal property. There were also six special cells which were dark and without light or furniture; these held the political prisoners. Occasionally, an inmate would be forced to wear chains. One was the clerk convicted of embezzlement who had to suffer the cumbersome irons for six weeks, but others, including those convicted of blood feuds, enjoyed a high degree of freedom and the wardens even left the prison gates open.

In the women's prison the doors and windows all faced outward and there was, again, no fence or wall to prevent escape. There were an estimated dozen or so female inmates at any one time. They could stroll around freely up to the boundary line marked by posts and trees and pass the time of day chatting and knitting. On feast days the male and female prisoners were allowed to see visitors and socialise together in the square outside the prison building. The revellers would enjoy a meal and drink brandy as they danced the traditional *kolo* to the accompaniment of the *gusle*.

These tolerant prison conditions had valid reasons behind them. Nikola considered the loss of liberty sufficient punishment and no added penalty was required once an offender was in prison. This was not only an illustration of his natural tolerance, it was also shrewd policy. For a Montenegrin to accept his or her punishment was to maintain honour and the most feared sentence was exile, which meant leaving the country probably never to return. This was a terrible fate for Montenegrins since it severed the cherished family and clan ties which made up their social and economic world.

"The Prince's ideal of government is a liberal autocracy in a conservative nation"[24]
William Miller

Although he was a benevolent ruler, Nikola was nonetheless an autocrat. His treatment of

Further pages and extracts from the commemorative albums from the weddings of Princess Milica and Princess Stane. Both marriages had great dynastic and political importance for Montenegro. Congratulatory telegrams from European royalty, notably Emperor Franz Josef of Austria-Hungary, were included in the albums, as well as some lively expressions of pan-Slav solidarity from the Russian newspaper 'The Citizen'.

"On May 20 [June 1] at 6pm, Princess Milena received this correspondence from His Highness the Emperor to Her Highness Princess Milena of Montenegro: 'I was glad to learn the news of the engagement of Princess Milica to Grand Duke Peter Nikolayevich, so I rush to express my and the Empress' sincere congratulations. Franz Josef, Vienna, Burgh, May 20 '."

"On May 20 at 11am, Princess Milena received the representative of Great Britain, Mr Butler Baring, who expressed to Her Highness the most sincere congratulations of HRH of Great Britain and India, Queen Victoria. Shortly after the Minister of the French Republic, Mr A Gerard, expressed the same sentiments in the name of the French Government. Later that same day, Milena received a telegram from the Prince and Master informing her that the wedding date was set for July 27 [August 8] in St. Petersburg."

"Metropolitan Mitrofan Ban [Head of the Montenegrin Orthodox Church] *to Princess Milica: 'I am profoundly happy because of the news of the engagement of Your Highness to the Grand Duke Peter Nikolayevich. Almighty God blesses your union, receives you and your fiancé under his holy patronage and protection, and guards your happiness and welfare under his holy right hand for many years. Metropolitan Mitrofan Ban'."*

The telegrams from Tsar Alexander III and Tsarina Maria Feodorovna expressing their happiness at the engagement of *"our darling daughter Milica"* naturally took pride of place. Being welcomed into the Russian nobility was an important event for the Petrović-Njegoš dynasty and an occasion of great joy for Princess Milena who sent this reply to St. Petersburg: *"The indescribable goodness of your Imperial Highnesses to myself and my family fills my heart with joy. I cannot find words to express my feelings. I can only pray most sincerely to God for Your Highnesses. Milena, Cetinje, May 19 [May 31]."*

(Left) An interesting interpretation of the significance of Princess Milica's wedding from the Russian newspaper 'The Citizen'. Although its pan-Slav sentiments are rather pugilistic, they nonetheless reflect an important aspect of the Russian connection for Montenegro, which was far more than just a dynastic or even political relationship. Milica's marriage to Grand Duke Peter Nikolayevich hardly had enough importance to cause a war, but it was an excellent opportunity for a robust expression of Russia's pan-Slav mission: *"Today, Wednesday, July 26 [August 7], 1889, an event of special political importance is taking place in Peterhof. That event is the wedding of Grand Duke Peter Nikolayevich and the Princess of Montenegro. The importance of this event is shown from the badly hidden discontent and irritation of Russia's enemies, as well as the joy of the whole Slav world. For the first time the ancient and celebrated House of Romanov is taking a Princess from a ruling and celebrated Serb house, celebrated for its martial virtues among many others. For the first time, with this joyful union, Russia is united in blood ties with the Slav world, after two hundred years of wandering through western deserts of the Roman-German world. From here on the 'Eastern Question' enters a new phase of its development, promising to the whole of Europe a beneficial and extended peace. If Roman-German Europe (excluding France) declares war on Russia, the consequences would be that around Russia would gather all Slav Europe, not least amongst which is the Serb nation. That is all doubled by the fact that Princess Milica is not only a Serb but also Orthodox Christian and educated in Russia. All Russia is united in joy because this celebrated union is the beginning of a new epoch, of a new bright and joyful life."*

Vojvoda Mašo Vrbica illustrated these traits as well as the political character of the ruler. Vojvoda Mašo was an old and trusted state employee whose career had begun under the patronage of Nikola's father, Vojvoda Mirko. He was also known for his boasting and self-aggrandisement and, even though their relations were cordial, Nikola sought to teach him a lesson through a practical joke.

A Montenegrin emigrant living in California sent Nikola a rock which contained gold and he decided it could be used in his scheme. As was his habit when he needed an errand, Nikola called over one of his subjects who was passing by the Palace. Handing over the rock Nikola said: *"Listen to my order very carefully! Take this rock and put it under your overcoat, go to Vojvoda Mašo, but do not approach him freely, show some hesitation. Then, pretending that you are scared, give him this rock and ask him if it is any good. And when he asks you where you found it, tell him in your yard while*

digging a well. And do not tell him even that much at once, do it in a roundabout way as if you are afraid."

The *agent provocateur* carried out his task so convincingly that when Vojvoda Mašo took the rock in his hand he began shouting: *"You bastard, you have stolen this, and I know where and from whom! Wait for me you son of a bitch, I will call the guard."*[25] As agreed the man ran away and reported back to Nikola that the trap had been set.

It was a warm summer evening when Vojvoda Mašo burst into the Prince's garden party exclaiming: *"God bless you Master and your country! Here we have God's gift."*[26] He excitedly explained to the gathered crowd that the gold was found in that village, in that man's

(Left) A framed portrait of Princess Milena. (Below) Milena's bedroom and (right) a close up of the dressing table with a portrait of daughter Jelena. Mother and daughter's greatest shared characteristic was their love of children, but both were also dignified and discreet consorts for their husbands.

Princess Milica (right) joined the Russian nobility after she married Russia's Grand Duke Peter Nikolayevich (below right). Milica's character has sometimes been subject to oversimplified analysis, due in part to a degree of religious mysticism on her part and the connection with Grigory Rasputin. However, she was also a benefactress to her homeland, personally paying for the construction of Cetinje's water system, while her linguistic talents were considerable, as was her knowledge of the Ottoman Empire and Asia.

yard, and how he had wanted to hide the truth, but Vojvoda Mašo had found out and unhesitatingly rushed to tell the Prince. The trap had been well laid and the assembled guests thoroughly enjoyed the joke.

However, Vojvoda Mašo's high-handed nature had a more serious effect on his career, which would end in personal disgrace.

In 1882 Vojvoda Mašo, then Minister of Home Affairs, was brought to trial at the Great Court. The charges were quite serious ones, *"plots with Austrians and some other business"* as Nikola off-handedly referred to them during the trial, but they were not used as evidence.

Nikola presided over the trial. To his left and right sat the officers of the State Council and the Great Court. The trial began as Nikola read from the 'Economic Society' rulebook, a foundation started by Vojvoda Mašo who was also its president. When he had finished, Nikola explained that Vojvoda Mašo had broken his own guidelines, even his own word, and he turned to the gallery and asked, *"Is that right?"* The chorus replied in unison, *"That is right Master."*[27]

Vojvoda Mašo stood motionless as Nikola continued with his prosecution, all the while calling for the gallery's opinion. To each and every charge the reply was in the affirmative. It was a strange way to conduct legal proceedings which a spectator at the trial, the Serbian writer Simo Matavulj, compared to the medieval trials of heretics. He noted that there was no passion or anger in the proceedings, only the anxiety of Vojvoda Mašo who behaved like a condemned man rather than a defendant.

Nikola had deliberately not used the main accusations against Vojvoda Mašo. Clearly those were matters he did not want to discuss further. He simply rose to his feet and pronounced sentence: *"As Vojvoda Mašo has abused my trust, from today he is no longer Minister of Home Affairs . . . Vojvoda Božo will replace him."* Vojvoda Mašo, shaking with emotion, bowed to the Prince and offered him his cap. *"Will you take my coat of arms away?"* he asked. *"No, no, you can keep that,"* Nikola replied.[28]

After a trial, it was customary to go the Palace with the Prince, but Simo Matavulj felt sympathy for the disgraced man and went with Vojvoda Mašo instead: *"I went to the Palace*

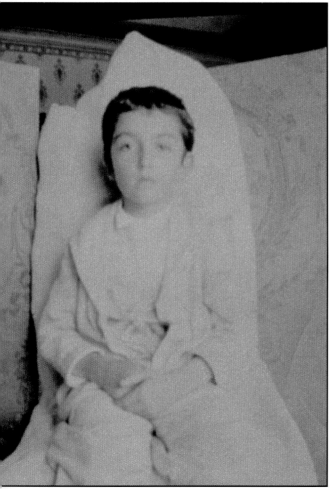

after lunch to report to the Prince. I found him pacing up and down the room very nervously. He approved of my Samaritan gesture and asked what I thought about the matter . . . I replied I was sorry that his old and faithful servant had suffered such degradation."[29]

A few days later Vojvoda Mašo fell ill. Nikola sent his personal doctor and also paid a visit, staying till late in the evening. After this gesture everyone visited and rumours even started that he would be reinstated, but he never was.

Nikola sincerely regretted having ended Mašo Vrbica's career. He was from Njeguši and had long enjoyed close relations with the Royal Family. He had supported Prince Danilo in his struggle with the Piperi tribe and had been one of Mirko's men in the famous siege at Ostrog Monastery in 1852.

While the political demise of the vojvodas was, over time, inevitable, Nikola's critics saw him becoming the tool of the court *camarilla*. An example of the potential for conflicts of interests was as close at hand as Milena's father, Petar. He had been accused of profiteering in the last war during the siege of Nikšić and of land grabbing after it.

An undercurrent of political violence also continued and the intolerance of opposition meant that a vocal diaspora denounced the Prince's rule. Many took refuge in Belgrade from where they were able to publicise their views. One such critic was the schoolteacher Marko Backović who, in 1895, published a denunciation of Montenegrin autocracy entitled 'Montenegro at the End of the Nineteenth Century'.

Backović made many accusations against the ruling circle, he even claimed to have been told by the Prince that repression was the only way the ruling dynasty could survive: *"I did not prepare Dano [Crown Prince Danilo] to be a modern ruler. The only way left to me now is to consolidate the throne for him and clear Montenegro of educated and liberal people, and leave him with only peasant highlanders who know nothing of the outside world."* Although one can question if the conversation actually took place as Backović described, his criticisms and his call for a change to a constitutional regime were a clear warning sign of the disillusion and anger directed at the Prince.

Nikola was far from being a bloodthirsty ruler, but he was prepared to be ruthless with political opponents and there were assassinations of political dissenters during his reign. As Marko Backović put it: *"They were swallowed by the darkness and none dared ask how they had disappeared."* Shortly afterward Backović would be among their number, although the facts surrounding his death did come to light.

Ranko Tajsić was a Serbian parliamentary deputy for the Radical Party who had links to Prince Nikola and a hatred for ĕx-King Milan. He was a maverick figure who was, apparently, so angered by Backović's attacks on the Prince's rule that he decided to organise his murder.

The political atmosphere in Serbia during the latter years of Obrenović rule was akin to that of a cauldron close to boiling point. Dynastic relations were also tense and both the Serb ruling houses believed that the other was conspiring to bring them down. In that context, for Tajsić and others, Milan's support for the Montenegrin opposition proved that Backović was an accomplice in Milan's schemes.

Tajsić needed to find a gun for hire and he heard of a bandit called Milan Brkić, who, it was known, wanted to relocate to Montenegro. Tajsić arranged to meet Brkić in the central Serbian village of Dragačevo, where he suggested to him that his best chance to be welcomed in Montenegro, and even rewarded, was to kill Marko Backović. Brkić thought it a reasonable proposal and Marko Backović was murdered in the autumn of 1896. The reward for the bounty was one hundred ducats.

However, the Serbian authorities were determined to find the culprits and a year later Tajsić and Brkić found themselves on trial. Brkić admitted his own guilt but denied any connection with Tajsić, who was therefore released due to a lack of evidence. Tajsić fled to Montenegro and the protection of Prince Nikola, giving ample reason to believe in the Prince's involvement. The case was reopened in Serbia the following year and, in his absence, Tajsić was sentenced to twenty years imprisonment.

Unwarranted though his murder was, Marko Backović would have been aware that he was swimming in dangerous waters. His well publicised opposition to Prince Nikola's autocracy had placed him in the Obrenović camp, which found the Montenegrin opposition in exile a very useful political tool.

In fact, ex-King Milan decided he could make further political capital from Backović's sad fate. Milan had abdicated, in 1889, in favour of his son Aleksandar, but he still had a good deal of political clout, which he gleefully used against Prince Nikola whenever an opportunity arose. With that aim in mind, Milan personally paid for the printing of a political pamphlet titled 'A few Bloody Pages from the Album of Petrović-Njegoš'. Its author, Savo Ivanović, was another Montenegrin exile and an associate of Marko Backović. It was hardly surprising then that Cetinje viewed Backović, Ivanović and their ilk as puppets of the Obrenovići.

Prince Nikola certainly did not shy away from involvement in the ugly side of politics but, certainly in comparison to the Obrenovići, he was a prudent and pragmatic ruler. However, one characteristic they shared in common was a dislike of political parties. In this context the Obrenovići were far worse off as they were in constant conflict with Serbia's developing parliamentary system; whereas Nikola, as an autocrat, could mould political relations to suit his own aims.

(This page and facing page, top) Princess Milica's elder daughter, Marina Petrovna Romanov.
(Facing page, bottom) Prince Nikola's youngest child Petar, who was born on September 10, 1889.

As a matter of general strategy, Nikola preferred to avoid direct confrontations with his ministers and held himself aloof from any particular policy they might be pursuing. This, of course, excused him if anything went wrong. He also played them off one against the other and let their stars rise and fall according to their successes and failures. This was guileful of him, infuriated the ministers and hampered consistent policy making, but also ensured that the Prince ruled the political roost. There would be no Bismarckian figure dominating the ruler; Nikola firmly believed he was by far the best man to guide the nation. He was certainly its most experienced politician and knew well how difficult keeping the ship of state afloat was.

"As you know, I do not enjoy travelling around the world camping on other people's doorsteps. I swear to you that if it was up to me, I would prefer to go somewhere between Lješkopolje and Danilovgrad in one of those little houses rather than these hotels and palaces. However, as I am forced to do these things I will."[30]
Prince Nikola to Princess Milena

Nikola's way of handling policy was most clearly seen in the state's notoriously irregular financial affairs. Patriarchal Montenegro had no official state budget, in fact the state as such had virtually no source of income. This ensured that power would be concentrated in the hands of Nikola and his few advisors, but their position was an unenviable one.

Reconciling personal and national finances was a perennial problem. The Russian subsidy was used solely for the Royal Family and the maintenance of the court, but as time went on it became less and less adequate. In 1902 Nikola wrote to Tsar Nikolai II: *"I said that I would not ask for more money, but can you imagine how difficult it is for me to answer all the needs that are becoming greater and greater? Sixty thousand florins, which is forty-seven thousand roubles, of income from my country and fifty thousand roubles of your help, that is all I have. And how many obligations! To support a family, a court, small, but even that still costs a lot, as well as official representations, marriages, travels, presents . . ."*[31]

It was possible to patch up the Royal Family's finances, but the state finances were a much larger problem and approaches were made to other powers in the hope of gaining loans. Austria-Hungary was prepared to help, but as ever there were political strings attached.

(Top) Princess Milica's third child, Nadezhda Petrovna Romanov and (above) her only son, Roman Petrović Romanov.

Although Nikola knew he needed Vienna's help he greatly resented being forced into economic dependency, all the more so as his personal views were strongly pro-Russian. Such sentiments were an article of faith for many Serbs, but Nikola still managed to surprise Čedo Mijatović with an anti-Austro-Hungarian tirade. It happened in the spring of 1882, during a stay at Nikola's favourite Viennese hotel, 'The Goldenes Lamm', as Emperor Franz Josef's guest.

Čedo Mijatović, who was at the time a member of the Serbian Government which had just concluded important and secret treaties with Vienna, was invited to dinner by Nikola. As they enjoyed the finest wines and the sumptuous cuisine, Nikola spoke long and passionately about the glories of

Russia and how the Tsar's forces would one day overwhelm Austria-Hungary. Mijatović recorded with dismay: *"He was the guest of Austria, and the great dinner, which we both heartily enjoyed, was paid for by the Emperor Franz Josef; yet he told me how Austria would be crushed and submerged as by a new flood, when once the waves of the great Slav sea of the White Tsar should break their boundaries and inundate Galicia and Hungary."*[32]

Personal sentiment had to be set aside. Nikola was too much of a realist to forget that he had to continue his financial begging and in this he enjoyed some success. During his trip to Vienna in 1889, after much frantic effort and the calling in of favours, a loan was agreed. Emperor Franz Josef, *"Big Mister"* as Nikola liked to call him, was a man one could do business with. Nonetheless, there could never be real friendship between the two countries and, although he took their money, Nikola was anxious to distance himself from the colonial clutches of Austria-Hungary.

He believed that a possible escape lay with French funds which could be used to pay off Montenegro's debts to Vienna, and to this end his cousin, Božo Petrović, was despatched to Paris. The French authorities did their best to help Božo find a bank which would make the loan. The banks naturally asked to see the state's financial records but there were none. In fiscal terms, the Montenegrin state did not exist and it was therefore impossible to underwrite a loan. Regardless of the amount being requested, every bank demanded Russian guarantees, but the Montenegrins could hardly expect St. Petersburg to underwrite loans from a third party. It was a lamentable situation and Božo's six months in Paris predictably came to nothing.

The Montenegrins had also asked France to allow the sale of a small amount of livestock. An agreement was made to export forty thousand head of sheep and goats, but under prohibitive conditions: the cargo would only ship via French boats, which would have a veterinary surgeon aboard to inspect and vaccinate the livestock. The French were worried about the proximity of the poorly governed and probably unhygienic Turkish provinces, so they also demanded that on arrival in Marseilles the livestock be checked again and kept in quarantine for a further five days. All these additional costs would be at Montenegrin expense. The whole exercise eventually unravelled when merchants started buying the livestock and Montenegrin farmers tried to raise their prices. Exporting became unprofitable and, even after prices dropped, the merchants still considered the cost prohibitive.

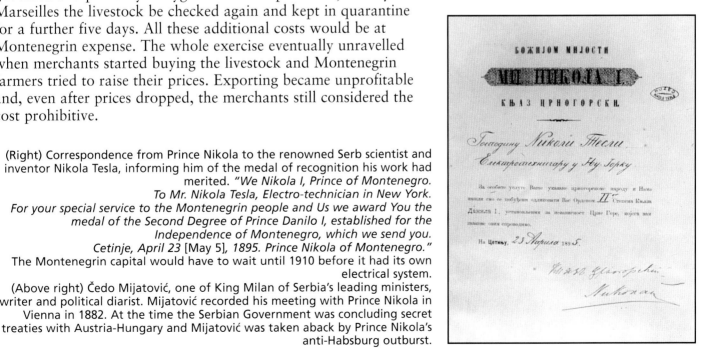

(Right) Correspondence from Prince Nikola to the renowned Serb scientist and inventor Nikola Tesla, informing him of the medal of recognition his work had merited. *"We Nikola I, Prince of Montenegro.*
To Mr. Nikola Tesla, Electro-technician in New York.
For your special service to the Montenegrin people and Us we award You the medal of the Second Degree of Prince Danilo I, established for the Independence of Montenegro, which we send you.
Cetinje, April 23 [May 5], 1895. Prince Nikola of Montenegro."
The Montenegrin capital would have to wait until 1910 before it had its own electrical system.
(Above right) Čedo Mijatović, one of King Milan of Serbia's leading ministers, writer and political diarist. Mijatović recorded his meeting with Prince Nikola in Vienna in 1882. At the time the Serbian Government was concluding secret treaties with Austria-Hungary and Mijatović was taken aback by Prince Nikola's anti-Habsburg outburst.

Behind these rather farcical episodes lay Montenegro's acute economic problems.

The territorial enlargement of 1878 had expanded Montenegro to include four substantial urban centres - Bar, Ulcinj, Nikšić and Podgorica - but the country was ill equipped to successfully assimilate new populations or develop these promising assets. Although Nikola, appreciative of their industrious nature, was keen to welcome his new subjects, communal relations were not always harmonious. By 1881, with the departure of Roman Catholic and Moslem communities, their combined pre-annexation populations of over twenty thousand had fallen to under ten thousand.

Bar's population fell from over four thousand to under two thousand, Podgorica lost two thirds of its population of seven thousand. The principality was markedly unable to replace these traditional trading communities with its indigenous population, but was hardly unique in this regard. Depopulation and deurbanisation were also evident in Serbia and Bosnia-Herzegovina.

All Balkan statesmen hoped that their economies could be created anew with the Ottoman yoke largely removed, but none had managed to transform agricultural and proto-industrial economies into dynamic engines of nineteenth century progress. Montenegro, which was trapped in a perpetual struggle for subsistence, had barely begun the process.

Resistance to change also contributed to the country's poor economic performance. A wary and suspicious nation remained far from convinced that the old ways should be discarded for the risks and vulgarities of trade and commerce. Furthermore, Montenegrins had a somewhat aristocratic disdain for 'business'. It was a noble posture they could claim to share with their Balkan antecedents the ancient Greeks; however, the economic consequence of these deeply rooted attitudes was very simple: Montenegrins were known

(Above and left) An Italian translation of Montenegro's Civil Law Code presented by Prince Nikola's daughter, Queen Elena of Italy, for the fortieth anniversary celebrations of her father's reign in 1900. It was in the same year that Elena and Vittorio Emanuele ascended the Italian throne after King Umberto I's assassination by an anarchist.

Palace interiors: (Above) Prince Nikola's bedroom and (right) the Prince's favourite reception room, known as the 'Red Salon' from its decoration and upholstery. Facing page: (Bottom right) The 'Indonesian Salon', used for receptions by the Prince's youngest son, Petar, and (bottom left) the modest family dining room.

to be good workers, but only in foreign lands. To work in the same fashion at home would be a keenly felt humiliation for a man and his family.

Nonetheless, Montenegrins loved their homeland and those who emigrated dreamed of returning with enough saved to buy a plot of land. A modest enough goal, but to be able to live as a peasant freeholder, even in Montenegro where good land was so scarce, was understandably preferable to the uprooted and hard life faced by emigrants in industrialised countries.

If this solved the problem of preserving family honour, it did little for the general economy. Continuing economic emigration sapped the manpower of the principality: between 1880 and 1900 as many as fifty thousand left, some twenty thousand settling in Serbia. Inevitably, in a country where

family honour meant more than national prosperity, trade and commerce was left to outsiders: Albanians, Dalmatians and the occasional entrepreneur from further afield.

Another problem was the unsystematic and, from the economic standpoint, badly implemented division of the new territories. After the territorial enlargement arable land had more than doubled and livestock had risen, by 1885, to more than seven hundred thousand sheep, one hundred thousand cattle and ten thousand horses.

However, the Prince's handling of agrarian reform did not help matters. Much of the new land was given to relatives, friends and those he felt were deserving. The benefit for the new territories was to replace feudal agrarian relations with peasant freeholds, but many felt the ruling circles had benefited excessively.

If the minutiae of its problems were home grown, the nation was not alone in struggling to reconcile itself to a changing world. Montenegro was a typical example of patriarchal-dinaric society, which could also be found in western Serbia and a large swathe of Bosnia-Herzegovina. The eminent Serbian ethnographer Jovan Cvijić described dinaric man as a rather contradictory character: valuing heroism and high moral standards but also being prone to egoism and laziness.

Prince Nikola did his best to change attitudes using symbolic gestures. He summoned the vojvodas to witness the Master planting a vine stock and commanded them to go home to do the same. He even had a blacksmith's workshop erected outside the Palace and hammered a horseshoe in front of his haughty subjects. They were not all that impressed; in such a conservative society attitudes were slow to change.

Even the reform minded ruler had his limits and baulked at modernisation which went too far. For instance, the Italian entrepreneur who asked for permission to open a gambling house in Bar was indignantly informed: *"I am the Prince of Montenegro not a casino owner!"*

Despite the difficulties, some progress was made and Nikola's contribution can hardly be overestimated.

One noteworthy achievement was an updated legal code which superseded the Code Danilo of 1855. The new code was designed as another step away from tribal society towards a modern civil society. Nikola told the nation: *"The Montenegrin is no longer only a soldier but now also a citizen. We are just beginning that process. We have to start with justice as the basis of the state . . . We have had the justice of the lonely man among his rocks living on the spark of his gun, but today there is a need for justice for the Montenegrin citizen in his village and town, for the merchant, sailor and peasant who has contact with his neighbours."*[33]

(Right) Vjera and Petar in a corner of the Diplomatic Salon and (below right) the salon as it looks today. The largest room in the Palace it was used for official receptions. Facing page: (Top) Prince Nikola and Prince Mirko attending the ceremonial blessing of a water well in Cetinje and (bottom) Princess Milena's salon, known as the 'Yellow Salon'.

To convert these principles into law, Nikola chose a good man in Dr Baltazar Bogišić, a native Dalmatian who held a chair at Odessa University. Dr Bogišić was a renowned legal expert and his work in drafting a new code based on traditional law has been highly praised as a marvel of concise wisdom.[34]

The infrastructure of the country also benefited, although Nikola's foresight would have counted for little without the aid of his shrewdness.

The problem of finance had been overcome by an agreement with Austria-Hungary, which had underpinned the road construction effort since 1881 through an annual

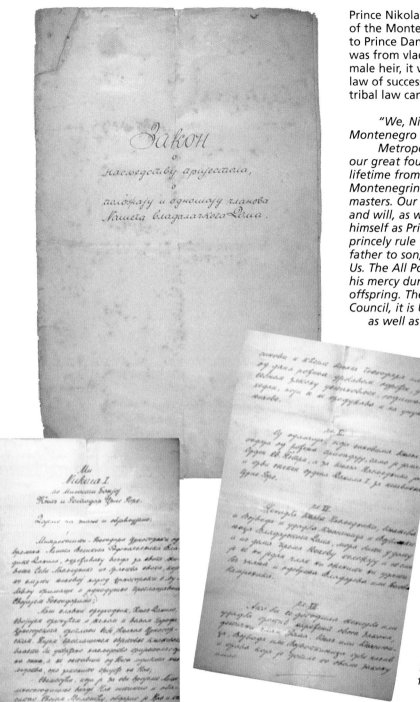

Prince Nikola's proclamation of 1902 declaring the line of succession of the Montenegrin throne to be based on male primogeniture. Prior to Prince Danilo's reign (1851-1860) the customary law of succession was from vladika to nephew. Prince Danilo having died without a male heir, it was left to his nephew, Prince Nikola, to formalise the law of succession. As with much of Montenegrin law elements of tribal law can still be seen, such as clause XVIII.

"We, Nikola I, with God's mercy Prince and Master of Montenegro Proclaim:

Metropolitans, the Masters of Montenegro since the time of our great founder Vladika Danilo, were appointing Heirs during their lifetime from within the brotherhood, whom after their death the Montenegrin people would accept with love and proclaim as masters. Our glorious predecessor Prince Danilo, thanks to his efforts and will, as well as the will of the Montenegrin people, proclaimed himself as Prince of Montenegro. With that proclamation of secular princely rule was established the law of hereditary succession from father to son, and, as he did not leave male heirs, by law it came to Us. The All Powerful, who has protected Us and bestowed upon Us his mercy during our long rule, blessed Us with many and happy offspring. Therefore, after listening to the advice of Our State Council, it is Us who has both the need and duty toward the future as well as the peace and progress of our State and Home, to set and establish this Law Of Succession of the Throne, position and relationship of members of our ruling house.

I. The Heir of the Montenegrin Throne is always the eldest son of the ruling Prince, who on his birth inherits the title Royal Highness Prince Heir to the Throne of Montenegro.

II. If the Heir to the Throne dies before he ascends the Throne, or abdicates, or has to abdicate (XII) the Heir becomes the eldest among his brothers, and if he does not have one, then a member of the family who is next in line (III).

III. If the Prince and Master loses during his lifetime his male heir, or does not have one, the Heir to the Throne becomes his eldest brother, after whom his children become the future heirs.

IV. Even if with this order of direct succession the Throne remains without an Heir, the inheritance goes to the one whom Prince and Master chooses as most capable from within the Petrović brotherhood, as was the custom accepted by the people from Vladika Danilo I until Prince Danilo I, and that branch of the family follows the same order as written above.

V. The Prince and Master announces a new Heir to the Throne at the moment of his birth, or if the position of the Heir is vacant, because of his death or abdication or by losing right to the Throne. (XIII & XIV)

VI. If the Throne is vacant the Heir becomes Prince and Master immediately, even if he is under age or by a permanent illness is prevented from accomplishing the Ruler's duties.

VII. In the case of VI the ruler is represented by the Regent of HRH Prince and Master, the eldest of age member of the house whose rule does not change the established rule of inheritance for the future.

VIII. If the Prince and Master is under age the Regency lasts until the day he comes of age, and if he is ill, until he heals or until God chooses to take him to eternity.

IX. The sons and daughters of the Prince and Master receive at birth the title of Highness Prince or Princess, the children of his sons the title of His Grace Duke or Duchess and their inheritance continues up to the seventh family line.

X. The Heir to the Throne, as well as the other sons and daughters of the Prince and Master, receive from the day of their birth, regulated by the State and special law, an annual income that is not passed onto their grandchildren.

XI. The honorary medals given to the sons of the Prince and Master on their birth are only the domestic medal of Saint Petar, and to the Heir to the Throne additionally the First Degree of the Medal of Danilo I for the Independence of Montenegro.

XII. Marriage of the Prince Heir to the Throne, Princes and Princesses, Dukes and Duchesses must be in and of a house equal to their position, and none can marry without the knowledge and approval of the Ruler or his Regent.

XIII. If a marriage against this law takes place, that member of the house, Prince or Princess, Duke or Duchess, loses the title and rights held until then.

XIV. If the Prince and Master is motivated by irresistible circumstance to approve an unequal marriage of the Heir, or other son or daughter, or his son's son or daughter, the betrothed would renounce in advance their title and rights, but still have the right to the income given by the State and their share of the inheritance.

XV. If the Prince and Master ascends the Throne still unmarried or becomes widowed he cannot make an unequal marriage. And if he does, abdicating the Throne, his children will have neither royal titles or rights as members of the Royal House.

XVI. If the Ruler makes an equal (second) marriage, the children from that marriage will have the same rights as the children from the first marriage, as their younger siblings.

XVII. The rights of the daughters-in-law of the Prince and Master are determined by their husband's status.

XVIII. If the widowed daughter-in-law of the Prince and Master wishes to remarry, she first has to renounce in writing the title and rights she has as a member of the Ruling House, after which she goes either to work or to her own house, and takes with her all the personal property she gained during her marriage as well as that which she has from the contract of marriage.

XIX. The sons and daughters of the Prince and Master, to whom the Royal House and State has since their birth given honours and income, are obliged to educate their offspring with love towards the Royal House and State, so that when the sons complete their education, they serve their homeland according to their education. And for daughters, even when they find their new homes, to make their homeland proud.

One copy of this law will have the Seal of State and be confirmed with our Highest signature and placed in the Court and State Archives. We order Our State Council to proclaim this law and to all we order them to obey it.

Cetinje, on St. Nikola's Day, 1902, the 42nd year of Our Rule. Nikola."

(Right) A portrait of Prince Nikola with his three sons. To his left Crown Prince Danilo, to his right Prince Mirko and with his father, Prince Petar.

(Above) Prince Petar with his father and sister-in-law, Crown Princess Milica-Yutta (formerly Augusta Charlotte of Mecklenburg-Strelitz).
(Facing page) Prince Nikola and Princess Milena with a teenage Ksenija and youngest daughter, Vjera, in the salon of the family residence in Rijeka Crnojevića.

subsidy.

However, it was one thing to overcome a lack of funds by calling on foreign aid, quite another to get around the people's dislike of manual labour. Nikola decided to apply both stick and carrot to this problem as he sought to galvanise his subjects into improving their own lot.

All he had to do was to wait for a lean year, which were common enough. He then distributed supplies of Russian grain to the people, but only on condition that it was earned by working on the roads.

Crude though this method was it made for progress and the roads, so vital to the mountainous principality, were duly constructed. They were Nikola's proudest achievement.

By 1898 ninety-six miles of passable driving road had been laid down, a further thirty-seven were usable and another thirty-seven planned. By the turn of the century it was possible to drive from the Adriatic coastline, starting at Kotor on the excellent Austro-Hungarian built road, then via Cetinje and Podgorica to Nikšić. It was also hoped to build a direct link between Nikšić and the coastline which would give a much needed stimulus to trade.

It was, unfortunately, as much progress as circumstance allowed as potentially beneficial economic relations were thoroughly tangled up with politics. The Ottoman threat had faded but now Austria-Hungary held Montenegro in a geographical, military and economic vice. The fortresses along the Herzegovinian frontier; the three battalions stationed in the Sandžak; the cannon commanding the Bay of Kotor and the warships which patrolled and threatened Montenegro's short coastline hardly made for a friendly presence. The principality was undoubtedly still isolated and vulnerable. If Vienna chose to impose an embargo the mountaineers could face starvation; the very same threat which the Pashas of Scutari and Bosnia-Herzegovina had wielded.

For the peninsula as a whole politics loomed large in all aspects of economic development. There was no shortage of governments or entrepreneurs keen to invest in the building of roads, railways and industry; however, the question of which of the Great Powers would exercise control, the possibility that the Balkan states would run their own affairs not being under consideration, made these projects intensely political affairs. The Balkan states lacked the means to catch up economically through their own efforts, but at the same time the region was assigned such strategic importance that proposed projects were intrigued over, blocked and cancelled more often than they were completed. Even so, Montenegro's economic performance was notably poor in comparison with its neighbours. Only the unfortunate Albania and Macedonia fared worse.

Somewhat ironically it was in Bosnia-Herzegovina, which had been under Austro-Hungarian administration since 1878, that the greatest advances were being made. The underlying economic, social and religious problems remained to be solved, but the province's considerable natural resources were beginning to be exploited. The ambitions of Montenegro and Serbia, as well as those of the Habsburg ruled South Slavs to the west, offered the prospect of liberation and were obvious threats to Austro-Hungarian designs, but none could guarantee to match Vienna's economic record and

Habsburg statesmen were optimistic that the loyalty of the province could be gained through the Empire's 'civilising powers'.

While the Balkan peoples could justifiably lay a good deal of the blame for their relative backwardness on centuries of imperial misrule and foreign interference, their own achievements had so far been modest. If Bulgaria, Romania and Serbia were expected to find their niche in economic affairs, many considered a transitional period of colonial rule by the Great Powers necessary if the remaining Ottoman provinces of Albania and Macedonia were to overcome their backwardness. In such a maelstrom, the opportunity created for Montenegro by the potential of its new territories and an extended period of peace could not be fully realised.

Montenegro, gradually emerging into the dynamic environment of early twentieth century Europe, also faced the converse danger of being overwhelmed by modernity before it could catch up sufficiently. Prince Nikola was well aware of the fragility of the nation's equilibrium and the destructive potential of too rapid change in a traditional society.

One often noted detrimental change was the undermining of the simplicity and austerity of the people. Foreign Minister Vuković observed that the centuries-old Spartan bravery of the tribal vojvodas was being slowly eroded: *"Some vojvodas come to Cetinje during the winter when travelling is risky, expecting a medal, reward or some other promotion."*[35] The idiosyncratic ruler actually encouraged them by giving gifts of money, much to the dismay of his ministers who reminded him that the state could not afford such royal largesse. Nikola was as discomfited as the vojvodas by this and one year he even resorted to a ruse to avoid the embarrassment of not giving the vojvodas their expected gifts: he took them off to Rijeka Crnojevića for a holiday! The people, however, did not appreciate this newfound thrift and came to the conclusion that the miserly ministers were getting in the way of the Prince's natural generosity. Reconciling the old and the new world would not be easy.

Vuković, while seeing much that was good in Old Montenegro, was pessimistic for the future:

"The harmony which exists between the ruler, the organs of power and the people will in future seem like a fairytale, but it is a genuine harmony that has reached an ideal level. How long can this ideal state last is not difficult to predict because our too patriarchal regime has no future."[36]

Nonetheless, a good deal had been achieved and, in 1902, Wyon and Prance saw grounds for considerable optimism: *"Under Prince Nikola's fatherly care the country improves in a wonderful manner from year to year. Roads are planned to connect the whole land, which only lack of funds are hindering from completion, and a railway is projected to connect the towns of Nikšić, Podgorica, and Rijeka Crnojevića with Bar and the sea . . . When Prince Nikola is called to his fathers, his son, Prince Danilo, will worthily carry on the work so nobly begun by his father, for he is a man imbued with the ideas of Western improvements and civilisation."*[37]

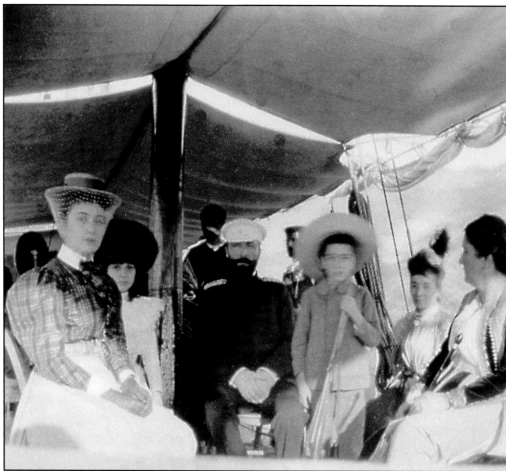

(Above) From left to right: Ksenija, Vjera, Princess Ana's husband, Franz Josef of Battenberg, Petar and Milena during a boat trip on Lake Skadar. (Below) Petar in Rijeka Crnojevića. (Left) Nikola and Milena's youngest child with his bodyguard and (top left) Petar and Franz Josef. (Above left) Petar in national costume.

(Left) Prince Petar in Darmstadt with Ana and Franz Josef.
(Below left) Cetinje: Petar in his salon in the Palace.
(Bottom) Petar with his parents in Nice, France, in 1902.

Both Petar's parents had realised that by not educating his two elder brothers abroad, their upbringing as future rulers had suffered. However, Milena was against Petar being educated in Russia. She remembered the untimely death of daughter Marija from tuberculosis, brought on, she believed, by the unhealthy climate in St. Petersburg. Nikola had already gone some way to gaining Tsar Nikolai II's consent for Petar to be educated in Russia, but Milena's worries saw the plan vetoed. Instead, in 1903, Petar was sent to Heidelberg, Germany, to be educated, where his sister Ana, living nearby in Darmstadt, could keep an eye on his progress.

Petar still managed to cause his parents some worry. Fortunately, it was not illness, but the typical problems of a teenager. In April, 1907, Nikola's trusted adjutant, Ilija Jovanović, was instructed to go to Heidelberg as Ana had sent word that Petar's studies were not going well. Jovanović asked to be given the authority to treat Petar as if he were his own son, to which Nikola fully agreed: *"I ask that you do so and I would damn you if you did not! Franz and Ana are there too, and if you need you can write to me personally."*

Jovanović caught up with Petar in Darmstadt. The young Prince was not pleased to see him as his previous perjanik, Djuro, had allowed him to do pretty much as he pleased. Jovanović was shocked at the state Petar was in: *"I found him in a bad way, he could not have looked any worse if he was a criminal. His hair was uncut and his nails were like eagle's talons. I asked him, 'For Gods sake, Prince, what has come over you'."* Petar had no reply so Jovanović took him to the local barber shop to be cleaned up. When they returned to Darmstadt Ana exclaimed: *"God praise you Ilija, lets hope that Petar will get better now."* A few days later Jovanović took Petar back to school in Heidelberg.

A month later the headmaster reported a big improvement, but Jovanović was soon dismayed again when he found out that Petar had been playing truant; worse still, he discovered that it had been going on for sometime. He confronted his charge and, for a fortnight, all seemed well again. However, when Petar lapsed back into his old habit, Jovanović decided he had to investigate. The reason was soon uncovered when he tracked him down to a local café, where he saw him exchanging intimate glances with one of the waitresses. He had found a girlfriend and his studies were suffering Jovanović concluded. No doubt to the young man's anguish, he did what any self respecting guardian would have. *"I am going to end this"* he said to himself.

Jovanović's firmness won Petar's respect and his studies improved. In June he accompanied him to the state exams in Studgart. They travelled together by train, arriving the evening before the exams began. Petar's nervousness prevented him from sleeping but in the morning, after a coffee, he was ready to do his best. At 2pm Petar returned from his trial with good news. *"I passed with flying colours"* he declared. They returned to Darmstadt to give Franz and Ana the good news, then travelled onto Venice to meet Nikola, Milena, Ksenija and Vjera. The family enjoyed a week long holiday in Venice to celebrate, after which they returned to Cetinje.

(Left) From left to right: Princess Zorka's daughter, Jelena Karadjordjević of Serbia, with her aunts Vjera, Ksenija and Professor Kovačević, tutor to the Royal Family, enjoying the pleasures of the cold Montenegrin winters. (Above left) Jelena Karadjordjević, Vjera, kneeling, and, behind her, Ksenija. (Above) From left to right: Vjera, Jelena Karadjordjević and Princess Milica-Yutta (Crown Prince Danilo's German born wife) during a trip to Italy.

(This page and page overleaf) Photographs taken during a visit by Vjera and Milica-Yutta to the Roman ruins of 'Old Bar'. (Left) The royal party with their bodyguards circumvent a local stream. (Below) Milica-Yutta and Vjera with the Archbishop of Bar and (bottom) a local Moslem woman with, from left to right, Vjera, Lady-in-waiting Miss Daubne, Milica-Yutta and Adjutant Popović.

Old Bar: (Above) A playful Princess Vjera poses amongst the bushes. (Left) From left to right: Vjera, Milica-Yutta and Miss Daubne amongst the Roman ruins, with the dramatic backdrop of Montenegro's karstic mountain ranges in the distance. (Below left) Princess Vjera and Princess Milica-Yutta with Bar's Catholic Archbishop. (Below right) The Concordat with the Vatican recognising Montenegrin jurisdiction over the Catholic Archbishopric of Bar. It was an important agreement as the country's territorial expansion brought with it Catholic minorities. (Facing page) Two striking portraits of Princess Vjera. Her mother, Princess Milena, preferred to wear the traditional national costume, but gave freedom to the daughters to wear beautiful western style clothes. Here, to compliment the outfit, Vjera wears a fashionable, wide-brimmed hat worn at an angle, trimmed with flowers and held by a decorative hat-pin.

A portrait of Princess Vjera taken in her salon. The youngest, most petite and, many felt, the prettiest of the Prince's daughters. Despite her obvious appeal, Vjera never married. Not having added to the family's dynastic connections, she contributed in other ways and was active in hospital and aid work during the Balkan wars and World War One. Like her elder siblings she was creatively inclined and a keen artist.

Facing page: (Top) Vjera's bedroom and salon. (Bottom) Princess Ksenija and, to her right, her salon and bedroom. Both of the youngest daughters had their own living space within the Palace, pleasant but modest, comprising of a bedroom and a salon for entertaining guests.

The Country & Its People

A doubling of territory in 1878 meant that Montenegro had grown, from a centre of resistance to foreign domination, into a multi-cultural and multi-denominational nation with several urban centres and a short stretch of Adriatic coastline. The Museum of King Nikola I has preserved many fascinating photographs from the late nineteenth and early twentieth century.

156

(Right) The Zetski Dom Theatre as it is today.
(Bottom) Cetinje's main street around 1900. Although the capital had grown from a village into a pleasant town, it still had a population of only around five thousand.
(Below) A view of the Palace around 1900.
(Facing page) Some of the local inhabitants viewing Cetinje from its surrounding mountains and (inset) veterans of the 1876/77 wars in national costume.

(Above) Officers and (above right) women in Montenegrin national costume. Many foreigners considered it the most splendid of all Balkan national costumes. (Right) Podgorica. Montenegro's greatest acquisition in 1878's Treaty of Berlin was the long coveted Podgorica, situated in the fertile Plain of Zeta. One of the country's few urban centres, it was even proposed by Parliament to move the capital there. However, Prince Nikola considered that a premature move and far too expensive. Podgorica, nonetheless, was the natural economic centre of the country and eventually became the capital in the twentieth century. (Below) A Montenegrin hotel. Foreign visitors noted that the facilities available were very basic but the hospitality very welcoming and (below right) a typical 'road'. Prior to Prince Nikola's road building efforts the country's roads were little more than horse tracks.

(Inset) Montenegro's main prison in Podgorica. The penal system was a distinctive and rather relaxed affair. At anyone time the prison population was less than a hundred. The majority of inmates had been involved in blood feuds, a crime but not a matter of personal shame. Harsher punishment was reserved for thieves and political agitators, some of whom would be made to wear shackles and be kept apart from the other prisoners. (Above) The male and female prisoners were allowed to socialise on holidays and feast days. In this photograph they are dancing the *Kolo*, the national dance.
(Left) Ulcinj bazaar. Montenegro's southernmost town was also its second port. Its potential was, however, undeveloped and the life of its mainly Albanian population continued much as it always had.

159

(Above and above left) Four views of Rijeka Crnojevića and its people. A favourite place of retreat for the Royal Family. Until the economic influence of Podgorica attracted trade away, the town was the sight of Montenegro's busiest and most colourful market days. (Left) Princess Milena in her salon in the royal residence in town.
(Facing page) Views of the town's royal residences. The main photograph was taken from across the lake looking toward Prince Danilo I's residence, which was later given to Crown Prince Danilo. The insets show past and present views of Prince Nikola's residence and, inset top, the royal carriage.

A view of Lake Skadar as it runs into Rijeka Crnojevića.
Princess Milena during an outing on the lake: (top) At the front holding an umbrella is the Lady-in-waiting, then Princess Milena and, at the very back, Djela Vuković, wife of Foreign Minister Gavro Vuković. (Above) The party relaxing after lunch, having been joined by Princess Ksenija, seated second from the right.

Milena with her pet dog, Vasko. (Above left and above right) The Royal Family in the sweltering heat of summer. Foreign visitors were struck by the amount of clothing Montenegrins wore during the summer months. The striking use of umbrellas appeared more logical; they were of great usefulness in providing shade and protection from the intense heat.
Facing page: Photographs taken during hunting trips. (Top right) The perjaniks are in the foreground with members of the Royal Family visible in the distance. (Top left) Montenegrins were known for their height and athleticism, which this party of perjaniks and younger additions to the hunt confirm. (Bottom) Danilo, seated, with Nikola and Mirko in Rijeka Crnojevića. Both Nikola and Danilo were renowned for their skills as marksmen.

(Main picture) A view *en route* to Vladika Rade's mausoleum at the peak of Mount Lovćen.
(Left) Mirko enjoying lunch in a restaurant above Cetinje. The beer he is drinking is from the brewery in Nikšić.
(Facing page) Princess Ana's husband, Franz Josef, during a hunting trip with the royal perjaniks.

(Right) The Palace as it is today, a museum to the nation's royal past. The scene of much of Montenegro's history, the visitor is struck by the simplicity and functionality of its exterior, that of a pleasant but not exceptionally large townhouse. The interiors reveal a fair degree of opulence, but the modest and homely nature of life in the royal household is apparent. (Below) The Royal Family with friends and ladies-in-waiting photographed during an afternoon of tennis.
(Facing page) Cetinje Park, where the children of Prince Nikola and Prince Petar Karadjordjević played together; idyllic days in the dynastic history of Montenegro. In the background *Orlov Krš*, the monument to Vladika Danilo I, is visible. (Inset) A nineteenth century postcard depicting a typical Montenegrin family.

Befriending the sons of "Europe's evil guest Orkan."

"Oh my mountains! What do you think of my journey? Is it not true that there is no shame in going to the great city of Istanbul? They replied: 'Of course we are not ashamed! You are going with head held high to see the Turkish Sultan, not to kiss his robe nor bring him taxes. You are without fault our son. The Emperor of Turkey will see as you arrive Tsar Dušan's eagle above your head, we have waited five hundred years to see that'." (Istanbul Diary, 1883). Prince Nikola's diaries from his state visits to Istanbul in the 1880's and 1890's provide insights into his development as both ruler and diplomat, and also show that the Prince hoped age-old foes might just be able to become friends. In contrast, Nikola's meeting with Queen Victoria in 1898 was very much a one-off affair; the occasion for a cordial meeting between two very different monarchs who, by all accounts, got along remarkably well. Whether in Istanbul or Windsor, Nikola managed to raise the Montenegrin banner in the hope that good personal relations would lead to political and economic benefits.

Given that Montenegro's oft-stated historic aim was the demise of the Ottoman Empire in Europe, it was only natural that Prince Nikola's diary from his first state visit to Istanbul, in the autumn of 1883, displays a degree of nervousness. Politically it was a sound enough undertaking and could even be presented as a matter of prestige: the first ruler of the recognised Montenegrin state had been invited by the leader of the imperial power which had historically claimed the mountaineers as their subjects. However, Nikola was concerned that South Slav sentiment could be offended and he noted that in Kotor *"they gave me a cold reception as if I had guilt toward them . . ."* Adding to his foreboding was an unfortunate incident during the sea voyage. Passing through Greek waters they hit and sank a Greek boat killing two sailors. Of the two surviving children, one had been orphaned by the accident, and they took him to the island of Corfu. Out of pity Nikola gave him some money.

Nikola was a poor sea traveller and spent as little time on boats as possible. The sea voyage was, therefore, an unwelcome necessity, but also a chance to broaden his geographical horizons. He was surprised by the appearance of the Greek islands: *"I imagined the Greek Islands differently: I had envisioned them as verdant, flower laden and beautiful, but they are sad and bare . . .*

170

I was angered by the Greeks because they did not take part in the last war, but I can see now that if they had, they would have been defeated. It is difficult to defend these faraway islands without great naval power." As they neared Istanbul he mused over the sad history of conflict between nations and the futility of war: *"God gave intellect to people to make agreements and anticipate evil."*

Nikola's apprehensions and a degree of loneliness (he had left Princess Milena and the family behind in Montenegro) caused him sleeplessness. Perhaps partly for this reason, his first impressions of Istanbul were somewhat reactionary. Apart from Dolmabac Palace, which surpassed his expectations, he was disappointed by the general squalor.

The youthful Nikola had found Paris very much of a culture shock, but the equally cosmopolitan Turkish capital, which was a poor and famously unhygienic city, provided an even more unwelcome surprise: *"Oh Istanbul! You scoundrel filled with of all kinds of dirt. When I was forced to walk your streets I had to hold my nose . . ."*

By way of contrast, Sultan Abdul Hamid II's charm made a good impression on the Montenegrin party. At their first reception his inquiries after the Prince's family, and his tactful recognition of Montenegro's territorial gains from Turkey, put Nikola at ease. It was especially pleasing that the absent Princess Milena was given a fulsome compliment; the shrewd Sultan no doubt being well informed

A view of Dolmabac Palace and (below) Istanbul viewed from the Bosphorus in the 1880's. (Facing page) Prince Nikola, Princess Milena and Prince Mirko during the state visit to the Ottoman capital in 1899.

of how close the Montenegrin royal couple were: *"I am following her work closely, please believe me, for my representatives were thriving whenever she acted as regent . . . Please tell her that I admire her."* Nikola's first impressions of Abdul Hamid were very positive: *"He is extremely capable and I saw that he is well informed and works hard. I have no doubt that he will solve Turkey's political problems no matter how complicated."*

After his initial misgivings for the state visit, Nikola could consider the whole endeavour a great success. Political issues were largely left aside as Abdul Hamid did his best to woo the Montenegrins with lavish gifts. It was politics of the old style. Abdul Hamid treated Nikola rather like a vassal ruler, to be seduced with compliments and pampered with gifts, to which the Prince and his entourage were more than susceptible. On the whole, both sides felt they had benefited and the Montenegrins relaxed enough to enjoy themselves. They even found time to enjoy the sights of the capital. Nikola's relative, Blažo, found the women of Istanbul particularly attractive and, with the aid of a pair of binoculars, viewed as many of them as he could find. He even composed a poem to their beauty which Nikola included in his diary.

"I am leaving with Maman for Istanbul.
We are taking this trip to thank HRH The Sultan for all the good he has done for us. Maman and I feel a real need to give him our heartfelt thanks."
Prince Nikola, August 12 [August 24] , 1899.

Istanbul. In the foreground is the Hamidie Mosque and, to the left, Yildiz Kiosk, the residence of Sultan Abdul Hamid II (above). Abdul Hamid's fear of assassination led him to construct his own labryinthine residence full of secret passages, the layout of which was only known to the Sultan himself.

Yildis et Mosquée Hamidie

It was not until 1899 that Nikola and Milena would see Istanbul together. Times had changed and the dark underside of Hamidian rule had become infamous through the Armenian massacres. Nikola's diary reveals his increasingly philosophical and conservative attitude toward life and politics, as well as a growing degree of detachment from the minutiae of government affairs. He was well aware of the true nature of his host's rule, but continued to show a personal liking for Abdul Hamid. Nikola had ample reason for generosity of spirit: his eldest son, Danilo, had just married the German Princess Augusta Charlotte of Mecklenburg-Strelitz (who became Milica-Yutta with her conversion to Orthodox Christianity), and Montenegro's international standing had continued to grow. Most notably, the previous year Nikola had made a successful state visit to England and gained the admiration of Queen Victoria.

The diary is also of interest for being dedicated to Nikola's daughter Milica and Milica-Yutta (nicknamed respectively by Nikola as Mika and Misja). The mood is humorous and irreverent; Nikola seems at ease with himself and the world and greatly enjoying family life.

Accompanying the royal couple were: second son Mirko, Foreign Minister Gavro Vuković and his wife Djela, Commander Mitar Martinović and Adjutant M. Vukotić. Tutor to the royal children Charles Puigget joined the party as Milena's secretary, along with lady-in-waiting Miss Noikom and Doctor Perazić.

They left on August 24, 1899, after a tearful parting from youngest son Petar: *"We left Cetinje at five o'clock this morning. Our little Pero [Petar] was very upset. If I had not told him the story of how the Sultan would have kept him in one of his schools if he came with us, his mother would still be occupied with him. Lying in his bed, rubbing his eyes from sleep, Pero called to me and asked: 'Papa do you think the Sultan would keep me there?' I replied: 'He certainly would and that would be a great honour and joy for us. Come with us darling.' Pero cried out: 'No, no I don't want to.' He is pleased to stay behind now. I know this because there were no more tears when he hugged me as we left."*

From Cetinje it took an hour and a half to reach Rijeka Crnojevića, then it was onto Crown Prince Danilo's residence, Topolica, nearby to the port of Bar, for dinner and an overnight stay to avoid leaving on Friday the thirteenth. To allay Nikola's superstitions they did not board the military cruiser *Ismir*, sent by Sultan Abdul Hamid, until just after midnight. While describing the departure, Nikola's affection for Milica-Yutta allows him to poke fun at her: *"I was a little bit uneasy at the foot of the stairs, worrying how solid they were and seeing the Admiral who waited at the bottom. I thought that the Admiral was at least 131 Kilos, I am nearly 120, and my little darling Misja is a bit plump (Please allow me to say that very quietly). If those steps start cracking under us . . . I commanded the Admiral to climb up before my daughter-in-law, who is rather more nimble."*

Obviously delighted at Danilo's choice of bride, Nikola also took the opportunity to consider names for their offspring. As they passed by Elbasan on the Albanian coastline he suggested Kosara (the Bulgarian wife of the unfortunate Zetan ruler Jovan Vladimir, 970-1016) for their first daughter: *"I like that name very much. If I had a granddaughter, and if Misja does not mind, I would give her that name."*

The sea voyage began well but Nikola's concern for Milena preoccupied him: *"The sea is calm without a ripple on it. Your mother is feeling so well that she goes to the deck between nine and ten, smiling and interested in everything. Dear, good Maman is full of the joy of life, she who started this trip with such fear . . . A great strain could maybe even kill her. So, night and day with a map in my hand, I am studying for a place where we can hide if need be, because I do not want to expose her to any danger. Her appetite is fine and the cuisine is good. When I tell Maman to return by train, via Istanbul and Bucharest, she does not want to listen and says that this way is the best for her. I would agree, so long as if on the way back the sea is as calm as it is now."* However, the voyage was not without worrying incident: the royal party had to change boats because of damage to the *Ismir*, which was serious enough that it could even have sunk. Nikola suppressed his fear of the sea and even ridiculed his own modest bravery at being the last to leave the *Ismir*.

The party arrived as planned in Istanbul, the day before the anniversary celebrations for Sultan Abdul Hamid's accession. Nikola was greeted as cordially as he had been on his previous visit. For a man as suspicious as Abdul Hamid, one might have surmised a glimmer of genuine friendship behind the offers of gifts: a new and larger boat and a horse for Mirko from the Sultan's own stable.

Nonetheless, both rulers were old hands at flattery. Abdul Hamid, the master of playing the Balkan powers one

A scene filled with the charm and, to Europeans of the period, the other worldliness of the 'mysterious east'.(Above) Istanbul 1900. A vendor of the famed, and very strong, coffee enjoyed throughout the Ottoman Empire.

against another to maintain his grip in Albania and Macedonia, told Nikola: *"You are the only one whose politics is real and sincere towards myself and the Empire."* With equal dexterity Nikola recorded: *"These kind words went straight to my heart. He asked how the journey went . . . and on this occasion I thanked him for his gift of the 'Timsa' boat. He replied: 'It is too small, I am going to give you another, bigger, so you can travel more comfortably with your family'."* Despite Turkey's political troubles, Nikola noted: *"It is strange that I found the Sultan not only more open and younger than during my last visit in 1883, but also much more cheerful and in a better mood than then."*

Inviting Nikola to view the processions before Friday evening prayers, Abdul Hamid made the gesture of not leading the procession of the Women of the Harem and, instead, joined his guest on the Palace balcony. Nikola found plenty to admire in the beauty and precision of the military parade: *"Especially the battalion composed of my friends the Albanians. I could not believe my eyes when I saw those people marching in step. What! Albanians and discipline together! Who would ever say so! After the parade I congratulated the Sultan."*

Nikola's jovial mood was broken on his return to the royal couple's rooms where he found an unwell Milena: *"Maman showed me her fingertips which had turned blue. I know that symptom, when it appears she usually has a high temperature and has to stay in bed for forty-eight hours. She went to bed at 3pm and I just had a nap. Tonight we will see how she is. At 7pm I took her temperature, 38.8 degrees. It is useless to tell her that she should eat something. So I left and went down to our apartments. We dined silently after which I returned to Maman. At 10pm her temperature had risen further so I called Doctor Perazić. However, looking at the thermometer he shouted loudly: '37.5!' Then Maman added: 'It is true.' During these crises there is unfortunately no help I can give, but I am used to it. Let God help her."*

By the following morning Milena had recovered and preparations were made for that evening's dinner with the Sultan. Nikola took the opportunity, in his diary to tease Mika and Misja for not sharing Milena's stoic attitude toward life: *"You would do very well, my little darlings, if you had Maman's will and courage. At exactly 2pm, despite her fever, difficult night and tiredness, she was receiving with charm and kindness the diplomats and their wives. The reception lasted three hours and, besides, she still intends to go to tonight's dinner."* The evening, too, was a great success. After the meal Abdul Hamid invited Mirko to display his musical talent. Nikola, aware of his son's pleasure at being the centre of attention, knew Mirko would give an enthusiastic performance: *"And this one [Mirko], of hardly a modest nature, agrees without hesitation, imagining that to lead the blind it is enough to be shortsighted. Still, he played very well."* Abdul Hamid's son returned the compliment by playing

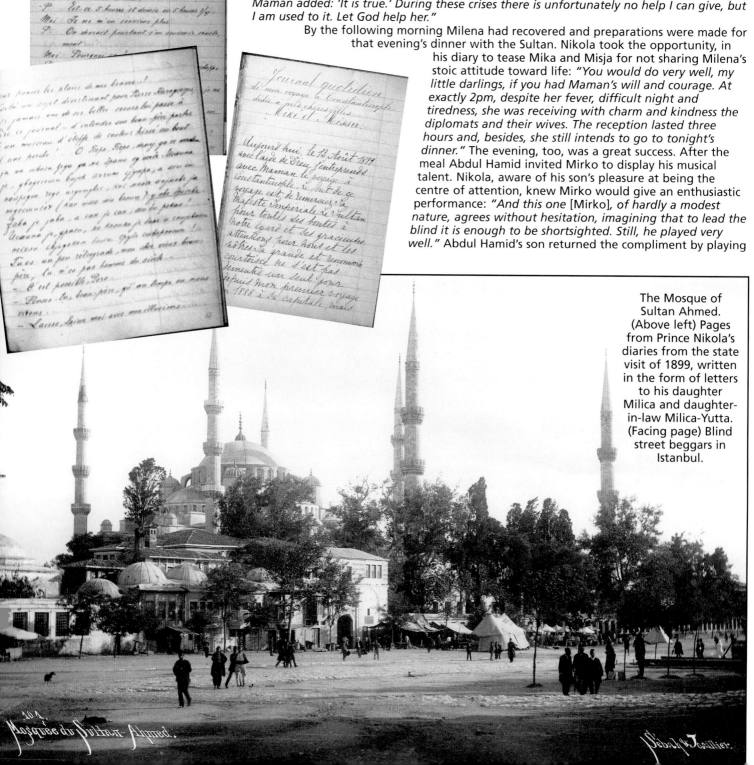

The Mosque of Sultan Ahmed. (Above left) Pages from Prince Nikola's diaries from the state visit of 1899, written in the form of letters to his daughter Milica and daughter-in-law Milica-Yutta. (Facing page) Blind street beggars in Istanbul.

the Montenegrin national anthem and both were given awards for their artistic endeavours.

Milena, still very much the village girl at heart who was always most comfortable when in Montenegro, had coped remarkably well during the visit. However, the thought of visiting the imperial harem proved too much for her.

Anticipating her trepidation, Nikola had made the arrangements beforehand and a bemused Milena understandably tried to avoid the engagement.

"You told me that today I have to pay a visit to the Sultan, but do I have to go to the harem? Is there anybody actually there?"

"Of course, the Sultan's wives."

"Is the Sultan going to be there?"

"Probably yes."

"Would you come with me?"

"I would volunteer but they do not let men in there."

"I hope the devil eats their dinner! Do other princesses, when they visit Istanbul, go there?"

"It depends. Those who want to go ask for permission and those who do not ask do not go."

"I did not ask to go!"

With a most serious look Nikola told his wife: "Of course you did."

"Where and when for God's sake?"

"I think it was the other night, you said you would love to see the harem."

"If I did let my eyes fall out!"

"Do not swear!"

"But I did not man! I know that I did not!"

"You forgot."

"Forgot! For God's sake are you insane!?"

"You have to go because you promised."

"Listen to him! I am not going there."

Nikola realised his ruse had run into trouble: "Aha, this is serious. Now I have to change my

approach, and slowly I tell her that it is the custom and that I asked for the visit . . . Later I found Maman busy with her toilette; quietly I was dying of laughter because of her scruples about visiting the harem. However, I did not dare to say anything fearing that she would again refuse to go . . . I told her, 'Now you are ready, good luck, you look fine in that dress'."

Fortunately Milena thoroughly enjoyed herself as Nikola found out on her return: "We had dinner without Maman and she returned after 9pm in a good mood, talking excitedly about what she had seen. She was delighted and I thought it was a good moment to tease her, but she only laughed. She said the Sultana Valide [Sultan Abdul Hamid's mother] was very kind to her, holding her hands and even caressing her face, repeating many times 'Gizen, Gizen' when Maman told her that Jabe [Jelena Karadjordjević], her granddaughter, had turned fifteen . . . During the visit the Sultana Valide mentioned that she had met Stane and had found her very beautiful and liked her very much. Maman saw the Sultan's daughters and many other ladies; some were playing musical instruments, others dancing, while they were serving refreshing drinks and marvellous coffee. One beautiful black woman with a wonderful voice was singing Arabic songs and many black men were serving the ladies."

For Nikola and Milena it had been a rare joint state visit and one which they both thoroughly enjoyed. Nikola could appreciate the company of Abdul Hamid and the considerable generosity he showed toward the Montenegrins without losing perspective. Nikola was fully aware of the realities of his host's often brutal rule and their friendship was strictly a political one, but his feelings for this rather strange man were genuinely cordial. They parted with the usual mutual flattery: "Sire, when I return to our dark mountains, this jewellery that you have given me will illuminate them." Abdul Hamid replied: "Your beautiful mountains will always be bright as long as you are their Master." Nikola saw the humour in it all and noted in his diary: "Was that not kind! In future nobody should dare to say bad things about my neighbour and friend the Sultan." Of course, Nikola personally abhorred Abdul Hamid's brutal treatment of the Armenians and dreamed of liberating the Empire's Balkan provinces, but he could also understand the many difficulties Abdul Hamid had to deal with. In fact it was only natural, given their two countries historic relations, that Nikola had a feeling and admiration for both the Sultan and the Turks.

For Nikola the Turks were "an elite, brave and noble race" which was no longer Montenegro's deadly enemy, but rather the victim of an unjust and hypocritical world order. As he departed Istanbul, Nikola pondered if the great war of the 1870's could have been avoided: "I think so, yes, of course: if Turkey had been better advised by the occupier [Austria-Hungary] of Bosnia-Herzegovina and if Cyprus wine was not so admired in Windsor Castle, an unfortunate war for Turkey could have been avoided." Nikola's empathy was excited by the struggles of the brave underdog the Ottoman Empire had become, for the crumbling state and the man that held it all together. Another, more humble, Montenegrin shared Nikola's views. Djuro, the servant assigned to the royal party during their stay, had become a true Turcophile during his years in Istanbul, and in his eyes Abdul Hamid's only shortcoming was his most un-Montenegrin lack of inches!

Cetinje to Windsor.

'I must now' whispered His Highness laughingly, *'compose my face and assume that expression of serious solemnity which I understand is correct in England!'*
Prince Nikola on his arrival in England: May, 1898.

Montenegro's political relations with Britain had not been close or particularly cordial. British imperial interests and Montenegro's allegiance to Russia hardly made friendship likely and, naturally enough, the interests of the tiny Balkan state hardly figured much in British considerations.

Relations improved after the country's recognition in 1878 and, soon after, with the election of a Liberal Prime Minister, William Ewart Gladstone. When difficulties arose over the implementation of the Treaty of Berlin, it was Gladstone who stepped in and helped Montenegro secure its two Adriatic ports of Bar and Ulcinj.

Through Gladstone and other vocal supporters of the Balkan states, notably Alfred Tennyson, whose famous poem glorified its historic heroism, late Victorian Britain took a romantic view of Montenegro. Gladstone sent Prince Nikola editions of his political works and Lord Tennyson his poetry, while the Prince reciprocated with his own literary works as gifts.

However, political relations were still rather ambivalent and an official visit was the ideal stage for the loquacious Prince's diplomatic talents. Nikola's lively wit and his light social touch could prove the ideal way to charm Britain's matriarch.

Nikola had dined with Queen Victoria in Nice, France, in March 1897, shortly before Princess Ana's wedding to Prince Franz Josef Battenberg in May, and dynastic relations had been steadily improving thereafter. Importantly, Ana's wedding had provided a family link through the marriage of Franz Josef's elder brothers: Henry to Victoria's daughter, Beatrice and Louis to her granddaughter, Victoria. Henry had been particularly close to the Queen until his death in 1896.

The first official Montenegrin visit to England had also taken place in 1897 when Crown Prince Danilo and Princess Jelena, by then Princess of Naples, were invited to Queen Victoria's Diamond Jubilee celebrations in June.

The following year the Queen's representative, Mr Raikes, arrived in Cetinje on St. George's Day, appropriately enough the patron saint of the Petrović clan, to present Prince Nikola with the insignia of a Knight Commander

of the Royal Victorian Order.

After the official banquet, Nikola asked the British Ambassador to Cetinje, R.J. Kennedy, to request the official permission from London to pay his respects to the Queen in person. Nikola told the Ambassador that it was a visit he had long dreamed of making.

Kennedy immediately sent a telegram and the following day an affirmative reply was received from Lord Salisbury. Nikola was invited to meet the Queen, either at Windsor Castle before she left for Scotland, in which case he would have to leave almost immediately, or to wait until late June, when she returned from Scotland. Nikola decided upon the former.

Preparations were hurriedly made to leave Cetinje for the Adriatic coast, as their boat was scheduled to leave Kotor on Tuesday, May 10. The party left Cetinje at 4am on the Tuesday morning, their personal belongings having been sent to the coast the previous Sunday.

Ambassador Kennedy described how he and his wife made haste to join the departing Prince: *"The long line of carriages rattling through the silent streets of the little capital, saluted by the faithful Montenegrins who had risen from their beds in order to wish their sovereign God-speed on his journey to unknown regions."*

The journey down to the coast was filled with camaraderie and Nikola certainly enjoyed himself: *"We were a cheery party as we drove away from Cetinje . . . On reaching the Bukoivica, which the traveller must pass between Cetinje and Kotor, the Prince left his carriage and made a short cut on foot, swinging over the rocks with that easy yet rapid stride so characteristic of all Montenegrins . . . looking as he moved along in his white tunic and scarlet and gold Zouave jacket, the 'beau idéal' of a mountain chieftain. At the village of Njeguši . . . we halted a few minutes to rest the horses and to drink a cup of coffee; then, crossing the frontier, we drove rapidly down the serpentine road to Kotor which, with its lovely bay, lay in full view three thousand feet below us. The Austrian Lloyd Steamer 'Graf Wurmbrund', specially chartered for the voyage to Fiume by the Prince of Montenegro, was waiting for us . . . at 9.30am on May 10 we were under weigh."*

One of the benefits of being Prince of Montenegro was the freedom it afforded the ruler. Nikola had none of the bureaucracy and protocol which European royalty had to contend with in their official duties. The visit to England was a personal initiative and, in effect, a holiday to a country he had never seen before. Nikola could,

figuratively and literally, travel light: the suite accompanying him to London consisted only of his aide-de-camp, his orderly officer and two servants.

(Above and left) Pages from the official programme for Queen Victoria's Diamond Jubilee in 1897, to which Montenegro's Crown Prince Danilo was invited. (Below left) 'From Cettinje to Windsor', a private edition commemorating Prince Nikola's state visit to Great Britain in May 1898. Facing page: (Top) A signed portrait of Queen Victoria commemorating her Diamond Jubilee, 1837-1897. (Bottom) The Queen during the celebrations at St. Paul's Cathedral on June 22, 1897.

The sea voyage to Fiume was a pleasant one. Nikola took the opportunity to spend a day with Prince Ferdinand of Bulgaria at the resort of Abazia, Croatia, after which the party met up again in Vienna. From where Nikola went onto Frankfurt to visit Princess Ana and Prince Franz Josef.

Then it was onto England via Brussels and across the English Channel from Calais. Nikola's fear of sea travel worried Ambassador Kennedy: *"I knew how much the Prince dreaded the ordeal of crossing 'votre terrible Manche' [the terrible English Channel]. I was filled with anxiety lest he should insist upon waiting at Calais for fine weather, and thus upset and complicate all the arrangements that had been made for his proper reception in England."*

Fortune favoured the Ambassador and it was on a clear and sunny day that they departed from Calais aboard the *Lord Warden*. Nikola was not a bad sailor in the sense of sea sickness, rather he had *"an undefined horror of being surrounded by a vast expanse of water, out of sight of land."*

On his Mediterranean travels that fear had given Nikola an excellent view of the Greek and Dalmatian Islands as he always insisted on sailing as close to land as was possible. Crossing the English Channel on such a clear summer's day he could, at least,

Queen Victoria with Franz Josef of Battenberg and his wife, Montenegro's Princess Ana. Franz Josef was related to Victoria through the marriage of his elder brothers: Louis to Queen Victoria's granddaughter Victoria, Henry to her favourite daughter, Beatrice.

take comfort from the view of the White Cliffs of Dover.

By the time they had docked, Nikola, who had changed into his national costume in preparation for the official reception, was in an excellent mood and joked: *"I must now compose my face and assume that expression of serious solemnity which I understand is correct in England!"*

As they disembarked the guns of Dover Castle thundered the salute to the first reigning Prince of Montenegro ever to set foot on British soil. The guard of honour presented arms as the Prince passed down the line and into the royal saloon carriage, which would take him to London's Charing Cross Station.

The journey to London allowed Nikola to view the beauties of the 'Garden of England', which Ambassador Kennedy observed *"delighted beyond measure the poetical and artistic sense of the Prince of Montenegro."* London, too, made a strong impression on Nikola: *"There are more omnibuses in one big London thoroughfare than in all Paris"* he observed.

Just after 5pm on Saturday, May 14, they arrived at Charing Cross Station. The Duke of York was waiting on the platform with a guard of honour composed of the Grenadier Guards. He had met the Montenegrin Royal Family some years previously as Nikola's guest in Cetinje and greeted him warmly. After the official introductions the Duke escorted Nikola to the royal carriage. As they left a small crowd of well-wishers, as well as the simply curious, cheered enthusiastically. Then it was onto Buckingham Palace via Trafalgar Square and Pall Mall. At the Palace the Prince of Wales paid a brief visit, after which Nikola asked to be allowed to dine alone after two tiring days of travel.

The following morning Nikola took the train from Paddington Station to Windsor. He was welcomed at Windsor Station by the Duke of Connaught and the Second Battalion of the Scots Guards playing the Montenegrin National Anthem.

On arrival at Windsor Castle, Nikola, escorted by the Duke of Connaught, was met by Queen Victoria at the Sovereign's Entrance. Victoria recorded her impressions of Nikola: *"He was wearing his beautiful, picturesque national dress . . . I found the Prince most kind and pleasant and pleased with everything."*

Nikola then joined Victoria in the Oak Dining Room for lunch, after which Victoria asked to speak with Ambassador Kennedy and the Montenegrin aide-de-camps Captain Radović and Lieutenant Zerović. The afternoon was taken up with a walk on the Castle terrace and attendance at St George's Chapel. It was Nikola's first experience of a church service in the English Protestant tradition and one which he greatly enjoyed.

Dinner, at 9pm, was the first real opportunity for Victoria and Nikola to converse. They seem to have got on very well and talked throughout the hour long meal.

The following day was busy and enjoyable. Nikola was given a guided tour of the State Apartments of Windsor Castle, the library and St. George's Hall. Inspecting the barracks of the Second Battalion of the Scots Guard, the Montenegrins took a keen interest. Nikola was highly impressed by the physique and appearance of the battalion. Ambassador Kennedy noted: *"Not a single detail escaped him, and the Colonel and the Adjutant gave him the fullest replies to all his many questions."*

The evening was the occasion for a large dinner party. The highlight came at the end of the meal with the entrance of four bagpipe players. Nikola had hardly been expecting to hear the skirl of bagpipes at the end of his meal, but once his surprise had passed he expressed his

pleasure at the wild strains of the Scots highlanders, which he felt had something in common with the Montenegrin *gusle*. It was a nice touch, particularly as Victoria was especially fond of the Scots.

The only official visit by a reigning Montenegrin prince to Great Britain had been a great success. Although there was no expectation that national relations, economic and political, could be greatly altered by Nikola's visit, it was a noteworthy personal success for him, and a further example of his talent for raising Montenegro's profile in the world at large. He had also enjoyed himself and found much humour in the English character. Ambassador Kennedy observed: *"There is nothing that the Prince likes more than to hear and retail stories more or less apocryphal, I hope, of our insular manners, habits and customs, for I know no one who has a keener sense of humour; but his 'chaff' is never unkind."* Certainly, Victorian England must have been as much of a novelty to Nikola as was the mountain chieftain to his hosts.

Nikola returned to Buckingham Palace where he enjoyed more royal hospitality. However, he was anxious to arrive back in Montenegro in time for the fortieth anniversary celebrations of the Battle of Grahovo and, therefore, he began his homeward journey two days later. From Brussels he sent Ambassador Kennedy a final note of thanks: *"I carry away the happiest recollection of my visit, and all my life I shall be grateful to you for having encouraged me in our conversations in past years to visit your country."*

Whatever else had been achieved, both Nikola and Victoria had found plenty to enjoy in each other's company. It was all very jovial and splendid, the romance of two very different rulers meeting whilst both were at the height of their renown.

A nineteenth century depiction of Windsor Castle, where Queen Victoria entertained Prince Nikola. (Above and facing page, bottom) Pages from 'Cettinje to Windsor', written by the British Ambassador to Montenegro, R.J. Kennedy.

Princess Zorka and the Serbian Pretender.

Chapter IX

Princess Zorka & the Serbian Pretender

I do not like Petar's travels. His way is too dangerous. Why will he not let things take their course?

Prince Nikola Petrović-Njegoš

Were it not for Princess Milena, I would not stay for one more day.

Prince Petar Karadjordjević

Although Prince Aleksandar Karadjordjević had been deposed and exiled from Serbia in 1858, his son, Petar, had long nurtured hopes of returning to reclaim the throne from the Obrenović dynasty. With this aim in mind he had spent much of the family's already diminished wealth in unsuccessful political and military escapades. Petar's failures were not due to a lack of ability or commitment. He had forged a distinguished military career for himself, joining the French Foreign Legion and fighting alongside the French Emperor Louis Napoleon in the Franco-Prussian war of 1870-1871. Most relevantly for his ambitions to the Serbian throne, he had fought as a volunteer in the Bosnia-Herzegovina uprising of the 1870's. His hopes to become the uprising's leader were stifled by Prince Milan Obrenović. Petar's military career testified to his bravery, but his attempts to raise himself to true pretender status had, as yet, achieved little. Worse still, Milan had successfully elevated himself to king in 1882.

Petar's lack of success affected his marriage prospects. A 'penniless prince' with little hope of reclaiming his throne, he could not be considered a good catch. Though he owned property in Romania and Hungary, these would not represent a sufficient dowry to satisfy European royalty with princesses to place on the marriage market. Petar's rather forlorn situation had a certain parallel in Prince Nikola's dynastic concerns. European princesses might be pawns in the royal marriage game, but they were also a responsibility and Nikola had three daughters of marriageable age, Zorka, Milica, Stane, and Marija, who was already thirteen. As their father, he was obliged to find suitable

(Left) Prince Nikola's eldest daughter, Princess Zorka. She was described by Montenegro's Foreign Minister as *"very intelligent, clever, energetic, with a touch of malice that is characteristic of the three eldest daughters . . ."*
(Facing page) The single-minded and determined Prince Petar Karadjordjević in Geneva. As the grandson of the legendary Karadjordje, leader of the Serbian insurrection of 1804, Petar's arrival in Cetinje in March of 1883 was enthusiastically welcomed by the Montenegrin people.

husbands for them but if he was unable to do so, then how could he support them?

Nikola's own finances were insufficient for the task. If, for lack of foreign princes with their own resources, he allowed his daughters to marry Montenegrins, it simply made matters worse. Locals marrying into the Royal Family would only create a multitude of native princes who would expect their father-in-law to provide for them. It would also bring their families too close for comfort to the throne.

The only other alternative was for them to remain unmarried, enter the church and become nuns. In this context, a monastery on the island of Vranjina on Lake Skadar had been earmarked as a permanent home if suitable husbands could not be found.

However, shutting them away from the world would have been a bad mistake on their father's part, for his daughters later proved to be his greatest asset.

The first inkling of the opportunities open to Nikola's vigorous daughters came when Petar became interested in the eldest, Princess Zorka. At their first meeting, Zorka was accompanying her mother in Vichy, France, he quickly realised that she surpassed his expectations. Understandably so: she was charming, intelligent and some twenty years younger than he. Petar lost no time in making his intentions clear.

On hearing the news, Nikola was intrigued but also

Prince Petar was joined in Cetinje by his two brothers, the athletic and well liked Arsen and Djordje, small, thin and of fragile health. Djordje was the family treasurer and restraint on his two more flamboyant siblings.
(Above) In front, from left to right: Princess Persida (Ida) Karadjordjević (the daughter of Prince Petar's eldest sister Poleksija), Princess Zorka holding her first son Djordje, Zorka's eldest child Jelena and Petar's brother Djordje. Behind, on the left, Prince Petar and on the right his brother, Arsen.
(Left) Princess Zorka with her three children. She is holding Djordje, next to her is Aleksandar and behind him is Jelena.
(Facing page) Princess Zorka in her wedding dress.

anxious as the proposal had complex political implications. The immediate problem was the difficulty of contacting Petar or his family, either

182

discreetly or, indeed, at all. Although he lived as an exile, Petar still studiously avoided the agents of King Milan Obrenović, as did the whole family. Petar's father, Prince Aleksandar, was under house arrest in Timisoara, Hungary, and his two brothers lived incognito in Paris. Fortunately, Petar had two old school friends in Cetinje who also happened to be Nikola's relatives: Božo Petrović and Stanko Radonjić. Petar contacted Božo with an enigmatic message: *"I beg Prince Nikola to send me a trustworthy person to give him some confidential information."* Mišo Popović, Nikola's most trusted adjutant, was sent to Hungary on the pretext of buying a horse for the court and while there he obtained Petar's address from Prince Aleksandar. Petar maintained the discretion and simply asked if he could come to Cetinje to visit his old friends.

Nikola still regarded Petar's arrival in Montenegro with some trepidation: he would have to make a decision whether or not to permit the marriage, but the proposal had come out of the blue and he had not had time to weigh the pros and cons. The majority opinion in the court circle was in favour of the marriage, even though it would raise Petar's status and thereby weaken Nikola's chances of ascending the united Montenegrin-Serbian throne. In compensation, the marriage would position Zorka as potential future Queen of Serbia if the much-anticipated fall of the Obrenović dynasty finally came about. So, despite his own misgivings, Nikola finally concluded that the benefits of the marriage outweighed the risks.

Prince Petar arrived in Cetinje in March of 1883, as the guest of Božo Petrović. Both curiosity and expectation were naturally focused on Petar as the grandson of the legendary Karadjordje, the leader of the Serbian insurrection of 1804. Petar was slim and quick-witted, slightly taller than average, with dark hair and the dark skin that revealed the gypsy blood the family was said to have. He also impressed with his good natured and friendly behaviour. Whenever he left Božo's house crowds would gather around him, and he had such an obviously enthusiastic following that some thought Nikola jealous.

The people certainly took to the romantic newcomer who liked and, even more importantly, showed great respect for the Montenegrins; this was not always the case with Serbian visitors. Petar spent his days socialising with the people of Cetinje, his evenings with the Royal Family. At the end of his stay he formally proposed and the wedding was scheduled for the summer.

Political considerations soon crowded in on the wedding plans and rumours started of a hidden agenda behind the marriage: that it represented a blow struck at King Milan and the Obrenović dynasty. Of course, nothing was ever officially admitted, and that, in its turn, only served to stoke the gossip. Eventually, Cetinje's *Glas Crnogorca* published a denial.

Nikola had good reason to show caution, as he explained to Minister Simo Popović: *"King Milan thinks that Prince Petar's wedding is against him and his dynasty, and he cannot forgive me for giving Zorka to Petar . . . even if Petar acted against him in the past, he would not do so again, being my son-in-law . . . Milan*

should put himself in my position."[1]

Although Nikola had some misgivings about the possible consequences of the marriage, he also hoped to make it the occasion of a grand gesture, visibly reconciling the rival dynasties. To this end, Nikola proposed that King Milan be godfather to the pretender's marriage, symbolically uniting the Serb royal houses. Milan simply saw it as an attempt to usurp his throne and his reaction to the news was a characteristic tirade: *"Could not that naked beggar from that hungry gorge spare me? Instead he dared to catch me in his perfidious, base trap, and asked me to be godfather to the murderers of Prince Mihailo."*[2]

At the least, Nikola managed to win over Tsar Alexander III who agreed to act as godfather. However, Austria-Hungary was not so easily persuaded and Vienna's representative, Baron Thommel, refused to attend the wedding as a sign of support for Milan.

Petar returned to Cetinje for the wedding with his two brothers: the athletic and well-liked Arsen, and Djordje, whose health was fragile. He acted as the family treasurer and exercised a restraining influence on his more flamboyant siblings.

The wedding took place in Cetinje Monastery on August 11, 1883, attended by diplomatic representatives from the Powers,

(Left) A young Prince Djordje proudly carrying his hunting trophy and (above) Djordje, standing, with brother Aleksandar during a visit to their Aunt Jelena in Racconigi, Italy.
Facing page: (Bottom) The Karardjordjević children in Geneva: Jelena, her brothers, and little Pavle, son of Prince Petar's brother, Arsen. Pavle would play a significant role in the future Yugoslav state. After King Aleksandar's assassination in 1934, he became Regent of Serbia from 1934-1941, until the lack of British and French support and a domestic revolt against his foreign policy forced him to step down and into exile. (Top) Portraits of a young Djordje and Aleksandar.

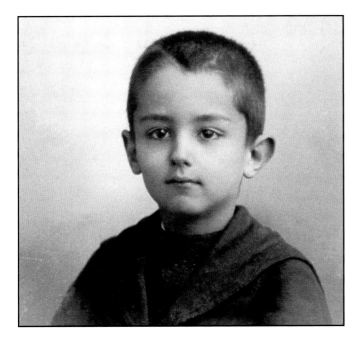

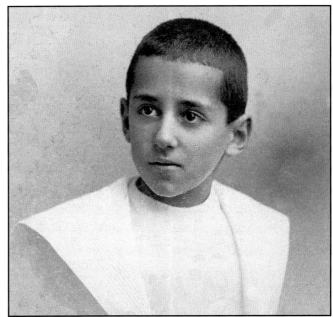

with the exception of the dissenting Baron Thommel. The wedding gifts ranged from the grand to the humble, from the splendid jewellery given by Sultan Abdul Hamid II to the offer of goats and oxen from the vojvodas. The latter were refused because Nikola knew the tribes could scarcely afford to give away the precious livestock they depended on.

After the wedding Petar and Zorka enjoyed a brief honeymoon. During their absence, Prince Djordje made ready a new residence for the Karadjordjević family in Cetinje. Two small houses across from the court were converted into a single dwelling and given to Zorka as her wedding dowry. She certainly preferred the simple life in Cetinje to travels in European society and happily returned home from the honeymoon as soon as the residence was ready.

Petar's zestful character, amply complimented by the intelligence and energy of his young wife, soon had a profound influence on court life in Cetinje, as well as the political life of Montenegro.

Zorka eagerly joined in with her husband's scheming to oust the Obrenović dynasty from the Serbian throne. To his dismay, Nikola realised too late the forces he had unleashed by permitting the marriage. He was pushed into the background as Petar laid the ground for an uprising and Montenegrins enthusiastically rushed to serve under the Karadjordjević banner.

Nikola found he had little choice but to go along with the popular mood and joined in with Petar's preparations. Together they travelled to Baden-Baden, Germany, to raise funds for a dynastic revolution, and Foreign Minister Gavro Vuković was sent to Belgrade, where King Milan's former premier Jovan Ristić promised a useful neutrality. It was decided that five to six thousand troops would be sufficient to escort Petar, who would, they hoped, be rapturously welcomed by the Serbian people. Vojvoda Marko Miljanov of the Kuči tribe was chosen as commander and volunteers from the Vasojevići tribe, from which the Karadjordjević family traced its roots, made ready.

The date was set for September 20, 1885. The troops gathered at Jelovica Hill near Berane. Then, at the last minute, Nikola decided to abort the uprising. Petar was infuriated and felt it was nothing less than a personal betrayal. However, Nikola had been warned by Vienna that he would be held personally responsible for an attack on the Obrenovići. Petar did not forgive Nikola his loss of nerve and only other, positive, events prevented an open breach between the two princes.

In four years Petar and Zorka had four children: two daughters, Jelena, born on November 4, 1884; Milena, born on April 28, 1886, who died the following year; and two sons, Djordje born on September 8, 1887; Aleksandar born on December 16, 1888.

It ensured that a link survived between Petar and Nikola, but their relationship had reached a watershed at Jelovica Hill.

Nikola, viewing himself as head of the two families, felt he had acted in the interests of both the dynasty and the country. A premature uprising could have been the ruin of them all.

For Petar it was an illustration of Nikola's *"Machiavellian politics: to take me by his side and, with his strict and malicious attentions, neutralise me to make it impossible for me to do anything against Obrenović."*[3] Nikola treated Petar's angry outbursts in diplomatic fashion, refusing to be provoked into an open conflict.

Petar had remained popular with the people and Nikola could not be too open about his own feelings. Instead, he tried to use social gatherings, where he would deploy humour and innuendo to indicate his thoughts; a strategy that also served to keep his son-in-law in his place, but one that the hot-tempered Petar greatly resented. A relative or a vojvoda were less exalted and were therefore obliged to accept Nikola's put downs meekly, but Petar in no way saw

(Top) A portrait of the young Jelena Karadjordjević and (right) enjoying a bicycle ride during a visit to her aunt, Queen Elena, in Italy.
(Facing page) The strikingly attractive Princess in her twenties wearing evening dress. Jelena was educated in Russia and went onto marry Grand Duke Ioann Konstantinovich. Shortly before the marriage, Tsar Nikolai II's daughter Tatiana wrote jokingly to her sister Olga: *"Perhaps you know that Ioanchik is engaged to Jelena of Serbia. How funny if they might have children, can they be kissing? What foul, fie!"*

(Below left and right) Portraits of Djordje, taken in 1903, and Aleksandar in military costume. Djordje's character was closer to his father's, being the more volatile and impatient of the two brothers. Aleksandar was more thoughtful and bookish, although he also showed, on occasion, his father's explosive temper. As adults the brothers would come into sharp conflict with each other over their rights to the throne of Serbia, which Djordje had reluctantly renounced in 1909. Ostensibly the reason was the death of a servant who had fallen after being struck by the then Crown Prince, but political reasons, with Serbia close to war with Austria-Hungary over the annexation of Bosnia-Herzegovina, played the larger part. Thereafter Aleksandar gave no thought to relinquishing his position. (Left) Petar Karadjordjević and (facing page) Zorka. Although she was actively engaged in her husband's schemes to reclaim the Serbian throne, Zorka also acted as a bridge between the Karadjordjević and Petrović-Njegoš families. After her premature death relations between Petar and Prince Nikola deteriorated and, instead of the marriage being a force for unity, there were three dynasties (Petrović-Njegoš, Obrenović and Karadjordjević) competing for the hearts and minds of the Serb people.

himself as having inferior prestige to, or being in the charge of his father-in-law.

These already strained family relations deteriorated further when Zorka died giving birth to a fifth child on March 4, 1890. The unfortunate child, a son named Andrija, only survived his mother by a month. It was a fearful family tragedy. Zorka had been dearly loved and when the Royal Family went into mourning their grief spread spontaneously throughout the country. Petar was shattered. For two days he remained alone in his room. On the third day Nikola came to see him and was met by an unshaven, emotionally exhausted and grief-stricken man. They talked together for over an hour. Petar's children had been waiting anxiously with their governess for some indication of their father's state of mind but as he left Nikola gave no clue as to what had transpired. No one ever knew what the two princes discussed, only that two days later Petar left Cetinje. There were rumours that Zorka's death had been partially caused by falling down the stairs of the family house, and even that in a fit of rage Petar had pushed her. The likelihood is that this was just malicious speculation.

For Petar his wife's death was a disaster. It signalled the beginning of the end for him in Cetinje, and even Milena's warm feelings toward him could not revive his relations with her husband. Petar became an isolated figure as he delayed his final departure until his children reached school age. He told Gavro Vuković: "*Were it not for Princess Milena, I would not stay for one more day.*"[4] Nikola tried to renew their friendship but to no avail; the embittered Petar saw double standards in everything he did and Nikola's overtures only made things worse.

Petar nevertheless continued with his plans to reclaim the Serbian throne. A conversation overheard by his eldest son, Djordje, revealed the continuing tension between his father and grandfather, and how Milena had tried to calm the situation: "*I do not like Petar's travels*" Nikola told Milena. "*His way is too dangerous. Why will he not let things take their course?*" Milena replied: "*Don't be unfair Niko, Petar cannot ignore what they* [Obrenovići] *are doing.*" Nikola's anger grew: "*But he should not leave the children. Young ones should be educated. They are going to start their schooling any day and he is spending on wars and politics . . . he has lost almost half of the Karadjordjević estate.*" "*The children are with us*" Milena reasoned, "*they will go to the best schools, we can do that for our Zorka . . . If their father cannot afford it, we will pay. I do not think that he has spent all the patrimony. Did you not say that the Obrenovići confiscated all their property?*" "*Yes*", Nikola replied, "*they did, their real estate, but the money and the gold is left, and he is spending it on wars . . . what is he going to leave for the children when they grow up?*" "*God is taking care of all of us. Zorka's property can go if necessary. That is for her children*"[5] Milena concluded philosophically.

Petar, however, had no intention of letting his children remain with their grandparents. They eventually left Cetinje with their father in 1894. Petar rented out the family house in Cetinje to the British Embassy and sold Topolica, the residence he had built near the port of Bar, to Nikola for one hundred thousand francs.

Returning to exile in Geneva, Petar continued to receive some aid both diplomatic and financial from Montenegro but, in the not too distant future, the Serbian Pretender and the Prince of Montenegro would become bitter rivals when the violent overthrow of the Obrenović dynasty brought a Karadjordjević back to the Serbian throne.

The union of the houses of Savoia and Petrović-Njegoš.

Chapter X

The Prince of Naples & the 'Montenegrina'

If you could only see how much they love each other. They are much more in love than at first, and they live entirely for one another. She is a real angel, a wife well suited for my son.

Queen Margherita to Colonel Egidio Osio, 1897.

The royal couple's fifth daughter, Jelena, was born on a rainy winter's day, January 8, 1873. Arriving only a year and a half after the birth of Nikola and Milena's first son, Danilo Aleksandar, the arrival of another girl was greeted in rather subdued fashion. Although Prince Nikola was an affectionate and caring parent he had some frustration as the possibilities for his daughters were as yet unknown. Fortunately, he soon set his initial disappointment aside and the precocious infant was given plenty of love and attention. Jelena's first steps were taken and her first words spoken under the watchful gaze of her parents, and her father involved himself fully with her early education.

Nikola was an accomplished writer and poet and he enjoyed reading to his children authors whom he admired and, whom he hoped, would instill a sense of national pride and patriotism in his offspring.

The Bosnian born Serb, Jovan Sundečić, and Nikola's father, Vojvoda Mirko, were family favourites, particularly Mirko whose songs were highly esteemed by his countrymen. Jelena's favourite South Slav poet was another Petrović-Njegoš hero, Vladika Rade. It was exactly the formative influence Nikola hoped to have on his children; he even read

his favourite clauses from the Penal Code, which had been drafted with a touch of the Montenegrin poetic muse.

If not all of the Prince's children had the Petrović creative gene they were all given ample opportunity to show their talent, and in Jelena's case her artistic flair was apparent from an early age. An anecdote, which became well known after her marriage, recalled her father's positive influence. One day his daughter presented him with some drawings but, unable to recognise what she had tried to depict, he saw the crestfallen Jelena burst into tears. Happily, Nikola realised his mistake and turned the pictures around the right way and saw that she had drawn the family house, Mount Lovćen and a dog chasing a sheep. Delighted by her efforts he sat her down and together they drew the scene again. After this drawing lessons were added to Jelena's daily studies. She learned quickly and, by the age of ten, had mastered the basics of drawing and begun using watercolours.

Jelena was a sensitive child but she was no wallflower, in fact rather the opposite. She was high-spirited, something of a tomboy, who liked best to play with her brothers Danilo and Mirko. She was a match for the boys with a rifle or a fishing rod and could walk and climb as far as they. Robust and energetic she soon developed into an athletic, attractive girl.

Jelena was also fortunate in that by the time she reached school age the path she should take was already mapped out. Her elder sisters, Milica, Stane and Marija, were already enrolled at St. Petersburg's renowned Smolny Institute and Jelena was sent to join them in 1883.

The Smolny Institute was a prestigious institution and, for women of the era, it gave a broad-based and enlightened education. The teaching ranged from the humanities and music, to mathematics and physics, while the more traditional feminine subjects of cooking, embroidery and housekeeping were also on the curriculum. The school regime was designed to develop discipline and self-sufficiency. Jelena was lodged next door to the headmistress, Madam Tomilov, in a sparsely furnished room and, like her fellow students, she slept on a hard bed, exercised first thing in the morning and washed with cold water. Although Jelena was a talented student who excelled in the arts she did not take to Russia the way her elder sisters had.

The Smolny era brought great benefits for the Prince's daughters, but for Jelena it ended prematurely due to an incident involving the Princess, a Karadjordjević prince and the future President of Finland. Speculation may have exaggerated the possibility but, were it not for the duel at the Yusopov Palace, Jelena might have become the next tsarina.

Education of the Montenegrin princesses was integrally linked to advancing their marriage prospects and Jelena's social debut at the Smolny College Ball of 1888 brought her to the attention of potential suitors of the highest rank. As Prince Nikola had hoped, Tsarevich Nikolai Romanov was taken with his elegant daughter and he chose Jelena for the opening dance of the evening. Gossip and rumour spread that the Tsarevich would take the Montenegrin as his bride. It

August, 1896. Prince Nikola, with youngest son Petar and, standing, Crown Prince Vittorio Emanuele and Crown Prince Danilo, hunting in Montenegro. Vittorio Emanuele had come for the official announcement of his engagement to Princess Jelena but he enjoyed himself so much he extended his stay for a week. Nikola subsequently became very fond of Vittorio Emanuele and felt very protective towards him. This was publicly demonstrated a few years later, in 1900, during King Umberto's funeral in Rome. There was a scare when the crowd forced its way into the funeral procession. For a moment it seemed that an attempt on the life of the newly crowned Italian King was being made. Nikola was next to Vittorio Emanuele and shielded him with his body. (Below) The Prince of Naples in 1896.
Facing page: (Top) 1896. The official portrait of Jelena, by 'Bambocci', which was published to announce her betrothal to Vittorio Emanuele. (Bottom) August, 1896. Lake Skadar. A Photograph taken at the time of the engagement. From left to right: Vittorio Emanuele, young Vjera and Petar, Jelena and, standing, Ana.

would certainly have been a remarkable boost to the prestige of the Petrović-Njegoš dynasty and for Russian influence in the Balkans, but Jelena would never find out whether or not Nikolai Romanov seriously considered her as a potential bride.

In 1890 Jelena was invited to a ball given by the Tsarevich's relatives, the Yusopovs. Among the guests were the Finnish aristocrat Carl Gustav von Mannerheim and a member of Serbia's former ruling family, Arsen Karadjordjević.

The two men competed for Jelena's attentions with almost fatal results and Jelena, as she later admitted to her sisters, felt she was partly to blame. Enjoying the company of Mannerheim she had refused Arsen a second dance, after which the two men fell out and fought a duel in which Mannerheim was badly wounded. His recovery was particularly fortuitous as he would eventually become President of Finland, but the scandal which ensued in the immediate aftermath put paid to any hopes of a Romanov-Petrović marriage.

The duel was reported throughout the European press and Mannerheim, who was influential at the Russian court, chose to blame

Elena & Vittorio Emanuele

Princess Margherita of Italy was just eighteen when, on November 11, 1869, she gave birth to her only son and the Heir to the Throne. At the time, the infant's grandfather, Vittorio Emaneule II, was King of Italy.

On January 23, 1871, the Prince and Princess of Piedmont, with their son, moved to Rome which had been taken by the Savoia, against the will of the Papacy, on September 20, 1870. The Papacy did not acquiesce and the Pontiff became the 'prisoner of the Vatican'. The discord between Papacy and Monarchy lasted until 1929, when the Lateran Treaty was signed.

Crown Princess Margherita and her husband, Crown Prince Umberto, were first cousins, being the offspring of two brothers: Umberto was the son of King Vittorio Emanuele II, Margherita the daughter of Ferdinando, Duke of Genoa. Vittorio Emanuele and Ferdinand's father was Carlo Alberto, King of Sardinia.

Umberto was also the son of two first cousins as Vittorio Emanuele II had married Maria Adelaide, the daughter of Ranieri, Archduke of Austria and brother of Carlo Alberto. The married couple had obtained the papal dispensation, as it was not permitted to marry within blood relatives.

Hardly unpredictable then that the infant, baptised Vittorio Emanuele Ferdinand Gennaro, was a frail child. To Umberto his son's fragility and poor health was a worry from the start; however, Margherita took heart from the beautiful blue eyes of her baby. Vittorio Emanuele was loved by his mother, but she was largely absent during his childhood as she chose to occupy herself with the social and cultural life she enjoyed so much.

When Vittorio Emanuele, who was given the title of Prince of Naples, was nine his grandfather, Vittorio Emanuele II, died and his father thereby became King Umberto I. Until the age of twelve Vittorio Emanuele was looked after by a governess, Bessie, of whom he was very fond. The young Prince was very kind and thoughtful, although his physical appearance, he was very short and of slight build, made him an introverted character who immersed himself in his studies.

His daily routine started early, at 7am each morning, and the day was a full one. His frailty made the daily riding lessons, which proved very painful due to his weak and thin legs, an unpleasant chore, and he much preferred his latin lessons and academic studies which allowed him to sit comfortably.

The choice of the Prince's tutor fell on the forty year-old Colonel Egidio Osio, military attaché at the Italian Embassy in Berlin. At the same time Vittorio Emanuele was enrolled in the famous Military College, the Nunziatella in Naples. Being a prince and having tutors at home, he was not obliged to attend regularly; however, a demanding life of studies and military training had started. Osio's stern educational regime ensured his charge was not only educated but thoroughly instilled with discipline.

Colonel Osio has been criticised as cold, efficient and authoritarian, of acting with Prussian severity toward the Prince, but the correspondence between the two illustrates the strong, warm and affectionate relationship which developed. Osio's influence certainly helped the diminutive Vittorio Emanuele to overcome his lack of confidence. The young man wrote to his tutor about the wonderful time he was having partying each night at a different house, " . . . *dancing the night away with the Duchess of Monteleone.*" There were malicious rumours regarding Vittorio Emanuele's reputed impotence and when news of his active social life was reported, King Umberto and Queen Margherita were relieved that their son was sowing his wild oats.

Emanuele Filiberto, Duke of Aosta with wife Helene and their children, Amedeo and baby Aimone

However, regarding the question of marriage Margherita wrote despairingly to Colonel Osio: "*Every time I mention marriage, he makes a face as if he had been given medicine . . .*" As the only son it was a vital issue that he marry and produce an heir. There was good reason for the Queen's anxiety as the young Duke of Aosta had ambitions to the throne.

Emanuele Filiberto, Vittorio Emanuele's cousin, tall and handsome, was the son of Amadeo d'Aosta, brother to Umberto I, and Maria Victoria, daughter of Carlo Emanuele, Duca del Pozzo della Cisterna.

Amadeo had been King of Spain for a short period (1870-1873). There was an uproar when, being a widower, on September 11, 1888, he married his young niece Letizia. However, Letizia became a widow after only two years when Amadeo died of pneumonia.

The dashing Emanuele Filiberto had great hopes to become King of Italy. His choice of a bride fell on Helene d'Orléans, daughter of the Comte de Paris. Helene was born in London, Twickenham, where her family lived in exile. She was very beautiful and Albert, Duke of Clarence, had fallen madly in love with her. Nothing came of it as he was a Protestant, she a Catholic. Mary of Teck was intended as Albert's wife, but in 1891, at the age of twenty-eight, he died.

After a year of delay, Emanuele Filiberto married Helene in England, at Kingston on Thames, Surrey, on June 25, 1895, in the Catholic church of San Raffaello. Present were his brother, Vittorio Emanuele, Count of Turin, and his cousin, Vittorio Emanuele. There had been strong opposition to the marriage because Italian dynastic tradition demanded that Vittorio Emanuele marry first and the hunt to find a bride for the Crown Prince intensified thereafter. Finally, to King Umberto and Queen Margherita's relief, Vittorio Emanuele found his match in Jelena Petrović-Njegoš.

Umberto I, King of Italy
(1878-1900)

Vittorio Emanuele II,
King of Sardinia (1849)
King Of Italy (1861-1878)

Published in 1878, *Le Bords de l'Adriatique* by Charles Yriarte was an interesting publication, an account of the journey the writer took along the Adriatic coast and Montenegro and the people he met, including Prince Nikola of Montenegro and his family. The book was dedicated and presented to Her Royal Highness Margherita of Savoia, Princess of Piedmont.
Facing page: (Top) Vittorio Emanuele, Prince of Naples, in 1877. (Bottom) A portrait of Queen Margherita of Savoia, born on November 20, 1851. Margherita had a beautiful face and blue eyes, a feature she inherited from her mother, Elizabeth of Saxony. However, she also was rather short, a fact she hid with sumptuous clothes, feathered hats and her famous sixteen rows of pearl necklaces.

Jelena for the incident. The Germanophile party, already indignant at the possibility of a Slav bride on the Russian throne, seized its opportunity and Prince Nikola was obliged to take his daughter back to Cetinje before her education was complete. Despite this unhappy episode, Mannerheim's feelings for Jelena lingered and there is a romantic story that he continued sending her roses on St. Helen's Day, July 24, for years afterward.

Although they had been cut short, the Smolny years were far from wasted ones for Jelena: she had matured into a highly attractive and presentable young woman; developed a refined hand for drawing; mastered landscape painting and her poems, written in both Russian and French, were published in a small magazine in St. Petersburg under the pseudonym 'Blue Butterfly'.

Returning to Cetinje, Jelena enjoyed seeing her family again, above all her younger brothers and sisters, but her thoughts were increasingly turned toward marriage. The Montenegrin capital could hardly satisfy the young lady who saw clearly that her prospects in European society were excellent. The young Prince Djordje Karadjordjević observed the restlessness of his maturing aunts Jelena and Ana: *"Jelena is eighteen and Ana is sixteen. They are both beautiful and dreaming of marriage and, having experienced big city life, are rather bored in Montenegro. They have nothing in common with their mother's ways and those old-fashioned beliefs will be forgotten by them as soon as they leave this region."*[1]

Prince Nikola still held out hopes to revive the Romanov project, but the news of Nikolai Romanov's engagement to a German princess, Alix of Hesse, closed the issue. In fact Russian relations had cooled somewhat. Nikola was invited to the funeral in 1894 of his old ally and patron Tsar Alexander III, but not to Nikolai Romanov's wedding which took place shortly after. Whether this was a personal snub or tact is not entirely clear. In Cetinje at least it was reported that Tsar Nikolai II wanted to spare Prince Nikola's feelings after his disappointment with Jelena.

One door had closed but another would soon open as the Prince's noted good luck intervened to brighten the horizon. On his return to Cetinje, Nikola learned that the Italian Ambassador to Montenegro, Count Sanminiatelli, had brought intriguing news: a new suitor had appeared from Italy's House of Savoia, no one less than the Crown Prince!

Vittorio Emanuele was under increasing pressure to find a suitable bride and a variety of potential consorts were rumoured to be on the shortlist. These included Queen Victoria's granddaughter, Maud of Wales, Louise of Schleswig and several ladies from the Habsburg and Orléans houses. However, Queen Margherita had already dismissed many of the more obvious candidates: *"The Orléans bring bad luck, the Belgians too, an Austrian girl is inopportune, and there are no eligible Saxons."*

Their increasing fame and their robust good looks had brought the Montenegrin princesses into consideration. This latter characteristic was particularly relevant in the Italian case, for the House of Savoia was suffering the hereditary effects of generations of inbreeding. Even Vittorio Emanuele's parents were cousins and fresh blood was badly needed to revitalise the family line.

The problem was that the Heir had shown little desire to get married and the Italian court was rife with gossip and innuendo as to the real reason. The culmination of the rumours was a story in a Parisian newspaper, *Le Gaulois*, which claimed Vittorio Emanuele was reluctant to enter into marriage because of his *"physical and moral handicaps."* Italy's Prime Minister, Francesco Crispi, was taking a keen interest in the Heir's progress and inquired if there was any truth in the story. He was relieved to be informed that Vittorio Emanuele had enjoyed relations with several ladies.

The Italian proposal to the Montenegrins had actually originated with Crispi. Italy's historic aim of a leading role in the Mediterranean had revived after national unification. In that context, Montenegro and Albania were viewed as natural spheres for Italian influence and it was hoped that Prince Nikola would be a useful ally on the eastern side of the Adriatic. The shrewd Crispi had earlier informed himself through Ambassador Sanminiatelli about the ruler's eligible daughters. The Ambassador had reported: *"Prince Nikola of Montenegro has two unmarried daughters, Princess Jelena . . . and Princess Ana . . . Jelena surpasses her sister in the sophistication of her features and gentleness of her expression . . ."* whilst Ana was noted as *"more dazzling but somewhat reckless due to her youth."*[2] Their charms confirmed, no small matter as the fastidious Vittorio Emanuele was notoriously stubborn and self-willed in the matter of marriage, Crispi began preparing the ground for a dynastic union.

In the early spring of 1895 Jelena and Ana were holidaying in Europe and their father decided it was a good opportunity to arrange a meeting with the Italians. Nikola sent Milena to join their daughters in Milan, after which the plan was to continue onto Geneva to meet with their Karadjordjević relatives. This ruse would bring them close enough

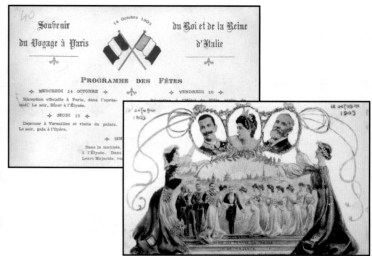

to meet up with King Umberto and Queen Margherita of Italy, who were staying in the north of the country at the royal residence in Monza. However, before Milena reached Trieste, news arrived that the Italian royal couple were on their way to Venice. Nikola telegrammed new instructions, to go onto Venice; he had concluded it would be an even better, less obtrusive, opportunity for an introduction.

Venice was celebrating the inaugural year of 'The Exhibition of Modern Art', and a painting by Giacomo Gross had caused a stir because of its depiction of the body of a young Don Giovanni surrounded by numerous naked mistresses. To spare royal blushes, the painting was displayed away from the main exhibits when King Umberto and Queen Margherita opened the exhibition on April 30. In all the excitement it seemed quite a casual happening for Milena and her two daughters to be in Venice at the same time as thousands of tourists and even Dowager Empress Maria Theresa of Austria had come to view the exhibition.

Milena and her daughters took lodgings at the Hotel Danieli and later went onto the Royal residence to pay their respects to King Umberto and Queen Margherita.

The Montenegrins were invited to both the formal and informal dinner parties and, with Vittorio Emanuele present, matters were progressing well. The highlight was an invitation to Venice's famed opera house *La Fenice* for the premiere of *Cristoforo Colombo* by Franchetti, where they were guests of honour in the royal box. Vittorio Emanuele was completely bowled over by Jelena, who was glowingly described by the Italian press as *"resplendent in a pink dress . . . a dark, olive skinned beauty."* Perhaps even more importantly, Vittorio Emanuele felt that Jelena was in no way prejudiced by his short stature and physical shortcomings, in her company he felt confident and at ease.

Jelena had also made a good impression on King Umberto and Queen Margherita, but politics

(Right) A portrait of the King and Queen in which Elena's slender, athletic beauty is captured. Her height exposed the shortness of her husband; however, that was of no importance to Elena. She was attracted to Vittorio Emanuele's character, his kindness, faithfulness and intelligence. (Inset) The wedding album. (Below) 1899. Vittorio Emanuele, Umberto I and Elena during a hunting excursion in Valsavaranche.

Facing page: (Top left) The official photograph of Elena di Savoia, taken just after the wedding in October 1896. (Top right) Postcards issued for the visit of the King and Queen of Italy to Paris to meet President Emile Loubet in 1903 and (below) a portrait of the young Queen. (Below right) The cover of the Italian publication of the Montenegrin national anthem presented to 'La Principessa Elena del Montenegro'.

intervened before relations could develop further. Italy's imperialist adventure in Ethiopia was going badly wrong and Vittorio Emanuele was recalled to Rome. The planned rendezvous with Jelena in San Remo had to be cancelled and the Montenegrins returned to Cetinje.

It would not be until the winter of that year that a new opportunity arose. Vittorio Emanuele planned to take a hunting trip in southern Albania via the island of Corfu. Ambassador Sanminiatelli was stirred to action once more and he despatched a telegram to the Montenegrin Ministry of Foreign Affairs: *"A noble hunter reported from Corfu that he would come to Montenegro, if the Prince were in Cetinje, to spend a couple of days there hunting on Lake Skadar."* Unfortunately, the coded message was wasted as neither Prince Nikola nor Foreign Minister Vuković were in Cetinje, and they were the only two who knew the identity of the *"noble hunter"*. Nikola was not informed for several days and, by then, it was too late to organise a meeting.

Such choice opportunities could hardly afford to be squandered, particularly as Italy's continuing troubles in Ethiopia led to the fall of Prime Minister Crispi.

The unthinkable had come about as the Italian army of General Baratieri was decimated at the Battle of Adowa. It provoked a major crisis. The King considered abdication, while Crispi wanted to send a further hundred thousand troops to finish the botched job. King Umberto pulled back from further madness and Crispi was forced to resign.

From the Montenegrin perspective the main political force behind the proposed marriage was gone. The situation was salvaged when *Glas Crnogorca* published an astutely pro-Savoia article. While Italy's foreign policy was criticised, the bravery of the Italian soldiers was praised, six thousand of whom had lost their lives at Adowa. The reality was that military arrogance and incompetence had played a large part in the *débâcle*, but the article served its purpose admirably, being commented on favourably and even reprinted in the Italian press.

The political crisis hardly lessened the pressure on Vittorio Emanuele to find a bride, but given his hesitant nature it could even be considered a blessing in disguise. Apart from the political considerations, an ambitious dynastic rival, the Duke of Aosta, had his eye on the Italian throne.

The much needed next opportunity for a meeting between Jelena and Vittorio Emanuele came at the coronation of Tsar Nikolai II in May 1896. Prince Nikola

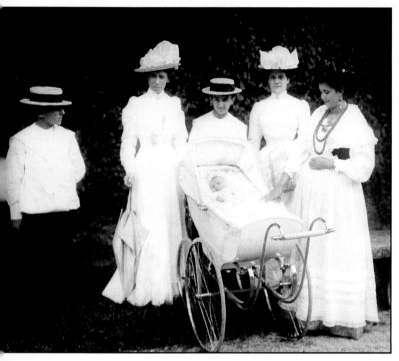

(Above left) Jolanda di Savoia, nicknamed 'Anda' by the family, was Vittorio Emanuele and Elena's first born. Here, at the age of one, she is enjoying breakfast and (above centre) the newly-born with her nanny. There is a story among the Savoia that tells of Vittorio Emanuele having bought a beautiful broche adorned with two large diamonds to donate to his mother on the day the heir would be born. When Jolanda was born he went to her residence, Palazzo Margherita, with the jewel. When he returned the broche was still in his pocket. Apparently Margherita, disappointed at the birth of a grand-daughter, had thrown the gift back at Vittorio Emanuele. Queen Elena treasured that broche all her life. (Above right) The King and Queen with Jolanda and baby Mafalda in 1902. (Left) Racconigi Castle. Baby Jolanda in the pram and her cousins, Djordje, to the left, and Aleksandar Karadjordjević, with nanny and governesses. (Below left) 1905. Four generations of the Royal Family. One year old Umberto, the Heir to the Throne, with Elizabeth of Saxony, the Duchess of Genoa, Queen Elena and Queen Mother Margherita. (Below) Queen Elena, Jolanda, Umberto and Mafalda.
Facing page: (Top Left) Queen Elena in 1902. (Top right) 1911, Tor Paterno, Verona. Queen Elena with her children, Jolanda, Mafalda, Giovanna and Umberto. With them are Sweden's King Gustav V and Queen Victoria. (Bottom) Vittorio Emanuele with Umberto at Villa Savoia. The photgraph was taken by Queen Elena.

accompanied by his two eldest sons, Danilo and Mirko, attended, and Jelena came as the guest of her sister Milica, while Vittorio Emanuele represented the House of Savoia.

During the coronation Vittorio Emanuele had finally made up his mind to propose, but it hardly showed. The twenty-one year-old Princess Marie, daughter of Queen Victoria's son Alfred and Maria Alexandrovna of Russia, observed both Vittorio Emanuele and Jelena at first hand: *"For all official processions the royal guests were paired off in couples according to precedence. It was Vittorio Emanuele who fell to my share . . . He was conventionally polite without being specially attentive or amiable. Abrupt of speech, he spoke in short, hacked sentences . . . We had not overmuch to say to each other, but I was interested in a dawning romance between he and his future bride, Princess Jelena of Montenegro, who made special friend with me because of my cavalier. Jelena was a tall, handsome girl with superb eyes and pleasant ways, she was both vivacious and amusing and not at all shy . . . I liked her very much, there was something fresh and spontaneous about her; she had, so to speak, retained a whiff of the breezes of her mountain home . . ."* Marie, however, saw little evidence of mutual affection between the two: *"I have no clear remembrance of how at that time young Vittorio Emanuele met the advances of the vivacious Princess."*[3]

Vittorio Emanuele was a very private person and most likely nobody knows, in spite of the many words written about it, the exact way in which he proposed to Jelena. That he did is evidenced by the short but significant entry he made in his diary on leaving Russia: *"I decide."*

"Knowing the affection you have for me I am happy to inform you that today I have become engaged to Princess Jelena of Montenegro. With great affection, V.E. of Savoia."
Crown Prince Vittorio Emanuele to Colonel Egidio Osio, August 18, 1896.

Elena & Vittorio Emanuele

In 1909 Tsar Nikolai II paid an official visit to the Italian King. Because of the fear of an attempt on the Tsar's life, the visit took place at Racconigi Castle. In this photograph the Tsar has just arrived and he is seen walking by the stairs with Vittorio Emanuele III. On the balcony, accompanied by their teacher, Miss Brompton, Jolanda and Mafalda have been allowed to view the arrival of the Tsar. The Tsarina (inset right) did not attend. (Inset left) Tsarevich Alexei in Russia with his pet donkey, a present from King Vittorio Emanuele and Queen Elena. (Below) The court photographer, Giuseppe Chialvo, took this official group portrait. In front, Vittorio Emanuele III, Nikolai II, Queen Elena and her maid of honour, Countess Francesca Guicciardini. Behind them are statesmen, diplomats and military officers. On his return to Russia Nikolai II wrote to his mother Maria Feodorovna: *"Livadia, 31 October, 1909. My dear Mama, it is a while since I have written to you . . . I enjoyed my visit to Italy, but I am pleased to be back . . . We were welcomed graciously at Racconigi, all the Italians seemed pleased to see us. The Queen and King were terribly affectionate and had a great simplicity of manner. They went out of their way to be very lively hosts but they left us plenty of time to ourselves, which*

was nice . . . Sometimes I went up to the nursery and played with their boisterous children. I brought them a Cossack village as a present which had to be put together. Elena helped us to do that and she was nearly late for an official dinner . . . I gave her, in your name, the order of St. Catherine and she expressed her thanks to you. The King, a very enthusiastic photographer, kept snapping . . . Mr. Tittoni [Ministry of Foreign Affairs] sends his regards to you . . . I met The Duke and Duchess of Genoa . . . One evening we listened to a concert. Everyone goes to bed early there, at 11 pm, and Vittorio Emanuele gets up at 6am. The Queen gave me a present for our children of a donkey and a cart from Calabria. I had to take him back on the train. The donkey arrived safely on the Standard at Yalta [Crimea]. He kicked furiously at Odessa when we were putting him on board the yacht, but then quietened down and felt quite at home on the straw."

Vittorio Emanuele's telegram to his tutor and lifelong friend, Colonel Egidio Osio, was sent two days after his arrival in Cetinje. It was typically undemonstrative, but Vittorio Emanuele had actually enjoyed himself greatly in the relaxed atmosphere of the Montenegrin court.

He had arrived after a rough sea voyage which had delayed him by a day. To the relief of Crown Prince Danilo, who was waiting to greet him, Vittorio Emanuele's small yacht, *La Gaiola,* docked in Montenegro's main port of Bar at eight o'clock on the morning of August 16. Danilo welcomed Vittorio Emanuele on behalf of Prince Nikola and embraced him as his brother.

They went onto Danilo's nearby residence, Villa Topolica, via the picturesque road which traverses the Sutorman Heights. During the journey Vittorio was struck by the coachmen wearing national costume, and by their remarkable skill in handling the horses even on the steepest slopes.

After stopping at Topolica, it was onto Cetinje via Lake Skadar. After reaching the village of Virpazar, the party boarded the small steamer which took them to the lake's terminus in Rijeka Crnojevića, where a honourary guard of perjaniks was waiting to escort Vittorio Emanuele during the relatively short journey to Cetinje. However, the narrow and winding mountain roads ensured that it was evening before they arrived in the capital. With the engagement still unannounced it was a rather curious event for the people and the Italian received a low key welcome.

After a short rest at Prince Danilo's residence, where he would stay for the duration of his visit, Vittorio Emanuele walked over to meet his future father-in-law at the Palace. Prince Nikola, flanked by his ministers, was waiting at the main entrance where he embraced Vittorio Emanuele. They then went inside to meet Princess Milena and the royal children in the Diplomatic Salon.

The next two days passed quietly, Cetinje was expectant, but there were no flags, no torchlight processions or music to give a clue as to the purpose of the visit. Finally, on the morning of August 18, the gathering of ministers at the Palace signified that an announcement would be made shortly and the people gathered in expectation.

At 11am, Prince Nikola, the Royal Family and the Prince of Naples with Princess Jelena by his side, appeared at the Palace balcony. There was a hushed silence as Nikola told the crowd that, with the consent of his father, King Umberto, the Prince of Naples had asked for the hand of Princess Jelena, to which he had given his consent.

Nikola's speech was very much that of any Montenegrin father announcing his daughter's betrothal; the grand titles aside it was a quaintly parochial scene. Most family heads, not having the luxury of the Palace balcony from which to promulgate the good news, would have gone to the town square, with their families by their side, from where they would make the announcement.

(Above) A charming photograph of Elena with a dedication to 'Lili', her sister-in-law Natalija, who married Prince Mirko. (Below) Elena was a keen photographer, as shown by this study taken at Castel Fusano.

As a sign of respect, the official engagement telegram had not been sent to Italy until after Nikola's announcement, but the engagement ceremony had taken place at the Palace an hour earlier. Vittorio Emanuele asked, in Italian, for Nikola's consent, which the Prince gave in Serbian. Then youngest sister, nine year-old Princess Vjera, gave a splendid bunch of flowers to Jelena and Vittorio Emanuele gave her a stunning diamond necklace.

The people were now free to show their enthusiasm: flags were waved from every window, the singing of the national anthem could be heard all over town and the people shouted *"zivio"* (hurrah) to Vittorio Emanuele and Nikola. Shortly afterward a service of thanksgiving was held in the Monastery and, as they left, Nikola and Vittorio Emanuele kissed the cross on the tomb of Vladika Saint Petar I.

Then something very foreign to Vittorio Emanuele occurred, one of those moments typical of patriarchal Montenegro, as Nikola went among the people talking familiarly to all about the organisation of the forthcoming festivities. Small tables were quickly placed outside the Palace and bottles of champagne and brandy appeared as the whole town celebrated. Vittorio Emanuele happily joined the party, mingling with the people, and when Prince Danilo took his hand as a sign of affection the cheers were deafening.

In the evening there was a dinner party at the Palace attended by the foreign ministers accredited to Cetinje, after which, at 9pm, the revellers went to Prince Danilo's residence to view the torchlight procession which had started from the Zetski-Dom Theatre.

The next morning congratulatory telegrams flooded in. Naturally, the first was from King Umberto and Queen Margherita, followed by Tsar Nikolai II of Russia. Soon the telegraph office was inundated as Cetinje basked in the good news, as did the Crown Prince of Italy. Vittorio Emanuele had anticipated spending just two days, but the warm hospitality he found ensured that he stayed a week longer.

(Above) Little Maria, born in 1914, with sister Jolanda at Villa Savoia. (Below) Italy entered the war on the side of the Triple Entente in 1915; this official postcard was sent to Italy's sailors, dedicated from the King's children with *'Best wishes and good luck.'*

ANNO DI GUERRA 1915

I figli dei Sovrani d'Italia
L.L. A.A. R.R. Princ. Jolanda, Mafalda, Umberto, Giovanna, Maria
Ai Marinai della cara Patria — Saluti ed Auguri

However, although the betrothed couple were deeply in love and family relations were excellent, the one remaining obstacle to the marriage was still considerable, namely the conversion of Princess Jelena to Catholicism. Religious sensibilities on both sides and the intrigues of the Italian court combined to threaten the marriage plans.

Queen Margherita had pledged: *"No woman will enter this house unless she is first a Catholic."* Meanwhile, the Italian Ambassador in Vienna, Count Nigra, being one of those opposed to the union, made his feelings clear with as little tact as he could muster. He informed Prince Nikola that King Umberto wanted a Catholic priest sent to Cetinje to instruct Jelena. Nikola was aghast at the thought of a Catholic priest daily visiting the Royal Family in his capital; Cetinje considered itself a shrine to the Orthodox Serb nation which had martyred itself at the Battle of Kosovo. Nikola prevaricated, replying that a formal offer of marriage was needed before such issues could be decided. King Umberto responded by offering to pay all the wedding expenses, but still required that Jelena be instructed in her new faith, if not in Cetinje then elsewhere.

(Above) Pope Pious XI gives the benediction to the crowds gathered in St. Peter's Square. (Insets) Vittorio Emanuele III and Pope Pious XI. (Right and inset) February 11, 1929. Cardinal Pietro Gaspari and Benito Mussolini sign the Lateran Treaty, sealing the reconciliation of the Holy See and the Italian Government. Benito Mussolini's domestic triumph, the Treaty resolved the 'Roman Question'. The ratification documents were signed by Cardinal Pietro Gaspari, on behalf of Pope Pious XI, and by Prime Minister and head of State, Benito Mussolini, on behalf of King Vittorio Emanuele III. (Below) 1929. The Sovereigns of Italy during an official visit to the Pope in the Vatican. Elena was escorted by Prince Francesco Chigi della Rovere, Commandant of the Noble Guards of His Holiness.

The religious issue was a genuinely emotive as well as a politically sensitive one for the Montenegrins. On receiving King Umberto's letter Nikola called a meeting. Milena, Danilo, Metropolitan Mitrofan Ban, the secretary to the Russian Ambassador, Professor Puigget, ministers Ilija Plamenac and Gavro Vuković were gathered to hear Nikola read his draft reply.

He proposed to tell King Umberto that Jelena's conversion should not be discussed before the

wedding, or even whilst she and Vittorio Emanuele had not ascended the Italian throne. Vuković could not contain himself at what he saw as an egregious error and interrupted: *"The issue of conversion is the most important, one which we have to accept and finish with before the wedding . . . There are many reasons but I will cite just one. Assume that a son is born before Princess Jelena converts. Although Italy is not a clerical nation it is at the very heart of Catholicism and Italians could never accept an Heir to the Throne from a marriage of mixed*

(Top) King Vittorio Emanuele with his son, the Prince of Piedmont.
(Above) Rome. King Vittorio Emanuele and Benito Mussolini.

religion. Perhaps anywhere else, but not in Italy . . . The Crown and the Throne of a Catholic country are in question and this must be respected. You, my Master, have to make those concessions unconditionally . . . it would be best if you left it to King Umberto's better judgement, but also let him know that the issue is a very sensitive one for yourself and Princess Milena, as well as the whole of the Montenegrin Orthodox nation, so that the conversion is done discreetly without great ceremony, and that Princess Jelena's religious instruction is not given now but after the wedding."[4]

The objections which Vuković had tried to circumvent were raised again. Metropolitan Mitrofan Ban objected to the conversion on the basis that it would be seen as anti-Russian. More tactfully, Milena, although it was well known that she opposed Jelena's conversion on religious grounds, waited to see Nikola's response. Nikola accepted the Foreign Minister's advice.

Some recompense could be found in the attitude of Vittorio Emanuele. He was not personally much inclined to any faith, as a Prince of the House of Savoia had little affection for the Papacy and was intent on marrying at the earliest possible date.

The domestic opposition was not restricted to Milena and Metropolitan Mitrofan Ban, there was open dissent, even in Cetinje. During Vittorio Emanuele's second visit in September, the protesters included Nikola's relatives Božo and Šako Petrović, both of whom refused to leave their homes until Vittorio Emanuele had departed.

Aside from religious issues, it was a reminder of the paramount influence of Russia in Montenegro. Skilled diplomat though he was, Nikola had to consider breaking off the engagement. Still, it would take more than the fraying of the Prince's nerves and some strained family relations to bring that about and the wedding plans went ahead.

The wedding party left Cetinje for Rome on October 16, 1896. Accompanying the bride and groom were Prince Nikola, Prince Mirko, Princess Ana, and the Duke of Genoa, who was sent to escort the bride on behalf of King Umberto. Breaking with wedding tradition, Vittorio Emanuele had gone to escort his fianceé as he wanted to pay his respects to Princess Milena, who, as a sign of protest against Jelena's conversion, had refused to attend the wedding. Milena and Jelena's farewell was a tearful one.

When they reached Bar the party boarded the royal yacht *Savoia* during a violent storm, to the salute of salvoes from the Austro-Hungarian and Italian cruisers. In the early hours of the following morning they were greeted in southern Italy, in Bar's sister port of Bari, by an enthusiastic crowd which had turned out despite the heavy rain.

At 10.30am the conversion rite of Princess Jelena was carried out aboard ship. The ceremony was held in a cabin with darkened windows, where Princess Jelena, instructed by the Archbishop of Bari, took on her new faith and began a new life. Whilst Jelena embraced her new faith, her mother went to the Vlach Church in Cetinje, where her daughter had been baptised, and offered a prayer for her. The other members of the family were not present either, they were taken aboard the warship *Francesco Morosini* to view the Italian fleet. Montenegrin feelings had been spared by the low-key ceremony and the Italians had the satisfaction of knowing that their future Queen's first step on Italian soil would be taken as a Catholic.

(Far left) On January 23, 1939, Maria of Savoia, Elena's youngest child who had her mother's Montenegrin looks, married Luigi di Borbone-Parma. They had three children: Remy, Guy and Chantal. On September 13, 1943, the family was taken by the Gestapo and deported to the concentration camp in Mecklenburg. Fortunately all survived the war. Maria and her husband lived in France and, strangely, after her marriage, she seems to have been forgotten by her family.
(Left) Jolanda. She married Count Calvi di Bergolo. They had four children: Ludovica, Vittoria, Guja and Pierfrancesco. On September 8, 1943, when Italy declared the armistice, Jolanda, her children, along with Roman and Prascovia Romanov took refuge in Switzerland.
(Below) Giovanna, who married Boris, King of Bulgaria on October 25, 1930. Political events saw Boris dying, it is believed poisoned at the hands of the Nazis. The Bulgarian monarchy was swept away at the end of World War II.

A honourary escort of forty carriages was waiting to take Jelena to the Basilica of St. Nicholas where the Grand Prior, the Abbot of the Benedictines, Oderisio Piscicelli-Taeggi, held Mass. Afterward Jelena returned to the *Savoia* for an emotional reunion with her family. That same evening they boarded the train for Rome, arriving after a twelve-hour journey.

The wedding contract was signed on October 18, 1986. The ceremony was attended by Božo Petrović, Prince Nikola's cousin and President of the State Council, and Minister of Justice, Baltazar Bogišić. King Umberto's representatives were the Minister of Foreign Affairs, Viscount Venosta, and Minister Giacomo Costa.The contract was placed in the Savoia archives.

The wedding took place on Saturday, October 24, 1896. The brief civil service was held in the Grand Salon of the Quirinale in the presence of the monarchs and Prince Nikola, representatives of the Italian Government and the Mayor of Rome. To Jelena's right were her father and Helene, Duchess of Aosta. The witnesses for Vittorio Emanuele were the Dukes of Aosta and Turin. The Marquis of Rudini, Francesco Crispi's successor as President of the Ministers Council, read the official marriage contract. Senator Farini recorded a confusion over the appropriate way for Jelena to sign. *"How will she sign, Elena Princess of Naples?"* King Umberto asked. *"No"* answered Farini,*"until the church ceremony she is known as Princess Jelena Nikolayevna of Montenegro."* Jelena resolved the problem by signing as Elena of Montenegro-Savoia.

By 11.30am the civil marriage service was concluded and the wedding cortège paraded through the streets of Rome to the church of *Santa Maria degli Angeli*. The bride was beautifully dressed in a white satin dress with silver embroidery and a wedding veil of Burano, a gift from Queen Margherita, held in place by a diamond tiara, a gift from King Umberto.

Santa Maria degli Angeli was the choice of King Umberto, who had refused to hold the wedding, as the liberals had suggested, in the chapel at the Quirinale. He hoped to use the occasion to improve relations with the Vatican and the ceremony was conducted by Prior Monsignor Piscicelli, dressed in the

Princess Mafalda & Prince Philip von Hessen

(Left) Mafalda, nicknamed Muti by the family, aged eight. She was of a fragile built and had the complexion of her grandmother, Margherita, with chestnut hair and very fair skin.

(Below) The wedding of Princess Mafalda to Prince Philip von Hessen. She had the blessing of her parents as well as the approval of Italian dictator, Benito Mussolini, who was looking favourably to a German dynastic connection. That link proved fatal for Mafalda.

Frau von Weber, as was recorded in the prison register of Buchenwald Concentration Camp, died on August 28, 1944. The truth was that no prisoner under that name had died. Towards the end of 1943 the Gestapo brought to the *lager* a woman with the name of Mafalda von Hessen née Princess of Savoia, on the order of imprisonment by Heinrich Himmler. A few days later her details were removed from the files and she was re-entered as Frau von Weber. During an Allied bombardment she was badly wounded. After a fatal delay, an SS doctor amputated her arm, but she died without recovering consciousness.

Thanks to another prisoner, a Czechoslovakian monk named Herman Joseph Tyl, who had recognised her body and rescued it from the crematorium, she was buried a few days later in Weimerand Cemetery and a rough plaque was placed on her grave with the writing 'unknown woman'. The monk made a note of the plot number, 262.

Mafalda, Vittorio Emanuele and Elena's second-born child, married on April 9, 1925, Philip von Hessen, who was the son of Margrethe, Princess of Prussia and Friedrich Karl Landgrave of Hesse. Margrethe was the sister of Kaiser Wilhelm II and the daughter of Victoria, Princess of Great Britain, who married Friedrich III of Prussia. Therefore, on his mother's side, Philip was a great-grandson of Queen Victoria. Philip and Mafalda had four children: three boys, Maurizio, born in 1926, Enrico in 1927 and Ottone in 1937; their daughter Elizabeth was born in 1940. Philip and Mafalda's marriage was a happy one.

Mafalda's unfortunate fate was sealed while World War II was raging and political life was racing towards the abyss for Italy. Benito Mussolini had been removed from office on September 3, 1943, prior to which his power base had already been crumbling. On behalf of the new Italian Government, General Giuseppe Castellano had gone to Sicily on August 31, 1943, to seal the final deal agreed with the Allies in Lisbon, Portugal, three weeks earlier. Castellano had asked the Allied representatives to delay the announcement of the agreed armistice until after their forces had landed on the Italian peninsula, as the Government was extremely fearful of German reprisals once news of the armistice broke. The Allies refused and Italy found itself the focus of German anger.

Adding further turmoil to the life of the Royal Family was the death of Giovanna's husband, King Boris of Bulgaria. The Allies accused Hitler to have had him poisoned. When Bulgaria's Minister Karadjoff advised the Savoia that Boris was gravely ill, Mafalda decided to go immediately to Sofia to give support to her sister. It was August 28, 1943, when Mafalda reached the Bulgarian capital. Boris had already died and Mafalda was unaware that her movements were being closely monitored by the Gestapo.

The Italian Government had asked for the armistice to be made public on September 12, but a telegram from President Eisenhower was received: the announcement of the armistice had to be made on September 8. Mafalda was left stranded in German occupied territory. On her return journey to Rome the train she was travelling on stopped at Sinaja in the Romanian countryside. At 3am Queen Mother Elizabeth of Romania boarded the train and advised Count Federico Avogrado di Vigliano, who was travelling with Mafalda, to inform the Princess that Italy had made public the armistice. With no indication received as to what to do Mafalda's only thought was to reach Rome and her children.

Meanwhile, in Rome, Mafalda's three younger children had been taken for safety to the Vatican on the request of Queen Elena, and were lodged in the apartments of Monsignor Montini, later Pope Paul VI. In Germany eldest son, Maurizio, had to stop college and join the anti-aircraft defence corps. On returning to Rome, on September 21, Mafalda visited her children. Returning to her residence she was informed that Prince Philip would call her at the German Embassy at 11pm that evening. It was a deception and she was arrested as she entered the Embassy. From there she was transported to an annex of Buchenwald Concentration Camp. The children, with the tacit agreement of Monsignor Montini, left the safe refuge of the Vatican for Germany on the pretext that they were joining their mother and father.

On the morning of April 14,1945, Vittorio Emanuele and Elena learned of Mafalda's death, which had taken place eight months earlier, from the newspaper *Il Giornale di Napoli*. Her children had heard the news only a day earlier.

Enrico von Hessen recalled that on April 12, 1945, Allied forces wanted to occupy the Castle of Kronberg where he and his siblings were staying with their grandmother, Princess Margrethe of Prussia, who was very ill with pneumonia. The American officer in charge initially seemed sympathetic to their situation, but on their return the soldiers threatened to shoot Princess Margrethe if they did not leave immediately. Margrethe was placed with some friends, the younger children, Ottone and Elizabeth, went to stay with their tutor in Schonberg, and Maurizio and Enrico stayed near the town of Kronberg. The following day they heard about Mafalda's death from the radio. A few days later an American officer sought out Enrico and told him that he had a lock of Mafalda's hair to give him. He promised to return but never did.

Mafalda had been unaware that her husband, Philip, had been arrested on Hitler's order. He was subsequently taken prisoner by the Allies and accused of being a Nazi collaborator. Between the Nazis and the Allies he spent fifty-two months in detention camps. In 1945 Philip learned that his beloved 'Mauve', his nickname for Mafalda, had died at the time he was in Pusteria as a prisoner of the Allies.

Since 1951 the mortal remains of Mafalda di Savoia have rested in the small cemetery of the Hesse family in Kronberg. Philip of Hesse died in 1980.

"If he had time to reign he could have been, perhaps, the best of the Kings of Savoia", a minister of the Italian republic said about Umberto II. Umberto Prince of Piedmont became King of Italy for one month, from May 9 to June 13, 1946. But he had inherited a tarnished crown, a burden more than an honour.

Umberto was born on September 6, 1904, at Racconigi Castle. He was put in the charge of the strict disciplinarian, Admiral Bonaldi. Like the last Tsar, Nikolai Romanov, he was not instructed in the political problems of the country. In the house of Savoia the saying was *"si regna una alla volta"* (only one reigns at a time). Like Nikolai II's father, Tsar Alexander III, Vittorio Emanuele III believed that only the reigning sovereign should take care of the affairs of state, the Heir had to wait his turn. Umberto's relationship with his father was not very close. Vittorio Emanuele was intelligent and cultured, but very authoritarian.

On January 8, 1930, Prince Umberto married Princess Maria José of Belgium. They had four children: Maria Pia, born in 1934, who married Aleksandar Karadjordjević, son of Regent Pavle of Yugoslavia; Vittorio Emanuele, born in 1937; Maria Gabriella, born in 1940 and Maria Beatrice, born in 1943.

Maria José was the daughter of King Albert I of Belgium and Elizabeth of Bavaria. Elizabeth's aunt was Maria Sofia of Bourbon-Sicily, the last Queen of Naples. Maria José was brought up in a family that was one of the most cultured among European nobility. Born at Ostende on August 4,1906, she was the third child and only daughter, having two brothers Charles and Leopold. From her childhood it was understood that she would marry Prince Umberto. From 1917 she spent two years studying in Italy at the College *Santissima Annunziata* in Tuscany. After her marriage Maria José became a controversial figure among the Savoia and she was said to have been active against fascism during the war.

Umberto and Maria José's marriage was not a happy one and in exile after World War Two she lived estranged from her husband. However, she always defended his courageous last ditch attempts to rescue the battered Italian monarchy.

Umberto was heir to the legacy of Benito Mussolini, a country stigmatised by two decades of fascism and destroyed by war.

After the Italian referendum of 1946 which deposed the young King, Umberto went into exile and chose to live in a villa on the Atlantic coast, in the town of Cascais in Portugal.

Asked in an interview if he had nostalgia for his country he answered: *"Nostalgia? Not exactly. There is a beautiful word in Portuguese, 'saudade', difficult to translate, but it means the joy of going back into the memory of things, one by one, things that are so far away now . . . our steps that resound in the streets, in the squares, in all the places that we run through again, now only with the heart. And I know my Italy, city by city, village by village . . . I love my country and it gives me joy even from afar."*

Umberto di Savoia died on March 18, 1983, his body was laid to rest in Portugal. Maria José di Savoia died on January 28, 2001, and was buried at Hautecombe Abbey, France.

August 1934. King Vittorio Emanuele and Queen Elena of Italy with their children and grandchildren. From left to right: Jolanda with son Pier Francesco, Queen Elena, King Vittorio Emanuele III, Mafalda, Giovanna holding her daughter Maria-Luisa, youngest daughter Maria and Umberto. Front row, from left to right, Princess Jolanda's children: Vittoria Francesca, Maria Ludovia and, on her Aunt Maria's lap Guia Anna Maria. The two boys are Princess Mafalda's children, Enrico and her eldest son Maurizio. Princess Maria José was not present for this photograph as she was pregnant with her first child, Maria Pia.

pontifical robes.

At long last, the Crown Prince had married and Rome burst into celebration. Prince Vittorio Emanuele and Princess Elena, as she was thereafter known, rode through the streets during the afternoon, as did King Umberto and Prince Nikola, the two rulers sharing a carriage. The Romans nicknamed the Montenegrin ruler by shouting *"Padre Nicolo"* (Father Nikola) and *"Zio Nicolo"* (Uncle Nikola).

The evening saw Rome illuminated and royal serenading on the *Piazza dei Cavalli*, all to the acclaim of the largest crowd Romans could remember. The wedding, as had been hoped, was a huge boost for the popularity of the Italian crown.

The near millennium of the House of Savoia, which traced its roots back to Umberto the White Handed in the eleventh century, joined with the Petrović-Njegoš dynasty, the reign of which stretched back a mere, but heroic, two centuries to Vladika Danilo I. The House of Savoia and the legendary warrior-princes of Montenegro now stood shoulder to shoulder and Prince Nikola had placed his family at the heart of European dynastic affairs.

Shortly after the wedding the newlyweds began their honeymoon, a wonderful opening to their married life of an extended cruise filled with sojourns in the choicest resorts and visits to the most historic sites. Aboard Vittorio Emanuele's newly christened yacht the *Jela*, in honour of his bride, they sailed from the tranquil waters of the Gulf of Naples to adventures in the North Sea and the Arctic Ocean.

These idyllic first few years of marriage ended abruptly with the assassination of King Umberto at Monza on July 29, 1900, at the hand of the anarchist Gaetano Bresci. Vittorio Emanuele and Elena were aboard the royal yacht in the Aegean Sea and only received an ambiguous report about the King's health. Disembarking at Reggio Calabria he was greeted as *"Your Majesty, King of Italy."* His response was *"This all feels unreal."* Feeling wholly unprepared for power, Vittorio Emanuele was crowned on August 11, 1900.

King Vittorio Emanuele III's reign would be a long and controversial one. Throughout Queen Elena proved to be the rock on which the 'Little King' relied. She was as every bit as suitable as Queen Margherita had anticipated.

The early years would be by far the happiest. Italy's political situation was relatively stable and the royal couple were able to continue enjoying their blissful home life. Elena provided Vittorio with the loving family environment he had never experienced.

Their greatest joy were their children, four daughters, Jolanda, Mafalda, Giovanna, Maria and a son, Umberto.

The Queen was also a vital asset to the Crown. The maternal characteristics which Elena inherited from her mother not only filled Vittorio Emanuele's life with a new contentment, they also made her tremendously popular with the Italian people.

It was, in fact, only her nature to concern herself with the welfare of others, above all children. In a rare interview she talked about her love of children: *"I was always motherly, even as a child I was a mummy to my dolls, loved them and took care of them . . . I know children's souls because I love them. It is enough to love them. I have always believed that those who do not understand children cannot do so because they do not love them. I used to hear from my friends or relatives how they do not know how to approach children, how they are unable to calm them down. I wanted to reply 'Love them!' I am no cleverer than other mothers, I just really love children, all children."*[5]

Elena's unstinting love would be her greatest gift to her husband throughout fifty-one years of marriage.

Vittorio Emanuele was a dependable, decent man, but his failure to offer any resistance to the rise of Italian fascism in the 1920's ruined the monarchy and brought disaster to the nation. It was a long, drawn out process in which the House of Savoia's famed caution succumbed to the more dynamic, opportunistic force of Benito Mussolini's fascism.

The chief criticism of Vittorio Emanuele is not so much that he allowed Mussolini, 'Il Duce' as he was grandiloquently titled, to come to power, for in real terms he could do little to prevent it without risking civil strife, but that, as the virulent nature of fascism became more apparent, he spurned opportunities to remove the demagogue. The best chances came during the early years when Mussolini's street theatre politics were still the basis of his power, public opinion was still undecided and fascism's grip on the nation incomplete.

Queen Elena of Italy.

Vittorio Emanuele disliked but also had a grudging respect for Mussolini, and he made the same mistake that so many monarchs have made by siding with the forces of reaction in times of crisis. Once established in power, Mussolini was a particularly ruthless politician with expansive ambitions which Italy could ill afford. Seeing the startling renaissance of German power under Nazism, he shackled the nation's fate to the heel of Adolf Hitler's jackboot.

Throughout Queen Elena kept a discreet silence and her personal popularity remained unaffected by political controversy. There is no indication that she had any liking for Mussolini, but her sense of propriety and duty meant that her relation to the ugliest political regime in Italian history was an ambiguous one. During the Mussolini era neither the King nor Queen made any public statement to distance themselves from the regime, and the demise of fascism did not spare the Royal Family. The deposition and exile of the monarchy in 1946 marked the final humiliating consequence.

Both the King and Queen died in exile: Vittorio Emanuele in Alexandria, Egypt, in 1947 and Elena in Montpelier, France, in 1952. To his dying day Elena remained the central figure in Vittorio Emanuele's life. When the end came she expressed her devotion simply and poignantly. On December 28, 1947, King Vittorio Emanuele III, after a few days spent in bed with a bad cough, suffered a paralysing heart attack. Queen Elena remained by his side and, as he passed away, her hand in his, she said quietly *"He was my son."*

Princess Ksenija and the problem of the Obrenović connection.

If the Prince promises anything to Queen Natalija remember . . . that it is I, as Mother, who has to be asked about the marriage of my daughters . . . I would never let my daughter marry an Obrenović, not even a king!

Princess Milena

Chapter XI

Princess Ksenija: Queen of Serbia?

With successful marriages for four of his daughters already behind him, sadly clouded by the death of Zorka in 1890, there was good reason for Prince Nikola to view Ksenija's prospects with optimism. When the possibility of her marriage to King Aleksandar Obrenović arose it seemed to Nikola a renewed opportunity for dynastic union between the Serb states. Furthermore, the sixteen year-old Princess, a very attractive and intelligent young woman, seemed to many the ideal bride for Serbia's nineteen year-old ruler. However, the Obrenovići were anathema to both Princess Milena and the Foreign Minister, while King Aleksandar's father, Milan, fully reciprocated their animosity.

Prince Nikola had been looking for an opportunity to thaw out relations with Belgrade after King Milan's abdication in 1889, but he was rather surprised to receive King Aleksandar's gift of the medal of Saint Sava for his literary work. It was read as a probable sign of interest in Princess Ksenija, particularly so as Archimandrite Dučić in Belgrade had written to Nikola's friend, Baltazar Bogišić, the previous year that King Aleksandar's mother, Queen Natalija, was aiming to marry her son to a Montenegrin princess.

It was actually not the sort of rapprochement Nikola was

(Facing page) Princess Ksenija. Along with her younger sister, Vjera, Ksenija did not enjoy a Russian education. She nonetheless received a broad and well-based schooling from her tutors in Cetinje, which she further enriched during visits to her sisters, Milica and Stane in St. Petersburg and Jelena in Rome. Her marriage to King Aleksandar Obrenović of Serbia (right) was the hope of Aleksandar's mother, Queen Natalija. If the match had transpired two possibilities can be speculated upon. Firstly, that Ksenija would, instead of Queen Draga Mašin, have died with Aleksandar in the *coup d'état* of 1903. A second, more positive, outcome might have been that the young Princess would have borne Aleksandar children, a vital failing from his eventual marriage to Draga Mašin, and that Aleksandar, with the help of his experienced Montenegrin father-in-law, could have navigated his way through the crises which ultimately led to his assassination. However, Aleksandar spurned the opportunity, while his father, Milan, worked tirelessly to prevent an Obrenović-Petrović-Njegoš union.

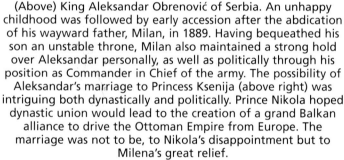

(Above) King Aleksandar Obrenović of Serbia. An unhappy childhood was followed by early accession after the abdication of his wayward father, Milan, in 1889. Having bequeathed his son an unstable throne, Milan also maintained a strong hold over Aleksandar personally, as well as politically through his position as Commander in Chief of the army. The possibility of Aleksandar's marriage to Princess Ksenija (above right) was intriguing both dynastically and politically. Prince Nikola hoped dynastic union would lead to the creation of a grand Balkan alliance to drive the Ottoman Empire from Europe. The marriage was not to be, to Nikola's disappointment but to Milena's great relief.
(Facing page) Princess Ksenija with her younger sister and brother, Vjera and Petar, in Rijeka Crnojevića.

anticipating. The prospect of an Obrenović-Petrović marriage proposal was strewn with potential problems: *"My unfortunate daughter Princess Zorka had two sons. If I agreed to give one of my daughters to the Obrenović family, from that marriage there could also be male children. Now, you think in which position I would place my own blood? What evil could come from those circumstances? Unceasing struggle and competing for power, no matter that . . . my grandchildren are still only children, nor have chance or party to be pretenders to the throne. Time can bring anything*

and if I mix my blood with Obrenović because of greed the Serbian nation would have reason to damn me."[1]

Baltazar Bogišić was disappointed at Nikola's response, but Foreign Minister Gavro Vuković firmly believed that the unpopular Obrenovići should be kept at arms length. Joining the families could, perhaps, save the ill-starred Serbian dynasty but he warned Nikola: *"I consider it a fatal prospect for the general interest of the Serb people. That is why we should leave the Obrenović dynasty to its fate, let it die naturally and others take its place . . ."*[2]

The arrival of King Aleksandar's envoy General Pavlović, in January of 1896, showed that a marriage proposal was, at least initially, not on the Serbian agenda, only closer political ties and an understandable desire on Aleksandar's part to emulate Nikola's adroit diplomacy. Even ex-King Milan, who thoroughly hated Nikola, had once said: *"I can understand everything except the skill of Nikola. How can he manage to be in good relations with both Russia and Austria at the same time? I could never have done it. When I was in good relations with one, evil came from the other, until my abdication."*[3] King Aleksandar was hoping that Nikola could help him regain Russia's favour.

Nikola, suffering from a bout of gout, entrusted the first contact to the Foreign Minister and Crown Prince Danilo, with the instruction to offer King Aleksandar diplomatic support with Russia. General Pavlović was invited to Danilo's residence, Topolica, to break the ice. He was surprised by the elegant and rather opulent residence, to which Danilo replied jokingly that there were many good things among their bare rocks, and the three men went on to discuss the lack of contact between the two Serb states and their dynasties. Danilo recalled meeting King Milan as a child, regretting that if he and Prince Nikola had ever met their relations could have been very different. A meeting of the Serbian and Montenegrin rulers was a proposal enthusiastically accepted by the General, while, for the Montenegrins, equally pleasing was the fact that there had been no mention of Princess Ksenija.

Nonetheless, as soon as General Pavlović left for Belgrade rumours of a marriage proposal started and Nikola had a denial issued to protect his daughter's feelings and reputation and, of course, there was no reason to fan the flames of speculation when King Aleksandar had not yet expressed an interest. More practically, Nikola began considering how to approach the hoped for new political era.

A split of opinion within the family soon opened up. Nikola was willing to make the first gesture of reconciliation by going to Belgrade before Aleksandar visited Cetinje, only requiring a confirmation that Aleksandar would return the compliment. However, both Milena and her father, Petar, disapproved, reasoning that Aleksandar's prestige would receive an unwarranted boost. Nikola met them halfway and Belgrade was added to his spring travel itinerary, making it one visit among several. The plan was for Nikola to take a cure for his troublesome gout in Baden-Baden in April, after which he would attend Tsar Nikolai II's coronation. On the return journey he would have time to visit Prince Ferdinand of Bulgaria and, lastly, King Aleksandar.

Aleksandar telegrammed his acceptance of the proposal while Nikola was in Baden-Baden, but during Tsar Nikolai's coronation the plans were upset when Prince Mirko fell ill with pneumonia. By the time he had recovered the round trip via Istanbul and Sofia had to be cancelled, and so it was straight onto Belgrade.

Nikola, accompanied by Danilo, travelled to Belgrade via Vienna, where he was joined by Foreign Minister Vuković. He greeted them with Milena's very thorough instructions on how they should conduct themselves: *"In any other court it would be easier for Montenegrins than in Belgrade. Every move and word will be criticised, that is why you must be very careful what you say both in private and in public, because every word will be reported to Queen Natalija. You have to show that you are gentlemen and that you are serious. Be kind to everyone and do not be tense because that will be seen as rudeness and ignorance. Tenseness is the mask of stupidity, be natural but dignified. When you talk do not shout or laugh too much. Do not forget that at all times you will be watched even when you think that you are not. During meals eat moderately and do not be too surprised or too critical. Be helpful to each other so they can see we have discipline and that the younger respects the older."*

As for any thoughts of discussing the marriage of Princess Ksenija, Milena's message was unequivocal: *"If the Prince promises anything to Queen Natalija remember . . . that it is I, as mother, who has to be asked about the marriage of my daughters . . . I would never let my daughter marry an Obrenović, not even a king!"*[4] Even though Nikola's views were close to Milena's, she, like his ministers, was afraid of his tendency to consider every possibility an opportunity.

The enthusiastic, cheering crowds of South Slavs - Serbs, Croats, Bosnians and Dalmatians - at Vienna and along the route as their train travelled through the Hungarian ruled

Vojvodina toward Serbia's northern border, allowed any anxieties to be put aside and the party were soon in a cheerful mood, particularly Nikola who would be seeing Belgrade for the first time in his life.

As they approached the border the wonderful position and panorama of Belgrade, with the impressive Kalemegdan Fortress and its converging rivers the Danube and the Sava, came into view. Nikola's emotions got the better of him and, as the train passed over the Sava Bridge, he stood up, took off his cap, crossed himself and prayed for the happiness and progress of Serbia and its people.

At 9am on June 26, 1896, they arrived at Belgrade station where King Aleksandar greeted them in Serbian military uniform decorated with the Montenegrin ribbon. As the band played the Montenegrin anthem the two rulers embraced and jointly inspected the guard of honour. The welcoming crowd was genuinely enthusiastic and the Montenegrins congratulated themselves on having made the opening gesture of friendship.

The first two days were taken up with ceremonial events, including *Vidovdan*, the commemoration of the Battle of Kosovo, that undying symbol of the national tragedy which Serbs felt was as much punishment for their own disunity as testimony to the might of their enemies. An appropriate moment then to show Serb solidarity and Nikola took the opportunity to place a wreath on the grave of his old friend, the assassinated Prince Mihailo Obrenović, as a gesture of respect and reconciliation. The two families also got to know each other and, helped along by the celebration of Crown Prince Danilo's birthday the following day, things were going surprisingly well.

However, indications of the difficulties which could arise from friendship between the two ruling houses were all too clear. Serbia was sharply divided politically, while the army was restless and

Princess Ksenija was an energetic and talented woman. (Left) Some examples of her work from the pages of 'The Near East Illustrated', published in 1907, partly illustrated with her photographs of Montenegro. The British author's desire to remain anonymous is explained by his strongly anti-German sentiments. The Kaiser's imperialist schemes, he believed, threatened the *"true interests of our Empire."* 'The Near East Illustrated' shows the astute means Prince Nikola could find to raise Montenegro's profile, although his son-in-law, by then King Petar of Serbia, took centre stage with his portrait on the title page. Nikola also composed a poem in honour of his British guest who, against his advice but much to his admiration, braved the wild mountains of Albania which even the Montenegrins were wary of exploring.
(Facing page) Ksenija was an excellent photographer as shown by this composition of Prince Nikola taken at Pjenavac, near Nikšić, in 1900.

ready to get involved in politics if the national interest or those of its officer class were threatened by the conflicts between the King and the political parties. King Aleksandar had already alienated many of his supporters with his assumption of full power in 1893, when he dismissed the three regents in a political *coup d'état.*

The Montenegrins could view at first hand the repercussions. At Belgrade station General Belimarković had paid only a fleeting visit to Prince Nikola due to his bad relations with King Aleksandar, and a former regent, Jovan Ristić, fulminated in private against the Obrenović family to Foreign Minister Vuković: *"King Aleksandar is no better than his father, but he has not had time to do as much . . . and he has a mother who nobody knows her real origins . . . She never loved her husband, nor her son, and Serbia she despises and hates."*

The dominant personality in the Obrenović family was still ex-King Milan and Jovan Ristić claimed to know that he had forbidden his son from marrying Princess Ksenija. He even showed Vuković a copy of a letter Milan had written shortly before the Montenegrins arrival: *"Who should let hungry Prince Nikola with his bunch of begging children occupy Serbia? They would gnaw it to the bone and nothing but skeleton would be left. His daughter, who is not only penniless and without even a shirt on her back, would parade as Queen at Serbia's expense. That cannot be and will not be as long as I live."*[5]

Milan had some grounds for his fears with the European press already anticipating Aleksandar's marriage. *"Princess Ksenija, a perfect example of Yugoslav beauty, should soon be the future wife of the young King of Serbia . . ."*[6] one German newspaper predicted. Although he knew Milan's anti-Petrović campaigning would continue, Vuković decided, for the time being, to keep Jovan Ristić at arms length. The positive response from the Serbian people had been a sign of the widespread desire for the two states to work together for the benefit of all Serbs; Prince Nikola's magnanimous gesture to visit first had been well judged and the possibility for a new era of co-operation now existed. The next move was Aleksandar's.

Despite the continuing disapproval of his father, King Aleksandar's visit to Montenegro went ahead the following year. On May 2, 1897, Aleksandar arrived in Bar where Crown Prince Danilo greeted him. Even though it was pure scaremongering, Milan had told Aleksandar that the Montenegrins would try to assassinate him. In fact, extra precautions were taken to ensure his safety and during the short car journey from Bar to Topolica soldiers were hidden all along the route to provide additional security.

Given his father's attitude, Aleksandar had hardly expected a genuinely warm welcome and he was surprised by the enthusiastic cheering which greeted him wherever he went, while the reception in Cetinje was as lavish and friendly as the court could provide. The Montenegrins were, however, rather disappointed that Serbia's ruler overlooked to bring a wreath to lay at Vladika Danilo's tomb to reciprocate Prince Nikola's gesture of respect to Prince Mihailo.

A slight hitch, but the diplomatic ground had been well prepared and the ministers immediately began discussing shared aims: nothing less than a grand Balkan alliance to drive the Turks out of Europe and share the conquered territory amongst themselves. Crucial to the hopes of all the Balkan states was the liberation of Macedonia, but it was the most complicated and divisive issue between them. Serbs, Bulgars and Greeks all claimed historic rights to the province and its division needed to be agreed prior to any military campaign. No easy task with a mosaic population of Albanians, Greeks, Gypsies, Jews, South Slavs, Turks and Vlachs, but their shared fear, the setting up of an autonomous Macedonia, the example of which could be a model for the other Turkish provinces, made co-operation a necessity.

The Montenegrins suggested that Serbia and Montenegro divide territorial gains on the basis of parity not population: the Sandžak which separated the two states would be divided fifty-fifty; the Macedonian town of Ohrid would go to Serbia; Prizren in Kosovo to Montenegro. Serbia would expand as far south as possible and Montenegro to the west. After lengthy discussions the ministers reached agreement, although the Montenegrins had doubts whether the Bulgarians would accept the Macedonian territorial division.

Protocols for both rulers to sign were hastily prepared. Prince Nikola was delighted by the draft agreement but wondered if King Aleksandar was aware of its extent. He would find out shortly as the whole house of cards the ministers had constructed was about to collapse.

In the Prince's favourite salon King Aleksandar and Crown Prince Danilo were talking over cigarettes. Foreign Minister Vuković was called over and asked to explain the agreement reached. To everyone's astonishment Aleksandar began shouting: *"How could my ministers agree to such a contract without my knowledge?"*

As Danilo hastily exited, Vuković asked the King if he had been unaware of the diplomatic talks. The tirade continued unabated: *"I told you before . . . that Prizren is in the sphere of my aspirations and I will never give it away freely."*[7] Vuković tried to make his exit, but Aleksandar followed, continuing his verbal assault, apparently oblivious to the fact that there were many watching the scene with dismay.

It was not, however, the theoretical loss of Prizren which had caused Aleksandar's agitation but fear of his father. The Montenegrins soon found out from Aleksandar's ministers that Milan had threatened to take action against his son if he made an alliance with them. It was no idle threat as Milan's rule had been based on the support of the army, with which he still had great influence.

After that evening's gala dinner Nikola, Danilo and the Foreign Minister met with Aleksandar and his ministers to try and salvage the agreement.

Nikola told Aleksandar: *"Last year I sent my Foreign Minister to Istanbul on a banal mission, as a cover for his true mission to Sofia and Belgrade. I had reason to start a great issue among the Balkan states and that is why I sent him to you, my brother King, and our brother Prince Ferdinand [of Bulgaria]. My suggestion was that before any trouble . . . the present Balkan states reach agreement regarding the Turkish territories in which our people live. I wanted to prevent an autonomous Macedonia or Albania and to stop the intervention of the Great Powers in solving the 'Near East' question. My brother, the Prince of Bulgaria, responded positively and we were only waiting for your visit to bring the project to life for all the Balkan states . . . Furthermore, when you visited Sofia last February you made a preliminary agreement with Prince Ferdinand regarding borders. I was informed about it . . . You all need to be aware of my proposal as otherwise we will leave ourselves and our people at the mercy of greedy great forces that will tear us apart, take pieces here and there and swallow us all. I am telling you, brother King, as I would to my own son, because it is my duty to Serbs . . . Take my advice, take this proposal and the Serb people will bless the day you visited me in my modest, martyrs capital."*

Aleksandar, shaking with emotion, replied: *"I would be ready to agree but the traditional politics of eighty years of my house will not allow me to give up Prizren."* Nikola had heard enough and angrily retorted that Prizren had been in the sphere of interest of Montenegro *"long before Serbia was established . . . but if the location of Skopje allowed it I would make that sacrifice for the general good. I would gladly give up Prizren and take Skopje, but in this case I remain with my decision. Prizren must be mine."* King Aleksandar was taken aback by Nikola's anger but could only prevaricate: *"Even with the best will I cannot decide . . . when I return to Serbia I will gather all the leaders of the political parties."*[8]

Aleksandar's behaviour was rapidly alienating the ministers he had brought with him let alone the ones he had left behind. The Minister of Finance, Mihailo Vujić, had also been on the receiving end of his tirades and would have resigned if it had not been a state visit. Nikola remained philosophical feeling he had done his duty for the good of the Serb people and both states, Aleksandar would have to make his own decision.

As for the possibility of asking for Princess Ksenija's hand, Aleksandar had hardly made a good impression with her, and his personal reputation was poor enough before he arrived. Milena remained pledged to prevent it: *"I would rather kill her with my own hands than give her to Obrenović . . ."* Conversely, Nikola still entertained hopes and marriage was certainly a prospect the Serbian delegation had been considering.

In fact, everyone, whether for or against, had been expecting a proposal, except Aleksandar who had other plans for his personal life. Serbia's Foreign Minister Djordje Simić made one last approach to his Montenegrin counterpart, who rebutted him: *"You had ample time and opportunity to talk to the Prince . . . the King saw Ksenija and that was the ideal moment to take the initiative."*[9]

Disappointment and recrimination all around, except for Aleksandar's father who anxiously waited in Vienna for his son's report. Seeing that Milan's influence would bar any alliance between the two houses, Nikola quickly informed Belgrade that Ksenija was already engaged to put an end to an affair which, by then, had become an embarrassment. Milan had triumphed and drove his victory home by holding the *débâcle* up as proof of Nikola's insincerity.

The near future would reveal the dire consequences of Milan's influence on his son and how fortunate Ksenija had, in fact, been. In the immediate aftermath he had made Aleksandar's relations with his ministers even worse and the Government resigned, after which Milan succeeded in having Vladan Djordjević appointed Prime Minister. Djordjević was wholly Milan's creature and he had no qualms about pursuing a vigorously anti-Petrović policy.

Princess Ksenija, to the right, with Natalija Konstantinović, who married Prince Mirko in the summer of 1902.

Franz Josef & Ana

The happy marriage of Princess Ana and Franz Josef of Battenberg.

The charming Princess Ana of Montenegro, who has been to me a sister, infinitely close and dear, a woman of rare qualities of heart and character.

Princess Marie of Battenberg

Immediately after the Obrenović *debâcle* came respite with the joyful marriage of Princess Ana to the German prince, Franz Josef of of Battenberg. A considerable consolation for Prince Nikola and an affair agreeable to all involved, not least the young couple. Ana, who had been the last of the princesses to be educated at the Smolny Institute in St. Petersburg, was the most vivacious of all Nikola's daughters, and also blessed with considerable intelligence, although it was said that she was somewhat lacking in diligence. With the engaging, lively Ana and the respected, likeable German, the prospects for the marriage were excellent, and if the dynastic implications were not immediately apparent, they were potentially considerable.

At first glance Franz Josef's lineage was not particularly important, but as a descendant of the morganatic branch of the House of Hesse he was related to many of the most important royal courts, including the German, Russian and British ruling houses. Two of his brothers married English princesses, Louis to Queen Victoria's granddaughter Victoria and Henry to her favourite daughter Beatrice, while the last two Russian tsarinas, Maria and Alexandra, had both been Hessian princesses. The Battenbergs were also related to the Habsburgs and Emperor Franz Josef had been the godfather at Franz Josef's baptism.

However, the family's history was also quite a turbulent and controversial story. Franz Josef's father, Alexander, had fallen

Emilsgarten. Princess Ana and Prince Franz Josef's residence in Darmstadt, Germany. (Facing page) A portrait of Princess Ana. (Background picture) A picturesque scene of the lake in the residential grounds.

from favour with Tsar Nikolai I. Initially he had served with some distinction in the Russian army and the Tsar wanted him to marry his niece, Grand Duchess Mikhailovna. Alexander refused and a year later, in 1851, he instead married Countess Julie of Hauke.

The Tsar angrily dismissed him and Alexander's career was only saved by the offer of a command from the Austrians, whom he served for a decade. It led to the family living a rather nomadic life, much of it spent in Italy where his children were born.

Franz Josef, the youngest of the five children of Alexander, Prince of Hesse, and Julie, who had been made Princess of Battenberg by Alexander's brother Grand Duke Louis, was born in Padua in September of 1861.

As a young man, Franz Josef was more inclined to academia than a military vocation, but gave in to his father's wish and served in the First Regiment of Foot Guards in Potsdam, Germany. After his brief military career, Franz went to Leipzig University to gain his doctor's degree.

(Above) Seeheim-Jugenheim, Germany: Franz Josef and Ana seated to the right, enjoying a day in the countryside with relatives. (Right) Franz Josef with Ernst, Grand Duke of Hesse and the Rhine. (Below) On the left, lying on the grass is Prince Henry of Prussia, next to him Ana. On the right Franz Josef, to his left, Henry's wife Irene of Hesse. Behind Anna is Ernst of Hesse

He also wrote and published a treatise on the economic development of Bulgaria. The family connection to Bulgaria had become one of special importance as Franz Josef's eldest brother, Alexander, had been placed on the throne, partially through the influence of their aunt, Tsarina Maria Feodorovna.

During Prince Alexander's reign (1879-1886) the two Bulgarian provinces had finally been united in 1885. It gained him the lasting gratitude of the people, but his politically independent tendencies, which lost him Russian support, proved his downfall.

The enlarged Bulgaria had torn a hole in the Treaty of Berlin and King Milan of Serbia rashly invaded seeking territorial compensation, only to be quickly defeated. The Great Powers, recalling the slide to war a decade earlier, were outraged and Russia decided to remove its protégé. Alexander was kidnapped by St. Petersburg's agents and taken into Russian territory, but the Bulgarian Government was brought down by the outcry and Alexander returned as the hero of independence.

However, having gained the throne through Russian influence, Alexander now decided his position was untenable and abdicated. Franz Josef had fought at his brother's side during the conflict with Serbia and had shared

his fate in the ensuing drama of the Russian kidnapping.

Prince Nikola could certainly ponder the possibilities of this interesting new connection, not only in regard to the Bulgarian throne where Alexander's successor, Prince Ferdinand of Saxe-Coburg and Gotha, was known to be apprehensive at the prospect of a Battenberg's marriage into the Montenegrin dynasty, but also in promoting the Petrović-Njegoš house as the premier Balkan dynasty which could be relied on to provide rulers for the region's not infrequently vacant thrones.

Franz Josef was no mere cipher in all this and certainly had designs on his brother's former throne. In 1887 he had sought the hand of an American heiress, Miss Consuelo Vanderbilt, which would have brought the needed funds. She, however, was understandably wary of Franz Josef's audacious plans to oust Prince Ferdinand and married the Duke of Marlborough instead.

Franz Josef's marriage to Princess Ana would be a very happy one, but at the time it was clearly a statement of intent: the Battenbergs would be positioned to reclaim former glory and Prince Nikola's dynastic hand in the

Ana taking a break from the kitchen, with her pet dog and a friend. (Inset) A page from the family photographic album. (Above left) Franz Josef and Ana with, on their left, sister Elena and her husband, Vittorio Emanuele. (Above) Anna reading and relaxing in Emilsgarten.

Ana and Franz Josef. The background picture is from the family photograph albums, a view of Heiligenberg Castle, the Battenberg family's summer residence by the village of Juggenheim.

region would be further strengthened.

Beyond the Balkans, Nikola hoped that the marriage would improve relations with Great Britain and Germany. After the resignation of William Ewart Gladstone in 1894, London had relapsed into its at best lukewarm attitude to Montenegro, and Berlin had still not accredited a representative to Montenegro after a diplomatic incident in Cetinje in 1878.

With regard to Queen Victoria there was a particularly hopeful connection as Henry Battenberg had been the male presence in the British royal household, compensation for the lonely Queen's loss of her beloved husband, Albert. Henry had been Victoria's advisor and confidant until his death in Africa in 1896, during the campaign against King Prempeh of Ashanti who was threatening British interests along the Gold Coast.

Prince Nikola quietly sought the approval of the Russian and British courts. In late February of 1897 Ana was invited to Nice by her sister, Grand Duchess Milica, who was holidaying with her husband and sister, Grand Duchess Stane. In March, Nikola came, ostensibly to visit his family, but he managed to pay a visit to Queen Victoria who was also staying in the riviera resort. Victoria's blessing for the marriage was gained and a new chapter in anglo-Montenegrin relations opened. It would lead to Nikola visiting Victoria at Windsor Castle the following year.

Ana and Franz Josef's wedding was slightly rescheduled due to the state visit of King Aleksandar Obrenović in April 1897, and it was put back until May 18. The short interval meant that there was no time for special preparations, only for the Serbian flags decorating the capital to be changed for the Hessen. The guests included Milica, along with her husband Grand Duke Peter Nikolayevich, and Stane, as well as Prince Petar Karadjordjević and his three children. The Russian, Austro-Hungarian and British courts accredited their ministers as representatives, as did Turkey's Sultan Abdul Hamid II.

Elena was an absentee as she and Vittorio Emanuele were touring the Italian cities for the first time. Also missing were Franz Josef's brother Louis and his wife Victoria. They had planned to come in April but were now unable to attend.

The ceremony was held in Cetinje and, in contrast to Elena's marriage the previous year, the religious question was resolved without Ana's conversion. The Orthodox ceremony was conducted by Metropolitan Mitrofan Ban in the

(Left) Emilsgarten: From left to right: Ana's brother, Mirko, with his wife Natalija, Ana and Franz Josef with a family friend. (Above left) Franz Josef and Ana enjoying a car ride. (Centre) Lunch at Emilsgarten. From left to right: Ernst, Grand Duke of Hesse, his wife Eleonore, Franz Josef, Irene and Henry of Prussia. (Top) Franz Josef and Ana.

Princess Ana of Montenegro

Monastery at which the godbrothers were Prince Mirko and Count Erbah Schenber. The Orthodox ceremony completed, the newlyweds simply walked over to the British Embassy where the Protestant ceremony was held. For Montenegro it was the first ever wedding in the Protestant tradition and the Hessen court had sent a priest from Darmstadt for the occasion. Prince Nikola and Princess Milena were present, along with representatives from the foreign courts and a few vojvodas. Ana keeping her Orthodox faith was particularly important for Milena, who had been so upset at Elena's conversion to Catholicism the previous year; the pragmatic attitude of the Germans had certainly helped.

Afterward Prince Nikola made a speech in French thanking Queen Victoria, then the festivities of gala lunches, balls and soirees began. It was the first marriage since Princess Zorka's in 1883 to be held in Cetinje and paid for by the state. No expense was spared. *"Spending as if we were English"* Foreign Minister Vuković observed, although he accepted that *noblesse oblige* demanded the state purse strings be loosened. Franz Josef's modest finances also meant that Nikola agreed to give Ana a dowry of five hundred thousand florins, which he, however, could only afford to pay in stages and at some interest.

Ultimately the promising union proved to be of little dynastic or political significance: Franz and Ana did not have any children and events in the Balkans took a different course after the turn of the century. However, Franz and Ana were undoubtedly a happy, contented couple whose greatest pleasure was to travel, whilst their Darmstadt home was an idyllic retreat for both family and friends.

If Ana's impact in royal history was a small one, her personal qualities made her an excellent wife and sister-in-law. Franz Josef's sister, Princess Marie, recorded her affection for Ana: *"The charming Princess Ana of Montenegro, who has been to me a sister, infinitely close and dear, a woman of rare qualities of heart and character . . ."*[1]

The Crown Prince and (facing page)
Crown Princess of Montenegro by
Paja Jovanović, 1903.

The unfulfilled promise of the reluctant Crown Prince.

Chapter XIII

The Reluctant Crown Prince

The Heir to the Throne, Crown Prince Danilo, was just twelve years old at the time, his second year in the gymnasium. He was physically and spiritually a wonderful child, with his mother's noble features.

Dr. Steven Cuturilo

To the royal couple's considerable relief their fifth child was a son, born on June 29, 1871. The arrival of the Heir was heralded as the guarantee of the line of succession and an ecstatic nation celebrated. The euphoria continued for three months, culminating with the baptism on September 20, when representatives from Europe's governments gathered for the event. The infant was baptised Danilo (after two of the Petrović-Njegoš dynasty's greatest heroes, its founder Vladika Danilo I and its first secular ruler Prince Danilo) Aleksandar (after his imperial godfather Tsar Alexander II).

Naturally, all efforts were directed to ensuring the Crown Prince's upbringing and education made him worthy of the high expectations surrounding him. At the same time, Nikola and Milena strove to keep Danilo as close to hand as possible. It was an anxiety brought about by the desire to oversee each and every detail of his upbringing, as well as the paternal fear of losing him to an accident or disease if he was out of their sight.

If that made Danilo's formative years somewhat provincial, his tutors were all highly competent and cultured men: the Swiss Charles Puigget instructed Danilo in mathematics and French; Colonel Ovsyaniy military studies and geography; Simo Matavulj, one of Serbia's finest writers, literature and Serbian language.

The young Danilo also had the physique, good looks and attractive persona to suggest that he could develop into a leading personality. One of his tutors described the positive impression he made: *"The Heir to the Throne . . . was just twelve years old at the time, his second year in the gymnasium. He was physically and spiritually a wonderful child,*

with his mother's noble features . . ."[1]

The last point, that Danilo's character leaned toward the Vukotić side of the family gene pool, was generally agreed upon, and therein it seems lay part of the problem. To inherit his mother's looks and intelligence were attractive traits, but to also inherit her more passive and reticent nature a problem. Danilo soon began to demonstrate that he lacked his father's strength of will and acuity, his physical strength and his determination. Even the doting father worried that his son was *"a big lazybones who would come to nothing."*[2]

The attention and praise constantly lavished on the young man further accentuated his tendency to indolence and Danilo came to feel that being the heir was enough in itself. Nikola and Milena were unable to bring themselves to be stricter with their son, who sauntered through his youth and early manhood enjoying the pleasures readily available to a man of his position.

Danilo's life was one of princely leisure and in that he excelled being an outstanding hunter, a talent which the people were much pleased by, and also an elegant, handsome young man well suited to the social whirl of *la belle époque.* His future secure, his desire for glory, if he had much at all, was only for the reflective kind.

There was, however, one aspect of duty which even Danilo could not be allowed to avoid. He had reached his late twenties and still showed no desire to take a bride. Left to his own devices it would probably have stayed that way but, fortunately, it required little effort from Danilo personally as his father and eldest sister, Grand Duchess Milica, set about placing a suitable bride in his path via the salons of St. Petersburg.

Her name was Princess Augusta Charlotte Yutta Alexandra Georgine Adolfine, daughter of the heir to the German duchy of Mecklenburg-Strelitz, Adolphus Freidrich. Augusta Charlotte's lineage was of some distinction and, like Princess Ana's husband Franz Josef Battenberg, it brought a link to Queen Victoria through her grandmother Augusta (the daughter of Queen Victoria's uncle, the Duke of Cambridge) and to Russia through her aunt, Maria Pavlovna, who married Vladimir Alexandrovich (the third son of Tsar Alexander II). Politically the principality had, fortuitously, sided with Prussia in the war of 1866 against Austria; a choice which brought it a privileged status within the German federation.

A further point of interest with regard to marrying into the Montenegrin dynasty was that the history of Mecklenburg-Strelitz had a strong Slavic connection. In the Middle Ages Slavic tribes settled the north-eastern region of Germany and the duchy actually took its name from a Slavic castle named Mecklenburg, which lies between the cities of Schwerin and Wismar.

Grand Duchess Milica brought the couple together by inviting Danilo for a personal visit to St. Petersburg. His first meeting with Augusta Charlotte took place at the residence of Grand Duchess Maria Pavlovna. Danilo may very well have been won over by the attractive nineteen year-old, but that can only be surmised. In any event his family rushed him to the altar, almost as if they were afraid that he might change his mind. The engagement was announced almost immediately and the wedding date set for July 1899.

The announcement of the Crown Prince's betrothal was the occasion for much celebration. Danilo and Augusta Charlotte left for Mecklenburg-Strelitz a few days later and were greeted with all the pomp and ceremony the principality could muster. Neustrelitz was decorated with the Mecklenburg and Montenegrin flags and poster pictures of the betrothed couple, who were deluged with flowers and good wishes at every step. In Cetinje, where Danilo's younger brother Mirko read Tsar Nikolai II's congratulatory telegram to cheering crowds, the response was equally enthusiastic.

Tsar Nikolai agreed to be godfather and his representative, Grand Duke Konstantin

Nicolo Giov. Gulli CETTINJE

(Above) Crown Prince Danilo's bride, Princess Augusta Charlotte Yutta Alexandra Georgine Adolfine of Mecklenburg-Strelitz, with her family. Seated to her right is her father, Grand Duke Adolphus Freidrich, and seated to her left is her mother Elisabeth Marie, daughter of the Duke of Anhalt. Standing right, elder brother Adolphus and, standing left, the Grand Duke's youngest child, Karl. (Right) Augusta Charlotte photographed in Cetinje. (Below) The procession through Bar for Charlotte Augusta's conversion to Orthodox Christianity; Prince Nikola can be seen behind the Metropolitan. The ceremony took place at the church of St. Nikola in Bar on July 26, 1899, and was performed by Metropolitan Mitrofan Ban. Charlotte Augusta took the Orthodox-Christian name of Milica-Yutta.
(Facing page) Shortly before their wedding day, Danilo and Augusta Charlotte in Neustrelitz, the capital of Mecklenburg-Strelitz, where the betrothed couple received a rapturous welcome.

Konstantinovich, arrived in Bar on July 24, along with Princess Ana and Prince Franz Josef, Prince Petar Karadjordjević with his three children, while Turkey was represented by Marshall Shakir Pasha. Grand Duchesses Milica and Stane were absent having remained in Russia to mourn the death of the Tsar's youngest brother, Grand Duke Georgiy Alexandrovich.

    The following evening Augusta Charlotte and her family sailed into Bar on the Lloyd Steamer, the *Vumbrand*, which was accompanied into port by the royal yacht.

    A rather splendid reception had been prepared for the Germans. Prince Mirko and Grand Duke Konstantin greeted them as the Kotor Orchestra, which had been hired especially for the occasion, played from the royal yacht in the harbour. In the surrounding hills

The wedding of the Crown Prince: July 27, 1899.
(Above) Newlyweds Crown Prince Danilo and Crown Princess Milica-Yutta exiting Cetinje Monastery and (left) Princess Milena and Franz Josef Battenberg lead the guests, amongst whom were Tsar Nikolai II's representative Grand Duke Konstantin Konstantinovich, Princess Ana, Prince Petar Karadjordjević with his three children and Turkey's Marshall Shakir Pasha.
Facing page: After the wedding ceremony. (Top) The wedding procession on the way back to the Palace and (bottom) Milica-Yutta and Prince Nikola in front of the Palace.

many fires had been lit to form one enormous flame and on Volujica Peak the letters ZDM were illuminated to signify 'Zivjeli [long live] Danilo and Milica' (Augusta Charlotte took the name of Milica-Yutta on her conversion to Orthodox Christianity). Danilo's arrival was greeted by cannon salvoes, fireworks and the ringing of Bar's church bells.

The next morning Augusta Charlotte disembarked ship and took her first steps on Montenegrin soil. Accompanied by her family and dressed in a beautifully decorated Montenegrin national costume she accepted the traditional offering of bread and salt. Then an honourary procession accompanied her to Bar's Church of St. Nikola, where the rite of conversion was performed by Metropolitan Mitrofan Ban and she received her Orthodox Christian name of Milica-Yutta.

All was now set for the wedding. In the early morning of July 27 the wedding party began the journey to Cetinje. At Vir, the small port which serviced Lake Skadar, they boarded the steamer *Danica* to Rijeka Crnojevića and then completed the journey to the capital by carriage.

Cetinje was resplendently decorated with flags, flowers, a military display and the guests and diplomats dressed in their finest apparel. Milica-Yutta, fatigued after her long journey, was nonetheless impressed by the glittering, picturesque capital. At 4pm Danilo and Milica-Yutta were married by Metropolitan Mitrofan Ban in the Monastery.

The future seemed bright as Danilo and Milica-Yutta settled into married life, while Nikola and Milena eagerly anticipated the day when their darlings *"Dano"* and *"Misja"* would have children.

Those and other hopes would be disappointed.

Danilo was a responsible man but his solitary and taciturn nature seems to have stifled the spirits of his young wife. Observers concurred that the Crown Prince's personal life was well organised, pleasant, even elegant, but also that it was a rather listless existence.

The couple's life was centred on their residence Topolica, which Prince Nikola had

(Top and facing page, top) Danilo and Milica-Yutta with Nikola and Milena in Cetinje. (Left) Milica-Yutta enjoying a swim and (above) with Princess Ana.
Facing page: (Bottom) Milica-Yutta in her residence, Topolica. (Insets) Two photographs of the Princess horse riding, (inset right) with Prince Nikola in Cetinje.

234

(Above) Milica-Yutta being attended to by a lady-in-waiting. (Below) Danilo, a renowned marksman, takes aim during a hunting trip and (right) relaxing at his residence in Ulcinj.
Facing page: (Top) Villa Topolica near Bar. The Crown Prince and Crown Princess' residence originally belonged to Prince Petar Karadjordjević, but was bought by Prince Nikola on his departure and subsequently given to Danilo. (Bottom) Milica-Yutta horse riding in the mountains.

bought from Petar Karadjordjević when he departed Montenegro. It was a rather opulent court, more in the European style than the Palace in Cetinje, and Danilo was a worthy master, being a stickler for order and etiquette.

German and English servants were employed to maintain the residence and prepare the French cuisine he so enjoyed, while Montenegrins were only employed as labourers. That detail illustrated another unfortunate characteristic of Danilo's: he did not think too highly of his earthy kinsmen and was most definitely not a man of the people.

His pleasures were to cultivate the court grounds. They were impressive with a large greenhouse, well tended woodlands, olive groves and farmlands for grazing cattle and also plenty of opportunity for car rides, horse riding and hunting. Guests were rarely invited to this idyll as Danilo preferred to live alone in the world of leisure and repose he had created for himself, but Milica-Yutta was not so happy with this secluded lifestyle.

Some of Danilo's failings no doubt stemmed from relations with his father and their disagreements over the political direction of the country and monarchy. Although he was aloof and

distant from the people, Danilo could still see the need for political reform to a constitutional system; whereas his father, while being much closer to the people, doubted the country was ready for such modernisation. Danilo's influence certainly helped Montenegro gain its first constitution in 1905.

Another point of dispute were Danilo's Germanophile tendencies. Prince Nikola's loyalty to Russia was, despite the necessary double-dealings of politics, sacrosanct. However, Danilo saw in Russia only a backward and primitive nation; the wealth and efficiency of Germany was far more to his taste. It is said that when he heard that the Japanese had taken Port Arthur in the Russo-Japanese War of 1904/05 he toasted their victory.

Inter-dynastic relations also served to disillusion Danilo. Attending King Petar Karadjordjević's coronation in 1904 he was told in no uncertain terms by his brother-in-law that the new Serbia wanted nothing to do with Prince Nikola's Montenegro. It was not, therefore, without reason or a degree of perception that Danilo saw the dynasty's future as a bleak one, its position as fragile as *"birds in the trees"*[3] he concluded. Conversely, if Danilo had inherited some of his father's fighting spirit that might not have been

(Left) A portrait of the Crown Princess signed "Militza 1914". (Below) Milica-Yutta on the Adriatic coast.
Facing page: (Top) Danilo and Milica-Yutta and (bottom), from left to right, Danilo, Ksenija, Nikola, Vjera and, standing, Milica-Yutta on the steps of Villa Topolica. Danilo and Milica-Yutta made an attractive couple and, as a constitutional ruler, Danilo could have brought positive attributes. However, he lacked the drive and dedication needed to forge a role for himself in post-1900 Montenegro and his political views were not of the traditional Russophile and pan-Serb sort which most Montenegrins held.

the case as there was still a good deal of prestige attached to the Petrović-Njegoš house.

In 1906 Danilo met the heir to the Habsburg throne, Archduke Franz Ferdinand, in Dubrovnik. The Empire's Croatian subjects were restless and, as Emperor Franz Josef was unwell, Franz Ferdinand attended military exercises in Herzegovina and Croatia, where he received a hostile reception. His doctor noted the contrast when the crowd saw the Montenegrin: *"The streets were decorated with flags, but exclusively flags in the national colours of Croatia. Not a single imperial black and yellow flag was among them . . . But when the Archduke returned with Prince Danilo at his side, the progress of the carriage was accompanied by enthusiastic acclamations . . . Crown Prince Danilo started on his return trip accompanied by the mighty cheers of the crowd."*[4]

A final disappointment, Danilo's marriage was childless. It was a great sadness for Nikola and Milena who, apart from their natural expectations, had great affection for Milica-Yutta.

Over time Danilo and Milica-Yutta's marital relations seem to have cooled, perhaps even to the point where she contemplated leaving him during the early years of exile in World War One. It was also suggested that Danilo's main reason for remaining married was to ensure he shared in his wife's inheritance.

The Crown Prince's role in Montenegrin history showed that the Petrović-Njegoš dynasty could not be an infallible source of inspirational leaders. Although he was far from incapable and his views during World War One showed a calmer temperament and better balanced views than some members of the ruling circle, Danilo demonstrated at every turn that his character was not that of a ruler.

Mirko and Natalija: the Prince's favourite son finds love at first sight.

Prince Mirko and the Colonel's Daughter

My father, tall, dark, handsome, typical Montenegrin . . . He had a talent for music. He used to play on the pianoforte classical music that I admired. I remember him playing Beethoven, Schubert, sometimes Mozart or Bach. My Mother . . . blond, very beautiful, big dark eyes, remained in my memory like a goddess.

Prince Mihailo Petrović-Njegoš

Nikola and Milena's second son, Mirko, was born on April 17, 1879. He was a playful and appealing child whose high spirits and exuberant nature ensured that he became the family favourite. A contrasting personality to his elder brother, he was an extrovert and a prankster who craved attention. He was also gifted with a marked talent for music. Prince Nikola's affection for Mirko allowed the creative, imaginative but sometimes reckless young man to indulge himself.

Mirko was brought up to believe himself destined for a great future, namely to occupy a Balkan throne, and he readily allowed himself to become the focus of speculation and rumour: which throne would he occupy and which bride would he choose? His travels and escapades throughout Europe, along with his self-publicising and boasting, gave the newspaper gossip columns plenty to write about.

He was suggested as the future ruler of Bulgaria, to replace the German born Ferdinand of Saxe-Coburg, of Serbia, with its heirless Obrenović dynasty and even as governor of the Turkish ruled provinces of Macedonia and Albania.

Many princesses were suggested as brides: from the House of Orleans, a Bonaparte, a Russian, a Greek and many others; their looks and potential dowry being of equal import in the many schemes built around young Mirko. In the end, however, it was his impulsive nature which determined his choice of bride rather than the hope of gaining a wealthy princess by his side.

Colonel Aleksandar Konstantinović was related to Serbia's King Aleksandar Obrenović through his mother Anka, the daughter of Jevrem Obrenović, brother of the dynasty's founder

The dashing and exuberant Prince Mirko and (facing page) with his bride, Natalija Konstantinović. After a brief engagement they were married in the summer of 1902.

241

Prince Miloš. Anka had been assassinated alongside Prince Mihailo in 1868.

Relations with King Aleksandar were, as was so often the case with the Serbian ruler, mutually hostile. Colonel Konstantinović had been forced to flee Serbia after criticising King Aleksandar's marriage to the controversial Draga Mašin. The family lived in exile, alternately between Nice and Vienna, materially provided for with a state pension they were not considered a political factor within Serbia.

That situation lasted until Mirko met and fell madly in love with the Colonel's daughter. An unplanned meeting in Nice was all it took for Mirko to forget his grandiose plans and determine to marry the beautiful, dark eyed Natalija Konstantinović.

If it was an understandable personal decision and a sign that Mirko had matured and was ready for the responsibilities of a prospective ruler, it was also a choice that created many problems.

King Aleksandar Obrenović's throne was far from secure and, after the notorious false pregnancy of Queen Draga, there were many who hoped, and planned, to be rid of him. Prince Nikola's daughter, the late Zorka, had married the Karadjordjević claimant to the Serbian throne and helped to ensure that Aleksandar had a determined Serbian rival close at hand. The unhappy Aleksandar, totally devoted to the otherwise unloved Draga, not without reason saw plots and intrigues in every action. No one imagined he would look kindly on Mirko's marriage plans.

Prince Nikola, however, surprised everyone when he took a more relaxed view and gave his assent, only asking that the marriage plans be kept secret for a period of time. Nikola's motives have often been debated: was it a lapse in his political acuity; was he simply indulging his favourite son or was it some strategy to place Mirko on the Serbian throne?

Whichever it was, a political hornet's nest was about to be thoroughly stirred.

Several of Nikola's ministers were suspicious of both father and son's innocent protestations of love. Simo Popović simply did not believe that Mirko was smitten with Natalija and, rather, he saw the matter as one of Nikola's intricate dynastic schemes. Of course he could not air such opinions openly and, worse still from his perspective, after Mirko had revealed his hopes to him, he was invited to lunch with father and son.

(Above) Natalija's mother, Mileva Konstantinović-Opujić, by Tito Aguiari. Facing page: (Bottom left) Mileva with her two children, daughter Natalija and son Vlada. (Top left) A portrait of Mileva and a teenage Natalija. (Right) After her marriage to Prince Mirko, Natalija was given the honourary title of Grand Duchess of Grahovo and Zeta.

After Mirko had left, Nikola raised the question of the marriage. Aware of the inevitable gossip about pretensions to the Serbian throne he told his friend: *"Konstantinović are from the female line and because the Obrenovići are on thin ice it is possible to say that I married Mirko to open his way to the Serbian throne. And I, as God is my witness and all of you that know me well, would never, even if it comes to that, allow it. Even if the Obrenovići are finished the throne belongs only to Karadjordjević, whose throne it was. Could I even imagine to take it from Pero, my son in law, and*

(Above left) Mirko in Cetinje and (above) Mirko and Natalija in 1902. (Left) Natalija with her father, Colonel Aleksandar Konstantinović. Although they were related to Serbia's ruling Obrenović dynasty, relations were not good and Colonel Konstantinović had gone into exile after criticising King Aleksandar's marriage to one of Queen Natalija's ladies-in-waiting, the divorcee Draga Mašin.

my Zorka's children, that I love so much."[1] Simo Popović remained unconvinced but he could at least share his worries with the Foreign Minister, Gavro Vuković, who had been kept in the dark.

Father and son had hoped to maintain a degree of secrecy and Nikola decided to use a visit to St. Petersburg, scheduled for November 1901, to sound out Tsar Nikolai II. The first that Vuković heard of the marriage plans was when he learned that Mirko wanted to go to Paris via Nice to meet with his fiancée. Adding to his misery, Mirko had been talking freely with the diplomatic corps. In this matter, at least, Prince Nikola and Vuković agreed and Mirko was firmly instructed to desist, although some damage had already been done.

After Nikola left, one of Vuković's contacts informed him that Mirko had told the Serbian Ambassador in Cetinje that the meeting in St. Petersburg was to discuss his accession to the Serbian throne. That was not only untrue, the visit had also been a closely guarded secret. How

Prince Mirko's escapades and affairs were well publicised and, ultimately, the cause of much personal sorrow. These love letters to *"Honey Heni"* (translations below), two years before his marriage, show the sort of romantic entanglements he got into. Mirko's affair with Mrs Vukosava Krsmanović was public knowledge and, before his daughter's marriage, Colonel Konstantinović acquired some of the most scandalous letters to protect Natalija's feelings and reputation. The relationship was later cited by those who doubted the sincerity of Mirko's professed love for Natalija.

> *Honey Heni,*
> *Please do not return my letters. No, I am not scared that my darling Heni would compromise me, but I was afraid of DK, not of you. Be happy, I am completely satisfied from DK. Tomorrow I will write to you a lot! My sweet darling is it possible that you think that I could be afraid of you!?*
> *At the very end of this letter you will see and be reassured that I am not the least afraid of you, and again I say that I am quite afraid of DK.*
> *My sweet darling I do not deserve that you harass me saying 'As you are asking me to return your letters it is a sign that you are getting bored with me and want to finish the relationship.' Please, my sweetheart Heni, do not tell me anything like that ever again. Kissing your hand I remain your faithful and devoted Prince Brigadier Mirko Petrović-Njegoš, Grand Duke of Zeta and Grahovo.*

Until we become honourably, truly and most sincerely . . . love you more than anything in the world.
PS. Tomorrow I will write to you and Anka very much.
Mrs Vukosava Krsmanović
Cetinje, February 1900.

> *Honey Heni,*
> *My sweet and dear happiness,*
> *Please forgive me for not writing to you these days, but I did not want to let 'B' go because he told me one day, five or six times, that 'R' is waiting for the letters and I let him go, but he did not go to 'R' but to see some singer. I would let him go to her with pleasure, and even more I would give him money because I accept that everyone is made of flesh and blood, and that every young man needs to make a 'speech about the unification of Serbs,' but I was very angry because he tricked me so meanly and nastily. I told you . . . young people talk about unification of Serbs and really that is how it is, it is true. For example I would die if I stopped talking about unification for thirty days. So you see, Honey, how good a patriot and Serb I am (now for certain you and Anka are laughing). Please do not tell anything to 'B', he would work out that I told you about him. I told Anka that tonight I cannot come, but now I think that after all I will. I hope that I will receive a letter from you, or from Anka, before I go. I have to leave tomorrow at noon . . .*
> *I hug your arms and legs and all of you.*
> *Your faithful and trustful speaker of unification.*
> *PS. Just a while ago, whilst riding, I met you with Anka and DK. I want to know immediately if you were walking with that Wanton Fellow and why was he around you. Please reply to me or tell Anka to reply.*
> *I forgive everything.*

would Nikola be received if the news leaked out? The primary purpose of the trip was actually to discuss military matters, which was tricky enough in itself, while Vuković's ongoing priority of improving Montenegro's relations with Serbia was undermined by Mirko's loose talk. In desperation he turned to the *"wise and understanding"* Princess Milena, but she could only commiserate, telling him *"what is done is done."*[2] Nonetheless, they combined their efforts to restrain Mirko.

Mirko, however, stuck to his own plan: to meet Natalija in Nice and then wait for Nikola's return. Milena argued long and hard with her son and finally forbade him from going until his father returned. He was determined so, finally, Milena turned to Vuković who, while realising he could not prevent the engagement, still tried to delay Mirko's departure. A telegram was sent to Nikola but he, to Mirko's great relief and Vuković's chagrin, approved of the trip and said he would join Mirko in Nice on his return journey from Russia.

Vuković was shocked, not so much at the marriage plans but at the conduct of the affair, in particular Nikola's benign view of the likely consequences. It was a clear illustration of the potential antagonism between the national and dynastic interest. For Mirko personally it was wholly understandable, but his irresponsible talks with the Serbian Ambassador could be enough to sever

Venice 1902. A series of pictures taken during the Venetian Festival. (Left) Natalija and her father, Colonel Konstantinović.
Facing page: (Top) Mirko and Natalija in their hotel room and (bottom) enjoying the spectacular view from the balcony.

already tense relations between Cetinje and Belgrade, which would bring serious repercussions.

Emigration to and migrant work in Serbia were essential for Montenegro: its own economy could barely feed the nation let alone fulfil the aspirations of the younger generation. If, as had happened in King Milan's reign, Serbia was closed to Montenegrin emigrants and workers it could spark political discontent, an economic crisis and an exodus further afield.

Vuković persuaded Nikola that it was best to approach King Aleksandar directly and he was despatched to Belgrade in February 1902. He sounded

out his old friend Mihailo Vujić, now Serbia's Foreign Minister. Despite his own misgivings, Vujić agreed to present Mirko's engagement to King Aleksandar as a love match which Prince Nikola, Princess Milena and Crown Prince Danilo all considered purely a personal matter.

King Aleksandar's response was unhappy but resigned. He told Vuković: *"Tell Prince Nikola to forgive me for my sincere speech. I have to admit this marriage would not be agreeable to me. The only thing I can promise is to remain indifferent towards the couple in love . . . our family ties are severed forever because the Konstantinović family have endlessly insulted myself and the Queen . . . I only beg Prince Nikola,*

Mirko and Natalija's wedding took place in Cetinje on July 25, 1902. For political considerations the celebrations were kept relatively low key; Serbia's King Aleksandar Obrenović was angered by the marriage, in particular its dynastic implications. (Right) Members of the Montenegrin Government resplendent in their national costume bring pageantry and colour to the occasion and (below) Prince Nikola with Princess Milena, Princess Milica-Yutta and Princess Ksenija.
(Facing page) The wedding procession: the bride and groom led by page boys with family and guests behind.

my brother, to keep that couple out of my sight. Your Master should know in advance, not to have any misunderstanding or cause insult to him later, that I will not receive his son or daughter-in-law . . . Your Mirko appears in the press a lot, he even proclaims to be a pretender to the Serbian throne. Neither I nor my nation can understand by which right he can even dream of the Serbian throne . . . Can you imagine what he will do now when he considers himself a relative through his marriage? That is why

I ask the Prince to protect me from his newspaper stories."

Vuković was relieved that King Aleksandar had accepted the inevitability of the marriage, but could hardly guarantee to silence the press and rather lamely suggested he simply ignore it. The King's reply was a perceptive one: *"That would be good if one could stay indifferent in the face of public opinion, but these days it is such a great force that it is equal to the English fleet. It should be considered most seriously."*[3]

The Foreign Minister's mission had been a success: he had secured King Aleksandar's agreement and prevented a political breach, thereby safeguarding the cornerstone of his policy. On February 21 he telegrammed Cetinje that the marriage preparations should go ahead.

In Cetinje attention was now focused on the important questions of a dowry and the choice of godfather.

The dowry was quite a thorny problem as Colonel Konstantinović was reluctant to have his comfortable exile disrupted, while the Royal Family's finances were already over-stretched. The agreement reached was for twelve thousand francs per annum from Natalija's father and forty thousand from Prince Nikola. However, the forty thousand francs could only be made up by taking thirty thousand francs from the state treasury.

Nikola had hoped that Tsar Nikolai II would agree to be godfather but the Serbian tangle, not least the fact that the Tsar was already godfather to Queen Draga, led to his refusal, while any hope that King Aleksandar would act as godfather had been shown to be wildly unrealistic. Finally, to spare Aleksandar's feelings, Minster Ilija Plamenac was chosen instead of Count Zici, who was considered unsuitable having been a friend of Aleksandar's estranged father, Milan. Given these circumstances, ostentatious celebration was avoided and the wedding was a relatively low-key affair.

It was eagerly hoped that Mirko and Natalija would have many children, particularly as Danilo and Milica-Yutta's marriage was as yet childless. In that regard the marriage got off to a hopeful start with two sons born in close succession: Stevan on August 27, 1903 and Stanislav on January 30, 1905. Sadly illness took both: Stanislav dying in January, 1908, and Stevan in March. Recompense came with Natalija's third pregnancy and another boy, Mihailo, born on September 14, 1908.

The death of their first children certainly had a detrimental effect on the couple's relationship, which was further strained by Mirko's selfish behaviour. Most damagingly, he was known to have taken several mistresses. His first lover was said to have been Prince Nikola's mistress also and the cause of many ugly scenes between father and son. The unhappy culmination was the scandal which eventually resulted from Mirko's pre-marital infatuation with the wife of the director of a travelling theatre company, Mrs Vukosava Krsmanović.

Their lack of discretion ended in an embarrassing scandal. Enjoying a game of 'Adam and Eve' in

Borovik, Mirko allowed his trusted servant, Mrgud, to take pictures of himself and his lover. These pictures along with many love letters later fell into the hands of King Aleksandar Obrenović. Eventually the Belgrade magazine *Zvono* published some of the less scandalous ones in 1910. The final blow to Mirko and Natalija's marriage was his lasting affair with 'L.P', from a respected Cetinje family. He paraded the relationship so brazenly that even Natalija's attempts to disregard her husband's infidelity, which had gained her admiration, became untenable.

Although Natalija gave birth to two more sons, Pavle on May 16, 1910, and Emanuel on June 10, 1912, the couple separated in 1913 when Natalija returned to live with her parents in Paris.

Mirko's response to the separation signalled a further deterioration in his behaviour. He wrote to his sister, Elena, now Queen of Italy, claiming that Natalija had seduced her husband, King Vittorio Emanuele, and had thereby been the marriage wrecker. Nikola was forced to intervene and, to appease both Natalija's family and Vittorio Emanuele, he placed Mirko under house arrest at his residence of Kruševac, Podgorica. Nikola used the newspaper *Glas Crnogorca* to tell the nation: *"In view of his personal troubles, Prince Mirko is withdrawing from public life to his court in Kruševac where he will remain in peace."*

Mirko was hardly in a state of mind to contribute much to the national effort in the prolonged period of war which began with the first Balkan War of 1912. Tragedy finally overtook him during the

Mirko and Natalija lead the wedding procession through Cetinje. Immediately behind the perjaniks are Princess Milena and Colonel Aleksandar Konstantinović. (Facing page) A portrait of the bride.

occupation of the country by Austro-Hungarian forces in World War One. Having contracted tuberculosis he was transferred to Vienna for treatment, but his condition deteriorated and he died in March 1918.

It was a sad end to a life which had promised much, for Mirko had positive and attractive attributes, but clearly not the temperament and sense of duty his status and circumstance demanded.

Family problems notwithstanding, Mirko's third son, Mihailo, remembered his parents fondly: "*My father, tall, dark, handsome, typical Montenegrin . . . He had a talent for music. He used to play on the pianoforte classical music that I admired. I remember him playing Beethoven, Schubert, sometimes Mozart or Bach.*" Mother Natalija he recalled as: "*Blond, very beautiful, big dark eyes, remained in my memory like*

a goddess. She used to repeat to me many times, 'do not imagine you are special because your grandfather is King of Montenegro'."[4] It was advice which Mihailo clearly heeded when, during the German occupation of Yugoslavia in World War Two, he was offered the poisoned chalice of a puppet Montenegrin kingdom. Instead he chose to support the Yugoslav ideal.

Caught up in a turbulent era, Mirko and Natalija did not find happiness in their relations, but their surviving children, who ensured a possible line of succession for future generations, and Mirko's musical compositions which are still enjoyed in Montenegro today, were a positive legacy from a brief and troubled marriage.

Portraits of Natalija Konstantinović. Prince Mirko was smitten at his first meeting with his future bride, highly understandable in that Natalija was considered one of the beauties of her day.
Facing page: (Top) Prince Mirko in his residence, Kruševac, near Podgorica. A portrait of Tsar Nikolai II can be seen on the wall behind. (Insets) Some of Mirko's musical compositions. Mirko's talents were creative rather than political or military, particularly as a musician and composer. (Bottom) An intimate moment for Mirko and Natalija in Darmstadt with Princess Ana, her husband, Franz Josef of Battenberg and a family friend.

Mirko and Natalija's first children were sons Stevan, born August 27, 1903, and Stanislav, born January 30, 1905. (Above) Stevan with his mother and grandmother. (Right) With his parents and (below right) With his father. (Left) Stevan with his doting grandfather and (below) a charming picture taken in Cetinje outside the Palace during winter. Facing page: (Top right) Stevan with Natalija in the court park in Cetinje, and (top left) Stanislav with his uncle, Prince Petar. (Bottom) Stevan with his mother and (inset) Stevan and Stanislav together in front of Prince Nikola's residence, Villa Ljeskovac, in Rijeka Crnojevića.

(Above left) Stevan with his nanny and (above right) Stevan and Stanislav under an aged and gnarled olive tree. (Below left) Natalija and Stevan and (below right) mother and son in Heidelberg. (Bottom left) Stevan and Stanislav enjoy a game in a haystack. The two boys were surrounded by a loving extended family and at the centre of much attention and affection; their premature deaths were a great sadness. During 1907 both caught tuberculosis and, on doctor's advice, were sent to the coast to stay with Slavo Romodonović, who lived near Prčanj in the Bay of Kotor. Stanislav was the first loss, dying in early January 1908. Mirko and Natalija took Stevan to Cannes, France, for further medical treatment. In February Princess Ksenija, accompanied by Adjutant Ilija Jovanović-Bjeloš, went to visit them. It had become clear that Stevan would not recover and Mirko took Jovanović to see him. He recalled: *"Stevan was lying on a veranda, his hands burning from his high temperature."* It was a tragic scene as Stevan, still cheerful and optimistic despite his condition, asked when would he be going home to Cetinje to see his grandfather and the rest of the family. Stevan died on March 15, 1908, aged four and a half. Crown Prince Danilo came and stayed for three days, after which the family took Stevan's coffin back to Cetinje. The Cannes authorities reserved a train carriage for the Royal Family and in Italy Queen Elena sent a boat with a cabin converted into a chapel. They were met in Kotor by Natalija's parents, after which the whole family continued onto Cetinje for the funeral.

Facing page: (Top left) A beautiful portrait of Natalija and Stevan. (Top right) Natalija at the family residence, Kruševac, and (inset) a portrait of Natalija. (Bottom left) Natalija during a hunting trip and (bottom right) a portrait of Mirko from 1905, dedicated to his 'Lili' (Natalija's nickname).

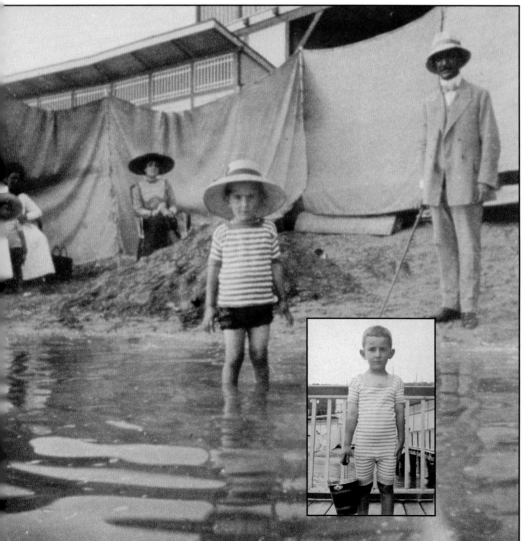

Facing page: A family day out to the beach in Abazia, Croatia, for Natalija and her third and fourth children, sons Mihailo, born September 14, 1908, and Pavle, born May 16, 1910. (Top left and inset) Natalija takes to the water wearing her sun hat. (Top right) Mihailo shows his younger brother, Pavle, who is king of the sandcastles. (Centre right and bottom right) Mihailo and Pavle. (Bottom left) Mihailo playing in the water as the family look on and (inset) Mihailo.

(Above) Mirko and Natalija's children. From left to right: Pavle, Mihailo and Emanuel. (Right) One of the family's last portraits. Mirko and Natalija's marriage was neither happy nor stable. Although they were deeply in love when they married, it proved to be a difficult relationship which lasted little more than a decade. Natalija went to live with her parents in Paris, shortly after the birth of their fifth son, Emanuel, in June, 1913. Moves for a divorce were begun in 1917, but Mirko died from tuberculosis in March 1918, before the annulment. In 1920 Natalija remarried.

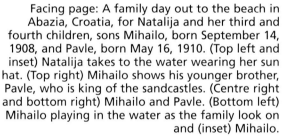

Prince Nikola by O. Basevi, 1900. The first decade of the twentieth century was a turbulent one for the Balkans and Europe as a whole. The final collapse of the Ottoman Empire was fast approaching, as was the demise of the European order which had existed in revised forms since 1815. In Montenegro the patriarchal era was coming to a close and Prince Nikola found himself in conflict with more modern currents of thought. An era of peace and modest progress gave way to one of instability and dispute. (Below) The Prince in Moscow. Allies were vital if the monarchy was to survive but ties with Russia were beginning to weaken.

Stalked by anarchy and assassination the Prince reluctantly joins the race to reform.

Ah! But what can I do? I am so helpless in the face of all the rivalries that abound among our Slav brethren and of the cruelty and oppression exercised by the Turks in regard to them. I do what I can, but how often have not events proved too strong for me?

Prince Nikola

Prince Nikola's perspective on Balkan problems and his place in the scheme of things was an accurate one. Despite his long and successful reign, his position on the European stage was still a minor and politically impotent one. Furthermore, unresolved problems were pressing. He had not yet succeeded in making Montenegro a viable economic state, even the borders were still ill-defined and worked against economic prosperity. There was also the thorny question of Serbo-Montenegrin unification, the eventual aim of both states but in what form and under which dynasty was still to be decided. All that could be left aside if the Ottoman Empire survived; an ironic fact considering that the Prince's throne was secure only so long as the Balkan status quo remained relatively undisturbed, but the nation's ambitions demanded liberation of the South Slav people throughout the Balkans.

By the turn of the century it was clear that the Ottoman Empire's internal problems were insoluble. Istanbul's remaining Balkan provinces, Albania and Macedonia, were restless while its nominal suzerainty over Bosnia-Herzegovina was a flimsy veil for Austria-Hungary's occupation. The region's other imperial power, Austria-Hungary, was also in decline and shared with Turkey an ominous appellation: ramshackle empire. It, too, was threatened by instability in its Balkan provinces which were dominated by South Slavs (Croats, Serbs and Slovenians) who were unhappy at their subordinate position within the Habsburg Empire.

There was another, alternative, prospect to empire: South Slav unification. This was also a problematic issue as the political programs advanced were varied and often antagonistic to each other. The shared but nonetheless distinct histories and cultures made union a complex matter; although the younger generation's enthusiasm provided impetus to the dream of a united South Slav state, embodied in what had become known as the 'Yugoslav Idea'.

Prince Nikola sought to navigate his way through this complex arena, placing his hopes in the Petrović-Njegoš dynasty's prestige and his own political skills. However, Serbia saw itself as the natural leader of the South Slavs. The result was that Belgrade and Cetinje competed to lead the unification movement, but neither had firm plans on how to achieve that goal. Instead, they vied with each other for prestige, a rivalry which was visible in the ongoing dynastic tension. In that regard, at least, Nikola had some grounds for optimism. The Obrenovići had failed to further the unification programme and their popularity was low, the Montenegrin ruler had the better image by far.

"You can see very well that I am a sick young man. I have been brought to this by the unhappy life of my parents and the continuous struggle with the love that I owe to both of them."[1]
King Aleksandar Obrenović

Since his accession, King Aleksandar Obrenović had struggled to stay on his unstable throne; his troubles were largely the legacy of his father, Milan.

If a ruling house ever needed a popular figurehead it was the Obrenovići after King Milan's reign. The family's achievements under Princes Miloš and Mihailo had been overshadowed by the political escapades of their successor, as well as the disputes between Milan and his wife, Natalija.

Aleksandar proved a personality wholly incapable of playing that unifying role for the dynasty. Much of the blame for Aleksandar's failings could be traced back to a troubled childhood and his feuding parents.

Milan's marriage had been an unhappy one. He had brought it on himself through his womanising and suspicions of his wife's supposed political ambitions, which ruined his relations with Natalija. In turn, she spurned him both in private and in public with a righteous wrath that could not be ignored. Their son was not spared as they also fought bitterly for control over his upbringing.

In 1887, when Aleksandar was just a boy of ten, Milan told Natalija he could no longer live with her and that she had to leave the country. She left for the Crimea taking Aleksandar with her. Milan was not satisfied, even though his wife was in *de facto* exile, and he had Natalija closely watched. He soon asked her to accept an official separation and to send Aleksandar back to Belgrade. Natalija, who was in Germany at the time, refused, and so Milan enlisted the help of Otto von Bismarck who sent the police to take Aleksandar from his mother by force.

What Milan really wanted was a divorce, but the couple's obvious incompatibility was insufficient grounds and he could hardly cite his own adultery as a cause. Instead, he used all his power and influence to force a divorce through, against the opposition of the Serbian Orthodox Church and public opinion.

Outside of his well publicised personal troubles, Milan's reign was filled with political controversy: a sharp shift of foreign policy from allegiance to Russia to subservient and secret arrangements with Austria-Hungary; a major peasant rebellion against his rule in 1883; a disastrous war with Bulgaria in 1885 and ongoing hostile relations with Serbia's developing parliamentary system.

It had all taken its toll on Milan personally. After divorcing Natalija and, rather surprisingly, giving the country a new and more liberal constitution, he abdicated in 1889.

However, while Milan departed to enjoy his favourite pastimes of gambling and womanising, he maintained an influence through his barely teenage son who ascended the throne under a regency. Any hopes that the nation was rid of its difficult monarch were soon further disappointed. Milan soon tired of his life of leisure and planned his return for when, as he confidently anticipated, democratic party politics in Serbia failed. Still, he would not have things all his own way as Natalija had not accepted the divorce or her banishment from Serbia as final.

The boy-King was also becoming an active factor and, in April of 1893 at the age of sixteen, he carried out a constitutional *coup d'état* by dismissing the three regents Parliament had appointed. Milan's influence behind the scenes was obvious, but Aleksandar was precocious and had his own agenda. Politically, at least, it was one which he shared with his father: to bring Serbia back under despotic rule. By the following year Aleksandar had brought Milan back to Belgrade and restored the more authoritarian constitution of 1869.

Natalija, with perhaps greater foresight, wanted her son to take a more conciliatory stance toward the political parties. Her opportunity came after Milan had run into trouble again, this time over some dubious mixing of politics and personal finance, after which he left the country in a huff. In May 1895, Natalija returned in triumph as friends and even former enemies rushed to greet her and the Government announced four days of public celebrations.

Natalija's influence over her son lasted a little over two years, until the autumn of 1897. She hoped Aleksandar would marry Prince Nikola's daughter Ksenija, but Milan worked hard to sabotage that possibility. Aleksandar was actually in love with one of Natalija's ladies-in-waiting, Draga Mašin. Natalija disapproved and the two women quarrelled. Draga resigned her post and Aleksandar decided it was time to bring his father back.

Aleksandar and Milan's duarchy of power lasted for three years until they too fell out over Draga, whom Aleksandar had resolved to marry. Draga was a divorcée, a widow and some ten years older than Aleksandar. Even worse than that, she was a woman with a past including, it was rumoured, a previous career as a professional companion to gentlemen friends. Several of Aleksandar's ministers and generals told him about Draga's past, one even claimed to have enjoyed her for a reasonable sum.

Conveniently disregarding his own chequered past, Milan was unequivocally against the marriage. A mistress was one thing, such a controversial woman as queen another altogether. He even wrote to his son that he would be the first to welcome his overthrow if he married Draga. However, the Obrenovići were always determined in matters of the heart and Aleksandar took no heed of the many warnings about Draga.

(Left) A French magazine's depiction of the constitutional *coup d'état* carried out by Serbia's sixteen year-old King, Aleksandar Obrenović, in April 1893. Influenced by his father, ex-King Milan, Aleksandar dismissed the three political regents and instituted an era of reactionary and divisive rule, which ultimately led to his own death. (Above) August 5, 1900: Aleksandar's marriage to the former lady-in-waiting to Queen Natalija, Draga Mašin.
Facing page: Portraits of (top) ex-King Milan and (bottom) Queen Natalija. The couple's stormy marriage ended in divorce, but they continued fighting for control over their son. It was a family melodrama which filled the columns of Europe's newspapers.

The last Obrenović rulers: Queen Draga (above) and (facing page) with her husband, King Aleksandar. Draga Mašin could hardly have been a more controversial and unpopular consort. Even Aleksandar's parents disapproved of Draga, to which Aleksandar, both in anger and fear of his domineering father, responded by threatening to have Milan shot as a traitor if he attempted to return to Serbia.

Milan resigned as head of the army and Aleksandar had finally become his own man. His father died a broken man, in 1901, and was buried in Vienna.

Aleksandar, like his father, was an intelligent man, but that was the best that could be said of the young King. He was also, predictably enough given his formative years, an emotionally unstable, nervous, insecure personality who soon proved to be a divisive ruler. Undoubtedly, he was deeply devoted to Draga and the more charitable observers thought her feelings were no less genuine. However, the royal couple's behaviour outraged and alienated public opinion.

Draga's fake pregnancies, which were revealed as deceits in 1901, finally ruined her reputation. It was pitiful for her to try and deceive her husband as well as the country in this way, but when rumours circulated that she hoped to pass off her genuinely pregnant sister's child as her own even greater scandal ensued. The personal lives of the Obrenovići had always made good copy for the press and the European public was now informed that the last legitimate Obrenović could not have an heir as long as he was married to Draga.

The royal couple continued in the same vein regardless. Draga was as determined as she was narrowly self-interested and she continued to forward the interests of members of her family whenever she could. Even more importantly, and fatally as it proved, Aleksandar had lost the loyalty of many army officers.

King Milan had based his rule on the support of the army and had treated its officers as an élite caste. They not only felt that Aleksandar had shamed the nation with an immoral marriage, they were also enraged by his high-handed attitude toward them. Serbia's financial difficulties meant that many were not being paid regularly and Aleksandar was blamed for not ensuring the Government understood its priorities. With more justification, they seethed at the King and Queen's personal vendettas as officers were refused promotion and others pensioned off early because of their suspected hostility to Draga.

Support for the King was dissipating, public anger was growing and many within the army did not want the onus of being seen as an unpopular and despotic ruler's only supporters. The long anticipated closing act of the Obrenović saga was finally at hand. It changed the destinies of both Serbia and Montenegro's royal families.

Having learned that a plot within the army was in motion, Aleksandar and Draga had become virtual prisoners within the Palace and Aleksandar surrounded himself with guards during the few public engagements he undertook. The conspirators therefore decided the only way to get to the King was to invade the Palace itself. On the night of June 10/11, 1903, they succeeded in having the Palace surrounded by troops, although many of the soldiers were not directly involved in the plot and thought that Draga was only going to be exiled. After heavy fighting with the still loyal guards, the conspirators forced their way in at around 2am.

The possibility of a rescue attempt had been removed and the conspirators searched the grounds for the King and Queen. A cruel twist of fate then sealed the affair. Aleksandar and Draga had hidden in a small alcove accessible only through a secret door in their bedroom. Through the window Draga could see the Russian Embassy, from where the Ambassador witnessed the drama, and in the garden below she spied the Commander of the Royal Guard, Captain Ljuba Kostić. Hastily opening the window she called out: *"Soldiers! Your King is in danger! For God's sake to the rescue, to the rescue!"*[2]

There were no loyal guards left, Kostić was also one of the conspirators. He looked up, saw Draga and fired his revolver. The conspirators rushed up the stairs but could not find the secret entrance to the alcove. An axe was brought and they began to destroy the bedroom wall. With them was General Petrović. Loyal to the King he had been wounded and taken hostage. Realising that the axe was about to strike where Aleksandar and Draga were hiding he broke his silence: *"Gentlemen, will you give me your word of honour that you will spare the life of the King?"* The increasingly agitated conspirators agreed and General Petrović went to the papered wall and knocked: *"Sire! Sire! Open! Open! I am your Laza. Here are your officers!"*[3]

Aleksandar appeared to find a crowd of angry officers. He demanded that they obey their oath of loyalty to the crown. *"Here is our oath of fidelity to him!"* one shouted as he opened fire on Aleksandar, who had stepped forward to protect Draga. The point of no return had been reached and the royal couple was murdered in a frenzy of violence. Draga was killed instantly by the first shots and, after the officers had mutilated her body with their sabres, thrown from the window into the garden. Aleksandar's end was even more horrid. Repeatedly shot, he was still alive as his body was lifted through the window. His fingers grasped onto the window frame, instinct and sheer desperation giving him the strength to hold on. One of the officers took out his sabre and cut off the dying man's fingers. The body, peppered with over thirty bullet wounds, was thrown down.

The corpses were left where they had fallen until, at 4am in the pouring rain, the Russian Ambassador came to view the situation. Greeted by the salutes of the conspirators he told them: *"For God's sake gentlemen, carry their bodies inside the Palace. Do not leave them here in the rain, exposed to the gaze of the public."*[4]

It was a gruesome murder and one of King Milan's former ministers, Count Čedo Mijatović, summed up feelings toward the atrocious act: *"I cannot describe the horrible, disgusting and ferocious conduct of some of those murderers. They seemed to emulate the exploits of Jack the Ripper on the dead body of the woman who was their Queen. I feel utter shame and humiliation that Serbian officers could have conducted themselves with such brutal cruelty."*[5] Nonetheless, hatred for Aleksandar and Draga was widespread and many viewed the regicides as patriots and liberators who had averted a civil war by their actions.

The news reached the Montenegrin capital via a telegram from the Vienna Correspondence Bureau. The disbelieving Foreign Minister, Gavro Vuković, decided to withhold the shocking news from the people because Prince Nikola and Crown Prince Danilo were in Bar on the coast. He even thought it might be a prank played by Prince Mirko and confronted him: *"What reason do you have for playing such a dangerous and crude joke."*[6] Mirko, of course, had nothing to do with it, but his dreams of the Serbian throne looked as if they might be about to come true.

Vuković, with Prince Mirko and Princess Natalija in tow, then went to ask the Serbian Ambassador, Miloš Vasić, an Obrenović supporter, if he had heard the news or had further information. He had received a coded telegram but

was unable, or perhaps reluctant, to decipher it. The fact that it was from a well known Karadjordjević supporter seemed to worry him as much as the news itself.

As the news spread, Cetinje began to buzz with rumour and anticipation. Believing, as did most of the capital, that Mirko would be elected to the Serbian throne the foreign ambassadors met over coffee to discuss the shocking events. The Italian Ambassador reported that he had never seen the capital so agitated and one newspaper even went to press with the story of Mirko's succession.

It only took until the morning of June 12 for these premature hopes to be dashed, when a telegram was received confirming that Petar Karadjordjević would be elected to the Serbian throne.

By June 15 Cetinje had caught its breath sufficiently to welcome Petar's accession, and Serbia's new ruler was genuinely popular with the Montenegrin people who liked to refer to him as *"our son in law."*

The capital was decorated with flags and a gala performance at the Zetski Dom Theatre hastily arranged. The Serbian Theatrical Company was in town and, like the Serbian Ambassador, had initially thought it appropriate to mourn the late King and Queen, but shook off their shock and embraced the new mood. They, too, now rushed to hail *"the accession of our beloved King Petar"* as the theatre programme announced.

The only representatives from the Royal Family to attend the performance were Prince Mirko and Princess Natalija. Having been so

King Petar Karadjordjević's coronation in 1904 (above) was attended by Montenegro's Crown Prince Danilo and his wife, Crown Princess Milica-Yutta. Also pictured with King Petar are his three children, daughter Jelena and sons Aleksandar and Djordje. (Insets right) The Illustrated London News reports Petar's sudden accession to the Serbian throne in June 1903, after the assassination of King Aleksandar and Queen Draga. Public opinion throughout Europe was outraged at the brutal murders, but Petar provided a sharp contrast to his predecessor by ruling as a constitutional and subsequently highly popular monarch. (Facing page) A signed portrait of the new King.

rashly celebrated as the next Serbian rulers, they were inevitably the centre of attention. Mirko's frozen features as he watched the performance amply expressed his disappointment.

The outstanding question for the Serb dynasties had been decided and, after all his shrewdness and patience, Prince Nikola's hopes had been dashed. At the Palace he discussed Petar's triumph with his ministers. With tears in his eyes he told them: *"I remember Zorka, if only she were still alive. I am even sadder because I believe that Petar will take her remains to Serbia. It is very hard for me to be parted from her."* Nikola was bitterly disappointed but went outside to make a speech welcoming Petar's election to the waiting crowd.

Worse still, although Nikola had obviously not benefited from the *coup d'état* he was rumoured to be part of the conspiracy. His feelings were expressed to an adventurous Englishwoman, Mary Edith Durham, who had become friendly with the Royal Family through her charitable work in the country. She was convinced of Montenegrin involvement and a conversation with Nikola only served to confirm her suspicions.

Nikola remarked: *"A sad affair was it not, Mademoiselle?"* - *"Very sad Sire, but perhaps necessary"* - *"My God, but you are right Mademoiselle! A thousand times right! It was necessary, and it is you alone that understand. Return, I beg you, to England. Explain it to your Foreign Office, to your politicians, to your diplomats!"*[7] From this audience and other hunches Durham concluded that Cetinje was part of the plot, but Nikola, in his loquacious and excitable manner, was only expressing a widely held view: the murders were atrocious but Aleksandar and Draga had been a disaster for Serbia.

The most obvious beneficiary was Prince Petar Karadjordjević and his involvement was also widely suspected. It was noted that the last Obrenović ruler was murdered on the thirty-fifth anniversary of the assassination of his great-uncle, Prince Mihailo Obrenović, a crime for which Petar's father, Aleksandar Karadjordjević, had been convicted of complicity. The long and violent rivalry between the two dynasties, Petar's Russophile sentiments and his relation to the Montenegrin Royal Family convinced many of his involvement.

However, Petar's politics stopped short of murder and he was not part of the conspiracy. He issued a statement to disassociate himself from the regicides: *"My opinion of the execution of the King and Queen of Serbia is this: I deeply regret that it has been thought necessary to shed streams of blood. I formally disapprove of the violent measures . . . It would have sufficed to force King Aleksandar to sign his abdication. He could have been bound, as had been done in other circumstances. It is a horrible thing to shed blood."*[8]

Undoubtedly, Petar had long hoped for the overthrow of the rival dynasty but the Serbian regicides were a force unto themselves. They had their own agenda and had not removed an Obrenović just to gain a Karadjordjević. Under the new regime several of the leading conspirators not

only went unpunished but continued to hold positions of power. Therefore, despite his genuine desire to be a constitutional ruler, Petar was for sometime regarded as a pariah by his fellow monarchs and for the first three years of his reign only Austria-Hungary and Russia recognised him. In the short term there was little he could do, except to watch his back and build up popular support among the people.

How much Petar or Nikola may have known of any conspiracy remains speculation, but Vienna and St. Petersburg both seem to have been aware of it. Some of the conspirators prepared themselves in Vienna with support from the Austro-Hungarian Ministry of Foreign Affairs and the Russian Ambassador's mute witnessing of the events amply demonstrated his country's attitude.

Official outrage from whatever quarter was not accompanied by genuine regret at the brutal murders. King Aleksandar and Queen Draga died as much from a lack of friends as from the regicides hands. Unloved in life they were barely mourned in death. They were buried a day after their murder, in an eerie early morning ceremony attended only by the clergy, the grave diggers and two conspirators who came to witness the burial.

The Obrenovići were soon forgotten and the closing chapter of their history generally considered, as a foreign journal remarked, *"merely a local effervescence of Balkan anarchy."*[9]

"The question of Macedonia is, I admit, an extremely difficult one. We have to govern a population so varied both in nationality and in creed, that there must of necessity be constant aggressions and outbreaks. It is said that we aid and abet the Greek bands in massacring the Christians. I totally deny this. We do not. Surely it is in our own interest to maintain peace and order in Macedonia and not allow outsiders to create disorder and dissension."[10]
His Excellency Mehmed Noury Pasha,
Secretary General of the Imperial Ministry of Foreign Affairs

Macedonia had become little more than a synonym for any territory in the southern Balkans that other states coveted; in that much the Sublime Porte's minister had a point, but Turkey's policy was also a cynical divide and rule exercise which most certainly included collusion with the armed bands terrorising the Macedonian peasantry. Austria-Hungary had proven strong enough to hold Bosnia-Herzegovina together; whereas Turkish authority in Macedonia, already notoriously corrupt and extortionate, had become so weak that its only policy was to try and ensure the rival claims of Bulgaria, Greece, Romania and Serbia were played off against one another. In the meantime Macedonia's multi-ethnic population, which included Albanians, Greeks, Gypsies, Jews, South Slavs, Turks and Vlachs, was trapped in a hellish arena of lawlessness and violence. Initially they formed local militias for self-defence, but that unity was soon lost in the internecine feuds between the various communities.

Among the Balkan states with interests in Macedonia, Bulgaria, Greece and Serbia had the strongest links to the province. In Bulgaria's case it was a burning frustration dating back to that great watershed for the Balkans, 1878's Treaty of Berlin. After Russia had dictated terms to the defeated Turks in 1877, 'Big Bulgaria' stretching from the Danube to the Aegean Sea and from the Black Sea to Ohrid was briefly created, but only on paper and until the Powers imposed their will at Berlin. Macedonia, tantalisingly gained and then torn from their hands, evoked as much emotion for Bulgarians as did the Battle of Kosovo among Serbs. No Bulgarian leader could ignore these national aspirations and Macedonian revolutionaries virtually terrorised Bulgarian politicians into supporting their activities.

Serbia saw Macedonia as historically Serb territory. The historical claim dated back to King Dušan's medieval empire, but that only meant the Bulgarians countered by recalling an earlier state encompassing the province, that of King Simeon of Bulgaria in the ninth century. Serbs and Bulgars also disputed over the identity of the Macedonian Slavs; neither nation having yet stopped to consider that they might have an identity of their own.

Greece also based its claims on ethnic ties, as well as the banner of Hellenic history and culture, creating particularly tense relations with Bulgaria.

The rivalry over Macedonia, combined with that between the Greek and Bulgarian churches for ecclesiastical rights over the Ottoman Empire's Orthodox Christian subjects, led many to believe there would be war between the two.

The three states, and to a lesser degree

(Below) A Bulgarian *četa* in Macedonia. The province was the battleground for militias - Bulgarian, Greek and Serbian - as the Balkan states jockeyed for position, anticipating the final fall of 'Turkey in Europe'.
Facing page: (Top) His Excellency Mehmed Noury Pasha, an eloquent apologist for Sultan Abdul Hamid's misrule and (bottom) Great Britain's candidate for Macedonia's governorship, Prince Arthur of Connaught.

Romania, citing kinship with the latin speaking Vlachs, competed through political, educational and religious propaganda and gave support to the ethnic militias.

Exactly how the population was divided between the many ethnic groups and cultures was the crux of the issue. It resulted in bribery and manipulation to the point of absurdity: whole villages would switch allegiance from one nation to another, even members of the same family would proclaim themselves belonging to different nations and, if these methods failed, threats and violence were used to coerce recalcitrants into giving their allegiance.

Montenegro, or rather its Prince's imaginative diplomacy, hoped to benefit from the imbroglio. Having lost the hope of gaining the Serbian throne for Prince Mirko, Nikola saw the possibility of making one of his sons ruler of the troubled province. Macedonia's partition through an agreement between the Balkan states seemed unlikely and Nikola had already explored that possibility unsuccessfully with the late King Aleksandar Obrenović. More realistic was increased autonomy under continuing Turkish suzerainty. It would mean the appointment of a governor or prince chosen by the Great Powers. Several candidates were forwarded, including both of the Montenegrin princes, Danilo and Mirko, a German prince, an Austrian archduke and England's Prince Arthur of Connaught.

Nikola used an interview to suggest that the Petrović-Njegoš dynasty could provide a solution to Macedonia's plight: *"It is a monstrous state of affairs . . . There is but one way, namely, for the Powers to call a conference and place Macedonia under a governor-general, who must be a European prince. The reforms would then be carried out and the Greek bands expelled from the country . . . how an innocent Christian population is being exterminated because of international rivalry, they would cry shame upon those responsible for this wholesale murder and outrage."*[11]

It was a reasonable proposal to solve an extremely difficult problem, and there were growing calls for Macedonian self-government, but volatile relations with their neighbours hardly recommended a Montenegrin prince to reconcile divided peoples. Crucially, Germany withdrew support for the princely option for its own imperial considerations. Nikola's diplomacy therefore had little impact for he was suggesting a nineteenth century solution in an increasingly nationalistic political environment.

While the Balkan states jockeyed for position in the run up to the Ottoman Empire's final fall, that process was not yet quite complete. Its delay was an important factor in the development of the political situation and a good deal of the credit for the Empire's survival lies with Sultan Abdul Hamid II, as does the blame for the bloodbath it culminated in.

The 'Red Sultan', as Abdul Hamid had become known for the Armenian massacres, had managed to survive for three decades, ruling over the twilight years of the Ottoman Empire with the

skills of a man born into a world of conspiracy and deceit. He had manipulated the competition between the Powers to his own benefit and, in latter years, gained the support of Kaiser Wilhelm II by using Germany's desire for economic hegemony in the Ottoman Empire to ensure his own position.

The world had learned about the true nature of Hamidian rule but, as a practical politician, Prince Nikola knew relations had to be maintained. Although his friendly relations with Abdul Hamid certainly harmed his public image, in private he shared the general outrage at the Sultan's policies. In 1899 he wrote to Queen Margherita of Italy expressing his frustration at the dual role he was forced to play: *"Regarding the gift of a yacht which I received from the Sultan, he who ordered the slaughter of the Armenians. If I could only separate my ruler's life from my private life, I would not even speak about this political present and would not be obliged to use it from time to time."*[12]

Abdul Hamid's talent was for political intrigue; his failing was that he lacked a positive vision for his ailing Empire. Aiming to become leader of the Moslem world he took a hard line toward his minorities and exploited the age-old tensions between Moslems and Christians. The Armenian massacres of the 1890's were the fruits of these policies.

Despite his best efforts to suppress reports of the atrocities the facts emerged and, in 1896, Montenegro's great friend William Ewart Gladstone roused himself for one last denunciation of the *"Unspeakable Turk"* whose rule should be *"rubbed off the map."* However, the uneasy balance of power in Europe meant that Abdul Hamid met with no sanction for his crimes against the Armenians.

(Above) Kaiser Wilhelm II, the embodiment of German imperialism and (right) a Russian caricature satirising Sultan Abdul Hamid II's growing economic and military dependency on Germany. (Facing page) An Ottoman officer with his men. The Ottoman army was equipped with German arms and trained by German officers.

When rebellion subsequently broke out in the Mediterranean island of Crete, which declared union with Greece, Greco-Turkish war followed in 1897. Instead of pushing Abdul Hamid from the throne the war saw Turkey score a resounding victory, which greatly boosted his prestige. Victory was made all the sweeter when Germany and Austria-Hungary refused to co-operate with the other Powers in imposing post-war reforms on the Empire.

The Macedonians also figured prominently in the list of those who had suffered from Abdul Hamid's stratagems. He had played Bulgaria, Greece and Serbia off against one another and encouraged communal hostility within Macedonia itself. Finally, he agreed to paper reforms knowing full well the misery and brutality would continue regardless.

More than two decades had passed since Nikola's first encounter with Turkey's tyrant and there was precious little left redeeming Abdul Hamid. Some felt his personal nature was neither cruel nor vindictive, but he was a paranoid autocrat in whose name horrific crimes were committed. The days when it seemed that he stood for a reinvigorated Empire were long gone and all that remained was the low cunning of the perennial survivor.

William Sloane, an American well acquainted with Hamidian rule, described the pernicious result: *"Between the ruler and the ruled there was an awful gulf which neither cared to bridge, such was the sodden inertia of the system . . . a sort of genial inefficiency permeates it all. Yet beneath is the volcano of indiscipline. Guile and the oiled feather first; then, if thwarted, fury and recklessness. Smooth promises with perpetual delay; then performance under compunction with the Parthian arrows of atrocious bloodshed."*[13]

Abdul Hamid's long reign had inevitably affected the development of the independent Balkan states. In Montenegro's case it had allowed political relations to stabilise but also stifled regional ambitions. The death of the 'Sick Man of Europe' and the liberation of the South Slavs had not come about. As standard bearers for Balkan freedom, the Montenegrins' historic mission had been to precipitate the Ottoman Empire's fall, and during the wars of the 1870's, when Russian forces almost overran Istanbul itself, they had made a notable contribution. Yet the Empire endured, enfeebled and horribly eroded by history but surprisingly tenacious.

The benefit of the extended peace had been to give Montenegrins the opportunity to broaden their horizons. The country had entered the world politically as a recognised state, cultural links had grown and economic ties had increased, albeit with as yet marginal benefits. Montenegrins increasingly looked to the north and west for aspiration and inspiration; fighting the historic enemy was no longer the all consuming occupation of yesteryear.

It was, therefore, only natural that Prince Nikola had also moved away from his youthful views to a broader view of Balkan problems. His eager anticipation had turned to philosophical resignation: *"Ah! But what can I do? I am so helpless in the face of all the rivalries that abound among our Slav brethren and of the cruelty and oppression exercised by the Turks in regard to them. I do what I can, but how often have not events proved too strong for me?"*[14]

Nikola well understood the realities around him and was frustrated that his experience was not called upon: *"It is very hard for me to say what I should do, but if I could talk on a footing of equality with Serbia and Bulgaria, and Montenegro were no longer the poor little principality it is today, then most certainly I should do my utmost to persuade all those within reach of my words and influence that they ought to do all that is in their power to prevent any conflagration, should such an unhoped for calamity arise, from spreading beyond its original limits."*[15]

Nikola wanted the peace to last and had set his sights on a royal elevation to strengthen his position, not least because the need for domestic reform was becoming increasingly apparent.

The Ottoman era was drawing to a close, as was its counterpart, the patriarchal era in Montenegro. As an alternative to foreign misrule Prince Nikola's patriarchy was attractive, but it hardly bore comparison with the opportunity and prosperity offered to the citizens of other European nations.

> *"Why do you laugh?"*
> *"I remember that story with the wolf Master."*
> *"You are wrong, I would be a good constitutional leader."*[16]
> Prince Nikola to Simo Popović

Successful though it was in many regards, Prince Nikola's rule was fast becoming a political anachronism. King Petar Karadjordjević, whose sympathy for republican ideals were well known, had gained popularity by ruling under a liberal constitution, and Serbia, along with the other independent Balkan states, had an active parliamentary system. If they all shared the same basic flaws, that of poor nations struggling to develop modern political systems, only Montenegro remained an outright autocracy.

Power had been centralised in the Prince's hands as far back as the 1870's, when the Senate's role had been reduced and its governmental functions taken over by ministers appointed by the ruler. It was a rationalisation of the governing institutions but also a move away from representative politics and, with the tribal system also weakening, a personal rule emerged.

Little surprise then that Prince Nikola was opposed to a constitution. He even used an unaccredited article for *Glas Crnogorca*, published in early 1905, to tell the nation: *"There is no constitution here, nor for the moment do we want one. What is a constitution? Often a constitution can be merely a piece of paper subject to changes of circumstance, to be used as a screen, but a transparent screen of the most unashamed absolutism and poltroonery. Then the affairs of state are worse than in the most isolated and primitive societies. The best constitution is justice and good sense, in our patriarchal monarchy we feel peaceful and happy."*

It was a position he could no longer sustain. Having long held faith in Russia as the model for his rule, events there proved pivotal in convincing him to reconsider his views. The shocking Russian defeat in the Russo-Japanese war of 1904/5, along with the failed revolution of the same year which forced Tsar Nikolai II to grant a constitution and a parliament, showed Nikola that change could no longer be put off.

The traditionalist now set out to prove he was not the implacable conservative his detractors claimed. Nikola invited his old and trusted friend, former minister Simo Popović, to his yacht moored in Bar. Over coffee he asked for his help: *"I would like you to write for me a 'little constitution' for Montenegro."*[17] However, Popović was not keen on the proposal and Nikola soon found out it was an opinion shared by his more experienced ministers. Undoubtedly, there was some self-interested calculation involved as their power and positions depended on the Prince, but there were also sound reasons for caution.

The apparently soothing balm of reform, they argued, might prove more of an irritation than a cure. Was Montenegro ready for a constitution, a parliamentary system and a free press after almost half a

century of autocracy? Where would the educated men to fill the parliamentary and governmental posts be found? While the young generation were gaining educations, it was mainly abroad and most often in Serbia, where many had become dissatisfied with the meagre opportunities available to them in Montenegro. Grinding poverty had created a diaspora of disaffected emigrants who felt that patriarchal rule was retarding the country's development.

Nikola's advisors argued that the freedom of a constitution would not check that anger but, rather, allow it free rein to wreak havoc. Both Simo Popović and Gavro Vuković cited Serbia's disputatious and polarised political society, made worse by its outspoken and partisan press, as further example of how troublesome liberal systems could be. Montenegro's less developed political life and still strong tribal loyalties could make for an even more volatile mix.

Crown Prince Danilo also became involved in the discussion, as an advocate of reform. Gavro Vuković tried to talk him out of encouraging his father's newly found reformist zeal, but a rising young politician, Minister of Finance Lazar Mijušković, had the Crown Prince's ear. Danilo was aware of the pressing need to reform the political system, particularly its finances, and Lazar Mijušković had already impressed him with reforms which had brought some stability to the public purse. Gavro Vuković, whose career spanned a sizeable portion of the patriarchal era, would help precipitate his own downfall in the conflict with the younger and more radical Mijušković.

Even Simo Popović, who had withdrawn from public life despite Prince Nikola's pleading, thought it a sufficiently important issue to draw on their long friendship to try and dissuade him. He stressed the possibilities for gradual reform which, he believed, would allow the Prince to end his reign peacefully and allow the Crown Prince to eventually take over the reins of power as a constitutional ruler.

Appealing to his sagacity, Popović recalled the story of Nikola's pet wolf which used to accompany him everywhere, until the day it attacked some sheep and was put down. He joked: *"The wolf can shed its coat but never its nature."* Nikola enjoyed the joke but was adamant that this particular old wolf would surprise his friend: *"You are wrong, I would be a good constitutional leader."*[18]

Montenegro's constitution was proclaimed on St. Nikola's Day, December 19, 1905, in a ceremony which ended with theatrical symbolism. As Nikola knelt to take his oath, he feigned inability to get up and his sons stepped forward to help their ageing father. The Prince was telling his people that, wearied by his long rule, he now wanted to share the burdens of power with his fellow countrymen.

Prince Nikola's belief in Montenegro's patriarchal tradition and his political conservatism inevitably gave rise to calls for a constitution and greater political freedom. (Right) A manifesto, from 1894, calling on the people to rise up against the Prince's personal rule. *"Brothers, It is not necessary to describe the sad situation in our homeland. Montenegro – home of glory, honour, integrity and bravery. Montenegro, home of great heroes, exemplar in the fight for freedom and the most beautiful, precious stone in Dusan's crown, is enslaved in chains by her first son, her Master, Prince Nikola, and his sycophants, with the chains of a most terrible absolutism, using the means of his tyrannical rule! Therefore brothers and friends, great and small, rich and poor, and above all dear youth, you the hope of our future, in the name of God let us fight for the civil rights and the constitutionality of our dear homeland . . . In the name of the Committee for a Constitution in Montenegro."* (Above) Foreign Minister Vojvoda Gavro Vuković, who, like the Prince but for slightly different reasons, opposed political reform, hastening the end of his ministerial career. (Facing page) Prince Nikola in Venice, 1903.

It was certainly something of a leap in the dark for all concerned as Nikola had resisted even minor reforms which would have encroached on his powers. In his opposition to the new constitution, Simo Popović's chief criticism was for its undue haste. He believed it represented: *"An unnatural jump*

(Above) Russian casualties from the Russo-Japanese war of 1904/1905 and (inset) Munsey's Magazine applauds American peacemaking efforts. Tsarism's troubles, military defeat and domestic upheaval, convinced Prince Nikola that reform was also needed in Montenegro.
(Facing page) Tsar Nikolai II with his mother, the Dowager Empress Maria Feodorovna. Prince Nikola had a share of influence at the Russian court through his daughters Milica and Stane, but Tsar Nikolai II was less enthusiastic than his predecessors toward the Prince of Montenegro. In 1907, as Montenegro's internal crisis was worsening, Nikolai wrote rather dispassionately about Prince Nikola's troubles: *"Dear Mama . . . this week we were expecting the Prince . . . It seems very peculiar that he left Montenegro and then disappeared. The rumour is that he fears an attempt on his life by some Serbs or Montenegrins who are studying abroad . . ."*

from the present state of your personal rule . . . there is an unbridgeable gap between the two which should be filled and flattened, so that one could cross over without danger . . . Not one in a thousand Montenegrins even knows what a constitution is."[19]

The foundations for parliamentary democracy had certainly not been laid: most Montenegrins were unfamiliar with the idea of political parties and in the first parliamentary elections votes were cast for Prince Nikola and even the Tsar of Russia.

Worse from Nikola's point of view was the free press which, despite his best efforts, he could not keep under control. Three new newspapers were started: *Ustavnost* (Constitutionality) in Cetinje; *Slobodna Reč* (Free Word) in Podgorica and *Narodna Misao* (National Idea) in Nikšić. *Ustavnost* and *Slobodna Reč* were pro-government newspapers and Nikola's friend, the Belgrade newspaper editor Stevan Ćurčić, sent trusted men to edit them.

The trouble was in Nikšić. The opposition spoke through *Narodna Misao*, edited by those disaffected young Montenegrins educated in Belgrade who became known as the *Klubaši* (Club Members). They were outspoken critics of the ruling clique, which they accused of *"shamelessly trading with the nation"* under Cetinje's famous elm tree where Nikola traditionally held his meetings.

Their anger struck a chord. If Montenegrins were unaccustomed to political parties or debates about economy and society, they could empathise with statements such as this from *Narodna Misao*: *"If we do not find a way to stop the horse-trading in parliament our destiny will be horrible. Our children will find their graves in the dark underground of American mines."*

Having started on the road to parliamentary democracy and a free press there was no turning back. Lazar Mijušković was Nikola's first choice as premier, but it soon became clear how difficult relations between the Prince and Parliament would be. The Mijušković administration was mildly reformist but still only survived until the following year.

In March 1906 a pamphlet was published in Belgrade entitled 'The Voice of Montenegrin University Youth on the Circumstances in Montenegro'. It was the most direct criticism yet of the Prince describing *"a personal rule of deceits and frauds"* with a sham constitution that showed *"the image of a supreme power, through which are organised the rights of an absolute ruler . . ."* Nikola was outraged and he instructed Lazar Mijušković to charge the students with insult and slander of the Prince and Government, while a *Glas Crnogorca* editorial called for the students to face trial.

In fact, Nikola was hoping they would be too afraid to do so, but, to widespread surprise, the students returned determined to defend themselves in court. This gained them public support and their case threatened to become a *cause célèbre* as young Montenegrins living in Belgrade, St. Petersburg and Moscow expressed their solidarity and offered to share the students' fate if they were convicted.

Court proceedings were begun but rather than continue with the trial, which could only bring more publicity and sympathy for the students' views, the charges were dropped. Nikola's improvised gesture won back public goodwill and reconciliation with the students took place at the Palace. The people of Cetinje gathered to cheer as one of the student leaders, Marko Daković, made a speech praising Nikola who in turn proclaimed *"Long live the students"* and gave them one thousand crowns to start their own political party!

Lazar Mijušković ended up as the scapegoat for the *débâcle*. The Prince and the students were, for the moment, on the best of terms and the crowd turned its anger toward the Government with demonstrations. In the usually tranquil port of Bar a dinner celebration was held for one of the student leaders, Djuro Vojvodić, to which a donkey named Lazar (in mockery of the Prime Minister) was invited with a place at table laid for him. Host Radjenović stood up and proposed a toast. *"Be in good health Lazar!"* he shouted as the donkey was forced to drink wine. By November Mijušković had resigned because of the Prince's lack of support, procedural arguments and the accusation that he had taken a bribe from the Italian company which held the tobacco monopoly.

Marko Radulović, a lawyer from Pažić near Danilovgrad, was proposed by Parliament and to show his goodwill Nikola accepted. He had again successfully used his populist touch and even managed to keep lines of friendship open with Lazar Mijušković.

In the same conciliatory spirit Nikola's cousin, Šako Petrović, was made President of Parliament, although their relations had not been particularly good. Nikola wanted to show his support for the parliamentary system and the new spirit led by the students, while the people hoped that Šako, being the Prince's relative, would have approval for his decisions. Hopes were raised when Nikola praised the appointment: *"You have acted as true Montenegrins who have always, in all circumstances, asked for a Petrović to be with you."* Šako certainly shared the popular if rather naive enthusiasm for the fledgling democracy, but he had also been disappointed when Nikola had not made him Army Minister. He saw an opportunity to reach his personal goals and was certainly prepared to side against his relative.

The next two administrations fared no better than the first. Marko Radulović proved too radical for the Prince: releasing prisoners who had not been given a trial in good time, proposing to introduce a new law for state finances and to move the capital to Podgorica.

Under pressure from both Prince and Parliament, Radulović resigned. Nikola personally appointed the next administration, which was comprised of only three trusted men. It was headed by Andrija Radović, who had close personal links to the Royal Family and had also been a member of Lazar Mijušković's brief administration.

The constitutional experiment was proving highly unstable and Nikola's behaviour hardly helped matters. Rather than stand above the political battle he tried to weaken the opposition by wooing, with some success, members of the *Klubaši*. The meetings held at the Palace quickly became public knowledge and rumours circulated that Nikola was dissatisfied with developments and would soon be dissolving the legislature. *Narodna Misao* accused him of disrupting democracy and Šako Petrović joined in the criticism by publishing a poem against the court party, whose members were so angered they called a meeting of Parliament. It did little to reconcile the factions as the *Klubaši* refused to apologise for their criticisms and the court party stormed out.

Nikola actually took some comfort from the outcome, feeling that he had divided the opposition, and he delayed the next parliamentary session until July. It never convened and, with the worsening crisis, Andrija Radović resigned. However, rather than share the fate of Lazar Mijušković, he now followed his own course and joined forces with the *Klubaši*. It was a portentous development.

Nikola appointed a new premier, Dr Lazar Tomanović, an old friend and formerly the editor of *Glas Crnogorca*. He was a well liked man who had not actually wanted the post, but Nikola's pleading had won him over.

Many thought that Nikola was reverting to the old pre-parliament style of government, and the inclusion of another friend, Vojvoda Lakić from Vasojevići, seemed to have little other rationale. The old man's loyalty recommended him, but he was a simple, illiterate peasant and hardly prepared for the business of government. Then there was Milena's cousin, Dušan Vukotić, who was made Minister of Finance. He was at least an educated man having studied in Zagreb, as was the new Army Minister, Mitar Martinović, who had studied military science in Italy. Pliant might have been the best description of the new administration, which was led by an old gentleman from the Bay of Kotor the people of Cetinje nicknamed *"Doctor Turtledove."*

In the meantime Nikola tried to deal a final blow to the opposition. Anyone suspected of *Klubaši* sympathies was now likely to lose their job. Even socialising with a *Klubaši* member could have severe consequences, as Brigadier Milo Djurašković found out when his brother-in-law by chance brought a *Klubaši* man to lunch. The Brigadier was promptly retired from service. A more substantive and worrying sign of discontent was the attitude of the Kuči tribe. Nikola had been making speeches calling the opposition traitors and he promised the Kuči he would visit them to explain his reasoning. The six hundred tribesmen who waited for him were dismayed when he did not even appear and angry words were spoken.

The situation soon deteriorated further as the campaign against the *Klubaši* escalated into violence. They had continued in their efforts to gain power, although they still claimed to be working for the crown and the nation. Nikola's response was to send Prince Mirko and his perjaniks to Niksić to destroy the opposition printing press. It was a bad omen for post-patriarchal Montenegro, particularly for a nation which had always proudly remembered that their medieval rulers had brought the first printing press to the Balkans. Inevitably the ravages of war had seen it destroyed, and more recently, in the 1850's, Prince Danilo had Vladika Rade's printing press melted down to make bullets. This destruction was in a different vein: an act of spite, a poorly judged punishment which even failed to silence the *Klubaši* who continued to publicise their views from Dubrovnik.

In Cetinje armed gangs searched out *Klubaši* members for punishment beatings. Terrified, they took refuge at the house of former minister Gavro Vuković who had become sympathetic to the opposition. For several days his house became an armed haven, as if some simmering blood feud had spiralled out of control.

The Prince's family also became caught up in the conflict. The dispute with Savo Serdar, who had been married to Nikola's late sister Gorde, ended tragically. In his memoirs Simo Popović retold the story of the events which led to Savo's death.

Savo was the parliamentary deputy for Ulcinj. He had joined the *Klubaši* and was one of the signatories of the 1907 political program which had denounced the Prince's rule. He ignored warnings to leave the *Klubaši* and even Nikola's personal pleading could not dissuade him. Nikola decided he would force the issue and he thought he could use the Mufti of Ulcinj to arrange an unpleasant welcome for Savo when he returned home. The Mufti was extremely unhappy to be given such an odious task, so Nikola told him to instead give the instruction to Ilija Srzentić who would get the job done; all the Mufti had to do was ensure his Moslem congregation went along with it.

A few days later Savo returned to Ulcinj. He was surprised to find only his servant waiting for him at the docks, who explained why a hostile crowd of local gypsies were nearby loudly banging oil drums. Savo stormed over to the Mufti's house, but he denied any involvement in the demonstration and told Savo to go to the courthouse and sort it out. On the way there Savo met Pero from Crmnica, an eccentric but usually friendly man who would often stroll through town singing.

However, he began singing a new ditty he had composed ridiculing the *Klubaši* and Savo in particular. It was odd because he had always shown Savo due deference, who now understandably became enraged and slapped Pero across the face, took him by the ear and demanded to know who had put him up to this provocation. Pero became hysterical and ran over to the courthouse while Savo, too embarrassed to be seen in court with the local fool, went home.

Shortly afterward a policeman called demanding he come to the court. Savo said he was ill but

Ilija Srzentić, President of the Court, sent the policeman a second and a third time. Srzentić also had a family connection to the tangle: he was married to Savo's niece and also grateful to Savo for helping him to get his job. It was a dire omen, for if Ilija Srzentić was against him Savo knew that the order must have come from the Prince. To avoid the humiliation of appearing in court next to Pero, Savo sent a statement accepting to be fined or imprisoned for his behaviour. Srzentić replied that the court would not proceed without his presence.

The next day Savo went to the courthouse where he was treated with disdain and told to wait his turn. In the past he had been greatly respected and often went to the court where even the judges would greet him. Eventually Pero appeared and was immediately called into court. Savo, realising that the court officials had waited for Pero's arrival to ensure they would go before the judge together, sat down on the staircase leading into the court, took his gun out and shot himself.

Nikola had wanted to demonstrate his displeasure with Savo and to ensure that the people of Ulcinj would not re-elect him as their deputy. However, the medieval humiliations heaped upon the old man proved too much and he took his own life. Nikola had not foreseen the pitiful outcome of his actions but his part in Savo's death was evident.

"But if a bomb explodes that is revolution! . . . He would become more constitutional than the Queen of England, as if she had breast fed him and not Stane from Bajice."
Nikola Vukotić to Vojvoda Simo Popović

A family schism even closer to home was that involving Princess Milena's nephew, Jovan Vukotić, who was imprisoned because of a letter sent from his brother, Nikola Vukotić. Nikola was living in Serbia and he wrote to his brother discussing the deteriorating situation in Montenegro. However, Jovan never received the letter but was still summarily sentenced without trial to three years and eight months in prison. Although the matter later took on a political aspect there were very personal feelings involved.

Nikola Vukotić had been angered when he was refused permission to marry Lina Petrović, the daughter of Prince Nikola's cousin Božo Petrović. The family pleaded to Metropolitan Mitrofan Ban, who had been obliged to refuse them as by law the couple were too closely related, and he asked Prince Nikola to change the law. The request was denied and Nikola Vukotić resigned his army commission and left for Serbia. In Belgrade, King Petar Karadjordjević helped him to enlist in the Serbian army and later helped him with some personal debts.

In Belgrade the thoroughly embittered young man openly vilified his royal relations. When General Putnik asked him to stop he was told that it was not criticism of the Prince and Princess but family affairs which he had witnessed living at the court. In Cetinje tempers were boiling and there was heated talk about putting an end to Nikola's activities. A friend wrote warning him to be careful, but Nikola had no intention of calling off his campaign and instead wrote to his brother, that same Jovan Vukotić, who ended in jail when the letter was intercepted. The father of the two young men, Princess Milena's brother Marko Vukotić, sold his house in Cetinje and moved to Podgorica to be nearer his imprisoned son. Milena, as ever faithful to her husband, told Marko she no longer considered him her brother.

If Prince Nikola did not have enough to contend with already, anarchism, that unpredictable force which filled the nightmares of European royalty and had done away with his Italian relative, King Umberto, as recently as 1900, now made its presence felt. Belgrade and Nikola Vukotić were again the source of the Prince's troubles.

At Belgrade's Hotel Balkan young Montenegrins would meet over beer and coffee to discuss politics, and their reports of the dire situation back home would sometimes end up in the Serbian press. They were determined to antagonise and harass Prince Nikola and sent him anonymous letters warning of plots against his life. The Prince had his agents in Belgrade who tried to keep him informed of any threats but, in this instance, the agent's identity became known and he was used to relay exaggerated stories of a plan to overthrow the monarchy and bring the *Klubaši* to power.

How serious all this was is hard to gauge, but, in Belgrade, Nikola Vukotić told Simo Popović: *"The Prince did so many bad things to so many people that I enjoy to see him suffer. He does not dare*

277

After the 1905 political reforms Montenegro's disputes became very personal. Princess Milena (above) ended by disowning her own brother, Marko Vukotić, whose son Prince Nikola had imprisoned.
(Facing page) Crown Prince Danilo and Crown Princess Milica-Yutta. Danilo was in favour of reform and worked to ensure his father moved from autocracy to a constitutional system.

to leave the Palace now. I remember when Savo Ivanović sent him letters . . . that someone would kill him and the Heir. His perjaniks had to check behind every bush and at the borders. Can you imagine how scared he will be now when there are so many malcontented people at home and abroad? . . . They only need one man to follow and they have Vojvoda Šako [Petrović] for that, he is prepared for anything. If it comes to that point he would even proclaim a republic . . . And then there is Andrija Radović, you know him as loyal and silent, but you should see him now. At one meeting he said, 'Bombs should start exploding everywhere, like in Russia'."

Popović was unimpressed and replied: *"You and your friends believe in everything you hear from Montenegro, even nonsense. Šako and a republic! He is a republican only after his head is emitting smoke after drinking brandy. Then Andrija and bombs! Why would anyone need bombs in Montenegro where everybody is armed?"* Although Popović could see that Nikola Vukotić had not thought the matter through, the young man remained defiant: *"That is different . . . But if a bomb explodes that is revolution! The Prince would think differently . . . he would become more constitutional than the Queen of England, as if she had breast fed him and not Stane from Bajice."*[20]

Nikola Vukotić's anger had something in common with the many disaffected young men in the Balkans, including those who would make their mark in Sarajevo in 1914 by assassinating the Habsburg heir, but was a Montenegrin revolution, or even regicide, part of their plans?

Replacing Prince Nikola with a genuinely constitutional ruler, preferably Crown Prince Danilo, was their first thought. By the autumn of 1906 the Belgrade diaspora were talking about the large tribes - the Bjelopavlići, Drobnjaci, Kuči, Piperi and Vasojevići - marching on Cetinje to bring the Government's resignation and force the Prince to listen to the people or abdicate in favour of his son. The reports of the coffee house conspiracy, as so far that was all it had amounted to, were nonetheless disquieting enough for the Montenegrin authorities to tighten up border controls.

The culmination of all this was the Bomb Plot of 1907; a convoluted affair which further soured Belgrade-Cetinje relations. Nikola Vukotić had finally got hold of his bombs and a certain Rajković, who used to work in Cetinje's printing house, volunteered to be the courier. His apparent *Klubaši* sympathies and his boast that he could get the bombs to Cetinje made him the ideal choice. Also involved was the student leader Marko Daković, whom Prince Nikola thought he had managed to make peace with. At the same time, before the bombs had even been taken to Cetinje, the conspirators placed a story in the Belgrade press that Prince Nikola had died.

Rajković travelled down to Kotor and contacted Andrija Radović in Cetinje who, either through a loss of nerve or fearing that some trap was being laid, literally jumped in the first car he could find and fled to Trieste. Rajković, despite the border controls and his hardly secretive travels, had little trouble reaching the capital and put himself up at the Lokanda Hotel. His first visit was to Vojvoda Lakić, Minister of Home Affairs, to tell him about the plot and the bombs. The startled minister demanded *"What bombs?"* - *"Those which are supposed to kill the Prince."* After sending Rajković away Lakić immediately informed Prime Minister Tomanović, who went straight to the Prince and asked for Rajković and some of the other conspirators, including Marko Daković, to be apprehended. Arrests were made in Grahovo and Vasojevići but rumour quickly spread that Rajković was really the Prince's *agent provocateur*.

If a conspiracy to assassinate the Prince had been uncovered why had Rajković been able to circumvent Montenegrin border controls and carry the bombs to Cetinje only to then confess his role in the plot? Had Prince Nikola arranged it all so he would have a reason to finally crush the *Klubaši*? On the other hand the fact that the bombs were manufactured in Serbia and had been obtained by *Klubaši* men supported the conspiracy theory. Had Rajković lost his nerve at the last moment and simply tried to save his own skin? Whether the *"bombs exploding under my nose"*, as the Prince put it, were a real threat to his life is doubtful, that they were to be used as a signal for an uprising is more plausible.

Prince Nikola was determined that the conspirators should be brought to trial; true or false the smashing of the conspiracy presented an opportunity to deal with those who had provoked his anger both politically and personally. He confided his feelings to Simo Popović in an emotional outburst which showed the true extent of the gulf between the Prince and the opposition, nothing less than a requiem mass for the patriarchal era.

"I thought Montenegrins would obey me as they always had, myself and my ancestors . . . They would have, poor men, but there were a few people from Palilula [a suburb of Belgrade where Montenegrin students lived] *. . . they filled their heads with ideas that every parliament in the world must have different parties and the one with a majority must form the government. They immediately*

formed the 'People's Party', as if the others are not with the people! Then they asked for parliamentary government so their party would take over. They caused quarrels in Parliament and attacked Mijušković so he had to resign . . . 'All right', I said, 'I will not name new ministers, you do that, whoever you name I will accept.' And do you know who made the new government? Mere children, unskilled, not fit to do even what was told, let alone run the country. But I let them do what they wanted. I did not want to stop them in anyway. I agreed to everything so as not to give them a reason which they could cling to later on when they hit the wall, so they could not say that I wanted to rule outside of the constitution, and then to resign for that reason. I knew it would come to that soon. And what did they do? Nothing and nonsense!

"That Parliament should not be called Montenegrin but Serbian [The Prince's response to the proposal was to agree on condition that he also be allowed to proclaim himself Master of Serbia-Montenegro], *the capital should move from Cetinje, as if that were as easy as tipping your cap and saying goodbye! One thing they did do well was to employ their supporters and get rid of those loyal to me. They were bringing one proclamation after another and I was signing them all. And do you know what I told them? - 'Do not touch the Heir, I will sign everything else.' Still, they resigned soon*

enough, to avoid being blamed for their incompetence. In their resignations they gave many reasons for their decision, all blaming me as if I had acted outside the constitution.

"Their empire did not last long but no one could have tolerated them for even that long except me. Their Palilula upbringing was exhausting my patience so many times I wanted to throw them out. They would come here, sit without being told to, cross their legs, lean on their elbows, light up a cigarette and blow smoke at me while they talked. Absolutely nothing Montenegrin about them at all; it was as if they had taken leave of their senses. God help me! How patient I was! I told them to form a new government of their own men but they did not want to.

"Then I placed my hopes in Andrija [Radović], that when he became Prime Minister he would follow my wishes because he was always listening to me and was a hard worker. But the devil intoxicated his brain and he began to dance to their tune to keep his popularity with them rather than to please me. In his confusion he thought that because there is a constitution now the Prince cannot do anything to him, good or evil, the Parliament is everything, the people are masters. Who could believe that Andrija, one that I cared for as if he was my own child and made a man of, would be the first one to shout for bombs? . . . I was crossing myself in disbelief at such a change in such a short time, at what is done.

"You remember what it was like in the past. As soon I would leave the court Montenegrins would gather around me and follow me. But lately there is nobody around. Now when I leave the court I look at them and they are walking away, or staying under the mulberry tree and no one moves. I thought to myself 'Let's see what they will do if I go to them with only a few perjaniks'. They, without turning at all, just glanced over their shoulders to see I was approaching and left for the Lokanda Hotel, the Vlach Church or the Kafana [Restaurant] to avoid standing with me or taking off their caps. And it is not like that only in Cetinje but all over the country.

"They have sown discord among the people. They have divided them with parties and who is not with the Klubaši is labelled a traitor. Tribes and brothers have suddenly become enemies. I let Andrija go but I feel bad about my relatives. I should say out loud like their ancestors did: 'Stop scoundrels! What parties, what a farce! Montenegrins belong with their Master, everything that we have gained was with him!' Instead, they withdrew to Nikšić like mice into their holes, in the houses which they would not even have were it not for my efforts. Allegedly they cannot be heard, but they are digging all the time and secretly whispering with the Klubaši."[21]

Nikola's unhappiness was understandable. Was it not through his efforts that Nikšić had been liberated from the Turks? Would the *Klubaši* have preferred to struggle for their rights as part of Bosnia-Herzegovina, which was now under Austro-Hungarian control? However, it was also clear that he had not kept up with the mood of the times. The younger generation looked to the constitutional democracy of Belgrade and, for them, the Prince's achievements belonged to the past, as did his patriarchal rule. Simo Popović had been right: the old wolf had not been able to change his nature.

There was, therefore, little ground for compromise and Nikola made sure that the trials of the bomb plotters went ahead. Those sentenced to death had their sentences commuted, but no pardons were given, although a gesture of forgiveness had been hoped for. Convinced that he could prove to the world Belgrade's complicity, Nikola demanded extraditions from Serbia and even Austria-Hungary. Their response was to hold trials which ended without convictions as, like the Cetinje trial, the evidence amounted to little more than hearsay.

The outcome of the struggle was inconclusive. Despite the publicity created by the trials neither side achieved its aim. The *Klubaši* had not forced the Prince to step down or to moderate his attitude toward them. For Nikola it did more harm than good. While muddying the waters may have partially discredited the *Klubaši* it also damaged his own reputation which had been dragged through the political sewer. Only events of international significance drew attention away from Montenegro's domestic crisis.

Emperor Franz Josef of Austria-Hungary. He was determined to maintain the imperial tradition of adding to the Empire's territory in his reign. He had, in fact, failed to hold onto its existing lands. The loss of the Italian provinces and expulsion from the German confederation meant that aggrandisement in the Balkans represented the last chance for an imperial renaissance.

"The future of the Monarchy is to be found in the Balkans, moreover the occupation of Serbia and Montenegro must follow . . ."
General Franz Conrad von Hotzendorf, 1906.

Vienna's politicians would have agreed with their bellicose General regarding the Habsburg Empire's future, but most baulked at the thought of an invasion of the Serb states. Although that dilemma created an ongoing tension within the Empire's Balkan policy, the basic aim of expansion southward remained constant. For Austria-Hungary, therefore, the administration of Bosnia-Herzegovina was merely seen as a stepping-stone to incorporating much of the peninsula.

However, the majority in the province were far from happy living under foreign rule. They had seen economic progress, but the peasantry had benefited little. Count Andrassy's promises, made as far back as 1878, for the reform of agrarian relations had not been carried out and the authorities continued to rely on the Moslem landlords as a ruling class. As a Catholic power Austria-Hungary also discriminated against the Orthodox Christians and the Serb element was the most radicalised, but discontent was spreading to all ethnic groups.

Nor could Vienna simply maintain the status quo. In response to the problems of running a multi-cultural empire, and the constant rivalry between Vienna and Budapest, a more strident policy was evolving. Its chief supporter was the Habsburg heir, Archduke Franz Ferdinand. He was unhappy with political dualism and determined to bring back power to Vienna by using the Empire's Slav subjects as a counterbalance to the Hungarians. In that context there was talk of a tripartite structure with a third Slav component, but there were major obstacles to these plans: Hungary jealously guarding its power within the dual-monarchy, the Empire's discontented Slavs increasingly thinking of independence and Serbia, a natural focal point for South Slav hopes and a nation with a renewed sense of mission since the accession of King Petar Karadjordjević.

Events were set in motion during 1908, but not by Vienna. The Young Turk political revolution, which began partly as a reaction to the fear of Macedonia being lost, had, by July 1908, forced Sultan Abdul Hamid II to pledge himself to rule as a constitutional monarch. Legal and religious equality for all was promised as, almost overnight, Ottoman subjects became, at least in theory, citizens. The prospect of a rejuvenation of the Ottoman Empire was quickly rebuffed in October. Prince Ferdinand declared himself King of Bulgaria, thereby relieving Bulgaria of its theoretical obligation of suzerainty to the Ottoman Empire, and the annexation of Bosnia-Herzegovina by Austria-Hungary was proclaimed.

Fearing that the Young Turks would try to reassert Ottoman sovereignty in Bosnia-Herzegovina, and to pre-empt any claims by the province for constitutional rights under the Young Turk constitution, Vienna had made its move. However, if one of the Great Powers were prepared to tear up the Treaty of Berlin the peace of Europe was threatened. Europe was shocked and alarmed by this unilateral action; even Russia which had made a tacit agreement with Austria-Hungary for compensation in the Black Sea Straits was taken aback. Tsar Nikolai II was shocked to find out that his grandfather, Alexander II, had agreed to the annexation in principle as far back as 1878. Emperor Franz Josef had written to Nikolai just before the official proclamation and the hapless Tsar could only remark to the Dowager Empress: *This letter has been in my hand for two weeks and I have not*

(Above left) Sarajevo, capital of Bosnia-Herzegovina. Since 1878 the Ottoman Empire had exercised only nominal sovereignty over the province, and its administrator, Austria-Hungary, had made a tacit agreement with Russia: Vienna would annex Bosnia-Herzegovina and St. Petersburg would be compensated in the Black Sea Straits. However, Austria-Hungary's unilateral action in October 1908 took Europe by surprise and outraged Russia. (Above right) Montenegro's main port of Bar. After having waited so long, until 1880, to gain access to the sea, Montenegro had not been able to realise the potential of Bar, its best chance to stimulate trade. Former minister Gavro Vuković felt that the blame was their own: *"Almost thirty years have passed since Bar was gained by Montenegro and we have done little to develop it, except for the road connecting it to the mainland, despite the fact that it is our only trading port and connection to the world at large."* In mitigation of that criticism, Montenegro hardly had the finances to develop Bar and did not even exercise sovereignty along its own short coastline. Austro-Hungarian warships patrolled and, on occasion, threatened Montenegro's two ports, Bar and Ulcinj. That latent conflict came to the fore in 1908 after the annexation of Bosnia-Herzegovina. Prince Nikola responded with a declaration that, in future, Montenegro would accept no limitations on its sovereignty and there were anti-Habsburg protests in Bar and other towns, some of which turned violent.

replied to it. I was not aware of such a secret document . . . What is there to say."

Prince Nikola had been around long enough to see it coming, in fact he had predicted it: *"Look at all she* [Austria-Hungary] *does in Bosnia. She is sure to annex it and Herzegovina. And do you think that the Slav populations of the peninsula will not rise in revolt against such a fact . . ."*[22] The Great Powers had, for neither the first nor the last time, taken little heed of the Prince's experience.

Austria-Hungary's action inevitably meant a showdown, and possibly a military one, with Serbia and Montenegro. From Vienna's perspective, if Montenegro could be kept neutral, or better still turned against its ally, the campaign would be against a landlocked Serbia surrounded by unfriendly neighbours. Whereas if Montenegro sided with Serbia it would create a second front and a real threat along the Adriatic coastline, most notably to the port of Kotor which could be attacked from the heights of Mount Lovćen. How much Austria-Hungary feared a united response to the crisis was shown by the preparations to deploy sixty-eight thousand troops against Montenegro: one Habsburg soldier for every four Montenegrins!

Against such daunting odds but ever the political opportunist, Prince Nikola tried to make the best of the situation and began negotiating for territorial compensation in Herzegovina. The Austro-Hungarian Ambassador to Cetinje, Baron Kuhn, quickly dismissed the idea but suggested that if Montenegro accepted the annexation there might be compensation along the coastline. A derisory offer considering Austro-Hungarian warships still patrolled Montenegrin waters, sometimes intimidating the local population, and, from the fortress of Spič, its guns overlooked the port of Bar. A furious Prince Nikola rejected the proposal, telling Baron Kuhn that international law had been violated and that, in future, Montenegro would exercise full sovereignty along its coastline hitherto restricted by article twenty-nine of The Treaty of Berlin.

On October 7, the day after Emperor Franz Josef had officially announced the annexation, Nikola issued his own proclamation. It was exactly what Vienna had feared to provoke as the Prince called on all Serbs to support their brothers in Bosnia-Herzegovina and Prime Minister Tomanović informed the foreign legations that Montenegro no longer considered itself bound by previous agreements.

Europe's intervention was hoped for and there were growing calls for an international conference. Representatives were despatched to plead Montenegro's case. Former Premier Lazar Mijušković was sent to Russia with proposals to resolve the crisis: autonomy for Bosnia-Herzegovina or a return to full Turkish sovereignty; the rescinding of article twenty-nine; territorial concessions to Montenegro, including the fortress of Spič, and free navigation along the River Bojana, the country's only significant river trade route. Sympathy and the suggestion of support were an encouragement: the French press was strongly pro-Montenegrin and Great Britain's Foreign Minister, Sir Edward Grey, gave assurances that he would not recognise the annexation.

While diplomatic positions were being staked out, Vienna tried another method to gain Prince Nikola's neutrality. His financial difficulties were well known and what amounted to little more than a bribe of five hundred thousand crowns was offered. The plan backfired when a Dalmatian newspaper published a story that the Prince's co-operation had been bought. In response Nikola issued orders for a partial mobilisation and called on émigrés to return to defend the homeland.

Vienna had grossly underestimated the anger the annexation would provoke. Cetinje saw demonstrations outside the Austro-Hungarian Embassy where a hostile crowd threw stones and shouted threats. The police intervened and only a few windows were smashed, but violent demonstrations also took place in Podgorica, Rijeka Crnojevića, Ulcinj and several other towns. Baron Kuhn warned Nikola that if the demonstrations were not stopped, Vienna would be prepared to take all necessary measures. For the sake of his diplomacy Nikola might well have wanted to use the demonstrations as a means of pressure, but he was not in control of public opinion.

The Herzegovinians working in Bar on port and railroad construction took an aggressive stance, as did the people of Nikšić. In Bar the Herzegovinians led the protesters on October 10 who announced that they would prevent Austro-Hungarian soldiers from disembarking their ships. Things turned violent when a large crowd of workers, joined by Montenegrin soldiers and police, attacked the Austro-Hungarian consulate. The Government's sympathy for the protesters could be seen in the treatment of Bar's chief of police, Djuro Ivović. He was sacked to placate Vienna only to be given the same post in Nikšić. In Nikšić a crowd several thousand strong listened to Stevan Kovačević, another Herzegovinian, call for Serb unity. The meeting ended with the pledge of 'liberty or death'. Kovačević found equally receptive audiences in Podgorica and Cetinje and was even praised in Parliament.

Prince Nikola was placed in a difficult position. Although he shared the protesters sentiments he could not openly support their means. Conversely, he would have faced a revolt if he had appeared ready to accept the annexation.

Tensions continued to escalate alarmingly. The Austro-Hungarian press was sabre rattling; the Montenegrin newspapers *Cetinjski Vjesnik* and *Glas Crnogorca* were banned from Austro-Hungarian territory; there was unrest along the Herzegovinian border as well as in the Austro-Hungarian occupied Sandžak buffer zone, which separated Montenegro from Serbia.

Prince Nikola kept his diplomatic options open while preparations were made for military action by the Vasojevići tribe and the Serbs of Novi Pazar in the Sandžak,

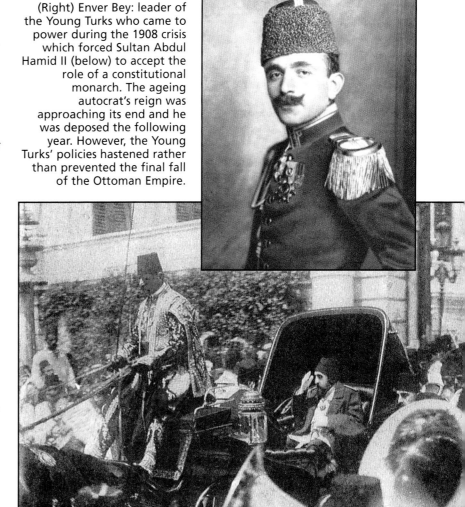

(Right) Enver Bey: leader of the Young Turks who came to power during the 1908 crisis which forced Sultan Abdul Hamid II (below) to accept the role of a constitutional monarch. The ageing autocrat's reign was approaching its end and he was deposed the following year. However, the Young Turks' policies hastened rather than prevented the final fall of the Ottoman Empire.

The lion's cage in *Tir Garten Zoo*, Frankfurt. The state visit to Russia in April of 1908 was a lonely and depressing chore, made worse by Prince Nikola's grief over the recent loss of his two grandchildren, Stevan and Stanislav, from tuberculosis. *En route* to St. Petersburg he stopped in Frankfurt where he passed his time window shopping and at *Tir Garten Zoo*. His thoughts were never far from his lost loved ones. He wrote to Milena: *"I went to the main street where I looked around the shops. I was in a good mood, but suddenly some strange feelings of melancholy and grief hit me, especially when I passed the children's shop selling clothes and toys. For which poor soul could I buy something? Where are those for whom last year I was buying gifts and who were cheering me up? Suddenly I met two little boys the same age as our two that are gone. They looked at me so gently as if they wanted to call to me and ask me, 'Who do we remind you of?' I was paralysed, everything was spinning around me. I thought to take a carriage back to the hotel but I could not. I decided to go to Tir Garten, to find among the animals distractions for my mind . . . I stopped next to the lion's cage as I always do . . . A small boy took my hand, his other hand holding his father's. He was looking, dumbfounded with fear, at the animal. Without thinking he had asked for my help, to unite with the help he naturally expected from his father. Vulnerable and upset he looked at me and I thought that with his sigh he was asking me for protection, as if to say 'Do not let me down, brother.' Oh poor me ! I am trapped in grief! I ran back to the hotel sadder than ever."*

while Montenegrin activists, on their own initiative, brought arms to Herzegovinian guerrilla bands.

November saw conflict of the economic sort break out. Montenegro imposed maximum tariffs on commercial goods from countries with which it did not have a commercial treaty; in real terms this only meant Austria-Hungary. Inevitably the gesture was reciprocated, which led Montenegrin merchants to boycott Austro-Hungarian goods. Given their negligible economy the hardship was much greater for the Montenegrins. Serbia was successfully defying Austria-Hungary in its own trade war, the 'Pig War' as it became known, but Montenegro's action could only be a symbolic gesture of defiance.

Despite the public anger and the political gestures, Austria-Hungary was standing firm. The strain was beginning to take its toll on Prince Nikola and during yet another frustrating meeting with Baron Kuhn, he lost his temper, drew his ceremonial sword and threatened the diplomat with a bloodletting. Vienna felt strong enough to let him bluster, but overplaying its hand could unite their victims, who were by now discussing the possibility of united action: an unlikely alliance between Montenegro, Serbia and Turkey seemed possible.

Princess Milena's cousin, Janko Vukotić, was despatched to Belgrade to deliver a letter to King Petar Karadjordjević, who had put aside his personal dislike of his father-in-law and agreed a plan for military co-operation. The mood was for war and Janko joined in the pan-Serb sentiment by making a speech from the balcony of Belgrade's Hotel Moscow calling for unification. However, an agreement with Turkey could not be finalised as Serbia wanted nothing to do with the Sublime Porte's plan to partition Bulgaria and, in the end, even a declaration of friendship proved beyond reach.

As the year came to a close, war still seemed the most likely outcome. Austria-Hungary's ire at the reaction in Serbia and Montenegro provided the counterpoint to their impotent rage. The more aggressive mood in Vienna boosted the militarism of General Conrad von Hotzendorf, whose views were gaining the upper hand over the diplomacy of the Foreign Minister, Baron Aerenthal.

Young Turk passivity in the face of the *fait accompli* finally decided the issue in Vienna's favour. By the close of February 1909 the Young Turks had proved themselves as malleable as Sultan Abdul Hamid II, signing away Bosnia-Herzegovina for financial compensation and an Austro-Hungarian renunciation of all rights to the Sandžak.

Montenegro and Serbia were now isolated. The Young Turks' capitulation had caught both by surprise and weakened their diplomatic position as Turkey could, at least legally, claim the greatest grievance against Austria-Hungary. Prince Nikola clung onto the hope of an international conference, or joint action with Serbia, and war still threatened as military preparations continued on all sides.

Adding to the weaknesses in the pan-Serb front, Russia, fearing war with Austria-Hungary, withdrew its support. Having lost the proxy war, Serbia swallowed its humiliation, dropped its demands for territorial compensation and pledged itself to neighbourly relations in the future. By April, Montenegro, too, had resigned itself to the inevitable.

Montenegro's relations with Russia had been at the centre of Prince Nikola's foreign policy since the late 1860's and he had benefited greatly by it: financially, militarily and also through the education and marriage of his daughters. However, times had changed since the days when Tsar Alexander III considered Nikola to be Russia's *"only sincere and loyal friend."* Tsar Alexander's son, Nikolai II, was on the throne of Russia and he took a more ambivalent attitude toward the Prince of Montenegro.

In late 1901 Nikola visited France, Germany and Russia. The French were toying with closer relations and, after Nikola's meeting with President Loubet, forty thousand army knives were supplied, arriving in Cetinje the following spring. Nikola then travelled through Germany and onto Russia. As his train neared the Russian border, Nikola discussed the situation with his adjutant, Ilija Jovanović-Bjeloš, who asked why the Prince was so keen to avoid the restaurant carriage where a member of the Russian Royal Family was loudly enjoying his lunch. Nikola explained why: *"That is Grand Duke Vladimir Alexandrovich, brother of Tsar Alexander III and uncle to Tsar Nikolai, mine and Montenegro's worst enemy, who can ruin the business for which I am going."* Nikola, kept well informed of the balance of forces in the Russian Government by his two daughters, Milica and Stane, was deeply unhappy that his long friendship with and loyalty to Russia were no longer held in such high esteem.

The shifting sands of time: Prince Nikola in Moscow during a visit to a wary Tsar Nikolai II and (inset) Tsar Alexander III (1881-1894), who considered Nikola a valued and trusted ally.
(Below left) Tsar Nikolai II's uncles, Pavel Alexandrovich on the left, and Vladimir Alexandrovich, one of Prince Nikola's political enemies, at the military manouevres held at Krasnoye Selo in August, 1899.

On the morning of December 21 Nikola arrived in Peterhof. He stopped off at the residence of Grand Duke Peter Nikolayevich and Grand Duchess Milica for a short rest before his audience with Tsar Nikolai II. The next day preparations were made for the audience in St. Petersburg and his adjutant was ordered to prepare his uniforms. However, the order came that the Tsar wanted to meet less formally. Nikola felt the slight keenly: *"You see, I am a contemporary of both Tsar Alexander II and Tsar Alexander III but I have to listen their grandson and son."* The effort still brought results as the Russians gave forty thousand rifles, munitions and grain.

Nikola's trip to St. Petersburg during 1908, shortly before the Bosnia-Herzegovina annexation crisis, was a more difficult and, for personal reasons, a much sadder affair. His grandchildren, Stevan and Stanislav, had died only recently and Nikola had little enthusiasm for state business. He was longing to return home and wrote to Milena: *"I think of you a lot . . . My God! How my old age is bending me towards you more and more, and today I think of you more than ever."* Making the burden even greater were the actions of some politicians. The Russian Ambassador to Cetinje openly told Nikola that he had sent negative reports to St. Petersburg and even admitted that they had been badly informed: *"If you knew what I wrote to my Government about yourself and Montenegro you would throw me out of the window."* Foreign Minister Izvolsky assured Nikola that the errant diplomat would be removed from his position, but it hardly made up for the damage already done. In St. Petersburg, Grand Duke Nikolai Nikolayevich warned Nikola of the opposition to him at the court and even suggested the Prince look to his *"friend"* Sultan Abdul Hamid, while Izvolsky gave a hint as to future Russian policy when he suggested that Montenegro make an arrangement with Serbia to allow it access to the Adriatic Sea. Despite his own depressed mood Nikola saw the job through: *"I am constantly working for our poor little country, enthusiastically and with high hopes for success. I put everything aside, the interests of our country come first . . . We are not yet rich enough to neglect those necessary duties."*

Nikola's luck had certainly deserted him in recent years: there was turmoil at home, the international climate was tense, relations with Serbia equally so and he had even been forced to take extra precautions during the journey for fear of assassination. The memory of his late grandsons and his sense of duty gave him the needed strength: *"No, I am not afraid because I am doing my duty and my conscience is clear, and I know that everybody has to die. Besides . . . I think about it less than ever, because I always have the feeling that next to me are those two little angels who are calling to me 'Grandpa we are here, do not be afraid Grandpa'."*

The ageing Emperor Franz Josef, who had vowed to add to his territory before he died, had his trophy. It was considered a triumph for Baron Aerenthal's aggressive diplomacy and a vital move toward complete hegemony in the region. However, the Balkans had often brought its conquerors more grief than joy and for Austria-Hungary it would prove to be a pyrrhic victory of historic proportions; its desperate imperial ambitions had created a foreign policy paradigm which would lead it to the fate Russia's Prince Gorchakov had foreseen three decades ago at the Berlin Conference.

The Kingdom of Montenegro was proclaimed on August 28, 1910. Although Nikola's reign had spanned fifty years, Europe's governments took a rather ambivalent attitude toward the Prince's elevation. From Europe's reigning royal families King Vittorio Emanuele and Queen Elena of Italy, King Ferdinand of Bulgaria and Crown Prince George of Greece attended. Russia was represented by two of Nikola's sons-in-law, the Grand Dukes Nikolai Nikolayevich and Peter Nikolayevich, and Tsar Nikolai II also made Nikola an honourary Russian field marshal. The other Powers, Austria-Hungary, France, Germany and Great Britain were more aloof, representing themselves only through their ambassadors. (Above) The Royal Family on the Palace balcony enjoy the acclamation of the people and (left) King Nikola with his daughter, Queen Elena of Italy.

The zenith of Royal Montenegro as Europe begins the descent into war.

To my beloved people . . . After accepting this proposal of the National Assembly and sanctioning it with my signature, in the name of God I proclaim our Country a Kingdom, and myself, by the Divine Grace, Hereditary King of Montenegro.

King Nikola I. Cetinje: August 28, 1910.

To coincide with the fiftieth anniversary celebrations of Nikola and Milena's accession, the Kingdom of Montenegro was proclaimed on August 28, 1910. It was a well earned accolade for both ruler and nation. As Nikola pointed out to the British *chargé d'affaires*, Henry Beaumont, he was only raising Montenegro to the same standing as other states whose independence was much more recent.

The coronation was followed by a tour of the country. The tribes greeted the King with enthusiasm and celebratory dinners, and Nikola made donations to schools and to the poor. In Grahovo the great victory of 1858 was remembered at a dinner for four hundred people; the party lasted all night.

It was an opportunity for

(Above) Crown Prince Danilo escorts his sister, Queen Elena of Italy, ashore on her arrival in Bar and (right) King Nikola greets his grandson, Crown Prince Aleksandar Karadjordjević of Serbia. (Left) An album commemorating the coronation.

reconciliation after the difficult recent years, to remember the shared achievements that had ensured Montenegro's independence and freedom. Nikola hoped the coronation would unify the nation by recalling those former glories, as he knew there were even more difficult times ahead.

Events of the year prior to the coronation had confirmed that the violent changes long in gestation, to sweep away the last vestiges of the Treaty of Berlin, were approaching. Montenegro was ill prepared to meet the challenge. The patriarchal era had ended badly for the nation, which had emerged from its internal struggle divided and embittered. Nikola had been working feverishly to keep his position as the dominant figure in political life. To that end, he had shown his opponents that he was prepared to rule harshly if necessary and this had sharpened the struggle.

By the autumn of 1909 the unity created by the annexation crisis was over and the movement to oust Nikola became active again. The 'Podgorica Committee', which was led by a postal official, Major Nikola Mitrović, prepared to overthrow the ruler. They planned to infiltrate government posts and call for an uprising before the year was out.

Their plans were derailed when one member, Petar Djinović, heard rumours that the conspiracy had been uncovered. Rashly, before consulting with his superiors, Djinović tried to pre-empt the Government by calling his men out and marching on the munitions depot at Kolašin. Troops were

quickly despatched and surrounded the depot, Djinović's men fled and the conspiracy was smashed. So soon after the 1907 'Bomb Plot', Nikola had been in no mood for leniency and of the accused only four were set free for lack of evidence, seven were sentenced to death and thirty-three imprisoned. Those who were able took refuge in Albania.

The Serbian press denounced Nikola and the anger of Montenegrin students in Belgrade was again raised to fever pitch. In response Cetinje claimed that Belgrade, if not masterminding the whole affair, had, at the least, its finger in the plot.

Although the tension between the two states was in some degree a consequence of Austro-Hungarian pressure, it was still a sorry spectacle: a public display of the chronic hostility which afflicted relations between Belgrade and Cetinje. Vienna's hope of turning Nikola away from his traditional loyalties now seemed more attainable than ever.

For Montenegro, almost entirely hemmed in by the cold efficiency of Austro-Hungarian rule, from the Adriatic coastline to its western and northern borders, there seemed only one remaining path of expansion: to the ramshackle remnants of 'Turkey in Europe' and Scutari town on the south-eastern tip of Lake Skadar.

Historically linked to Montenegro, as the capital of the early Zetan state as well as during the Balšići era, its population of thirty-six thousand signified its contemporary importance. If Scutari were gained, Montenegro would control Lake Skadar and Prince Nikola would reclaim the glory of his forefathers, as he had in the wars of the 1870's.

(Above) The coronation ceremony of King Nikola I. The coronation and its celebrations were also noteworthy for having being filmed and these pictures are probably taken from the original film. (Left) Nikola during the ceremony, behind him Queen Elena of Italy. Facing page: (Top) From left to right: Prince Petar Petrović-Njegoš, King Vittorio Emanuele III of Italy and Crown Prince Aleksandar of Serbia with Montenegrin generals and (centre) King Nikola with veterans of the 1876/77 wars of liberation. (Bottom) King Nikola with his son-in-law, Grand Duke Peter Nikolayevich.

The considerable stumbling block lay in the fact that Scutari's population was overwhelmingly Albanian. They naturally looked to the possibility of an independent Albanian state rather than joining with Montenegro. However, it was not quite as cut and dried as that. The Young Turk revolution had, somewhat ironically, opened up possibilities for Montenegro in northern Albania.

The Albanians were potentially the Ottoman Empire's last loyal European subjects and they had welcomed the proclamation of the new constitution in August 1908 with tremendous enthusiasm. Their joy had turned to anger and dissatisfaction as it soon became clear that 'Osmanli' citizenship amounted to little more than forced 'Ottomanisation'.

Alongside the backward economic and social conditions, the issue of education was, as it had proved in Turkey's other Balkan province, Macedonia, an intractable and incendiary issue. Albanian language schools were the demand but the authorities knew all too well that they were a breeding ground for nationalism. The official response was the repression of the Albanian language, which only strengthened the people's resolve to gain their cultural and political freedom.

Rebellion and reprisals followed. The Moslem Albanians of Kosovo Province had rebelled in 1909; although they were still loyal to the Sultan they had refused to pay tax unless the revenues were spent within the province and military service only be given locally. The Young Turks responded by claiming that the Kosovars were refusing educational opportunities and sent the army in to enlighten their unhappy subjects. Kosovo simmered until the spring of 1910 when a more violent rebellion broke out which took until June to quell. The Catholic Albanian tribes also rebelled in 1910.

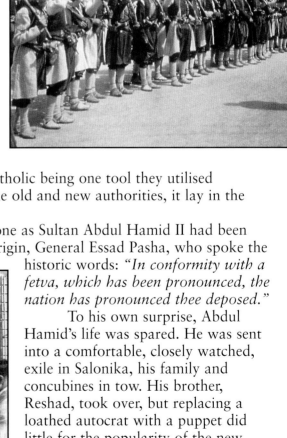

The Young Turks' punishment of the Albanians was firmly in the Hamidian tradition: setting Moslem against Catholic being one tool they utilised alongside military force. If there was a difference between the old and new authorities, it lay in the arrogance and clumsiness of the Young Turk leadership.

They no longer had the excuse of a tyrant on the throne as Sultan Abdul Hamid II had been removed in April, 1909. It was a Young Turk of Albanian origin, General Essad Pasha, who spoke the historic words: *"In conformity with a fetva, which has been pronounced, the nation has pronounced thee deposed."*

To his own surprise, Abdul Hamid's life was spared. He was sent into a comfortable, closely watched, exile in Salonika, his family and concubines in tow. His brother, Reshad, took over, but replacing a loathed autocrat with a puppet did little for the popularity of the new regime.

The Young Turks were now the

289

(Left) To the left, Princess Natilja and, third from left, Princess Vjera, with ladies-in-waiting. (Below left) Crown Prince Aleksandar Karadjordjević with his aunt, Princess Ana. (Below right) Prince Mirko and Prince Petar. (Bottom left) Three kings chatting during the military parade on Cetinje Field. From left to right: King Vittorio Emanuele of Italy, King Ferdinand of Bulgaria and King Nikola. King Ferdinand's son, Prince Boris, is standing behind them. (Bottom right) General Mitar Martinović poses with young Austro-Hungarian soldiers outside Cetinje Monastery.

focus for the people's anger. A Scutari Albanian, watching the celebrations for the accession of the new Sultan in April 1910, summed up the sour post-revolution mood: "*Look at them the devils! That is where our money goes. There used to be one big thief; now there are a lot of little ones.*"[1]

Lacking Abdul Hamid's formidable talent for playing race against race and religion against religion, the Young Turks were driving the Empire toward dissolution. The result in northern Albania was that the desperate Catholic tribes looked to Montenegro for help.

Against this backcloth, Nikola saw an opportunity to recuperate his damaged credibility. As he cast his eye toward Scutari, he had determined on proclaiming a Montenegrin kingdom to raise himself to the same status as his fellow Balkan rulers. If those two goals could be achieved, Montenegro had a chance for economic viability and the Petrović-Njegoš dynasty a new lease of life.

However, Nikola must surely have wondered if he had not been too patient and waited too long. During the celebrations of the dynasty's bicentennial, in 1896, he had written optimistically about the future to Prince Ferdinand of Bulgaria: "*All things come*

to he who waits."[2] By 1910 another old maxim may well have plagued his thoughts: *'he who hesitates is lost'*. Those peaceful means he much preferred had not secured the dynasty or the country's future.

While keeping a watchful eye on northern Albania, the diplomatic moves to have his royal elevation accepted by the Great Powers were begun.

Vienna had been willing to help so long as it further divided Belgrade and Cetinje. Conceivably, even the bond between them could finally be broken?

The question Vienna so eagerly sought a response to seemed to have been answered in its favour as Prince Mirko took the initiative, telling the new Austro-Hungarian Ambassador to Cetinje, Baron Giesl: *"Montenegrins are not Serbians, nor cowards, nor traitors, nor regicides . . . we do not want to have anything to do with Serbia."*[3]

Nikola went a step further, suggesting acceptance of a Viennese protectorate: *"There are only four of us . . . a single bomb can kill us all."*[4]

The King receives the acclaim of war veterans. (Below) Nikola and Milena leaving the Palace. (Inset below) From left to right: Generals Martinović, Vučinić, Nikolić and Bećir.

Next, Crown Prince Danilo made a formal request that the heir to the Habsburg throne, Archduke Franz Ferdinand, be asked directly for his approval of Nikola's royal elevation.

It was a promising development for Vienna and talks began for a commercial treaty as well as the delimitation of the border around Grahovo; although the Foreign Minister, Baron Aerenthal, remained sceptical of Prince Nikola's sincerity.

He was right. Nikola's true feelings toward Austria-Hungary could easily be surmised with a new *"greedy Great Power"* having taken over from the Ottomans in the Herzegovina, one of the heartlands of the Serb people and, of course, the Njeguši tribe. However, political unity had fractured and the Petrović-Njegoš dynasty, under siege at home and vilified in Belgrade, saw little choice other than to place its own survival first.

The Great Powers viewed the whole affair with ambivalence but, not wanting to give others opportunity to gain

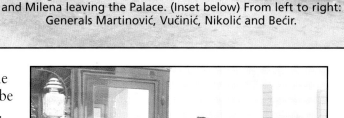

A stunning panoramic photograph of the celebrations. In the centre are King Vittorio Emanuele, King Ferdinand and King Nikola. (Left) King Nikola and Crown Prince Aleksandar Karadjordjević inspecting the troops.

Veterans of the 1876/77 wars parade through town. (Left) Queen Milena and (below left) the Queen's cousin, General Janko Vukotić.

undue influence, all gave their assent. The Kingdom of Montenegro was proclaimed amid a degree of controversy. It was another testiment to Nikola's political skills, but also a further complicating factor in the region's political affairs.

Reflecting its mixed reception, the guest list for the celebrations in Cetinje was appropriate, if slightly less than overwhelming. King Vittorio Emanuele III of Italy, King Ferdinand I of Bulgaria and Crown Prince George of Greece attended. Russia was represented by two of the Prince's sons-in-law, Stane and Milica's husbands the Grand Dukes Nikolai Nikolayevich and Peter Nikolayevich, and Tsar Nikolai II also made Nikola an honourary Russian field marshal. The other Powers were more aloof, representing themselves only through their diplomatic corps.

Serbia's representation proved a difficult issue. Prime Minister Pašić had threatened to resign if King Petar attended without him, but Pašić was far too unpopular in Cetinje to be invited. King Petar, therefore, excused himself through a convenient illness and sent his father-in-law a cordial greeting. Crown Prince Aleksandar Karadjordjević ended up by default the only representative from Serbia, but as Nikola's grandson he was a suitable envoy and well received. It did not, however, heal the rift between the two families.

More unpleasantly still, on the day of the coronation an honourary performance of 'The Empress of The Balkans' at Belgrade's National Theatre was the scene

King Nikola and Queen Elena, followed by Queen Milena and King Vittorio Emanuele, lead the dignitaries; in the background Cetinje Monastery and the Biljarda.

of an angry anti-Petrović-Njegoš demonstration.

Nikola had demonstrated that he was not prepared to play a secondary role in South Slav politics, regardless of how much it exacerbated his Serbian brothers. In that vein, and to publicise the rapprochement with Vienna, Emperor Franz Josef's congratulations were published in full by the Montenegrin press.

However, the new relations were not well grounded. It was all, to borrow a phrase from Turkish times, a matter of 'asiatic hypocrisy' on both sides. As the Viennese press were hailing their new ally, applauding his cleverness and astute diplomacy, Nikola was proving them right by negotiating a military convention with Russia, an annual subsidy of six hundred thousand roubles and promising to place the army at St. Petersburg's disposal.

Indeed, no amount of diplomatic hypocrisy could erase the real causes of mutual hostility. A fact which had been illustrated by a border incident in July in which two Austro-Hungarian soldiers were captured on the wrong side of the border near the village of Vršuta. They were quickly released but complained of rough treatment from their captors. Nikola had quickly apologised, but Baron Aerenthal still had to restrain his military from retaliating.

Despite all the complications, the newly crowned King could congratulate himself on his political acumen. Having forged new relations with Vienna, while keeping the goodwill of his Russian patron, and elevated the principality to a kingdom, Nikola prepared to seize the moment in northern Albania.

(Above) King Nikola meeting guests and (above right) the party in Cetinje Park: Princess Ksenija and, partially shown, Princess Milica-Yutta skating. (Right) A commemorative postcard from the coronation celebrations. (Inset) The special edition of *Cetinjski Vjesnik* with its rousing eulogy to the heroism of Montenegro, heralding the dawn of a new era for the nation: *"We salute the Kingdom of Montenegro on the dawn of its restoration with all the passion of our patriotism, we salute HH King Nikola I and HH Queen Milena and their sacred home with all the power of our delight, we proclaim to the restored Kingdom of Zeta. Kingdom of Montenegro live in happiness and fame! Long live HH King Nikola!"*

(Above) King Nikola looks toward the Albanian town of Scutari, Montenegro's primary war aim in the Balkan Wars of 1912-1913.
(Below right) Montenegrin forces crossing the River Lim *en route* to joining up with Serbian forces in the Sandžak and Kosovo Province.
(Facing page) A view of Scutari town and its fortifications, the formidable Taraboš Fortress.

"However adverse His Majesty may be from disturbing the peace of Europe, there was nothing left for him but to take up the sword, for his hopes of liberating the Serbs of Turkey without bloodshed had proven in vain. Montenegro, therefore, declared a Holy War, inspired by the noblest intentions of preventing the final extermination of its brethren."
Declaration of war by King Nikola,
October 9, 1912.

The Catholic tribes of northern Albania, the Malissori (Highlanders), had much in common with the Montenegrins with whom they shared their mountain ranges. Without having developed as great a degree of political autonomy, they were nonetheless equally sure of their identity and status as free tribesmen. They had never been ordinary subjects of the Ottoman Empire and even the Montenegrins were wary of venturing into their mountain strongholds, where blood revenge retained an even stronger hold. Having often fought against their South Slav neighbours they were driven by the actions of the Young Turks to forge an alliance with Montenegro.

The Malissori uprising, which began fully in 1911, was claimed by the Young Turks to have been instigated by outside forces, but was in reality a genuine attempt to secure a degree of autonomy. The Vali of Scutari succeeded in turning the Moslem Albanians against their Catholic countrymen and, as the fighting raged to brutal levels, Catholic villages were burned out. The result was a flood of Albanians crossing into Montenegro for protection. The handful of refugees from the Hoti and Gruda tribes in the autumn of 1910 had risen to five thousand by the following spring. Malissori dissatisfaction and Montenegrin ambitions converged with Scutari town as their focal point.

Only one thousand men had garrisoned Scutari and, if the Malissori had been sufficiently united and well armed, the rebellion could have succeeded. The disappointed rebels, who gathered in and around Podgorica, pleaded with Queen Milena's cousin, the burly, imposing General Janko Vukotić, for arms. By nature a man of the war party, he was eager to help but only dared give them weapons clandestinely. The larger tribes - the Kastrati, Skreli, Hoti, Gruda and Klimenti - were the best armed and had kept up a guerrilla resistance, but Turkish reinforcements were arriving too quickly.

Adding to General Vukotić's problems were the tactics of the Malissori fighters who fought as individuals rather than as an organised force. To return from battle with a new rifle and more ammunition was considered a success in itself. Vukotić sent some of his officers to advise them, and also to ensure that he would not be taken by surprise and miss the moment for direct intervention if Scutari fell.

Political considerations notwithstanding, King Nikola genuinely sought an alliance with the Malissori in the hope of persuading them to unite with

Montenegro. The chieftain of the Gruda tribe, Sokol Batzi, acted as his advisor throughout the Malissori uprising. In his youth Sokol Batzi had been a member of the Sultan's Imperial Guard, but he had become an Albanian freedom fighter in the 1876-77 wars. Thereafter Sokol and his wife became fugitives until they found refuge in Montenegro, where they were given a house and some land.

King Nikola could not raise the pan-Serb banner for the Malissori, but he could rightly claim to be their protector and denounce the brutality of the village burning carried out by General Turgud Pasha's forces. A Montenegrin newspaper editorial sarcastically commented: *"Blessed is the nation that lives in a land where such civilisation is carried out. This is the work of an army led by a civilised Young Turk leader!"*[5]

The diplomatic pressure was growing. Austria-Hungary and Russia concurred that the Malissori problem needed to be suppressed and the other powers could all see a dangerous escalation of conflict close at hand. Russia even threatened to cut off its military subsidy if Montenegro did not maintain a strict policy of neutrality.

Nonetheless, preparations for intervention were stepped up. By the summer of 1911 artillery tracks were ready for an attack on Taraboš Fortress, which defended Scutari; the long delayed carriage road to Andrijevica was hurriedly completed and two battalions were sent to Podgorica.

Mary Edith Durham, who had befriended the Malissori, recorded in her diary: *"Rifles are being distributed to all over eighteen, and everyone is agog. We are on complete war footing. Every man has orders to hold himself in readiness, with five days provisions and two pairs of opanke [raw hide sandals], to start at any moment. The ćetas [battalions] are being raised from one hundred to one hundred and fifty men . . . All work is at a standstill. Extraordinary state of nervous tension. Place crammed with state officers."*[6]

Expectations proved unfounded. Although there had been reports, false as it turned out, of successful uprisings in southern Albania, and Janko Vukotić was confidently boasting that he would take Scutari in a mere ten days, the Malissori uprising was failing. In desperation, they addressed a letter to the Great Powers who had ignored their plight: *"We have resisted for three months troops twenty times superior to ourselves . . . we are now pressed against the Montenegrin frontier, where our miserable families are refuged, camped often in holes in the rocks. Exhausted by the terrible campaign, we address ourselves to the Western Powers, in the name of our children, our families and our brethren of Albania and beg for an intervention on behalf of our rights as men and citizens. We beg for a large autonomy, which will permit us to be an active and fertile unity."*[7]

The opportunity for the Malissori had passed: they had risen before they were adequately prepared and their Montenegrin allies had been brought to heel.

Crown Prince Danilo gave a newspaper interview assuring Europe of Montenegro's pacific policy: *"We Montenegrins, who most sincerely desire peace, speedily re-established and lastingly assured, do all we can by giving both sides friendly advice . . . My father is most anxious to prove to the Turks the sincerity of his desire to live with them in true friendship . . . It grieves my heart to see these brave, uncultured mountaineers suffer and die for the liberty of having their own schools for their own children."*[8]

However, the battalions in Podgorica were not demobilised. In fact there were rumours of Bulgaria joining Montenegro if the Turks attacked, and of an assassination plot against General Turgud Pasha. In Scutari thirty thousand troops had been hurriedly assembled. However, to general surprise, on August 2, the news arrived that peace had been agreed. The Young Turks were offering tempting concessions: an Albanian speaking Christian governor; the tribes to be allowed to carry arms; the opening of Albanian language schools; roads to be built into

the mountains; the burned out villages to be rebuilt; enough maize to feed the refugees until next harvest and each male over fifteen to receive one Turkish pound on his return home.

A meeting between the Malissori chieftains and Young Turk officials, with General Vukotić and Sokol Batzi on hand, was called. The chieftains were scornful of the offer, which they did not even credit as genuine intent and considered a trap. They called on Sokol Batzi not to betray them and, in a tense atmosphere, the officials left for private talks. General Vukotić, desperately and futilely trying to convince the Malissori to go home, pleaded to Mary Edith Durham for help: *"Things had all gone wrong. He [Vukotić] had been all for war. The right moment had been lost; the Turks had taken all the positions. Those fools of Maltsors [Malissori] had begun too soon! With all the eyes of Europe attracted, what could one do? . . . The Maltsors must be sent back somehow, he and all the Montenegrin authorities had failed to persuade them."*[9] She could only note to herself the absurdity of the army commander, who was also the Queen's cousin, pleading with a foreign female relief worker who held no official authority, to make terms with the insurgents his own Government had supported.

The alliance was coming to an end as General Vukotić threatened to forcibly disarm the Malissori, in which case everyone knew bloodshed would be unavoidable, and to cut off food aid. Finding themselves between a rock and a hard place, the tribesmen had little choice but to return home, fully believing their lives were in danger as soon as they crossed the border. The Malissori struggled through the winter of 1911-1912 awaiting the fulfilment of Turkish promises for relief and reconstruction of their homes. An old Albanian woman in the devastated Skreli Valley saw the madness of it all: *"The Sultan is the stupidest man in the world. First he spent a lot of money to burn down our poor houses. Now he must spend a lot more to build them up again."*[10]

The Vali of Scutari knew where his priorities lay and left the Malissori to their miserable lot; a winter of misery and starvation would cool their tempers. If the Young Turks saw little reason to aid their Catholic subjects, the defences of Scutari were worth fortifying: mile upon mile of barbed wire was brought in for the construction of trenches and walled defences; weapons were distributed amongst the Moslem Albanians and troops from Asia Minor were hurriedly brought in.

In the meanwhile, King Nikola, who was being strongly advised by his ministers that the dynasty's future depended on gaining Scutari, continued to draw on his experience and diplomatic sleight of hand, skills which were soon to be of vital use. The other Balkan states also saw the clock running down on their ambitions and the grand alliance which had proved so elusive finally began to take shape. It was still a project fraught with difficulty, but the sheer force of events would overcome all obstacles and give rise to the Balkan League.

Italy provided the impetus for the Balkan states to unite. Rome had its own designs on the Balkans and, in particular, Albania. The dynastic connection for Montenegro of King Vittorio Emanuele III and Queen Elena on the throne did nothing to alter those facts, even though Vittorio Emanuele was wary of his politicians' plans for an Italian protectorate over Albania. What mattered to the foreign ministries in both Rome and Vienna was the belief that whichever nation held the Gulf of Valona had control of the Adriatic Sea. The impoverished Albanian provinces fully shared the general Balkan burden of being designated as strategically significant.

More immediately, Italy had its own imperialist ambitions in Turkish North Africa and, in the autumn of 1911, the Italian army set about conquering Tripoli under the pretext of protecting economic interests. Italy's haste, belatedly seeking its place in the imperial sun, further destabilised the Ottoman Empire, while Young Turk brutality and negligence dashed any hopes that the Albanian provinces could return to relative tranquillity. How little the Albanians of Scutari now cared for the Young Turks was demonstrated when they were called on to defend the fatherland from Italian aggression and only one hundred and sixty men volunteered.

King Nikola, exploring each and every possibility with desperate urgency, suggested an alliance with Italy for an invasion of Albania. Chastised by Vienna he then promised to stick with Austria-Hungary through thick and thin. He even offered the Young Turks a territorial adjustment. Ultimately his only real chance lay in William Gladstone's old war cry of *"The Balkans for the Balkan people"* and, as the Italians occupied Tripoli, the Balkan states began discussions in earnest for a military alliance. Nikola would play a significant role in the formation of the Balkan League, as both secret diplomatist and military *agent provocateur*.

"The bankruptcy of this comedy between the so-called Concert of Europe and the Sublime Porte was already foreshadowed by the Balkan War . . . The Balkan League sprang into being and acted suddenly and vigorously. The Great Powers were left talking in helpless and ridiculous postures."[11]
R.W. Seton Watson

If a provocation to commence war were going to be needed by the Balkan states, Montenegro could readily supply it. The Albanian border was a continuing source of tension and, in January 1912, Foreign Minister Dušan Gregorović warned that Cetinje's patience was running out. In the meanwhile secret talks were taking place across the Balkans. Bulgaria was the centre of activity, greatly aided by a remarkable Irishman, the journalist J.D. Bourchier of The London Times, who worked tirelessly to bring the often disputatious states together.

With the liberation of their brethren living under the Turkish yoke within reach, Cetinje and Belgrade were not even on speaking terms. Serbian sentiment had been doubly offended: by Montenegro accepting an Austro-Hungarian loan and the Patriarch of Istanbul choosing their candidate as the new Metropolitan of Prizren. Both states were pleased with the dismissal, although only a temporary respite as it turned out, of Austria-Hungary's hawkish General Conrad von Hotzendorf. At the least that suggested a more placatory policy from Vienna, but even that could widen rather than bridge the breach.

As the Balkan League finally became reality, Belgrade was still refusing to include Montenegro in Serbo-Bulgarian talks and King Nikola's relations with King Ferdinand proved vital in bridging the impasse. Indeed, without Bulgarian determination and the efforts of J.D. Bourchier in bringing Bulgaria and Greece together the alliance could have been stillborn through the mutual jealousies of its members.

The Balkan League's masterstroke, no doubt a lesson learned from long and bitter experience, was to take the Great Powers by surprise, pre-empting any moves to stifle their plans. Rather than raise suspicions by meeting in their own countries, King Nikola and King Ferdinand held their talks under the noses of Emperor Franz Josef's statesmen in Vienna. Their joint appearance in the Habsburg capital, during June of 1912, came as something of a surprise, neither having been officially invited. However, it was assumed they had come for talks with the new Foreign Minister Count Berchtold, Baron Aerenthal having died from leukemia in February. In Cetinje, Ambassador Giesl could note for his memoirs that the goodwill visit was a gross fraud; his masters were thoroughly duped by the two wily monarchs.

Perhaps the years of chronic but manageable crisis had deadened the foreign ministries of Europe to the possibility of an alliance amongst the Balkan states, but the harvest sown at The Treaty of Berlin was finally about to be reaped. In Montenegro's case it pitted South Slav against Albanian, a direct result of the loathed treaty, as Mary Edith Durham knew from first hand experience: *"The frontiers drawn by the Treaty of Berlin were so impossible that in many places they could not be defined, much less enforced. As the borderers themselves described it 'The frontier floated in blood' . . . . solid Albanian districts which hated all things Slav were handed over to Montenegro, and solid Slav districts, which asked nothing better than to be Montenegrin or Serb, were handed over to the Turkish Empire . . . I climbed with the Captain and some soldiers up Mount Džamija where stood the Montenegrin frontier kula [borderhouse], a very stiff ascent, and thence saw the frontier, complicated beyond belief, coiling in and out, one valley Montenegrin, one Turkish, tongues of land so narrow that a rifle bullet could carry right across and kill on the way . . ."*[12]

By August of 1912 the Balkan League was almost ready for action. During talks held at King Ferdinand's hunting lodge, Montenegrin requests for financial aid were accepted. In return Montenegro pledged to be ready by September 28 and to provoke war by an unacceptable ultimatum. Public opinion, too, was all for war, particularly after villages of the Vasojevići tribe were burnt out along the border, after which a public demonstration held in Cetinje called on the Government to take action.

With Bulgarian preparations falling behind schedule, the commencement of hostilities was delayed, giving time for a belated Serbo-Montenegrin agreement to be reached by October 2. Significantly it was not only directed against Turkey but Austria-Hungary as well. Article one of the military convention stated: "*In case of war with Austria-Hungary, Serbia and Montenegro will adopt a series of defensive tactics which does not exclude, in certain directions and at favourable moments, strategic offensive measures.*" Once begun, hostilities could quickly escalate.

It was an important moment of reconciliation, but the potential for disagreement remained and one clause in particular would later cause trouble among the allies. It was agreed that no town should be occupied by troops from more than one nation; in practice that would prove to be contentious not only for the Serb states but for Greece and Bulgaria too. There were potential disputes amongst the allies in Albania and Macedonia, particularly the much coveted port of Salonika, while Montenegro aimed to be the first to take Prizren, as did Serbia. At the least, Scutari was solely King Nikola's for the taking and expected to fall quickly.

Although he had pledged to the Great Powers that he would never fire the first shot in any conflict, circumstance demanded that Nikola fulfil his obligation and make the first move. A royal proclamation informed Europe: "*However adverse His Majesty may be from disturbing the peace of Europe, there was nothing left for him but to take up the sword, for his hopes of liberating the Serbs of Turkey without bloodshed had proven in vain. Montenegro, therefore, declared a Holy War, inspired by the noblest intentions of preventing the final extermination of its brethren.*"[13]

On the rainy morning of October 9, 1912, the Vladika of Ostrog was called to bless the military standard in a private ceremony for the Royal Family, after which the King accompanied by his sons, Mirko and Petar, went to Gorica Hill (from which Podgorica takes its name) to start the campaign. As the rain cleared and the sun broke through the clouds, the King, in his national costume, made for a romantic figure as he watched his youngest son fire the first symbolic shot toward the walled camp on Mount Dečić. With the highest expectations, Montenegro set out on the greatest offensive campaign of its modern history.

Its army was by far the smallest, as well as the least prepared, of the four Balkan League members. Bulgaria brought 300,000 infantry, 5,000 cavalry and 720 field guns; Serbia 220,000 infantry, 3,000 cavalry and 500 field guns; Greece 130,000 infantry, 1,000 cavalry and 180 field guns. Montenegro could only raise 35,000 infantry, had no cavalry and only 130 field guns.

The Balkan League's combined forces were significantly greater than their enemy, totalling 685,000 infantry, 9,000 cavalry and 1530 field guns. Turkish forces and armaments were numerically inferior with 340,000 infantry, 6,000 cavalry and 850 field guns; equally importantly morale was low and the loyalty of the soldiers was open to doubt. Nonetheless, Turkish victory was widely anticipated in Europe.

The Montenegrin army was divided into four divisions. The King acted as Commander-in-Chief and General Veljko Lazović as his Chief-of-Staff. Three divisions were readied in the south-east for the assault on Scutari and the fourth, under General Janko Vukotić, for action in the Sandžak and Kosovo Province. The Scutari campaign plan had General Martinović's forces attacking the town from the south-west, while General Bošković and Crown Prince Danilo's forces completed the pincer movement by an advance from the north. After taking Scutari they planned to join forces with General Vukotić.

Early victories gave grounds for optimism. General Vukotić's forces soon overran Bijelo Polje and, by October 16, Berane had also fallen. The Scutari campaign, too, opened briskly. Planinica succumbed hours after Prince Petar had fired the first shots on October 9, and Rogom had fallen by the following day. The next objective of the camp at Mount Dečić proved a tougher task and the mysterious death of General Bošković also suggested problems within the army command. Officially it was reported that he had committed suicide after a failed night-time attempt to take Mount Dečić, but rumour circulated of a dispute with one of the princes and of assassination. Whatever the truth, Crown Prince Danilo was now in command.

Mount Dečić fell shortly after. The combined assault by Malissori, who had rejoined the fray, and Montenegrin forces was so sudden the Turks fled leaving their guns behind, only to be mown down with their own weapons. The fearless, reckless bravery of the Montenegrin soldiers was remarkable, but militarily a mixed blessing: "*They rushed like a pack of wolves, howling war cries, and had no notion of how to take cover or spread. It was this which brought about Montenegro's high death roll.*"[14]

Aided by Malissori tribesmen, who had gone ahead to burn out Moslem villages in revenge for the previous year, Montenegrin forces closed in on Tuzi. It was the vital point *en route* to Taraboš Fortress and Scutari. The Turks responded with an ambush at Široka, firing from the mountain heights, and even used guns mounted on the steamboats of Lake Skadar. However, Tuzi's defences were not strong and its commander tried to negotiate a withdrawal of his forces to Scutari. The Montenegrins responded by moving their guns closer and bombarding the town from six positions, bringing a hasty surrender on October 13.

It was the occasion for a dramatic scene of wartime triumph. As evening fell, an orange sunset was turning to a deep red and the skyline was illuminated crimson by fires from the burning villages. Crown Prince Danilo mounted his white charger to the strains of the military band and set out to accept the surrender. As the Montenegrins reached the bridge on the way to Šipčanik Fortress, Tuzi's commander and his defeated troops met them. He dismounted, came forward on foot and offered his sword to the Prince, who returned it as the soldiers of the frontier posts Tuzi, Vranje, Nenhelm and Rogom, trudged forward to surrender. Over the next five days as many as five thousand prisoners were taken and Montenegrin hopes for a quick victory soared.

Ominously, casualties were steadily rising. Montenegro had entered the war with virtually no preparations for field treatment, let alone a sufficient number of doctors, nurses and quantity of drugs to care for the wounded. Remarkably, it seems that the authorities had not anticipated so many casualties, at least not so many still living ones. Yet, in the first week of war alone, a thousand were either killed or wounded.

The only hospital was in Cetinje, some forty miles away from the frontlines and reachable only in carts, over bumpy, badly kept roads, then by steamer to Rijeka Crnojevića, and finally, offering the wounded some respite, via motor-omnibuses to the capital. Many of the casualties had broken legs and arms, shrapnel wounds and horrific injuries caused by flying fragments of glass, iron and zinc. Still, they were Montenegrins and accepted their suffering with that famed warrior's spirit, smoking and joking despite the pain.

Within two weeks Montenegrin forces were closing in on Scutari. However, the weather and the nature of the task, a gruelling war of attrition to take Taraboš Fortress which lay at the top of a two thousand foot ridge which rises from the southern shore of Lake Skadar, now confronted them. Heavy rain had turned the roads into quagmires and General Martinović could view a desperate scene: *"The roads covered with wounded men, riding in creaking carriages, and mules laden with ammunition and stores struggling through the mud, while every small cottage flew the Red Cross flag, all outward and visible signs of the desperate struggle going on before Taraboš beneath a pall of fog which hid the bombardment from the onlookers on their mountain top."*[15] Conditions were treacherous: the mud was waist high in places, the water chest deep in others. It was fortunate that the heavy guns had been brought up before the rains came, while caravans of ammunition laden mules valiantly continued to struggle from base camp at Bar to the Taraboš heights. By late October all were eager to make a final assault on the gloomy fortress.

General Martinović's forces were keeping up a heavy bombardment, but the bulldog resistance of the Turks took him aback. They were *"fighting like madmen"* he told journalists. It was heroism which the General admired as much as it infuriated him; both sides still felt there was honour and glory in the bravery of war.

An English journalist filed this evocative report on the unfolding struggle between the age-old foes: *"Hour after hour the heavy bombardment continues, drawing but perfunctory replies from the great sullen stronghold . . . The huge fort-crowned hill stares grimly at me two miles away across the valley. Minute by minute the Montenegrin guns on my right thunder out, and shells go ringing over the deep ravine . . . In the distance the Adriatic gleams like molten silver. Over this exquisite panorama speeds the wailing of the messengers of death, the only other sound being that made by a solitary shepherd who is drawing a monotonous tune from a rude and ancient gusle . . . Between each crashing series of gun-shots the wild complaint of the clumsy instrument quavers out amongst the sun baked rocks."*[16]

Even though Crown Prince Danilo had pleaded with him not to take risks, King Nikola, anticipating victory, had taken a small boat onto Lake Skadar, inviting the correspondent of The London Times and the Austro-Hungarian attaché to join him and gain a distant view of the fighting.

Events of the the same day proved his hopes were overly optimistic. A Turkish force of some ten to twelve thousand, led by Scutari's new Vali, General Hussein Riza, launched an attack on General Lazović's forces, which included among their number both Princes, Danilo and Mirko. It was an act of desperate defiance. Scutari was almost completely surrounded and the only line of retreat for General Riza would have been to cross the River Drim and traverse Mirdite territory, where the Catholic tribe would hardly have welcomed him. Instead, he attacked the Montenegrins, who retreated rather than take more casualties; still confident of victory their tactic now was to wear down the defenders. A Turkish attempt to retake the Široka Heights above Taraboš failed and Montenegrin forces managed to occupy Obleka, south of the fortress, but it was still not enough to bring Scutari's surrender.

The Montenegrins had found a worthy opponent in General Riza. Born in Baghdad he had learned his warcraft in Istanbul and Berlin and was one of Turkey's better commanders. His rise through the ranks had been under Sultan Abdul Hamid II, a fact which was enough to make the Young Turks suspicious of him, but he was genuinely patriotic and saw the defence of Scutari as a matter of the highest military honour. To that objective the town was placed under the severest martial law and its population treated as virtual prisoners. To prolong the siege General Riza commandeered food, clothes, wood; whatever the people hoped to keep back for their own survival was taken from them. Taxes on future sales were brought forward to force shopkeepers to hand over their goods; the churches were told to raise money from their congregations; wood collected from villages two days walk away was confiscated as the desperate people first begged and then cursed the unyielding soldiers.

An Italian correspondent reporting clandestinely from within Scutari described how compliance was ensured: *"Anyone who refuses to accept the new order will be shot. Therefore, silence is golden, be silent and pay. If you complain you will be beaten, imprisoned and still have to pay."*[17] By the end of November many were ready to accept capitulation as a preferable outcome to starvation; General Riza announced that if they attempted to surrender he would execute the traitors by the thousand.

General Riza had prepared as well as circumstance allowed, and his pledge to King Nikola's envoy was a defiant one: *"The word surrender will never pass my lips . . . If ever Istanbul ordered me to haul down my flag I would refuse, for as long as I live I will not permit any dishonour to the flag I have sworn to defend . . ."*[18]

Terror reigning from without and imprisoned by their so-called defenders, the townspeople had become pawns for the belligerents. The Montenegrins had begun by targeting the Moslem districts, but as their frustration grew indiscriminate bombardment and then the deliberate targeting of civilians became the strategy. General Riza took no notice of civilian casualties and kept an eye on the Montenegrins. He had even decided that if the town fell, he would concentrate his troops at Taraboš Fortress and bombard Scutari himself.

The siege was tightened as Crown Prince Danilo's forces occupied positions east of the River Drim and General Martinović's along the River Bojana, but the final push was still needed.

It was General Martinović's task to besiege Taraboš Fortress, whose defenders were not only able to resist any assaults, they even managed to threaten Montenegrin lines of communication and supply with guerrilla tactics. The twenty battalions which attacked Taraboš in mid-October were repulsed with heavy losses, and an attempt by Turkish agents to blow up the munitions depot at Bar was partially successful.

General Riza had done enough to frustrate Montenegro's war effort, while the sieges of Janina in Epirus and at Adrianople in Thrace, where the triumphant advance of the Greek and Bulgarian armies had also been halted, further demonstrated that there was still some fight left in the 'Turk'.

Nonetheless, the death of 'Turkey in Europe' was finally at hand. Balkan League forces had routed armies which were often lacking in conviction, cohesion and strong leadership. General Vukotić had contributed amply to those victories: within a month he had taken

Montenegro's campaign in the south-east began well and the fortresses of Rogom and Tuzi (above) fell within a matter of days. (Below) Turkish deserters and (facing page) several thousand prisoners of war were captured. Montenegrin hopes for Scutari town to fall as easily soared.

almost all of the Sandžak and half of Kosovo. By November his forces were free to join the siege of Scutari.

Marching his army over the snow covered mountain ranges to save two vital weeks, they had to overcome peaks as high as the six thousand foot Alto Vallico in freezing temperatures and torrential rain. By the time General Vukotić arrived south of Scutari, on November 20, an unfortunate few had succumbed to the cold and exhaustion and been lost in the snowdrifts.

The Serbian army was prepared to assist, but King Nikola, having being beaten in the race for Prizren, was desperate for a personal crowning glory to end the campaign. To that end, the Montenegrins brought fearlessness, patriotism and a stoic fatalism. They were qualities sorely needed for, alongside the atrocities of war which were committed on all sides, Scutari's besiegers faced the ravages of nature, constant snowfall and storms in sub-zero temperatures.

One battalion was posted three thousand feet high on Mount Kraja; without tents they slept in crevices in the rocks but still protected their guns and ammunition with their greatcoats rather than warm themselves. The womenfolk shared the hardships of war too; undeterred by the raging storms they carried supplies up to their men and braved the trenches to recover the bodies of dead relations where, inevitably, some were cut down by Turkish bullets.

No matter how selfless, such sacrifice could not make up for other Montenegrin failings. Despite their bravery they lacked the organisation, co-ordination and discipline of a modern army. Mary Edith Durham considered the Montenegrins to have *"the physical courage of wild boars"*[19] but gave them little chance of success and another war correspondent observed: *"Living as I have done for a week with the Montenegrin army in the field, I realise what a peculiar mix of tribal and military system prevails. I see a commandant of a battalion order a private to do something or other, and I*

observe that the man argues with much vigour as to the advisability of his doing it; the commandant, equally vigorous, entering by no means unwillingly into the wordy combat. Perhaps, the soldier agrees to do what he was told, perhaps he does not. In the latter event he walks off, apparently unconvinced as to its desirability or necessity. The officer turns aside with a gesture, and either leaves the thing undone or asks another man to get on with it."[20]

It had never been an easy task to take

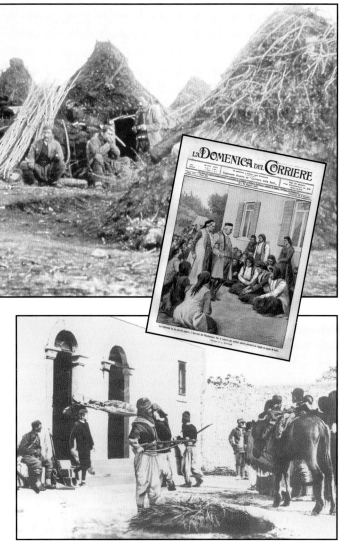

a fortified town as Montenegro had found out by its own attempts in the past. Nikšić and Podgorica had finally come their way in 1878, but resistance rather than conquest was Montenegro's true strength. The difficulties of the local geography, which the Turks had always struggled to overcome, now confronted the Montenegrin army.

In Scutari's case the campaign was made all the harder as the surrounding country was cut into four by the rivers Bojana, Drim, Kiri and Lake Skadar itself. General Riza had made good use of them too, diverting the Drim into the channel of the Bojana and causing it to flood, thereby preventing the Montenegrins from bringing their forces nearer.

Delay and survive, always the best hope for the besieged and a tactic which had become second nature to Turkish commanders, was General Riza's strategy. He had carefully husbanded his ammunition and supplies; even as Montenegrin shells drove into the heart of the town the response was always the minimum required to keep the enemy at bay.

However, the bombardment had succeeded in bringing an intolerable pressure to bear on the townspeople. As the exhausted, near starving population clamoured for action, General Riza had to put down several mutinies amongst his troops, as well as conflict between his men and the reserve troops led by General Essad Pasha. The civilian population as a whole was at the end of its endurance, while the Catholic and Moslem communities were

almost at each other's throats. Only the General's iron discipline and the fear of a vengeful Montenegrin army taking retribution against them held the terrified town together.

At Scutari a military stalemate had been reached, but as a whole the Balkan League's campaign had been a triumph which shocked Europe.

The hub of the whole matter was the Bulgarian campaign, and after the victory of Lule Bargas in Thrace, the largest battle of the war, Bulgarian forces had threatened to advance on Istanbul itself. King Ferdinand's generals, who had proved so efficient and

After the successful opening campaign, the limitations of Montenegro's war readiness soon became apparent. (Top) Making camp often meant little more than huts made from mud and straw. (Inset) Italy's *La Domenica Del Corriere* depicts *"The sadness of a little kingdom"* as King Nikola and Queen Milena visit war widows. (Above) The wounded being cared for in Podgorica. The Italian Red Cross (right) and other international relief agencies were on hand, but (above right) much medical help had to be given in the theatre of war, where supplies of drugs and medical personnel were lacking. Facing page: (Top) As winter set in the soldiers had to endure sub-zero temperatures and violent snow storms. (Bottom) Montenegrin soldiers entering Peć in Kosovo. The combined campaign with Serbian forces was a considerable success and brought Montenegro a large territorial enlargement.

ruthless, now faced a conundrum similar to that of the Russians in 1877 at the Siege of Plevna. With the Chatalja Fortifications still to overcome, cholera had broken out, while the Turks were taking heart that Adrianople could still be held and that even a counter-offensive might become possible.

Greece had enjoyed success in Macedonia, Epirus and the Aegean Islands, while its naval contribution had been a vital aid to the Bulgarian campaign, preventing the movement of Turkish forces from Asia Minor and Arabia. Greek forces had grabbed Salonika before the Bulgarians; it was an issue which would cause trouble between the two nations later on. For the Greeks, as it would also prove to be for Serbia and Montenegro, the Great Powers insistence on an independent Albania would be an obstacle to their territorial ambitions.

Serbia enjoyed its greatest victory at Kumanovo in northern Macedonia, celebrated as revenge for the Battle of Kosovo. In the Sandžak and Kosovo, in co-operation with General Vukotić's forces, Serbia took the cities of Novi Pazar, Prizren, Peć and Djakovica. Macedonia would also draw Serbia into conflict with its allies and an outlet to the sea still remained elusive, although Serbian forces advanced into Albania taking Durazzo, Tirana and Elbasan. Having neutralised Turkish resistance against them, the Serbians were free to assist at the sieges of Adrianople and Scutari but, given the tangle of Serbo-Montenegrin political-dynastic relations, that was not purely a military matter.

The Russian revolutionary Leon Trotsky, on journalistic duty in the Balkans after escaping his Siberian prison, considered the King's dilemma: *"King Nikola is not willing on any account to let the Serbs have the glory of taking Scutari. The Serbian forces have played no part in the battles for this fortress, although the first army was free to do so . . . In Montenegro itself there is much dissatisfaction with the doubtful successes won by the country's forces which have suffered heavy losses . . . It may be expected that this war will lead, in Montenegro, as in Turkey, to internal reforms which will put an end to the tyranny and financial indecencies now reigning on the Black Mountain. Whether Nikola Njegoš will be able to hold out is difficult to forecast. But anyone has the right to consider the need for a distinct Montenegrin dynasty not proven . . ."*[21]

Within the besieging army war weariness and disillusionment were setting in. A Montenegrin artilleryman on leave had no desire to return to his post: *"First we have to fire a shell into the Christian quarter to frighten the people. Then the officer watches through his glass which way the crowd of women and children runs and then we have to fire a big shell into the middle of them. I am sick of shooting at women and children!"*[22] All the King could offer in response was to praise the bravery of his soldiers: *"King Nikola expresses his admiration of the endurance and sacrifice of the soldiers, whose iron wills, he says, have never for a moment faltered throughout the continuous fighting . . . It is our duty and right to annex the homes of our ancestors, and to assemble around their graves. For that it would be a joy for us to die."*[23]

Time was fast running out. The Great Powers, desperately trying to exercise some control on events, had, by mid December 1912, gathered the diplomats in London to discuss peace proposals. Montenegrin hopes of gaining Scutari found little support: an independent Albania was demanded by Austria-Hungary and Italy and the other Powers showed little sympathy for Cetinje's claims. It could have been very different, if only Scutari had fallen in time.

Macedonia had been conquered and its partition amongst the Balkan League allies accepted, only the delimitation needed to be decided. Even Adrianople, sight of the magnificent mosque built by Sultan Selim II and considered their holy city by the Turks, was

considered an acceptable war trophy for the Bulgarians. Likewise, Kosovo and the Sandžak, where Montenegro, too, stood to gain, were considered legitimate spoils of war.

Rumour had it that King Nikola's desperation to gain Scutari was so great he had his daughters Milica and Stane bribe Grigory Rasputin to advocate an anti-Habsburg policy at the Russian court. There were always plenty of rumours, usually exaggerated, surrounding Nikola's schemes, but it was true that Scutari had assumed a disproportionate importance. He was faced with the starkest of choices: assert Montenegro's claim to Scutari against the will of the Great Powers or back down and risk the loss of his throne.

Within Montenegro anger toward the Royal Family was rising. In October, Lazar Mijušković and Ilija Plamenac had told Baron Giesl that the dynasty was likely to fall if the war was unsuccessful. As the year's end approached with only Tuzi, Medua and a few villages taken, resentment over the sacrifice and privations of war were being openly voiced. Anti-dynasts, especially republicans, were denouncing the King, his sons and even Princess Ksenija, who, as her father's personal secretary, was held to blame for the military failures.

As both Montenegrins and Albanians dug in to share a Christmas of misery and mutual hatred, Nikola decided to fight on for the dynasty's survival.

In London the Montenegrins vainly protested that as 'Turkey in Europe' no longer existed, nor did its Albanian provinces. A self-serving argument, but hardly less so than that made by the newly found champions of an independent Albania, a state of which the primary purpose would be to prevent Serbia securing an outlet to the sea. Austria-Hungary saw the death of its Balkan ambitions if Serbia succeeded in that aim and Italy equally hoped to use Albania and Montenegro to stifle Serbian expansion.

As the diplomats parleyed, the belligerents, on the natural enough assumption that possession constituted nine tenths of the law, scrambled to gain or recover whatever territory they could.

Despite the December armistice, by February 1913, hostilities had resumed. In March Adrianople and Janina finally fell. Two of the three fortresses which were thought to make up the impregnable strategic core of European Turkey had fallen.

Adrianople proved to have been a military bluff. The forts consisted of brick covered with earth, there were no cement walls or protective constructions, the gun emplacements were hollowed out of the ground and many of the guns were antiquated; indeed, had they known the real state of the Turkish defences, the Bulgarians could have decided the issue in January. If the fall of Adrianople had come too late to allow Bulgarian forces to advance on Istanbul and realise King Ferdinand's personal dream, he could still consider

(Above) Crown Prince Danilo with his officers. Danilo was placed in command of one of the three armies besieging Scutari. (Left) The battalion of the Kuči tribe celebrating the tribes *Slava* (Saint's Day).
(Facing page) One of the few comforts of war was strong black 'Turkish' coffee.

the campaign a triumph.

Janina, like Scutari, had been expected to fall quickly. As early as November it had been rumoured that its garrison of twenty-five thousand troops was ready to surrender rather than face starvation. The reality was that, in ignorance of Turkish defeats with some even believing that the Sultan's armies were advancing on Sofia, many were prepared to fight on. Resistance was strengthened by the arrival of an additional ten thousand troops and, during December, hopes to halt the Greek advance briefly rose. However, by the turn of the year the Turks had been unable to force the Greeks back and, with as many as ten thousand wounded and less than two weeks food supplies remaining, the fall of Ali Pasha Teppeleni's legendary stronghold was imminent.

In February, urged on by the Austro-Hungarian Consul, Janina's defenders made one final attempt to lift the siege. The Greek response, on the orders of Crown Prince George, was a massive bombardment on March 4 of ten thousand shells into Turkish positions, followed by a further fifteen thousand the following day. On March 6 Janina surrendered.

With celebrations taking place in Athens, Crown Prince George triumphantly entered Janina. The London Times reported: *"As a result of this fresh feat on the part of the Crown Prince, which adds another important province to Greece, and the bravery shown by the other princes during the war and the assistance rendered by the princesses, the dynasty may now be considered to be naturalised*[24] *and definitely linked to Greece."*[25]

In contrast, the fighting at Scutari had never ceased but the Montenegrins had only succeeded in maintaining their stranglehold, while General Riza had succeeded in bringing fresh supplies during December. To the outrage of the Balkan League and the diplomats seeking peace in London, he claimed to have had no knowledge of the armistice, thereby justifying his continuation of hostilities. Montenegrin hopes rested militarily on the belated arrival of Serbian troops, and politically on the widely held assumption that if Scutari fell before the peace treaty was finalised it would be impossible to deny their claims.

Within Scutari conditions were deteriorating further. General Riza's iron fist had terrified the town's inhabitants into submission, but there had been mutinies among the troops.

A growing danger came from General Essad Pasha and the reserve forces. The two commanders had nearly fought a duel over the unequal distribution of food rations between their men and it was only the intervention of their officers which prevented bloodshed.

General Riza's intransigence finally proved his undoing. He was murdered, but by whom is not entirely certain. On the evening of January 30 he had dined with Essad Pasha until around 8pm. Declining his host's offer of an armed escort back to his residence, he left accompanied by a single officer. The two men made their way across town together until they reached the main square and the General dismissed his companion. He had only taken a few steps alone when three men appeared before him. He demanded to know who they were; the only reply he received was three gunshots.

The prime suspect in General Riza's demise was Essad Pasha, who now assumed control of Scutari. However, as Albanian custom held the host personally responsible for his guest's safe passage home, would Essad have risked embroiling himself in dangerous enmities with such an obvious assassination? Conversely, and more convincingly, his personal ambitions were a very plausible motive, and Essad had considerable ambitions.

His Young Turk sympathies were waning as he saw the possibility of becoming the leader of an independent Albania. Toward that aim he was prepared to take a pragmatic approach to the territorial claims of the Balkan League and was ready to accept an immediate armistice.

However, the Montenegrins initial response was to resume full hostilities. The news of General Riza's death was a considerable boost to morale, as was, on February 6, the capture by Serbian forces of the village of Bušatlija seven miles south of

Scutari. In support of Serbia's advance, the Montenegrins bombarded Brdica and Taraboš Fortress. At the same time, General Vukotić launched an attack from the north against Turkish positions at Bardanjolt Hill and, by February 9, he had dislodged the defenders from their positions.

Militarily it was a step forward but the death toll was heavy. Upwards of three thousand were lost storming Bardanjolt Hill. The Montenegrins charged too soon and the Serbian bombardment stopped too quickly during the assault. The Montenegrins were left exposed and many were cut down by the Turks. Serbia also lost around a thousand men to enemy guns when they found themselves bogged down in the muddy plain around Brdica. As dawn broke they were an easy target *"struggling in the mud as helpless as birds in lime."*[26]

As for tending to the growing number of sick and wounded, little if anything had been learned from nearly six months of war. Mary Edith Durham described the scene in Podgorica: *"A number of the foreign doctors had left; the hospitals were blocked with the sick. The wounded, many of whom had had no food for three days, and had not had their wounds dressed properly, were thrown in heaps on the dirty floors of every drink-shop, empty house and shop . . . Men almost too weak to stand, just recovering from enteric, were turned out into the streets to make room, and crawled about begging shelter, driven pitilessly from every door, for the Montenegrins are terrified of infection."*[27]

A fortnight after the Bardanjolt engagements, Cetinje was struggling to care for over one thousand seven hundred sick and wounded men. However, rather than being disheartened the Montenegrins were now enraged; the stubborn resistance of Scutari had become unbearable.

To enable the next stage of operations the barbed wire defences protecting Scutari had to be destroyed. General Martinović had no trouble finding one hundred volunteers for the task. They were armed with twenty bombs, which they had

(Top) Scutari town. Any hopes of a quick Montenegrin victory were soon shown to be ill-founded. The town was well defended by Taraboš Fortress, miles of barbed wire trenches and the ruthlessly effective command of General Hussein Riza Bey. (Above) Scutari after a shell has just struck and (left) a Turkish trench near Bardanjolt Hill, the scene of an important Montenegrin victory.
Facing page: (Top) Montenegrin troops wait to attack Scutari but (bottom) more effective militarily was the heavy bombardment of the town.

to take right up to the enemy positions and detonate. They caused considerable damage but twenty or so paid for their boldness with their lives.

In London the question of Scutari had the Great Powers lining up against one another: Austria-Hungary and Italy supporting Albania and Russia supporting Montenegro. It was a trial of strength, conflict by proxy, in which Berlin stood behind Vienna and Paris and London stood behind St. Petersburg. The diplomats could, therefore, at the least agree on the need for a settlement to avoid a European war and, by February 25, Russia had resigned itself to an Albanian Scutari. An international force under the command of Britain's Admiral Burney was despatched to take the necessary action to bring compliance.

Montenegro's political isolation only served to reunite public opinion behind the King. Nikola talked angrily of *"setting Europe ablaze"* over Scutari and in Podgorica an angry crowd greeted the collective note from the Powers with defiance: *"We will take Scutari with the last drop of our blood, and then avenge ourselves on Austria by marching into Bosnia."*[28]

Montenegrin frustration, although directed toward the unfortunate people of Scutari, was not without foundation. A more reasoned exposition of the country's position was presented by its three man delegation in London: *"Scutari is a vital question for Montenegro. The Treaty of Berlin itself recognised the fact when it stipulated by a theoretical and ill-contrived provision that Turkey should give Montenegro access to the sea through her territory. The sacrifices we have made to attain this object are enormous . . . The diplomatists of the Great Powers, with Russia at their head, may come to any agreement they like among themselves on paper, but we shall see if their people allow us to be stifled . . ."*[29]

A further assault against Taraboš Fortress on April 4 was unsuccessful and brought five hundred casualties. Seemingly, all Montenegro could do now was to prevaricate and delay in the hope of Scutari's belated fall. On April 20 it was even claimed that the ultimatum delivered by Admiral Burney had not been received and the Government requested that another be sent! Another blow came with the withdrawal of Serbian assistance; fearful of losing the goodwill of the Great Powers, Belgrade resigned itself to accepting Montenegro's loss of Scutari.

However, something was certainly afoot judging by events of the following day: there were rumours of a boat with a white flag leaving Scutari to parley; the Montenegrin frontier was closed; foreign nationals were forbidden to leave and even the foreign ambassadors were prevented from communicating via telegrams to their governments. Austria-Hungary's military attaché tried to leave, but was stopped at Njeguši where his car was confiscated. He continued on foot to the border, but once there was still refused permission to leave.

The protracted struggle was finally over, but with a whimper rather than a bang. A deal had been struck. The horrors of famine and the pragmatic ambition of General Essad Pasha brought Montenegro victory.

In the early hours of April 22, 1913, the firing of cannons and the ringing of bells announcing the fall of Scutari awoke Cetinje. The King and his family went to the Palace balcony to the acclaim of a small crowd, the capital being half deserted due to the war effort, singing the national anthem. The following day Essad Pasha handed over control of Scutari to Crown Prince Danilo. Ignored by the townspeople, its defenders trudged out. In the late afternoon, the almost equally exhausted Montenegrins

(Above) Crown Prince Danilo confers with his officers over their next move. Danilo's view was that heavy bombardment was the best way to force Scutari to surrender. However, his later promise to Austro-Hungarian representatives not to occupy Scutari brought about a revolt among his troops. (Inset) *La Domenica del Corriere's* romantic depiction of the storming of Bardanjolt Hill in February 1913: a success but at the high cost of several thousand casualties. Facing page: (Bottom right) The camp of a battalion posted near Bardanjolt Hill and (bottom left) Montenegrin troops after capturing a Turkish trench. The death toll was high, but a military stalemate was the only result and (top) all King Nikola could do was to praise his war weary soldiers bravery whilst Europe's diplomats deliberated in London on the future map of the Balkans.

marched in, greeted by neither protests or visible signs of anger, only despondency.

The diplomats were as outraged as Montenegro's allies were jubilant. Belgrade and Sofia went mad with joy while Russia could not stop itself from joining the celebrations. In contrast, Austria-Hungary's statesmen winced as the Croatian press offered congratulations to their fellow South Slavs.

While Vienna's *Fremdenblatt* hoped: *"This brutal attack upon the authority of the Great Powers will have the effect of raising Europe from her lethargy . . . that Europe will employ sharper methods in order to restore her damaged prestige and to break the resistance of Montenegro,"*[30] Zagreb's *Narodne Novosti* rejoiced: *"With our whole heart at this success, which proves again that our Montenegrin brethren still possess the heroic qualities of their glorious ancestors."*[31]

King Nikola had taken Europe by surprise with a masterful stroke of *realpolitik*, in which Essad Pasha's hopes to become the leader of an Albanian state had been the key. The terms of surrender were suitably generous. Essad Pasha was allowed to leave Scutari with his army of forty thousand intact, the weapons, except the heavy artillery, and supplied with provisions for the march to Tirana. The London Conference had recognised a government led by Ismail Kemal as the provisional authority in Albania, but, on reaching Tirana, Essad Pasha proclaimed himself head of an autonomous Albania under the protection of the Sultan.

As Montenegrin troops took control in Scutari a vital question hung over their conduct: would they be a civilised occupying force or vengeful, plundering conquerors? The terms of surrender stipulated that the town's inhabitants would receive food and medical relief, be free from molestation and have their religious rights respected. However, the mood of the troops was ominously ugly and resentful, even members of the Royal Family were venting their anger.

In Cetinje, Prince Petar had a donkey, dressed in black and labelled *Neue Freie Presse,* driven through the streets to the Austro-Hungarian Embassy. Although the young Prince's anger was political, directed toward Vienna and the Austrian press, how would the army treat the people of Scutari after such a long and bloody conflict?

During the war the Government had tried to prevent excesses. General Martinović had been particularly determined in banning trophy hunting, the horrific nose and lip cutting that some soldiers still indulged in. It was an issue that even divided the soldiers themselves, in particular many of the young men who had returned home to fight were shocked at the brutalities committed by some of their kinsmen. In Scutari the new authorities did their best by policing the town with the most disciplined battalions.

The occupying army found very little active resistance. After months of bombardment the once picturesque and busy town was a devastated shell from which Essad Pasha had been happy to withdraw. He had become a virtual prisoner to the desperate and dying civilians who surrounded him each time he left his quarters, even his troops had been surviving on one bread biscuit each a day. The townspeople had survived on whatever could be found: tortoises, frogs, hedgehogs, even plants had been eaten, some of which were poisonous. The bombardment had also caused enormous destruction

and the damage to schools, churches, hospitals, the Catholic Cathedral and the British Consulate evidenced the claim that civilians had been the targets of the shells.

The new authorities made a good start by giving flour to the leaders of both the Catholic and Moslem communities for distribution amongst their congregations, but there was some plundering and the harassment of civilians was already noticeable.

The new Governor of Scutari, Petar Plamenac, was an educated man and eager to show that the Montenegrins were a civilised army capable of administrating the town equably. However, the Albanians had no faith in him and offered little co-operation. As General Janko Vukotić had found during the Malissori uprisings of 1910, Plamenac found himself with nowhere to turn except to a contemptuous Mary Edith Durham, to whom he offered, in effect, to share power with. Durham only saw it as further proof of Montenegro's inability to govern the town. Instead she demanded to be allowed to help all regardless of race or religion. Plamenac's honour was offended by her implied accusation of prejudice and she was given full authority to go and do as she pleased.

Plamenac aimed to persuade Scutari to join Montenegro but, given the overwhelming Albanian majority and their religious division between Catholic and Moslem, this was nigh on impossible. Talk of a plebiscite, attempts to win over the Archbishop, even the irrefutable fact that the town was in Montenegrin hands made little difference. Scutari considered itself Albanian, even in ruins, under occupation, awash with spies and King Nikola's entrance being prepared for. The news filtering in that the Great Powers were preparing action if the Montenegrins did not evacuate further stiffened the townspeople's resolve to resist.

In Cetinje the pressure on King Nikola and his ministers to withdraw was coming from all sides. The Russian Ambassador warned that Montenegro ran the risk of direct action by Austria-Hungary, in which case Russia would not intervene; even Bulgaria warned its ally of the dire

consequences if Scutari were not handed over to the control of Admiral Burney.

Despite the diplomatic unanimity that the Montenegrins must give in, the question of Scutari had brought Europe to the verge of war. If Cetinje refused to comply, military action by Austria-Hungary would follow, in which case it seemed impossible to avoid wider consequences. The London Conference would break up and the pressure on all governments to take sides would become irresistible.

Finally, King Nikola yielded. Realising that he had little prospect of holding onto Scutari and hoping that Montenegro's honour had been salvaged by the brief occupation, he chose peace rather than to set Europe ablaze. A meeting of the King and his ministers was held to discuss the withdrawal. His insistence that there was no longer any choice but to evacuate Scutari led to the resignation of the cabinet and General Martinović.

Undeterred, Nikola announced the withdrawal via Britain's Ambassador in Cetinje, Count John de Salis, telling Europe: *"I once more affirm with my people our rights which are consecrated by history and by conquest. As my own dignity and my people's does not allow me to submit to isolated summonses, I leave the fate of the town of Scutari in the hands of the Powers."*[32]

Under the 1905 constitution foreign affairs remained the King's preserve, but the decision was hugely unpopular with his subjects. Nikola's only hope was that the Great Powers would appreciate Montenegrin sacrifices and not let the country go unrewarded; by backing down at the last minute he could justifiably claim to have *"rendered an inestimable service to European peace."*[33] On May 14 the keys to Scutari were handed over to Admiral Burney.

Although the soldiers had, for the most part, behaved decently during the occupation, there was a parting act of vengeance which could not be prevented: the burning of the town's bazaar. A little after midnight, on May 14, a fire mysteriously broke out in three places and, it was claimed, the guards prevented the bazaar's shopkeepers from raising the alarm. Mary Edith Durham saw: *"The crowd of Montenegrins, officers and all, were laughing, as pleased as punch. The shopkeepers near the fire tried vainly to save their goods, the greater part of which were looted by the Montenegrins."*[34]

The question of Scutari had been resolved but there was one more twist in the tale to come. Sultan Abdul Hamid II had blamed the chauvinism of the Young Turks for uniting the Balkan states and, to a large degree, he was right. Driven by the rise of the Young Turks and Austria-Hungary's annexation of Bosnia-Herzegovina, they had finally set aside their differences. Now the Balkan League allies set about reminding Europe why they had remained under foreign domination for so long.

The Balkan League had already begun to unravel during the London peace talks. In Macedonia and Epirus there had been clashes between Bulgarian, Greek and Serbian forces, whilst the Albanians complicated matters further as they struggled against being partitioned between the feuding allies. It only needed Bulgarian resentment over once again losing out in Macedonia, and in particular Salonika, combined with the military arrogance brought on by victory to ignite a second war.

The Second Balkan War saw Bulgaria's attempt to become the predominant Balkan power quickly thwarted by a combination of its former allies and the hitherto pacific Romania. Serbia, still denied an outlet to the Adriatic Sea, had asked for a revision of the territorial division, citing the fact that the war had been continued for four months to allow Bulgaria to take Adrianople as evidence of previous good faith. However, Bulgaria's leaders saw the opportunity to maximise their gains and remained inflexible, claiming that their contribution to the campaign had been the greatest. They counted on Austro-Hungarian support but had not reckoned with the intervention of Romania, which now expected reward for its neutrality.

Fresh hostilities commenced in the summer of 1913 with battles even more brutal than the Turkish campaign. There were casualties of at least of one hundred and twenty thousand killed and wounded in less than two months. In June Montenegrin troops fought alongside Serbian forces in a crucial victory. A fourteen thousand strong Montenegrin force advanced beyond Prizren to join the Battle of Bregalnica, in which Bulgaria lost some twenty-five thousand and the Serb states over sixteen thousand men.

The balance was decisively tilted against Bulgaria by Romania's entry into the war and, by July 31, Bulgaria's former allies were within twenty miles of Sofia. An armistice was hastily agreed but Sofia's arrogance had not only cost it dearly in the Balkans, it had also allowed Turkish forces, led by the Young Turks' best commander, Enver Bey, to attack from Thrace, retaking Adrianople and advancing, briefly, into Bulgaria itself.

The failure of the Treaty of London had partially caused the Second Balkan War and the Treaty of Bucharest which followed it also paved the way for further trouble. The Bulgarians fared badly considering their major role in defeating the Turks. Sofia still gained something, the smallest portion of Macedonia and a section of the Aegean coast, but was forced to cede territory to Romania while Turkey reclaimed Adrianople. Greece fared considerably better, gaining more than half of Macedonia, southern Epirus and some Aegean Islands. The border with Albania in the Epirus remained a point of dispute, as were the Aegean Islands with Turkey.

The Serb states gained considerable territories. Serbia gained around a third of Macedonia and a common border with Montenegro through the Sandžak. Montenegro had not gained Scutari but was compensated in the Sandžak, including the towns of Pljevlja, Bijelo Polje, Peć and Djakovica. The Serbian Government considered unification of the two states to be in the long run inevitable and, with that thought in mind, saw good reason to help Montenegro's expansion. However, the Macedonian rivalry with Bulgaria had ruined the possibility of building a Balkan federation around a Belgrade-

(Right) The Montenegrin flag flies above Taraboš Fortress and (inset) the Italian press utilise Mario Rolo's depiction of Essad Pasha, who had taken command of Scutari after General Riza's assassination, surrendering to King Nikola. The keys to the town were formally handed over to King Nikola in a ceremony held on Lake Skadar, but Essad Pasha had surrendered Taraboš Fortress to Crown Prince Danilo on the morning of April 25, 1913. The Italian correspondent, Gino Berri, described the scene: *"At ten o'clock the sound of trumpets heralded the arrival of the troops . . . Prince Danilo appeared from the hills in front of the Customs House. The crowd was relatively numerous as a military band, at the entrance of the Bojana Bridge, played the Montenegrin anthem and the Prince advanced in the shadow of his national flag. He rode a white horse with an incredibly beautiful long tail . . . followed by General Martinović, General Vukotić, Prince Petar, Minister Plamenac, many officers and about fifty cavalrymen. As the cavalcade progressed along the bridge over the River Bojana, so clear against the background of the large river, it was a spectacular and picturesque sight greeted with many hurrahs! From the town bazaar the Prince rode up to the entrance of Taraboš Fortress and dismounted. Soon after he was greeted by an ashen faced Essad Pasha, flanked by two officers. The Prince and the Pasha shook hands. 'You will understand' Essad told the Prince, 'the pain I feel in this instant that I hear the dear voice of my dead who will be left behind in this land. However, I have the comfort to have been conquered by a brave enemy, the most heroic in the world.' Danilo replied chivalrously: 'He who has a clear conscience having done his duty should not feel regret. I tell you this as I have been your fierce enemy, but also as one who has admired the bravery of yourself, your officers and your soldiers'."*

Facing page: (Inset) *La Domenica del Corriere* depicts Cetinje celebrating the fall of Scutari. The capital had been woken in the early morning of April 22 by the ringing of bells and the firing of cannons, after which the King made the announcement to a small crowd from the Palace balcony. The capital had been emptied by the transferral of men and women to help with the war effort and (top) children play in the near deserted streets. (Bottom) The bombardment of Scutari reduced the town to a devastated shell inhabited by a starving and terrified population.

Montenegro's determination to hold onto Scutari (left) brought Europe to the brink of war, but the Great Powers finally managed to agree that the town should be part of the newly created independent Albania. A naval force under Britain's Admiral Burney was sent to administer the transition. (Inset) Admiral Burney arrives to take up his duties. King Nikola's desperation to gain Scutari and parts of northern Albania played a considerable role in his downfall; however, his objectives were coherent ones: economic viability and survival of the dynasty. This letter from the 'European Trading Company' (below), a few months before the start of the Balkan Wars, underlines how much control of Scutari and, thereby, control of Lake Skadar could have meant economically to Montenegro.

Your Royal Highness! Merciful King and Master!

I had an opportunity last year to travel throughout Your Highness' beautiful land and, as much as a visiting foreigner is able, study the circumstances of the state that, under the blessed sceptre of Your Highness, is rapidly developing on the path of enlightenment and civilisation. On my travels I have been all over the world and seen many beauties of nature, so I can, courageously, claim that the natural beauties of heroic Montenegro are worthy of comparison to any! Montenegro's mountains and plains, lakes and all her other natural charms beg the question: 'How is it that a torrent of millions of foreigners has not swarmed to the country, bringing with them greater prosperity and turnover to that splendid and dark land?'

Your Royal Highness! No doubt that turnover of visitors to Montenegro would increase greatly if that issue was given serious attention. What the turnover of visitors can mean to a country is shown by Italy, Spain, the French Riviera, the Tyrol, Egypt and Switzerland. The population of Montenegro would, if the flow of foreigners were directed into the country, benefit greatly by it, and with the growth of industry, home trade and business would flourish and, therefore, would increase the tax paying capacity of the population. It is clear that the state as a whole would benefit from these increased tax revenues.

For myself and my business partners we would be happy to dedicate our experience and great material means to a large company dedicated to increasing the turnover of foreigners, naturally, only with the mighty moral support of Your Highness for the company, because without that support success would not be possible. We are ready to build at the appropriate place (probably on Lake Skadar) a fashionable tourist centre like Monte Carlo, along with a chain of modern hotels and climate sanatoriums. We are ready to invest a large capital sum for roads, electric railways, lighting, steamship services, and we would obligate ourselves to invest an initial capital of five million American dollars in companies which are related to the venture. We would undertake to employ native workers for the above mentioned construction and also contribute with at least one million francs to the state budget of the Kingdom of Montenegro from the profits of our Montenegrin companies. All this we would be able to do if Your Royal Highness is merciful enough to give to our consortium for the turnover of foreigners throughout Montenegro the concession and monopoly to build casinos for foreigners with the rights that the casinos of Monte Carlo enjoy. Of course that concession would have to be irrevocable for at least forty years, so a large capital investment could be amortised. The execution of the project would be given to one Montenegrin-American society which we would found on the basis of the King's concession with the capital of aprox twenty-five million francs.

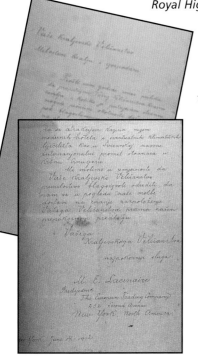

We modestly beg Your Royal Highness to forgive us for daring to come directly to the Sublime Throne of Your Royal Highness with our humble plea. Knowing that Your Royal Highness, as a real father and master of the land who, with his vigilant eye, oversees the development of Montenegro, and, knowing that the Sublime Person of the Holy Master energetically takes part in everything that concerns the development of the country, we think that we took the best path for our project addressing directly the serene face of Your Royal Highness. If Your Highness mercifully approves our humble suggestion in principle, we would again humbly plea that Your Royal Highness orders us to present more elaborate details on that subject before the Government of Your Royal Highness. At the same time we are humbly pleading Your Royal Highness allows our representatives an audience before the Sublime King's presence in which they would present our intentions verbally. We do not want to conceal that this undertaking of ours and our American capital is the result of business intentions, but still it cannot be denied that for Montenegro and its population it would be of boundless value if, with the attraction of casinos, a chain of modern hotels and eventual climate sanatoriums as in Switzerland, the turnover of foreigner visitors is directed toward Montenegro.

We humbly plead to Your Royal Highness to mercifully order that we be informed of Your Royal Highness' response to our humble suggestion.

Your Royal Highness' humble servant
M.E. Lacenaire, President of the European Trading Company
232 Second Avenue, New York, North America
New York: June 14, 1912

SIGNATORIES TO THE TREATY OF BUCHAREST

Sofia axis and that ongoing tension would lie behind future Serbo-Bulgarian conflicts.

For Cetinje, Belgrade's generosity was something of a double-edged sword. The Treaty of Bucharest gave Montenegro some eight thousand two hundred and forty-eight square kilometres of new territory and doubled its population, but these gains only further strained the resources of the war weary nation. Its largest urban gain, Djakovica, illustrated the problems. The town was considerably larger than the capital, which, it was clear, would struggle to administer its new territories effectively. Djakovica also had a large Albanian population and guarantees had been given that the rights of minorities would be respected; it was a pledge easier to make than to enforce in the aftermath of war.

The country's economic and social difficulties were exacerbated by its gains and the growing prospect of unification made King Nikola's position even more precarious. Montenegro's mission of liberation was its historic *raison d'etre*, which many now considered to be near completion and, therefore, what purpose did a separation of the Serb states serve? Serbia's economic and political development was far in advance of Montenegro; the smaller state could only benefit from full political and economic union. In that context, for many, the dynastic question was already a closed issue. King Nikola should be allowed to see out his reign after which the Serbs would all unite under the Karadjordjević banner.

King Nikola's patrons, Austria-Hungary and Russia, were also sensing the end of the Petrović-Njegoš dynasty. Vienna was, finally, considering accepting Serbo-Montenegrin unification so long as the ports of Bar and Ulcinj were handed over to ensure its control of the Adriatic coastline continued. After unification, Vienna's long-term aim would be to absorb the united state into the dual monarchy. Russia anticipated the creation of a larger South Slav state as a more powerful Balkan satellite than the fractious smaller states which had been open to influence by the other Powers. King Nikola's usefulness, particularly to Russia, was now of questionable value.

It was hardly the outcome Nikola had hoped for or anticipated; every new development seemed to inexorably undermine his grip on the throne.

However, Montenegro and the Balkan peninsula's troubles were those of a wheel turning within larger wheels, all of which were spinning out of control. Time was fast running out, not just for the Balkans, but for the European order itself. Economic and military superiority had enabled the European powers to extend their reach around the globe as imperialist nation states, but their competing ambitions had become irreconcilable.

Admiral Burney's men look on as Montenegrin troops evacuate Scutari. (Above) August 10, 1913. Signatories to the Treaty of Bucharest which concluded the Second Balkan War. Initiated by Romania, which had played a decisive role in Bulgaria's defeat, the treaty benefited Serbia, Greece, Romania and Montenegro, in spite of its failure to gain Scutari. The Bulgarians signed reluctantly, still hoping that there might be revisions in their favour if the Great Powers intervened.

(Left) The heir to the Habsburg throne, Archduke Franz Ferdinand, with his wife, Countess Sophie Chotek, and their children. (Inset left) The Archduke's assassin, Gavrilo Princip, in his prison cell and (bottom) a wartime tribute to the Serbian soldiers who died during the retreat from the Central Powers' invasion in the autumn and winter of 1915/16. (Below) Two propaganda postcards from World War One. The 'Forces of autocracy' - Kaiser Wilhelm II, Sultan Mehmed V and Emperor Franz Josef - and the flags of the Triple Entente and Italy, which defected from the Triple Alliance in the belief that Austria-Hungary had been the aggressor against Serbia and its treaty obligation was only binding for defensive reasons. (Facing page) Wartime French propaganda postcards utilising the Montenegrin and Serbian flags respectively.

Opening the floodgates of history: from Sarajevo to exile.

Chapter XVII

From Sarajevo to Exile

Why do not the German Emperor and the King of England fight out their quarrels alone? Why drag thousands of men from their homes and farms to fight their quarrels?

A Turkish deserter in Montenegro, circa 1902.

The anti-war views of a Turkish soldier, who had taken refuge in Montenegro around 1902, were recorded by two intrepid foreign travellers; merely the musings of an unnamed deserter, but sending the world's leaders off to the remote pacific island of his imagination to settle their differences would have been a more peaceful, and even honourable, resolution of international rivalries. However, pacifism of any sort was hardly on the agenda in 1914 and the two Balkan wars had pushed Europe closer to the brink of disaster: concluded by an unsatisfactory peace settlement and, more vitally, with the balance of power further disturbed.

That Europe had become a powder keg of conflicting interests and that World War One was the culmination of national, imperial and economic rivalries is generally agreed upon. That events arising from the tangled politics of the Balkans would light the fuse was not inevitable, but it was certainly appropriate. Europe's statesmen and generals only required an event which would force or, as it turned out, allow the first move to be made to plunge millions into the horrors of war. A young Serb from Herzegovina named Gavrilo Princip provided the spark.

His brief life story is full of interest and also has a strong Montenegrin connection; indeed, the Serbs of Herzegovina and the Montenegrins considered the borders which separated them as the artificial creations of their enemies. Princip, whose family roots were Montenegrin, played an historic part in eradicating those borders.

The Princips lived on the Montenegrin-Herzegovinian borderlands of Grahovo. The family traced its roots back to a centuries old *zadruga* belonging to the Jovičević clan, which had migrated from the rocky Montenegrin side of the border to Grahovo Valley in Herzegovina at the beginning of the eighteenth century.

The family settled as *kmets* (serfs) and Gavrilo's grandfather, along with his sons and their families as well as his unmarried daughters, all lived communally in the one house. It was only a few kilometres away from the historic junction of Tromedja, where the frontiers of the Venetian Republic, the Habsburg and Ottoman Empires had once converged. Inevitably, the Princips were caught up in the precarious existence of the military frontier and are recorded as having fought on both sides of the divide,

Montenegro　　　*Serbie*

as Turkish police and as Serb rebels.

In the 1875 peasant revolt Gavrilo's grandfather, Jovo, and his family had joined the uprising. Jovo was initially in a difficult position as he was at that time employed as a policeman by the Turkish authorities. One story has it that the Princip family house was burnt down by the rebels; whether this was for military-defensive reasons or to coerce the family into joining the insurgents is unclear.

Jovo, along with his brother Todo and his two sons, Petar and Ilija, were members of the rebel bands based at Crni Potoci. Ilija's bravery earned him a medal from Prince Petar Karadjordjević, who was fighting alongside the rebels in Bosnia under the pseudonym Petar Mrkonjić.

The Princip family's loyalties were undoubtedly with the Serb *kmets* and their political allegiance to Montenegro and Serbia. They shared the widespread anger, which led to armed resistance, when the province was given over to Austro-Hungarian administration after the war ended in 1878. However, if it was another form of foreign domination, in contrast to the Ottoman era economic opportunities were also part of the new regime. Bosnia-Herzegovina even came to be regarded as the economic model for the improvement of the Balkans.

At the same time the traditional life of the Balkan *zadruga* was breaking down and becoming economically unsustainable. Petar Princip was the last communal family head, after whom the *zadruga* was dissolved and its land divided. Petar gained about four acres and it was in this modest homestead that his son Gavrilo was born on July 13, 1894.

Gavrilo was a bright but rather withdrawn boy. He was fortunate to attend the primary school in Grahovo as his father had wanted him to become a shepherd, and it was only his mother's insistence which ensured he received an education. On finishing primary school he resolved to continue his studies in the Bosnian capital, Sarajevo. Among his motivations for leaving Grahovo were certainly his demoralising experience of the declining communal life of the zadruga, as well as, in a vague way, the desire for personal advancement.

Gavrilo went to Sarajevo on the advice of his brother, Jovo, who was energetically working his way up the social ladder. Still in his early twenties, Jovo had already become his own boss and a small-scale businessman. He had initially suggested that Gavrilo enter Sarajevo's Military School, but fearing that a military career could lead to his brother becoming the most despised kind of professional soldier - a represser of his own people - he instead arranged admission to the Merchant School.

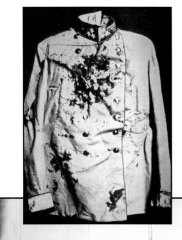

(Above) Franz Ferdinand and Sophie Chotek during the fatal royal tour of Sarajevo. (Left) The Archduke's blood-soaked jacket and (below) the royal car which fatally stopped outside Schiller's delicatessen, giving Gavrilo Princip his opportunity. (Facing page) The young conspirators on their way to trial. From left to right: Trifko Grabež, Nedeljko Čabrinović, Danilo Ilić and Gavrilo Princip.

Gavrilo was a good pupil who lived an uneventful life, commuting to and from his brother's house a few miles outside Sarajevo to school. However, in spite of Jovo's example, Gavrilo shared the widespread disdain among the youth of Sarajevo for business and he switched to the Classical School. Following his graduation from the fourth grade in 1911, aged seventeen, he became involved with the anti-Habsburg student groups which had formed as a reaction to the province's annexation in 1908. The students of Sarajevo were inexperienced as political activists, but many were strongly attracted to the 'Yugoslav Idea'. Gavrilo took an active part in the demonstrations of February 1912 and his student years ended with expulsion. The idealistic young man was on his way to becoming a dedicated Yugoslav patriot and revolutionary. Regardless of any economic benefits it had brought, he hated Austro-Hungarian rule and his sentiments were shared by many among his generation.

Serbia, enjoying a revival under King Petar Karadjordjević, had again become the great hope for the South Slav cause and Gavrilo decided to go to Belgrade. It was natural for him to view Serbia romantically and it is said that on crossing the border he knelt down and kissed the soil of a free Serb state. Ironically enough Serbia seemed to have little use for him. After a failed attempt to restart his studies in Belgrade, he tried to enlist in the army to fight in the First Balkan War but was turned away on account of his frail build.

It was one of the Obrenović regicides and a member of the nationalist society *Narodna Odbrana* (National Defence), Major Vojin Tankosić, who had refused him. They could certainly have made use of such a determined young man, who shared their conviction that only positive and violent action could liberate and unite the South Slavs. Despite his disappointment at missing the war, Gavrilo still dreamed of a great act in the national cause.

The general feeling in Serbia was that war with Austria-Hungary was inevitable, and success in the Balkan wars had encouraged the feeling that the country was ready to liberate Bosnia-Herzegovina. Gavrilo began spending much of his time in the environs of Belgrade's café society. Always a meeting place for political discussion and plotting, they were now also filled with victorious war veterans. Accompanying the nationalist sentiment there were many advocating political terrorism.

As fervent as they were, Princip and his group of Bosnian friends were hardly leading candidates to contribute much in that regard. They were, in fact, a notably naive bunch who could not even afford to purchase their own weapons. These were procured courtesy of the same Major Tankosić who had turned Gavrilo away from the army. He had become aware of their anti-Austro-Hungarian views and happily added them as a peripheral link in his chain of conspiracy. It was a loose association and a day of shooting practice, with a few words of advice on how to use their bombs, was all the training they received.

The one great strength the Bosnians all shared was an emotional one: the feeling that they each had little to lose and the belief in the greatness of the cause they were preparing to sacrifice themselves for. This was especially true of Princip who had a nihilistic aspect to his personality. He told his friend, the group's eldest member and organisational brain, the schoolteacher Danilo Ilić: *"After me the flood and I do not care."*

In that arbitrary vein their eventual victim, Archduke Franz Ferdinand, was only one potential target among many. The regional governors were more obvious targets and several attempts had already been made in Bosnia-Herzegovina and Croatia. Bogdan Žerajić had become a martyr figure through his attempt to assassinate Bosnia's Governor Varešanin in 1910, while an attempt to kill Croatia's Governor, Count Cuvaj, had narrowly failed in 1912.

Although he was hated as a symbol of foreign rule, Franz Ferdinand was aware of the urgent need to restructure the Austro-Hungarian Empire. He was also a restraint on the military and had his share of run-ins with the Chief of the General Staff, General Franz Conrad von Hotzendorf.

Most notably Franz Ferdinand had opposed the annexation of Bosnia-Herzegovina, believing that if war ensued it would be the end of the

(Above) The Sarajevo assassins at trial. From left to right: Grabež, Čabrinović, Princip, Ilić, Čubrilović. Austria-Hungary used the group's links to Belgrade to implicate the Serbian Government. (Left) An Austrian postcard of Emperor Franz Josef's letter to Kaiser Wilhelm II from July 5, 1914. The Emperor's conviction that the Serbian threat must be extinguished is expressed in some detail: *"The attack directed against my poor nephew is the direct consequence of the agitation carried on by the Russian and Serbian pan-Slavists . . . it is no longer an affair at Sarajevo of the single bloody deed of an individual, but of a well organised conspiracy . . . the Monarchy must expect in the future to deal with the irreconcilable and aggressive enmity of Serbia. In these conditions the Monarchy must tear away with a strong hand the net in which its enemy seeks to entangle it."*

monarchy. Relatively liberal though he was, he was also strongly opposed to South Slav nationalism. In that much he shared his impatient General's views, but he disagreed on the means by which Serbia and Montenegro could be brought to heel.

Franz Ferdinand was an interesting mixture of conservatism and progressive tendencies. And whilst being a devout Catholic, he realised that the condition of the Slav subjects of all faiths had to be ameliorated. However, his views had enjoyed little publicity and therefore meant nothing to those already seething with hatred toward the Empire.

Of all the Habsburg provinces, Bosnia-Herzegovina was considered the most backward and primitive, peripheral both territorially and culturally, but strategically vital. The strong-arm tactics of its governors had turned the people against the monarchy and the Habsburg aura counted for little. Emperor Franz Josef had paid only one fleeting visit in 1910, comprising of two brief security riddled stops in Sarajevo and Mostar which had been more like an inspection of an occupied territory than a royal tour.

Franz Ferdinand's visit to Sarajevo planned for June 1914 was, therefore, of the utmost political importance and, of course, a great provocation to his opponents.

His advisors had warned him of the tense situation in the province and of the potential danger to his life, but security for the visit would not be rigorous. A surprising omission, especially so given the extensive police and spy network the authorities could have utilised. Bureaucratic inertia was the cause: a mass of information had been collected but it had not been systematically analysed let alone acted upon. In addition, Bosnia's Governor, General Oskar Potiorek, had little feeling for the mood of the people and underestimated the undercurrents of violence the intelligence reports warned of. Any would be assassin had good prospects of at least one direct attempt on the Archduke's life.

Gavrilo Princip and his fellow conspirators planned to make their attempt on the last day of the Archduke's tour: Sunday, June 28, the most symbolic date in Serb history when Miloš Obilić redeemed himself through an act of regicide at the Battle of Kosovo.

Their journey from Belgrade to Sarajevo was relatively incident free. Much was later made of the tacit help they received from the border guards whilst crossing back into Bosnia, but the border was porous and they were unremarkable travellers among the agitators, spies, smugglers and the like who went back and forth with relative ease. The fateful day found all six assassins in Sarajevo at their assigned places along the royal route, armed with guns and bombs, each carrying a phial of cyanide with which to commit suicide after the Archduke's assassination.

It should have been easy as the safety of Franz Ferdinand and his wife, Countess Sophie Chotek, had been left to a security force of one hundred and twenty men in a city with a population of over fifty thousand. The conspirators were able to mingle freely with the crowds lining the wide avenue, the *Appel Quay*, awaiting the royal couple. Their plan was simplicity itself: for each in turn to try to kill

Franz Ferdinand as his car made its way toward *Franz Josef Strasse*.

Fortunately for the Archduke and his wife they were also remarkably amateurish. The first conspirator the royal car passed by was the young Moslem Mehmed Mehmedbašić. He failed to throw his bomb, probably through a loss of nerve. Next it was the turn of the youngest, Vaso Čubrilović, who held back out of pity for the Countess Cvetko Popović also suffered a loss of nerve, but, as he faltered, Nedeljko Čabrinović threw his bomb.

However, Čabrinović had released his bomb too soon and it bounced off the car roof and only exploded as it fell to the street. The car was momentarily stationery and, now, Gavrilo Princip had a chance, but he failed to recognise the Archduke and allowed the departing car to speed past without firing a shot.

Given one botched assassination attempt it would have been only prudent to abandon the rest of the tour, but events brought Franz Ferdinand and Gavrilo Princip together again. Habsburg pride and personal bravery only strengthened the Archduke's resolve to complete his itinerary, despite his own conviction that there would be more trouble before the day was over.

Governor Potoriek and his Chief of Police, Edmund Gerde, were undecided how to proceed and he hardly wanted to admit that his reassurances for the royal couple's safety had proven so ill founded. Franz Ferdinand, therefore, decided himself in what manner the tour should be completed. As precautions he demanded a change of route to avoid narrow *Franz Joseph Strasse* and, instead, to continue along the *Appel Quay* to the military hospital. Secondly, he demanded that his wife would not be with him. In both instances his wishes were not carried out. Countess Sophie refused to be parted from her husband's side and Franz Ferdinand reluctantly accepted that they would face the danger together. It was, however, the confusion of communication over the change of route which made the tragedy possible.

The column of cars made its way back up the *Appel Quay* and, for the seventh time in an hour, the Archduke passed by an assassin. Trifko Grabež was standing near the Kaiser Bridge. He had seen the car approaching but failed to react. A hundred yards after the Kaiser Bridge, Chief of Police Gerde's car turned right into *Franz Josef Strasse* and the Archduke's car followed suit, the chauffeur apparently not having been instructed of the change of route. Governor Potoriek shouted at them to turn back.

The chauffeur broke to a halt by the curb outside Schiller's delicatessen and prepared to reverse. Gavrilo Princip, who had changed position in the hope of gaining a second opportunity, disbelievingly saw the Archduke's car stop only a few feet in front of him. He stepped forward, hesitated momentarily on seeing Countess Sophie, and fired two shots at Franz Ferdinand, although he turned his head away as he did so.

The car sped off to the Governor's official residence, but the assassin's aim had been deadly. Countess Sophie was fatally wounded. The first bullet penetrated the car door, cut through her corset and into the right side of her body. The second bullet severed Franz Ferdinand's jugular vein and ended up lodging itself in his spine. Both were unconscious as they were carried from the car into the residence and, within a few minutes, were pronounced dead. At 11.30am the bells of Sarajevo's churches rang out in mourning.

Immediately after he fired his gun, Gavrilo Princip had been knocked to the ground and badly beaten. Most of the other conspirators were also soon caught. Their interrogations would reveal the details of the conspiracy, giving Austria-Hungary the pretext it needed for a strike against Serbia.

Relations between Serbia, the Balkan Piedmont, and Austria-Hungary, Otto von-Bismarck's *"Eastern Empire par excellence"*, had been a long and acrimonious debate on whether or not the two states could find a way to co-exist. All means except open warfare had been utilised, but now the war party in Vienna had finally been given its chance to deal the fatal blow.

France

Russie

Angleterre

Wartime French postcards of the Triple Entente allies: France, Russia and England.

(Facing page) Serbian Prime Minister Nikola Pašić. Austria-Hungary realised that by implicating the Serbian Government in Franz Ferdinand's assassination it had found the justification for war against its Balkan neighbour. In his desire to avoid that war, Nikola Pašić accepted almost all of Vienna's demands, except those that were felt to infringe too greatly on Serbia's sovereignty, which he suggested be arbitrated under the Hague Convention. Serbian compliance should have allowed the crisis to be resolved peacefully.
(Above) The Kaiser and Kaiseren. Even Germany's Kaiser Wilhelm II thought the Serbian Government had shown sufficient goodwill to make military action unnecessary. However, Vienna had decided on war, which was declared on July 28, 1914.

"Here comes war."
King Nikola, June 28, 1914.

As the cataclysm approached, Europe's leaders did themselves little credit. Emperor Franz Josef believed a limited war would be feasible and decided to risk the Habsburg dynasty rather than let the Serbian miscreant go unpunished; Kaiser Wilhelm was at his summer residence in Potsdam and saw no serious chance of war; Tsar Nikolai, remembering the Russo-Japanese war, had pledged he would not "be responsible for a monstrous slaughter" but events proved beyond his control; President Poincaré and Prime Minister René Viviani carried on as if there was little to fear and departed for a ceremonial visit to St. Petersburg and, at the Foreign Office in London, Sir Arthur Nicolson doubted that Austria-Hungary would take serious action.

King Nikola responded with a good deal more realism and alacrity.

In late May he had left for a holiday in Venice and Germany. Accompanied by Ksenija and Vjera, who were on their way to Russia to visit Milica and Stane, he enjoyed a four-day cruise aboard the royal yacht *Rumija*. In Venice he was met by Danilo and Milica-Yutta. Then it was onto Germany by train where Danilo visited his in-laws at Neuestrelitz, while Ana and Franz Josef Battenberg paid a visit to Nikola, who stayed in Munich.

The journey home began on June 26. Accompanied by Ana and Franz Josef, Nikola enjoyed two days in Salzburg on the Austrian-German border, after which, on the morning of June 28, he boarded train for Trieste.

At a stop *en route*, Adjutant Ilija Jovanović-Bjeloš was sent to buy the morning newspapers. On the platform he overheard people talking about Franz Ferdinand's death at the hands of a Serb. Back on board the train, Nikola could hardly believe his ears, but at the next station they saw the billboards and his reaction was concise and unequivocal: *"Here comes war."*[2]

A revealing response as many considered the Archduke's murder an isolated act carried out by extremists within Bosnia-Herzegovina and, more generally, European rulers had learned to view death at the hands of the political assassin as an occupational hazard. Few concluded that it signalled war between Austria-Hungary and Serbia let alone an even greater conflagration, but five decades on the throne had taught Nikola well where politics ends and war begins.

As the crisis escalated into all out confrontation between Vienna and Belgrade, Emperor Franz Josef hoped that it need not mean all out war, but his military were straining at the leash. They found justification in the conspirators connections with Belgrade, although the Serbian Government itself had nothing to do with the plot and Prime Minister Pašić had even tried to warn Vienna of the potential danger.

The democratic Serbia of King Petar Karadjordjević and the vocal nationalist societies it tolerated proved a combination which was Belgrade's undoing. Within Serbia there were those who saw the country's role in a more militaristic vein; they believed violence would be needed to achieve national union. That some of these were the regicides involved in the murder of King Aleksandar Obrenović hardly improved the country's image. Their views were aggressively publicised through the journal *Piedmont*. A despotic regime might have suppressed *Piedmont*, along with the nationalist societies *Narodna Odbrana* and the soon to be infamous *Crna Ruka* (Black Hand), but a constitutional monarch, one also still wary of dealing with the regicides, was in a difficult position.

That said, Serbia's domestic complications were irrelevant to Vienna except as corollary justification for war. The delay between the assassination and a declaration of war was only extended by the incompetence of the official investigation in Sarajevo. As the links to Belgrade eventually surfaced during interrogations of the conspirators, the opportunity to implicate the Serbian Government presented itself.

In Cetinje, King Nikola was frantically doing all he could to calm the situation, while Austria-Hungary's diplomats tried to ensure his neutrality. On returning to the capital he had immediately paid his respects at the Austro-Hungarian Embassy, offered to send Crown Prince Danilo to Franz Ferdinand's funeral and *Glas Crnogorca* had condemned the assassination. The Archduke's death was actually the occasion for genuine sympathy within Montenegro, but latent anti-Austro-Hungarian feeling soon resurfaced when the brutal reprisals against the Serbs of Bosnia-Herzegovina began. The mood turned ugly and Nikola had to intervene personally when a crowd several hundred strong demonstrated outside the Austro-Hungarian Embassy.

The situation was volatile and one of the Sarajevo conspirators made Montenegro's position even more difficult. Mohammed Mehmedbašić had evaded capture and fled to Montenegro where the police arrested him on July 12. Austria-Hungary demanded his extradition but before an agreement was reached he escaped from Nikšić prison. Another potentially incendiary political problem, it had been conveniently defused by Mehmedbašić's disappearance. The authorities went through the motions of punishing the guards for dereliction of their duty and even searched the houses of three members of parliament, but Vienna still suspected official connivance. If true, it was certainly in the age-old tradition of harbouring fugitives and saved Mehmedbašić's life.

Despite the growing crisis, King Nikola's approach was the same as it had always been: to avoid war but to forward the national cause if an opportunity arose. It was a strategy he had been pursuing since the 1870's. If Vienna wanted his neutrality he would demand a tangible gain, still nothing less than Scutari and part of northern Albania. As Austria-Hungary could not have delivered these even if it had wanted to, for Rome would never allow Vienna a *de facto* protectorate of Montenegro, it was of little use except in keeping the King's options open.

In the meantime the march to war was gathering pace. Claiming the conspiracy had involved official Serbia, Austria-Hungary presented an ultimatum which no sovereign state could accept. The Government did its best to comply and accepted all demands except allowing Austro-Hungarian officials to be present during the investigations within Serbia. Even Kaiser Wilhelm II thought Belgrade had done enough to placate Vienna, but the ultimatum ensured, as it was designed to, some objection, even if only on a detail, and allowed war to be declared.

Gavrilo Princip could not have predicted the awesome consequences which followed the murder of Franz Ferdinand, but he had, nonetheless, fulfilled his pledge and opened the floodgates of history. It was an illuminating statement which illustrated the gulf between his revolutionary impulse and the conservative King who believed that he alone stood between Montenegro and the unbridled forces of history. King Nikola also liked to quote the well-worn phrase, but to his ministers as a warning of what could happen to Montenegro after his reign ended.

"Serbia may rely on the brotherly and unconditional support of Montenegro in this moment upon which depends the fate of the Serbian nation, as well as on any other occasion." King Nikola to Nikola Pašić: July 11, 1914.

A month after Franz Ferdinand's assassination, on July 28, 1914, Austria-Hungary

(Above) Montenegrin troops preparing for battle. Serbia and Montenegro's armies were placed under a joint command and in the first phase of the war captured territory in Bosnia-Herzegovina and along the Adriatic coast. (Below) A Montenegrin gun fires across the mountain ranges.
(Facing page) Serbian infantry covering the movement of troops at the second line at Vračar, east of Belgrade. Serbia's early victories in the war prevented the Central Powers from securing the land bridge between Europe and Asia.

declared war on Serbia, which responded by calling for the liberation and unification of the South Slavs. Thereafter, as the military machines rolled into action, the descent into European wide war was as predictable as a muscle reflex, although the masses and many of their leaders had little awareness of what it would mean in death and destruction.

That immutable slide to war was also taking place within tiny Montenegro. On August 1, the same day that Germany and Russia declared war on each other, an emergency session of the Montenegrin Parliament was called. The vote was unanimously in favour of a declaration of war, but the King sought to forestall the inevitable.

In the afternoon he received the parliamentary deputies to ask them to remain calm and to leave the final decision in his experienced hands. It was a characteristic prevarication, diplomacy of the 'Old World'. Perhaps the King was hoping for a last minute reprieve or for last minute negotiations, or perhaps it was simply the fact that three of his children had not yet returned from enemy territory in Kotor.

Whatever his personal reasons, Nikola was also neither warmonger nor militarist and enough of a realist to understand that European war would be a cataclysm. He cast diplomacy aside to tell the Austro-Hungarian military attaché: *"God is my witness that I never willed the war, for I know what is at stake, but destiny fulfils itself; it is stronger than the human will."*[3] His desire for peace counted for nothing; indeed, to many, it appeared disingenuous and even a betrayal of the national cause.

Montenegro declared war on Austria-Hungary on August 6, 1914, and the Serbian and Montenegrin armies were placed under a joint command.

Despite the calls for South Slav liberation, the response from the South Slavs in the Austro-Hungarian provinces was not hopeful; mobilisation went smoothly and the first battalions sent against Serbia were comprised of up to fifty percent Croats and twenty-five percent Serbs. The Empire was clearly not about to collapse from within.

Statistically, Serbia and Montenegro's position appeared dire. Their populations of four and a half million Serbians and half a million Montenegrins opposed the fifty-two million of Austria-Hungary. Furthermore, the conflict in the Balkans was of secondary importance to the Triple Entente alliance of Great Britain, France and Russia, for whom the German threat was the primary concern.

With the odds apparently so much in its favour, Austria-Hungary's first assault was a striking failure. Serbian forces inflicted the first defeat against the Central Powers at Cer and they even managed to advance into the Hungarian ruled Vojvodina. It was a morale boosting beginning with the Russians also advancing into Austrian Galicia, but Serbia's resources were already overstretched and Belgrade was lost and regained in a fortnight of frantic fighting.

Montenegro also enjoyed early successes in the first stage of the war. Its forces occupied parts of the Adriatic coastline and advanced into the interior to within sight of the Bosnian capital, Sarajevo. In November a force of five thousand Montenegrins joined fifteen thousand Serbians to drive back the Austro-Hungarian army which had advanced across the River Drina.

Left to their own devices, Serbia and Montenegro might have been able to frustrate Austria-Hungary, but as the war widened and the neutral nations chose sides, the situation for both deteriorated rapidly. Turkey joined with the Central Powers in the hope of regaining lost territory, as did Bulgaria with the promise of Macedonia and territory in Greece and Romania.

Italy's entry into the war on the Triple Entente side in May 1915 should have been a boost to Serbia and Montenegro, but was actually of highly dubious benefit. It was a coup for the Triple Entente as Italy had been allied with Austria-Hungary and Germany; the price was the secret Treaty of London in which Italy was promised extensive gains, including areas with large South Slav populations: Carniola, Istria, Trieste and part of Dalmatia. Italy, therefore, had little incentive to aid Serbia and Montenegro and, instead, planned to bide its time until circumstances favoured annexation of the promised territories.

The worst turn of events was the agreement concluded in the summer of 1915 between the Central Powers and Bulgaria. In October Serbia faced a renewed attack from a combined force almost a million strong. Resistance was quickly overwhelmed as Bulgarian forces barred the route to Salonika, threatening to trap the army and force a complete surrender.

A retreat through the Albanian and Montenegrin mountains was the only way to keep Serbia in the war. The divisions which stayed to slow the Austro-Hungarian advance faced certain defeat and likely death, while their comrades had to cross hostile and anarchic Albania. As the enemy advanced and, in terror, much of the population fled, it seemed like the end for Serbia as a military factor and, possibly, even as a nation.

> *"If I were asked to give the death of Serbia in a few sentences, I should tell of a tearless woman besides the shreds of her little boy, struck down by an aeroplane bomb for 'moral effect'; of old men and young men, old women and young women, boys and girls starving, starving hopelessly in a frozen wilderness; of the Serbian army groping and staggering into Scutari; and of the wounded at Kruševac. One does not get rid of such pictures."*[4]
> *Fortier Jones (American journalist)*

As the Central Powers advanced the Serbs went south once more toward the Adriatic through Albania, only this time it was in a desperate struggle for survival. One legacy of the Balkan wars was that the Albanians saw little reason to welcome them. The Balkan League had envisaged a final partition of the Ottoman Empire's European provinces; the Albanians, who occupied a sizeable portion of those territories, were credited with neither national consciousness nor the right to form their own state.

It was an insensitive stance from their neighbours, but it was also true that the Albanians were badly divided amongst themselves: between religions, Catholic and Orthodox Christian, Sunni and Bektashi Moslems; by region and dialect between northern Ghegs and southern Toscs; socially and economically between landowning *beys* and resentful peasants. Still, they had no desire to exchange Ottoman rule for assimilation by their neighbours.

The fledgling Albanian state had disintegrated into violent chaos after repeated incursions by foreign armies and in-fighting among the ruling élites. In March 1914 the Great Powers had installed a little known European prince, Queen Elizabeth of Romania's nephew William of Wied, as

sovereign. Controversially and foolishly he appointed Essad Pasha as War Minister and Interior Minister, but by September the Government was discredited and the Prince stepped down and left to join the German army.

Essad Pasha's dream of becoming Albania's next ruler now seemed attainable and he set himself up in central Albania with Serbian and Italian support; a rival movement called for a return to Ottoman allegiance and a third, led by the experienced former Ottoman politician Ismail Kemal, claimed legitimacy from the provisional administration of 1912. To compound the misery with a touch of irony, Albania attempted to remain neutral when war broke out only to be occupied at different times by the forces of almost every Power.

Although Essad Pasha offered some assistance to the starving and exhausted Serbs, they found little sympathy from the Albanian tribes. In the urban centres some semblance of mercy and food could still be found, but in the freezing mountains even firewood was scarce and assassins and bandits lay in wait. The treacherous snowbound mountain passes also claimed their victims as soldiers, women and children fell to their deaths in the deep gorges.

The remnants of Serbia's army finally found salvation on the Adriatic coastline. From a force of three hundred and fifty thousand around one hundred and thirty-five thousand made it to Corfu and the protection of the Triple Entente. Among the victims were also many women and children. From the thirty thousand young boys who had fled the enemy advance and tried to cross the mountains on their own, only fifteen thousand made it to the coast. Serbia would rise again, but the retreat to safety seemed more like the exodus of a vanquished nation than a tactical retreat.

Montenegro's contribution to Serbia's military survival was vital. The modern warfare of the Balkan wars, heavy artillery, trench fighting, and the military mistakes made during the campaign to take Scutari, had brought higher casualties than the guerrilla wars Montenegrins were accustomed to. The nation was exhausted, but one last act of Serb solidarity was still needed and in the Battle of Mojkovac, a series of engagements which took place between December 30, 1915 and January 21, 1916, that task was accomplished under the leadership of General Janko Vukotić. It was the last great battle fought by 'Old Montenegro' in which several attempts by the Austro-Hungarian army to intercept the Serbian retreat were repulsed.

The final push to the coast took the Serbian army through Scutari, which Montenegrin forces had retaken in 1915 with some jubilation. However, that was during the early successes of the war and it would yet again prove to be a short lived gain, as alone Montenegro could not withstand the onslaught of the Central Powers.

In the wake of the Serbian retreat, the surrender of Cetinje and the country's military capitulation was inescapable. As the enemy forces approached the capital and took up positions around Mount Lovćen, King Nikola sought to encourage his army encamped nearby. From Cetinje he went to Njeguši and Krstac, both of which had already been evacuated and from where Austrian troops could be seen in the mountains. The King initially thought they were Montenegrins until his adjutant fetched a pair of binoculars; a despairing moment of revelation with the enemy army approaching and their airplanes circling above. The order was given to retreat to Cetinje and representatives sent down to Kotor to negotiate the peace.

Vienna demanded that the Montenegrin army lay down its arms at Virpazar, Danilovgrad and Nikšić; that all commanders and officers should be surrendered as prisoners of war and the handing over of all Serbian officers and soldiers on Montenegrin territory. Nikola could not accept such a *diktat:* "*The first two points I can accept; however, the third I cannot because I was always fighting for Serbdom and the Serbian people. I do not want to betray them and enslave them now.*"[5]

Prevaricate, delay and hope was the only remaining option as the evacuation of the capital was ordered. On January 9, 1916, the Royal Family left for Rijeka Crnojevića with their servants and belongings. The King stayed behind in Cetinje and Metropolitan Mitrofan Ban was instructed to meet the Austro-Hungarian command at the capital's entrance so as to allay the people's fear of the occupation.

When he felt he had done all he could, Nikola made ready to go to Rijeka Crnojevića. Before he left he paid a visit to the aged Ilija Plamenac: "*Vojvoda, I am going to Rijeka for a few days. I think I will be back soon. Be well.*" Plamenac could see what Nikola refused to acknowledge, that he would not return. He replied: "*Goodbye Master, you and I will never meet again.*"[6] At 1am on the morning of January 10, Nikola left Cetinje.

His last few days in Montenegro were taken up with futile negotiations over the terms of surrender while Austro-Hungarian forces steadily advanced. They entered Cetinje immediately after the King's departure as the majority of the army surrendered its weapons.

Nikola retreated to Prince Mirko's residence, Kruševac, and again sent his delegates to negotiate. However, the terms of surrender would not be relaxed and the enraged King retreated to his salon to write a letter to Emperor Franz Josef, a spark of defiant optimism remaining: "*You will see what is going to happen now!*"[7] he told his adjutant. Franz Josef's reply was predictably disappointing but pathetically poignant, considering Austria-Hungary had unleashed the war: "*Your Highness, I am deeply sorry that I cannot satisfy your wishes. My supreme command has decided, and that is how it must be.*"

Nikola's last hopes for an honourable peace had been dashed. In a mood of bleak despair he thought of making a last symbolic stand with his army at Carev Laz, where Vladika Danilo I had routed the Turks two centuries ago. However, the soldiers were a spent force and the commander of the Zeta battalion reported that his men were so exhausted they could barely fire a single shot.

(Above) A depiction of Austro-Hungarian troops traversing Bosnia-Herzegovina for the invasion of Montenegro and (inset) Italy's favourable depiction as an ally of the Triple Entente. However, the Allies gave no tangible support to enable Montenegrin resistance to continue. (Right) Montenegrin women repairing the roads to facilitate the movement of troops. Insets: Contemporary reporting of the war in the Balkans: (left) the Austrian army advancing through Montenegro and (right) the Serbian retreat to the Adriatic coast.

Facing page: King Petar Karadjordjević seated on a gun carriage drawn by bullocks during the Serbian retreat. The Central Powers brought a million men to the Balkan campaign in late 1915. The Serbs fled southward across the Albanian and Montenegrin mountains, finally finding refuge on the island of Corfu. Casualties from starvation and disease were high: from 350,000 soldiers around 135,000 made it to safety. (Inset left) An anti-Bulgarian propaganda postcard; an appropriate representation of Serbian sentiment as King Ferdinand's allying with Germany and Austria-Hungary enabled the Central Powers to overwhelm Serbia. (Inset right) Belgium's fate was similar to Serbia's in that it took the brunt of the German assault in 1914/15, but French and British support prevented total disaster.

Stores, Shells and Shattered Men near Scutari

(Above) Montenegrin troops marching out from Cetinje. The capital was defended by antiquated guns, the soldiers were war weary and, unlike earlier would be conquerors, the Austro-Hungarians had the benefit of air power. When this picture was taken Cetinje had already been bombed. The 'Gibraltar of the Balkans' would fall shortly after the Serbian army had reached safety. (Inset) Montenegrin troops around Scutari town and Lake Skadar. In the first year of war Montenegro recaptured Scutari, which subsequently proved vital in enabling the Serbian army to reach the Albanian coastline.

Despondently, Nikola sent Milena, Ksenija and Vjera down to Scutari to make ready to leave for Italy and, with his two sons Mirko and Petar, returned to Kruševac. The Supreme Commander of Montenegrin forces, Serbia's General Pešić, was instructed to leave Montenegro immediately with his officers and army to prevent their capture. Finally, Nikola departed with Petar to join the family, while Mirko stayed behind to maintain the royal presence in the country.

Already notable by his absence was Crown Prince Danilo. Having disagreed with Nikola's decision to declare war on Austria-Hungary he had left for France in July using the pretext of poor health.

On January 18 Nikola departed for Scutari where his cousin, Božo Petrović, was in command. The journey over Lake Skadar was a dangerous one as the enemy had taken the islands of Virpazar and Vranjina. Nikola spent a night and a day in Scutari as Božo took steps to organise his departure for Italy. When the news came that Italian warships would be docking at the port of *San Giovanni di Medua*, Nikola decided to leave Scutari on January 20.

Departing at 6pm from the village of St. Nikola, which lies at the mouth of the River Bojana, the ageing King was given Božo's carriage while his entourage had to manage as best they could. Crossing war torn Albania was risky, as the sounds of gunshots from the nearby Montenegrin volunteer battalion testified.

For travelling it was, fortunately, a clear night, but this also allowed the party to see the casualties of war lining the route from Scutari to Lješe. It was a gruesome sight: the road was strewn with the dead bodies of soldiers, horses and, even sadder, many in the last stages of dying. Near Lješe they stopped and a fire was made for the King to warm himself. They continued on through the night as, although the journey was taxing, Nikola wanted to arrive at *San Giovannni di Medua* by dawn.

The following morning they duly arrived at the coast but the Italian warships had not yet docked. Although Nikola was fatigued he did not want to sleep and his adjutant was asked to contact Božo Petrović in Scutari.

There was some good news, that Prime Minister Lazar Tomanović had also escaped the advance, alone on a little boat via the River Bojana. Unfortunately, Božo was unable to help with the request to send Nikola money and informed that enemy forces were already entering Scutari. Božo was very anxious that the Italians arrive soon as he had his own family to consider. He had entrusted his son and two nephews to Nikola's adjutant to ensure that they reached the protection of Queen Elena in Rome.

Nikola had finally given in to tiredness and slept for half an hour. After waking and receiving the news from Scutari he had a coffee and went down to the dock. It was raining lightly so he was given a chair under the twisted roof of an old warehouse to avoid the rain. A little later Regent Aleksandar Karadjordjević arrived from Lješe. He joined his grandfather and, as they watched the Serbian army boarding the steamships to Drač and Corfu, they talked.

Aleksandar was now effectively Serbia's ruler as King Petar had made him regent for political reasons in 1914. He was preparing to go to Corfu with the remainder of his army and organise Serbia's government in exile. He had already proved himself a brave and effective military commander and would soon prove to be a shrewd and tough politician.

Around 10am the Italian warships arrived. A small steamboat brought the Captain ashore with the news that the King could not leave before noon. Nikola and Aleksandar talked a little more until a steamboat came to take Nikola to join his son Petar, who had already boarded ship. Aleksandar walked his grandfather to his transport and kissed him goodbye. It was the last time they would meet.

Nikola's departure was filled with ill-portent and his mood became even more melancholy on seeing the dead bodies of volunteer soldiers in the water. All aboard removed their hats as a sign of respect as Nikola, with tears in his eyes, paid homage: *"We pray to god for these martyrs."* He crossed himself and went down to his cabin to be alone, his countenance as *"black as the earth."*[8]

With death and destruction all around there was every reason for despair, but also some reason to hold out hope for the future. Only the addition of German and Bulgarian forces had enabled Austria-Hungary to overrun Serbia and Montenegro, and Nikola had used his experience to ensure it was a hollow victory: the King and his ministers escaped, there was no signed instrument of surrender and the state of war was never formally terminated. The Austro-Hungarian army had taken control of the country, but only as despised occupiers harried from the mountains by guerrilla bands.

Nikola left *San Giovanni di Medua* at 12am on January 21, arriving at the Italian port of Brindisi in the late afternoon. The following morning he took the train from Brindisi to Rome, where Queen Elena was waiting to take her father to the Villa Margherita. Elena took into her care Božo Petrović's son and two nephews, as well as the son of Adjutant Ilija Jovanović-Bjeloš. Three days later Nikola left for France, arriving in Lyon on January 25, 1914.

(Inset below) The fall of Montenegro was strategically important. In particular the surrender of Cetinje and Mount Lovćen, in January 1916, were vital to the Central Powers. The port of Kotor was secured against possible bombardment from the mountain heights and giving assistance to the guerrilla bands, which continued to harass the occupying forces, became nigh on impossible. (Inset, below right) A French propaganda postcard from 1914 showing the Triple Entente and allied nations. From left to right: King Petar Karadjordjević, King George V, President of France, Raymond Poincaré, Tsar Nikolai II, King Albert of Belgium and, centre, King Nikola. (Below) The King on the Adriatic coast shortly before his final departure. After the country's occupation, Nikola followed his family down to the coast where Italian warships took him to refuge, firstly in Italy and then France. The military capitulation was one of the most controversial moments in Montenegrin history. The King felt justified in seeking the protection of the Triple Entente, as had his Serbian relations and King Albert of Belgium. However, opponents accused him of offering a separate peace to the Central Powers, although no formal peace was ever signed, and of preventing the Montenegrin army from escaping with Serbia's. The accusations and counter-accusations would continue, but the King would never see his beloved homeland again.

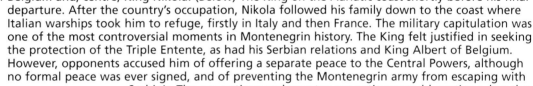

Page 607

The War Illustrated, 12th February, 1916.

King Nicholas Seeks Refuge in Friendly France

The arrival of King Nicholas of Montenegro at Lyons. Together with King Albert and King Peter, this venerable monarch goes into friendly exile to await the moment of his country's liberation from Teuton tyranny.

A Montenegrin soldier, who was one of the bodyguard of King Nich... billeted. He is about to sample some of the soup for w...

MAI UNA PACE SEPARATA

The final struggle for crown and country.

Chapter XVIII

The Final Struggle: 1916-1921

A peaceful revolution: peaceful because it was made by the almost unanimous consensus of the population and without any resistance.

Andrija Radović (former Montenegrin Prime Minister)

I can see that Montenegro will not be taken like a maiden without a dowry.

King Nikola

In the immediate aftermath of the capitulation of Montenegro it was clear that the country had been let down by its allies: that it had been given neither the military nor logistical support needed to withstand the enemy onslaught. Most debilitating of all had been Italy's failure to give assistance and one newspaper, *Il Secolo*, considered its lack of support particularly unjustifiable: *"Who is responsible for the crushing of Montenegro? . . . The very fact of having left the defence of the Bay of Kotor to the obsolete artillery of the Montenegrins very nearly constitutes an act of treason."*[1]

Italian politicians argued that saving Montenegro would have been a considerable military operation and, in January 1916, Foreign Minister Baron Sonnino gave this appraisal of events to the British Parliament: *"The invasion of Montenegro has been the inevitable consequence of the Serbian retreat. It was said that Italy could have, ought to have, sent a military expedition to protect Montenegro, but this argument cannot stand the most elementary criticism, if the tactical and strategical position on land and sea is taken into account."*[2] It was estimated by the Italians that two to three hundred thousand troops would have been needed to prevent Montenegro's fall.

Whilst there was a degree of truth in that excuse, it was also true that Italy's leaders had concluded that giving help to Serbia or Montenegro at this point in the war would not further their ambitions along the eastern Adriatic coastline. For those reasons the food supplies for the Serbian army that the Allies had sent to southern Italy were held up. It was only after Tsar Nikolai II and President of France, Raymond Poincaré, interceded that the supplies were released.

An anecdote in France's *Le Journal* publicised King Nikola's views on the fall of Montenegro. During Nikola's stay in Rome his grandson, Prince Umberto, had asked him why he seemed so downtrodden: *" 'I have been beaten all over my body by my enemies: on the arms, on the legs, on the chest and on the head.' Then the Prince said to me in a sad voice: 'You had by then nothing left to eat in your country.' Thus my twelve year-old grandson summarised the cause of our defeat better than all the diplomats!"*[3]

The King's last days in Montenegro were a controversial issue. Although it was obvious that Montenegro would have to surrender and

(Below) King Nikola's flight from the Central Powers by Luj Rajmakers. Facing page: The King's arrival in France makes the headlines and (inset) an Italian postcard declares that the Allies will never conclude a separate peace. From left to right: President Poincaré of France, Tsar Nikolai II of Russia, Regent Aleksandar of Serbia, King Vittorio Emanuele III of Italy, King Nikola I of Montenegro, King Albert I of Belgium and King George V of Great Britain.

starvation was fast becoming a danger, Nikola was accused of having handed over Mount Lovćen without a fight, preventing several thousand soldiers escaping with the Serbian army and of offering a separate peace to Austria-Hungary. However, it is unlikely that Nikola expected anything from Vienna and certain that he would have been a match for the conquerors in diplomatic duplicity; there was no shame in that for *"Once again in freedom you cannot be held to engagements you were forced to make while in captivity."*[4]

Nikola claimed that it was the Commander in Chief, Serbia's General Pešić, who had called for the surrender. *"Henceforth all resistance and all fighting against the enemy is impossible. There is no chance of the situation improving, ask the enemy for peace,"* he told the King. For his part, Pešić denied that was the case and laid the blame for the capitulation squarely at Nikola's feet. Furthermore, the Royal Family was accused of aiding the enemy: Prince Petar had gone down to the coast to negotiate peace terms and had been warned to surrender post-haste or face aerial bombardment after which, it was rumoured, he had given vital military information that caused casualties. The truth is mired in circumstance, political manoeuvrings and the subsequent propaganda.

Nikola also faced criticism for not continuing onto Corfu with his son-in-law and grandson, King Petar and Regent Aleksandar of Serbia, in a show of dynastic unity. He declined as, although both royal families had accepted French protection, relations with Serbia and its powerful Prime Minister remained poor. Nikola certainly wanted to keep his freedom of action and his hands would be tied if he fell under Nikola Pašić's sway. In the circumstances there was little to be achieved by sharing the Serbian army's exile and, by placing himself firmly in the Allied camp, he had avoided becoming a tool of the Austro-Hungarian occupation and ensured the opportunity to forward Montenegro's interests. Nikola's main objective for the duration of the war would be to ensure the Triple Entente's support for his post-war return.

The Royal Family had left their belongings in Scutari and the only money they had brought with them were one hundred thousand perpers in gold and bonds. The King stayed in Lyon while financial arrangements were discussed with the French authorities. The people at least raised Nikola's spirits, greeting him with shouts of *"Long live the King, long live Montenegro"* wherever he appeared in public. It was a gratifying acknowledgement that Montenegro's plight had not been forgotten; that he had been right to place his faith in the Triple Entente's ultimate victory and that the Allies would honour their pledge to fight on until three small, brave nations - Belgium, Serbia and Montenegro - were restored.

After spending a month in Lyon, the Royal Family were settled in *Chateaux Merignac* near Bordeaux and a new cabinet appointed from the ministers who had made it into exile. However, problems soon arose as the long running disputes and jealousies within the ruling circle continued in exile. Lazar Mijušković returned as premier but his term would again be cut short. His most positive act was the negotiation of a subvention from the Allies based on the number of government officials in exile, from which an apanage for the Royal Family was also taken. Mijušković saw himself as the legitimate political authority, having led the ministry formed in December 1915, but some, including another former premier and currently the Minister of Finance, Andrija Radović, refused to accept this state of affairs. Mijušković, therefore, set about trying to remove those he considered his political enemies.

They included the King's personal secretary, Miloš Živković, and the court priest, Leontije Ninković. Both were accused of being Austro-Hungarian spies. Mijušković also objected to Princess Ksenija's influence and she, too, was threatened with punitive measures. Unsurprisingly, he soon found himself the victim of some retaliatory backstabbing. After a heated argument with General Ante Gvozdenović he was forced to step down and Andrija Radović was proposed as his replacement.

Given the prominent role he had played in Montenegro's pre-war political disputes, Andrija Radović's loyalty was questionable, but the King was persuaded by the advice of another former minister, Petar Plamenac, who assured him: *"Master, you know well how faithful I am to you, but I give you my word that Andrija will be even more so than I."*[5] Certainly, Radović's political skills were needed and he successfully formed his cabinet as a coalition between the *Klubaši* and the royalist party, the *Pravaši*.

Matters took a more positive turn. Radović persuaded the French to relocate the Montenegrins to *Neuilly-sur-Seine* near Paris. The Royal Family was settled in a villa in *Rue Victor Hugo* and the Government took two floors of a house in *Rue Ansel*. It was an important step: Russia, France, Italy, Great Britain and Serbia all recognised the Government's legitimacy; a Montenegrin Red Cross office was organised, with Queen Milena as patron and King Nikola's old friend, Simo Popović, as president; the energies of the King's youngest daughters, Ksenija and Vjera, were directed toward helping Montenegrin POW's and an administrative office was found in the *Champs Élysée*, from where the collection and distribution of donations was organised.

This unity of purpose survived until late 1916. For Serbia, Montenegro and the Habsburg ruled South Slavs war also meant that the general aim of a Yugoslav state needed to be defined. That, in turn, demanded a reconciliation between the Karadjordjević and Petrović-Njegoš dynasties. Andrija Radović prepared a proposal; whether King Nikola actually requested he do so or if he went ahead on his own initiative is disputed. Either way it failed and brought about a decisive break between the King and his talented but headstrong Prime Minister.

Radović tried to create a formula acceptable to both states and treated the ruling houses as equals. He proposed that King Petar and King Nikola abdicate in favour of their sons, who would then share an alternating royal dignity in the united state. Regent Aleksandar would be Yugoslavia's first king but be succeeded by Crown Prince Danilo, then Aleksandar's male heirs, after which the princes of both dynasties would rule in turn.

The Royal Family gathered to consider Radović's proposal, including Crown Prince Danilo who was called from his isolation in *Cap d'Antibes* where he had rented a villa. Danilo had little belief in the survival of an independent Montenegrin state and raised no objections, but he kept his thoughts to himself while the family deliberated. Their reaction was not what he hoped for. The strongest rejection came from Ksenija, who thought it an insane idea and lobbied her father to dismiss it out of hand. Her influence, along with that of Italian diplomacy behind the scenes, was decisive. Nikola summoned the Prime Minister: *"Andrija, although you have worked hard in preparing this proposal, you must understand that, as long as I live, the crown will never leave my head. You can go now."*[6] Radović offered his resignation, which the King accepted without hesitation. It was a crucial rupture and a major mistake on the part of King Nikola.

So long as Serbia had been ruled by the Obrenovići, Nikola would have been the first choice for the unified state and even a future Yugoslav state. In contrast, the Karadjordjevići had proven popular rulers and Serbia had prospered during King Petar's reign. They also had the support of Prime Minister Nikola Pašić, a hugely experienced politician and the dominant figure in Serbian politics.

Andrija Radović's departure gave a hostage to fortune that King Nikola could ill afford. It was a turn of events Nikola Pašić was closely involved in. Radović, who would later justify his actions by asserting that the King had reneged on a promise to place his crown at the service of Yugoslav unification, gladly accepted Serbian financial support for his anti-Petrović campaigning. It marked the beginning of a process of political disintegration for the *Pravaši*.

One of Radović's first post-resignation acts was to convince the French authorities to reduce the financial subsidy to the Montenegrin Government. More damaging still was the virulent propaganda he disseminated through the Serbian funded Montenegrin Committee for National Unification, which claimed to be the true voice of the country. In future, each and every step taken by King Nikola would be repudiated and denounced as treachery.

Nikola now turned to Simo Popović to form a ministry but he declined, pleading old age and exhaustion. The truth was that, along with others in the ruling circle, Popović was looking for a way out. He had fled Montenegro along with the King and had hoped to help his cause, but their long political collaboration and close friendship was finally coming to an end. Popović also resigned from the Montenegrin Red Cross, breaking his remaining link with the King.

Like Lazar Mijušković he objected to the influence the Royal Family had in political matters. The *Pravaši* felt it showed gross ingratitude and subsequently claimed that the memoirs of his years in Montenegro, which were published in Belgrade in the 1920's, were written with an eye to pleasing the Karadjordjevići.

The more immediate significance of these departures was to demonstrate to the Serbian and Montenegrin communities in exile, as well as to the Allies, that King Nikola's position was precarious.

(Left) President Poincaré and Tsar Nikolai II. Both men were strong advocates of the Triple Entente, but France and Britain were criticised for demanding too much of the Russians and thereby helping bring about the downfall of Tsarist Russia in 1917. (Below) King Vittorio Emanuele of Italy and Crown Prince Danilo have a distant view of the Montenegrin war front in 1915. Danilo had left the country before the Austro-Hungarian invasion citing poor health as the reason. However, most concluded that it was anger at his father's decision to declare war which prompted his early departure. Nikola and Danilo's relations would become increasingly distant during exile as Danilo had little desire to continue the struggle to return to Montenegro. (Facing page) The Montenegrin Government was initially installed in Bordeaux, later moving to *Neuilly-sur-Seine* near Paris.

It was also precisely the wrong moment for Nikola to lose the support of some of his most prominent advisors, with the debate over the future of the Balkans and Central Europe coming to the fore.

Emperor Franz Josef had died in November 1916 and been succeeded by his nephew Karl. The young Emperor had tried to negotiate a separate peace to save his throne, but he was unable to free himself from the German alliance and his well meaning attempts to offer greater autonomy to his subject nationalities only accelerated secessionism. Preserving the Habsburg Empire as a buffer state in Central Europe seemed increasingly impractical to the Triple Entente and other options came under consideration.

For King Nikola the loyalty of his ministers had become the most immediate issue. With that priority in mind, Evgenije Popović was appointed Prime Minister. Formerly the Montenegrin Consul in Rome, he had also been a Garibaldian freedom fighter in his youth and was a man whose integrity Nikola had confidence in. They decided to attempt to renew co-operation with Serbia.

An opportunity came with Nikola Pašić's visit to Paris in July of 1917 for the allied conference, which was debating whether or not to continue the Balkan military front. Pašić had little to offer the Montenegrins; instead he asserted that, during 1916, Russia had given Serbia a free hand to reconstitute the map of the Balkans. In turn, the Montenegrins accused Pašić of funding Andrija Radović's unification campaign with the sole aim of destroying the monarchy. He rebutted the charge and called on King Nikola to abdicate in favour of his grandson, Regent Aleksandar. The only concessions he offered were guarantees to the Royal Family for their property and of lifelong apanages from the future unified state.

Pašić was determined to ignore their objections and wanted to demonstrate that he was not under any compulsion to compromise. It was a bluff and he was taken aback by an unwelcome surprise. As the meeting ended, Evgenije Popović told him that he had also been invited to the conference: *"You? At the conference without an army!"*[7] Pašić exclaimed in both ridicule and exasperation. He certainly had major obstacles to overcome without the unwelcome stubbornness of the Montenegrin royalists adding to them.

Serbia needed to ensure the Triple Entente did not withdraw from the Balkan front. The army was exposed and potentially a prime target for the Central Powers. By the end of 1916 a mainland foothold had been regained in Bitola, in Serbian Macedonia, but the army was strung out along a thirty-seven mile front and close to collapse. Despite Pašić's efforts, Britain removed

its forces for operations in the Middle East, although the French confirmed that they would continue to provide support. Serbia was in a precarious position as, while the Allies gave general assurances, no formal agreements were concluded.

Pašić also had to give his attention to the details of South Slav politics. Relations between Serbia and Montenegro were just one example of the problems general to the Yugoslav movement. While Regent Aleksandar and Pašić both believed in Yugoslavia their political instincts were strongly centralist, which created tensions with the other South Slav groups.

Pašić was rather more pragmatic than the young and ambitious Aleksandar about the Yugoslav project. He believed that the overriding priority for Serbia was to unite with Bosnia-Herzegovina and Montenegro in a centralised Serb state, but if wider unification was to be achieved it had to be through a unitary rather than federal state. A political detail perhaps, but also one of great importance to the South Slavs.

Serbian aims, either minimal or maximal, were not proving easy to achieve, but progress was being made. The Corfu Declaration of July 1917 sealed an agreement with the Yugoslav Committee. It had been created after a meeting in Italy of Croatian exiles and Serb politicians from Bosnia-Herzegovina. They agreed that the Habsburg Empire's South Slavs needed an agency that would present their case to the Allies. It had virtually assumed the status of a provisional government and was preparing plans for the political organisation of prospective Yugoslav territories, as well as helping the war effort through its links with émigré communities in America. At Corfu Serbia and the Yugoslav Committee agreed that the state would be comprised of three constituent parts under the Karadjordjević dynasty.

The Corfu Declaration was an important step forward for Yugoslavia, but hardly the last word on the matter. It was, in part, a reaction to the earlier declaration in May by another agency, the Yugoslav Parliamentary Group. Led by a Slovenian, Anton Korošec, it also aimed to represent the Habsburg South Slavs but called for unification within the Habsburg Empire.

None of these developments augured well for Montenegrin independence. The Government had not been consulted about the Corfu Declaration and, most ominously of all, Montenegro was not even considered as an autonomous component of the projected state in the agreement. It was clear that unification with Montenegro had become a prerequisite for Serbia and genuine allies ready to help oppose that process were proving hard to find.

Although political issues were creating a good deal of friction, as events unfolded, all involved would find that they needed Serbia. As much as Austria-Hungary and Italy wanted to forestall the creation of Yugoslavia, it was actually that pressure which made Serbia vital to the other South Slavs. Despite their objections to centralism, Croat and Slovene politicians would soon see the need to accept a Serbian led unification to protect them from their former Austro-Hungarian masters and, most urgently, the ambitions of Italy, which the Triple Entente had encouraged through the Treaty of London.

If the final outcome to the struggle was uncertain, the tide of events appeared to be turning against the Montenegrins who found themselves increasingly marginalised and overlooked by both their fellow South Slavs and the Allies.

Family matters were also not helping King Nikola's cause. In September, Nikola, very active despite his age, suffered a recurrence of his troublesome gout. During his illness, Crown Prince Danilo came to Paris to visit his father at the *Hotel Meurice* in *Rue Rivoli*. Relations between father and son had been poor since they fell out over Montenegro's declaration of war in 1914 and they now had a heated exchange over the course of the war in front of the Minister of Defence, Niko Hajduković. His voice filled with passion, Nikola demanded: *"Dano, how does it go?"* - *"Well, Daddy! One can still not predict anything for certain, war luck can change."* Nikola had a point to make: that he had been right to side with Serbia and the Allies in 1914: *"Dano, I predicted it a long time ago. If you do not understand let the Minister of War explain to you what things are like on the battlefield."* Danilo replied defensively: *"I follow events too, but it is too early to predict the victory of either side."* Nikola had heard enough: *"For God's sake Dano! The sheep does not see far when it is lying down!"*[8]

In fact the divergence in outlook was deeper than father and son's opinion on war strategy; it was rather the case that Nikola's flock were straying from the paths he had long trod. Nikola was flexible as a politician but his basic loyalties remained constant; whereas his sons had grown up as dynastic relations came into sharper conflict and none really shared their father's pan-Serb or pan-Slav sentiments. The same could be said of the younger daughters. They were Montenegrin princes and princesses first and foremost. Danilo's disenchantment meant that he kept as far away as possible from the ongoing struggle; he had become detached from the national cause and had no taste for the political battles his father unceasingly waged. While Nikola was right about the ultimate course of the war and Danilo's views saw him branded as the *"German of Cetinje"*, Danilo's cynicism toward the Allies, who he dismissed as *"The unstable and pompous French, the perfidious and cunning English, and those poltroons, the Machiavellian Italians"*[9], would be proved fully justified.

As long as these differences of opinion were kept within the ruling circle the damage was limited. However, Danilo had made little effort to conceal his admiration for Germany and his disdain for Russia. Further harm was being done in Montenegro, where the King's representatives, although under their own initiative, explored the possibility of a separate peace with Austria-Hungary. The later accusations of treachery on the part of the Royal Family became all the more plausible when their personal views and secret diplomacy, which was being carried out by all the warring nations and factions, became public knowledge.

By the summer of 1918 the end of the war was in sight. The final campaigns of the protracted struggle on the western front were underway, but in the Balkans the Central Powers were still in control. Since the Serbian army had reopened the Balkan front in Macedonia, the Triple Entente had done little except to support the pro-Entente Prime Minister of Greece, Eleftherios Venizelos, who forced the prevaricating King Constantine into exile in late 1917. Almost the whole peninsula awaited liberation from the deprivations of the Central Powers' occupation.

In Serbia and Montenegro it had been brutal and vindictive. So much so that in some cases the occupying troops had deserted rather than follow orders to mistreat their captive neighbours. Nonetheless, the Austro-Hungarian authorities interned one hundred and fifty thousand, many of whom died in concentration camps, while others were used as forced labour. Serbia was stripped of its industry, shops were looted, forests decimated for timber and natural resources exploited recklessly. Montenegro had less economy to exploit but suffered greatly too. As early as January 1916 the German press had reported: *"In Montenegro there is no more bread, no flour, no tobacco, no salt and no oil . . ."*[10] By the end of 1917 reports of famine and starvation were being received.

Relief came through the military campaign in the autumn of 1918 which brought about a sudden collapse of the occupying forces.

Despite the fact that public opinion had not been hostile to Serbia, Bulgaria's King Ferdinand had led his country into war alongside Germany after the promise of large territorial gains. Discontent had steadily risen as the war effort took its toll and the massive allied attack, launched from Macedonia in September 1918, proved too much for Bulgaria's weary forces. Following the military collapse, the Government was forced from power and the King forced to abdicate. His son Boris, who was married to Queen Elena of Italy's daughter, Giovanna, came to the throne and a coalition government was formed to try and restore order. Bulgaria's defeat had a knock on effect. Austria-Hungary's military presence unravelled and the retreat left Italy and France in control of Albania and much of the Adriatic coastline. Germany soon followed suit. By November, as French and Serbian troops crossed the Danube, Romania felt confident enough to resume hostilities and German forces began to withdraw.

The Central Powers collapse in the Balkans had been preceded by defeat on the western front and, in quick succession, each sued for peace: Turkey on October 30, Austria-Hungary on November 3 and Germany on November 11.

The deliberations for the future of Central Europe and the Balkans were now matters of the utmost urgency, dictated by the need to fill the power vacuum and the fear of revolution spreading from Bolshevik Russia.

Nonetheless, Yugoslav unification was ultimately not the work of the diplomats and politicians; rather a rare moment when the centripetal forces of South Slav unity proved strong enough to overcome both the designs of their enemies and their own internal divisions.

When the Habsburg Empire finally fell, actually through a process of disintegration rather than revolution, any hopes of resurrecting it as a bulwark against Communism disappeared. In the Balkans a unitary Yugoslav state, which in real terms could only mean one built around Serbia, offered France and Great Britain the best guarantee against revolution as well as a bar to the machinations of Italy or Germany. Having a focal point for unification and the support of powerful allies, the pieces fell into place. In the final process, which culminated in a flurry of activity from November 1918 through January 1919, the unitarists were the beneficiaries.

(Above) 1917: King Nikola celebrates his seventy-sixth birthday in Paris and (inset) the official state calendar for 1918. Although the King and Government were still recognised by the Allies, the pro-unification movement had gained ground and the Corfu Declaration of July 1917, by Serbia and the Habsburg ruled South Slavs, formalised agreement to form the Yugoslav state. The Montenegrins were not represented at Corfu and it was clear that Belgrade considered unification of the two states as a non-negotiable necessity.

A less turbulent historical moment might have allowed the federalists to gain the upper hand, as was demonstrated by the Geneva Conference of November 6-9. Nikola Pašić was forced to soften his centralist line after general opposition, which, to his embarrassment, included members of the Serbian delegation. At the same moment the French made it clear that a show of Yugoslav unity was needed. It brought a political defeat for Pašić, who was forced to acknowledge the recently formed National Council in Zagreb as the lawful government of the Serbs, Croats and Slovenes in the former Habsburg provinces. He also accepted that the new state would be the joining of three separate entities, the Kingdom of Serbia, the Kingdom of Montenegro and the State of the Serbs, Croats and Slovenes. He signed the declaration with tears in his eyes, feeling that much of his earlier work had been undone and that, having sacrificed all for national unity, Serbia was not being allowed to lead Yugoslav unification.

However, events on the ground were more influential than the nuances of state building. Social disorder was on the increase as demobilised soldiers returned to their war ravaged homelands. Lawlessness, looting and violence were spreading. Slovenia remained relatively calm, but in Croatia order had largely broken down and in Bosnia-Herzegovina, Macedonia and Kosovo the situation was even worse.

Adding to the urgency, Italian troops were advancing beyond the agreed demarcation lines on the Adriatic coast. Croats and Slovenes realised that their differences with Serbia had to be overcome quickly. In mid-November the provisional authorities in the Croatian port of Split, close to the Italian zone of occupation, informed the National Council in Zagreb that the formation of a common

government for the entire state must be agreed with Belgrade. Other regional authorities were also sending the same message and, by November 23, the National Council had decided to send a delegation of twenty-eight members to Belgrade to finalise the terms of union with Serbia and Montenegro.

While the other South Slavs patched up their differences, Montenegro's internal strife had developed into a bipolar divide between its desire for unification and its tradition of independence. The allegiance of the highland regions and the territories acquired in the Balkan wars was increasingly toward Serbia, while resentment against Belgrade in 'Old Montenegro' saw a resistance movement with its centre in Cetinje and Katuni Nahi.

Having been on the victorious side but also forced to the sidelines, King Nikola made it his first priority to return home. French troops had taken control of the country after Austria-Hungary's withdrawal, while the Montenegrins in Paris were given reassurances that they were only restoring order in preparation for the King's return. Time was clearly of the essence and Nikola tried to force the issue.

He called the French and Italian envoys to his Paris hotel suite. The King, alone, greeted them in full military costume. France's envoy offered pleasantries, but only repeated that Nikola should be patient and that he had nothing to fear as long as French troops were in control of the country. Infuriated, Nikola asserted that he must be allowed to return immediately, but he was then told that France would consider this a hostile act. If Nikola insisted, the most help that would be given was a train to take him to the Italian border or one of France's southern ports, from where he could take a refugee transport ship or hire a boat of his own.

Italy's envoy, the Marquis of Montigliari, proposed an Italian train from Paris to an Adriatic port, from where the King could wait for the appropriate moment to return home. Nikola pointed out that if he accepted such an offer, he would be snubbing France, formal protector and occupier of his country, and Italy was not even guaranteeing his return to Montenegro. Montigliari asked if the King was demanding an Italian boat to take him home; Nikola retorted that he was simply asking to return via the same route by which he had departed.

Personal diplomacy having failed, Nikola still thought there was a chance he could return through his own efforts and he told his ministers to discuss ways and means. They were more cautious as hiring a boat to sail via the heel of Italy with the Mediterranean Sea still full of mines, warships and submarines would be highly risky. They also believed, although they had not informed the King, that a group of Serbian students were planning to assassinate him.

Nikola was prepared to take risks and thought that, in this matter at least, Crown Prince Danilo could help. Danilo had played a negligible role in the affairs of government, but his shrewdness in financial affairs had paid dividends personally. He had made a deal utilising the French subvention to buy the villa he was living in. It was owned by a rich Spaniard who had agreed for Danilo to buy it in instalments, which the monthly rent neatly paid for.

The Spaniard also owned a yacht, which Danilo hoped to buy as soon as he was compensated for the sinking of his own yacht in Bar earlier during the war. Nikola assumed the yacht was already Danilo's. In fact he had only registered it in his name. Worse still, it was not even seaworthy: the hull was covered in seaweed and shells and the engines were badly in need of repair.

Nikola was undeterred and he scoured the political horizons for other possibilities. His hopes were raised with Italian troops entering Bar, Ulcinj and Kotor in November 1918, and by the Marquis of Montigliari's renewed proposal to move the Government to Italy prior to its return. Rome's desire to set up satellite states in Albania and Montenegro was obviously an attempt to limit the extent of

Yugoslav unification, but Nikola was, by now, in direct opposition to Serbia's unitarist aims and had nowhere left to turn except Italy.

His opponents had been active as well, and with far greater results. France had allowed Serbian and Montenegrin troops, both under the control of the Serbian Government, to begin the reoccupation of the country, and they dealt harshly with anyone showing loyalty to the King. Leading figures that could have campaigned for Nikola's return, such as Mitar Martinović and Lazar Tomanović, kept to the sidelines and others were ready to openly throw in their lot with Serbia.

Furthermore, events during six years of almost continuous war and privation had convinced many that unification was necessary and, in some respects, had already taken place: the practice of joint military commands had been in evidence since the Balkan wars and Montenegro's internal affairs were currently in the hands of General Janko Vukotić, who favoured unification and placed the country under Serbian guardianship.

There was also a good deal of bitterness toward the King, of which Nikola and Milena had been informed of by Niko Hajduković's wife. *"Master, if you wish me to be honest, I think that there is no hope of return for you because the people are very sour towards you"*[11] she told them. That feeling was the key to Nikola's dilemma: he still had supporters, mainly among the older generation, but there was no great demand for his return.

At the least, legality was on Nikola's side. With the promulgation, in early 1918, of President Woodrow Wilson's 'Fourteen Points' a sliver of hope remained that the principle of self-determination could be called upon to save Montenegro's independence. Each nation's right to decide its own future could hardly be disputed and, despite the effective propaganda campaign to undermine his position, Nikola felt that in this regard he could claim to occupy the moral high ground and win back popular support.

Hope could also be found in the criticism which Serbia's unitarist policies were still drawing from the Slovenian and Croatian representatives on the Yugoslav Committee, as well as from the pro-Yugoslav British lobby made up of diplomats and intellectuals. However, Belgrade could not afford an ambivalent, let alone a negative, outcome for Serbo-Montenegrin union, particularly after Nikola had proclaimed his own federalist vision for Yugoslavia in October of 1918. The struggle was finally coming to a head.

The Great National Assembly, held in Podgorica from November 24-26, 1918, decided the issue; it was the expression of the popular will or a political fraud depending on which side of the bipolar divide it was viewed from.

Formally the Assembly was constituted by the free elections of deputies from each electoral district, who then voted on the unification of the two states

King Nikola with Britain's General Douglas Haig on the western front during 1917. General Haig became infamous as the 'Butcher of the Somme', the battles of 1916 in which French and British forces lost over six hundred thousand men to gain a mere twelve kilometres of ground. In 1918 he commanded British forces in the successful campaigns which led to the final Allied victory. Many consider Haig as one of the most culpable of First World War generals; others that his tactics were largely forced on him by the tactical decision to sustain pressure on the German defences at any cost. King Nikola's wartime conduct was also much criticised, in his case for, allegedly, seeking a separate peace with the Central Powers. His tour of the western front in December of 1917 was an opportunity to help raise moral, but the King's mood was bleak and he told his entourage that he felt it was an appropriate moment for his death.
(Facing page) Regent Aleksandar Karadjordjević of Serbia. King Nikola's grandson became King of the Serbs, Croats and Slovenes in 1921, the state usually known as Yugoslavia, which it became officially in 1929.

Evgenije Popović, Montenegrin Prime Minister from 1917-1919. For King Nikola, after the resignation of Andrija Radović, it was Popović's loyalty which recommended him. He took a pragmatic attitude toward Montenegro's political plight until finally resigning in February 1919. His successor was the Italian sponsored Jovan Plamenac, who was prepared to take military action to regain independence, even if that meant fighting against the emerging Yugoslav state.
(Facing page) Montenegrin troops on the 'Salonika Front'. Serbian and Montenegrin forces combined with Allied forces liberated the Balkans from the Central Powers in the autumn of 1918; a decisive blow in the final campaigns of the war.

and the future of the monarchy. In practice it was a highly unsatisfactory affair which accentuated already existing divisions. Even the green and white ballot papers revealed the split between the heartlands and the borderlands. The 'greens' in effect represented the *Pravaši*, the 'whites' the *Klubaši*.

The 'whites' enjoyed the support of the Serbian authorities and Andrija Radović's pro-unification cadres had begun campaigning in early November. They utilised some dubious campaigning tactics, such as gaining votes by distributing flour in Nikšić. King Nikola had not been consulted prior to the convening of the assembly and neither he nor his supporters participated in the electoral campaign. However, in Cetinje, the centre of resistance, the 'whites' were given such a hostile reception that they withdrew from the polling station.

Predictably enough, given control of the electoral process by the pro-unification faction, the 'whites' scored a resounding victory and, on November 26, the Great National Assembly voted to depose King Nikola by one hundred and sixty-three votes with none opposing and three absentees. The unification of Montenegro and Serbia was proclaimed.

The reality behind the official outcome was that Belgrade had funded and supported the pro-unification faction in their struggle against King Nikola. Of the Assembly's five executive members, three had been convicted for involvement in the Bomb Plot of 1907: the King's *Klubaši* opponents were finally settling some old scores.

The fact that the new authority was convened in the urban centre of Podgorica rather than the capital also illustrated the country's divisions. In 'Old Montenegro', particularly among the tribes of Katuni Nahi, but also among some of the highland tribes such as the Moračani, Rovci, Piperi, and Nikšić's Rudinjani, unification was seen simply as Serbia's annexation of Montenegro. The 'whites', however, with strong support amongst the Bjelopavlići, Vasojevići, Drobnjaci and Grahovljani tribes celebrated the outcome.

A fully fair and free electoral contest would have demonstrated these divisions and, therefore, it was politically vital for Serbia to have King Nikola deposed by an overwhelming majority. Andrija Radović even went a stage further and announced: *"A peaceful revolution: peaceful because it was made by the almost unanimous consensus of the population and without any resistance."*[12]

From that quarter it was a predictable statement, but Nikola was also reaping the harvest he had himself been sowing since the political conflicts which had begun after the promulgation of the constitution in 1905. It was telling that among the deputies selected to present the Montenegrin crown to King Petar Karadjordjević was one of Queen Milena's brothers, Stevo Vukotić.

Neither faction could really believe that it had a large majority supporting its program. The Great National Assembly represented a political manoeuvre forced on Serbia by circumstance and designed to achieve a specific goal. It was successful in that, but King Nikola and the remaining die-hard loyalists could continue to dispute its legitimacy as, under pre-war Montenegrin law, it was an unconstitutional body.

The new authorities sent notification to Nikola – ex-King Nikola as they now referred to him - of his deposition, the confiscation of his property and the other decrees that had been passed. In Paris, Foreign Minister Pero Šoć brought the historic documents to the King and Queen.

Nikola and Milena were surprised to find Stevo Vukotić's name among the signatories, although, as Nikola noted, he had not signed as a vojvoda. He asked Pero Šoć if he was certain that it was definitely his relative. As he did so, he stole a glance at Milena, who remained unhappily silent. His doubts now raised, Nikola also noticed that the signature of Priest Petar Hajduković did not appear to be genuine. Was it a forgery? And, if so, were there more forgeries and could that be a way to invalidate the document? The truth was more innocent. The Priest's friends had signed on his behalf as he was in hospital. Nikola was also trying to ease Milena's pain caused by her brother's disloyalty, by implying that Stevo's name could have been forged.

Milena interrupted and said quietly: *"I do not know what is going to happen next but, God be blessed and merciful, we are not alone, there are so many who are gone. The great and powerful Tsar Nikolai II of Russia has been dethroned and killed somewhere in Siberia along with his whole family and they do not even know where their graves are. That is much more tragic than our fate. And Sultan Abdul Hamid II, the once so powerful, is in prison on the Bosphorus, and, besides these victims, there are so many others."*[13]

If Milena was trying to steer Nikola toward philosophical resignation, the reactions of the French and British suggested to him that there was still hope. Count John de Salis, Britain's former Ambassador to Montenegro, had raised serious doubts about the conduct of the November elections, while the French pledged to Nikola that referendums would be held in all the prospective Yugoslav territories; with a French commander, General Vennel, still the military authority in Montenegro there was nothing to fear they assured. Pero Šoć was not convinced and he reminded the Allied diplomats of their moral culpability for detaining the King in France while his opponents had a free hand in Montenegro.

Belgrade had successfully pre-empted King Nikola's strategy, but in so doing had raised the political stakes. A few weeks after the Great National Assembly had dethroned the King, conflict broke out as the struggle for Montenegro reached its culmination with the 'Christmas Uprising' of December 1918 (by the Julian Calendar).

> *"I can see that Montenegro will not be taken like a maiden without a dowry."*[14]
> *King Nikola*

The more temperate men among the King's ministers were by now concerned with avoiding a final ignominy: that of being the last prime minister of independent Montenegro. Prime Minister Evgenije Popović had excused himself through a convenient illness and a reluctant Niko Hajduković had taken over his duties.

Within the King's shrinking circle of advisors the controversial figure of Jovan Plamenac, formerly Minister of Education and of Home Affairs, came to the fore. Plamenac was now the leader of the Montenegrin Independence Party. He publicised his more extreme version of Montenegrin nationalism with the help of the Italian press and organised his followers, amongst whom were several

(Left) Washington DC, 1917: US President Woodrow Wilson pictured with his second wife, Edith Bolling Galt. Wilson was Montenegro's last hope at the post-war Paris Peace Conference. King Nikola claimed to have correspondence with Wilson dating from July of 1918 in which the President wrote: *"I am confident that neither you nor the noble people of Montenegro will allow yourselves to be cast down by the present untoward situation but that, on the contrary, you will have implicit confidence in the firm determination of the United States Government and people that in the final, certain and assured victory, the integrity and the rights of Montenegro will be recognised and safeguarded."* One of Wilson's advisors, Stephen Bonsal, wrote about this enigmatic correspondence: *"President Wilson recalls an interview with the Montenegrin envoy at about this time and also that he spoke encouraging words to him, but he has no recollection of having sent the cable, although he is not willing to deny that he sent it. This may be another instance of a typewriter near at hand and a dislike of secretarial assistance having resulted in embarrassment for our chief magistrate. The failure of a mail copy to authenticate the cable is not remarkable. At this time King Nikola had taken refuge in Italy and mail to the Allies, owing to the activities of the U-boats, was most uncertain and precarious. The King is determined to show the cable to President Wilson and is insistently demanding an opportunity to do so. And nothing could be more understandable. The Italians are withdrawing the slender support they at first gave to the father of their Queen, and unless help, indeed real assistance, comes from Wilson, the King's chance of returning to his battle-scarred kingdom is slight indeed."* Bonsal was right: the King's enforced exile; the fact that many of the his opponents were prominent Montenegrins and the failure of the 'Christmas Uprising' for which the King was held responsible, all contributed to the Peace Conference's Supreme Council finally declaring, in December 1919, that it would no longer recognise Montenegrin representatives. (Below) President of France, Raymond Poincaré, pictured with King Constantine of Greece in Paris. Constantine had an acrimonious battle with Greek premier Eleftherios Venizelos and, like King Nikola with Austria-Hungary, was accused of pro-German sympathies before being forced into exile in 1917. His son Alexander reigned until his death in 1920. Thereafter Greek political leaders wanted Alexander's brother, Paul, to succeed him but he refused and, despite Allied hostility, Constantine managed to return by winning a resounding victory in the plebiscite held in November 1920. Ultimately he was forced to abdicate in late 1922. President Poincaré's hostility to King Nikola was well known, although he had officially pledged support for Montenegrin integrity. On November 24, 1918, as the King was being deposed by the Great National Assembly in Podgorica, Poincaré wrote: *"The presence of Allied troops . . . will contribute no doubt to hasten this moment which Your Majesty's every wish is awaiting. As soon as it has arrived, the Government of the Republic will be happy, Your Majesty, to facilitate your return voyage."* The reality was that Franco-Italian rivalry resulted in Paris supporting Belgrade's unitarist policy and Rome giving assistance to the more extreme faction within the Montenegrin exiles, in the hope that it would further its territorial aims along the eastern Adriatic coastline.

former ministers, in the southern Italian towns of Gaeta and Formia. Plamenac was widely considered to be vain, ambitious and unstable, something of a loose cannon; even the Crown Prince warned Nikola against him. Danilo had always been infuriated by his father's *"trick of meddling"* and it was that characteristic which led Nikola to think that Plamenac could be a useful tool. If anything the reverse turned out to be true.

It was Plamenac who instigated and organised the 'Christmas Uprising' and the full extent of the King's involvement, for events of which he was held responsible, is not entirely clear. Although Plamenac lacked judgement he did not lack guile, and he had told Nikola exactly what he wanted to hear: that, if he managed to return to Montenegro, the people would welcome him with open arms. Nikola was also well aware of Plamenac's Italian connections and, particularly with the French preparing to end their subsidy, how vital they might be.

For Nikola it was an uneasy alliance borne of desperate circumstance; one in which Plamenac was even accused of motives of revenge against the Petrovići. In Vladika Rade's poem, 'The Tower of Djurišići', Plamenac's grandfather, Markiša, was accused of betraying Montenegro to the Turks. It was an old point of dispute between the two clans, but probably courtiers' gossip to suggest that the Crmnica man's schemes were diabolical enough to use the King only to destroy him.

The tangible outcome of their relations was that Montenegrin 'greens' and 'whites' clashed in Cetinje on Christmas Eve, 1918. It was a date chosen with self-conscious symbolism: the day of the 'Montenegrin Vespers' when in Vladika Rade's great poem, 'The Mountain Wreath', Vladika Danilo expunged the Moslem presence. Both the poet and the first Petrović-Njegoš ruler must surely have been turning in their graves as Montenegrins took up arms against one another over the question of Serb unification.

Jovan Plamenac and the other 'green' leaders used their agents to stir up the loyalist tribes and, briefly, it seemed as if they might achieve something. Several towns, including the capital, were besieged. However, the poorly armed insurgents were soon overcome: in Nikšić the siege was easily broken by the Bjelopavlići; the casualties were minimal with only one killed and one wounded.

It was only in Cetinje that the fighting took on a more serious aspect. Eight hundred and eighty-seven well armed defenders were in a nervous stand off with the numerically superior rebels. The Kuči, Piperi and Bratonožići tribes had set out to lift the siege, but were persuaded to turn back to avoid greater bloodshed. 'White' casualties were sixteen killed and sixty-three wounded, the 'greens', by all accounts, considerably more. The survivors returned to their tribal heartlands or fled, along with Jovan Plamenac, to the Italian zone of occupation.

Although it was a military failure, the uprising did force Serbia into reconsidering direct negotiations. It had also brought the conflict to the attention of the Paris Peace Conference, which asked King Nikola to make a proclamation calling for peace. Having being advised that he needed to show his pacific intentions he did so, but made sure that a note from the Great Powers, to the effect that Montenegrins would soon be able to decide freely about their future, was also included.

Nikola's hopes briefly received a further boost when Regent Aleksandar asked to see him. A last chance for the two dynasties to work together, the meeting never actually took place and only served to confirm that their paths could not converge again. Nikola saw it as an opportunity to resume diplomatic relations broken off in December 1918, but Aleksandar claimed he had only planned a personal visit. Aleksandar could not afford the former; the latter would, for Nikola, be accepting as a *fait accompli* the decision of the Great National Assembly.

The aborted meeting was still a minor tactical victory for the King's ministers who felt that it was yet another diplomatic trap. A further small sign of hope was gleamed from Belgrade where one of the King's old *Klubaši* enemies, Marko Daković, withdrew from Parliament in protest at the policy in Montenegro. The country was clearly restless in its post-war misery and even the pro-unification faction was disgruntled.

However, events on the ground conspired to ensure that the call for peace on the basis of future elections was not fully communicated to the people. Rather than ask the French authorities in Cetinje, or perhaps Metropolitan Mitrofan Ban as head of the church, to be his messenger, Nikola asked his cousin Božo. The result was that when France's General Vennel received the telegram in Cetinje he simply threw it away. Apparently, he thought that as Božo was on the list of those suspected of involvement in the 'Christmas Uprising' it was not an officially authorised communique.

It was a rather dubious explanation and it seems that, apart from the Americans, the Allies made little effort to ensure the joint communication was received. Nikola's sympathiser, Stephen Bonsal, an American journalist and also President Wilson's advisor, noted: *"It is difficult to say exactly what happened . . . Both were radioed from the American, the British, and other naval vessels that were patrolling the Adriatic, but the French and the Italian ships, which were far more numerous in these waters than ours, showed little zeal in bringing news of the peace policy to the distracted country . . . the call of the King, addressed to his people to return to their homes and refrain from active hostilities, secured in some way a much wider circulation than did the assurance of the Powers that the harassed mountaineers would be given an early opportunity to decide for themselves what form of government they preferred . . ."* Through the émigré grapevine Nikola soon learned that many believed he had called for a complete surrender: *"And of course that was the very last thing I wanted them to*

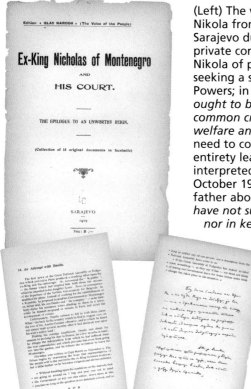

(Left) The virulent denunciation of King Nikola from a pamphlet published in Sarajevo during 1919. The Royal Family's private correspondence is used to accuse Nikola of political crimes, fraud, and of seeking a separate peace with the Central Powers; in short of being a man who *". . . ought to be judged and convicted like common criminals, in the interest of social welfare and the defence of the nation."* The need to condemn the Royal Family in its entirety leads to each and every letter being interpreted in the worst possible light. In October 1918 Princess Ksenija wrote to her father about the plight of the people: *"We have not succeeded in looking after them; nor in keeping them informed, nor in rousing their enthusiasm. If it is not too late for heaven's sake send them some food and clothing."* Her accuser fulminates: *"The dutiful daughter of the Montenegrin potentate imagines that the conscience of a people can be bought for 'some food and clothing'."*
(Below) One of Montenegro's American defenders, Whitney Warren's 'Montenegro, the Crime of the Peace Conference' in its first Italian edition of five thousand copies, published in 1923. A solid if partisan defence of the King, Warren considered Montenegro a nation betrayed but questioned what had been gained through such *realpolitik*: *"President Wilson went to Europe with a briefcase bulging with peace plans, any or all of which he was willing to trade for support of his League of Nations. When the diplomats had gone through it nothing remained but the League. They left that to the very competent hands of the United States Senate."* A salient point as the peace settlement proved an historic mistake which played a major role in the rise of Fascism and the League of Nations was instituted without the participation of the USA, due to the isolationist Senate's opposition.
(Facing page) From left to right: Vjera, Milena, Nikola and Ksenija.

do . . . I am a fighter, they are fighters. I wanted them to fight for the freedom of the Black Mountain to the last man."[15]

In Paris, despite the obvious failure of the uprising, Jovan Plamenac was continuing the struggle. *Le Temps*, the semi-official mouthpiece of the French Foreign Ministry, was paid a substantial sum in return for favourable coverage. The propaganda campaign backfired because the information received from Plamenac's agents in Bar and Kotor was unreliable, exaggerated and soon discredited.

In the meantime, Evgenije Popović had finally reached the end of his tether and resigned in February, after which the oldest member of the Government, Milo Vujović, briefly took over.

The moment was ripe and, with the support base of angry exiles and Rome's political clout, Jovan Plamenac now seized his chance. Nikola knew his options were rapidly dwindling. When he was told that Rome considered Plamenac the only choice to head the Government, his reaction was nothing more than a wry smile. The shift from the French to the Italian sphere of influence had been completed.

Italian patronage was of little positive use. Looking to find ways to disrupt the Yugoslav movement's state building drive, by forcing Plamenac on Nikola it only served to further tarnish the King's image.

Once installed in power Plamenac set about marginalising the old guard. He only wanted men who shared his views; whereas Nikola wanted a coalition to include the more moderate supporters. Plamenac simply shuffled the ministerial portfolios around to consolidate his control.

The ministers were called once more to the *Hotel Meurice* where they were informed of their new jobs. As they took the oath of allegiance, Niko Hajduković, who had been given the portfolio for the Ministry of Agriculture, could not prevent himself from smiling at the absurdity of his new position. The King observed his friend's amusement and afterward they shared a joke.

"Nikolaides, have you become the Minister for Vegetables?"

"Yes, Master. I am the Minister of Salad."

"Let it be."

It was an irrelevant post in a ministry of which Jovan Plamenac proudly asserted: *"I am the Government, the rest are just clerks."*[16]

There was still one important task to carry out: a last ditch opportunity to bring Montenegro's plight to the attention of the Peace Conference, which was still divided over its position on Yugoslavia. King Nikola made a dignified presentation; despite all the controversy he had a strong case based on international law and agreements made between recognised governments.

On March 6, 1919, General Ante Gvozdenović read the King's statement to the conference. The case for new elections as a genuine expression of the popular will was made and Serbia was accused of an *"audacious and forcible coup d'état."* It was followed up by a request for the admission of Montenegrin representatives to the conference. President Wilson asked for the issue to be resolved but the diplomats could only fumble to a new formula, 'Yugoslavia including Montenegro', which still implied the issue was already closed.

Diplomacy dragged on until, in late September, Jovan Plamenac threatened to make a separate peace with with Germany, Austria and Bulgaria and, on December 1, 1919, the Supreme Council of the Peace Conference responded by delivering the *coup de grâce* to Montenegrin independence with a unanimous decision to disregard Plamenac's communication.

The last Prime Minister of an independent Montenegro had proven unable to see the larger issues beyond his own schemes. He had been foolish enough to believe he could reverse the tide of events by organising an armed uprising and, thereafter, continued on the same blinkered course. It ensured that Montenegro's case was lost in the controversy of accusation and counter-accusation.

He and King Nikola's twilight wanderings through the darker recesses of politics only accelerated the demise as they became the unwitting allies of their enemies. Nikola should have, in fact, did know better. *"If it is the will of the Allies that we should cease to exist, you cannot stand against it . . . "* he had told his son. That fatalism would have served him far better than intransigence; the final choice he faced was to accept defeat with grace or fight to the bitter end. Choosing the latter not only ensured the ruin of his reputation, it also brought him into conflict with his own beliefs and Montenegro's mission. The romantic ruler ended his reign vilified as the *"cloven hoof"* of the Yugoslav movement.

The issue of South Slav unification had, albeit in an unsatisfactory way, been laid to rest as Yugoslavia was finally born. An historic triumph for the South Slavs, structurally it was a flawed creation with several dangerous fault lines already apparent. The new state had been created by the sacrifice of the people and it represented the popular will for independence, but imperfectly. From the unitarist perspective the country hardly needed two dynasties adding to the complications of state building; for others the deposition of the Montenegrin monarchy only served to further prove that state centralism had been imposed on the South Slav brotherhood.

As the initial idealism of the Peace Conference gave way to the horse-trading of national self-interest, Montenegro found that, although it still had sympathisers, for the Allies the thorny but minor question of Serbo-Montenegrin relations had been resolved. King Nikola had lost the battle for his throne and, in disgust, he turned his back on diplomacy: *I shall write no more notes of remonstrance to the Powers who are unworthy to receive them, but I will write and rewrite the songs of my people, and these songs will hearten and sustain them until once again the light of freedom and of liberty shines down upon them from the summit of Lovćen."*[17]

King Nikola hoped till the very end that he would return to Montenegro. He never did, but, in October 1989, his mortal remains were brought back to the homeland. (Above) Bar: Montenegro hails the return of the King. (Below) The people of Cetinje pay homage to the King and Queen. (Left) The King with Princess Ksenija shortly before his death in March 1921.

The King's death marks the end of an epoch.

And now my dear son remember this: if I die in exile, give me a simple funeral service in the tradition of our church, and let my body lie intact in a temporary grave, until my remains are taken to our beloved homeland and buried there . . . Let God bless you and all our family, let him be helpful to our nation, let those forgive me if I, unknowingly, harmed them. Amen.

King Nikola: Last Will and Testament.

In December 1920 King Nikola's loyal adjutant, Ilija Jovanović-Bjeloš, received a telegram calling him to *Villa Lisseron* on the French Riviera. It was a cry for help from the Royal Family: the King was ailing and, they feared, close to death. Jovanović had his own troubles to deal with as Prime Minister Jovan Plamenac was trying to force him to take his family to Italy. For the émigré community in general financial support was running out and Plamenac wanted to relocate the whole diaspora. Out of loyalty to the King, Jovanović decided to stay on in France.

With the exception of Queen Elena still secure in Italy, all of the Royal Family were in exile; the network of dynastic connections which had supported them had been swept away by war and the

(Right) Ćipur Church, where the King and Queen were laid to rest. Their youngest daughters, Ksenija and Vjera, were also laid to rest in Cetinje, in the court cemetery by the Monastery. It had taken sixty-eight years since the King's burial in the Russian Orthodox Church in San Remo, Italy, to return him home. The intervening years had seen the King's memory both honoured and desecrated. Shortly after Queen Milena's burial in 1923, the municipality of San Remo erected a monument to King Nikola in the 'Noble Garden' at Villa Hormond: a bust on a pedestal, and nearby a figure of a Montenegrin soldier in national costume. The dedication was to the *"Warrior, poet, hero"* of Montenegro. For the family crypt, from 1921 to 1951, the House of Savoy paid rent to the Russian community. In 1942/43 negotiations were initiated to bring the bodies of the King's three sons to San Remo, but the war and the subsequent fall of the Italian monarchy prevented a successful conclusion. In 1947 the crypt was desecrated by burglars and, towards the end of the decade, it was left unattended. For these reasons Princess Jolanda of Savoy transferred the bodies of her grandparents to the estate of her husband, Count Calvi di Bergolo. In the 1970's, complying with the wishes of the Savoy and with the permission of the San Remo municipality, the mortal remains were returned to their original burial place and Vjera and Ksenija were also brought to rest in San Remo. Above the tombs of the princesses the icons of their patron saints were placed. In 1989 the Italian authorities agreed to Montenegro's request for the Royal Family to be returned to Cetinje. In the same year, at the entrance to the Russian Orthodox Church were placed busts of King Vittorio Emanuele III and Jelena of Montenegro. Created in 1939 by the sculptor E. Monti, the pieces had been in storage since the fall of the Italian monarchy.

(Left) King Nikola's granddaughter, Jelena Karadjordjević, with her Russian husband, Ioann Konstantinovich. In World War One Jelena ran a field hospital from the frontlines and Ioann served in the Horse Guards Regiment. During the Russian revolution Jelena escaped, but Ioann was murdered, along with his brothers Konstantin and Igor, by the Bolsheviks on the night of July 18, 1918, in the Urals town of Alapayevsk. With them were three other members of the Romanov nobility: Grand Duke Sergei Mikhailovich, Prince Vladimir Paley and the Tsarina's sister, Grand Duchess Yelizaveta (Ella) Feodorovna. (Right) A portrait of Ella, whose husband, Grand Duke Sergei, at the time the Governor General of Moscow, had been the victim of political terrorism in 1905. King Nikola's daughters, Milica and Stane, were more fortunate, escaping the revolution along with their husbands, Nikolai and Peter Nikolayevich aboard the *HMS Nelson* in April 1919. (Below) March 1921: Milica and Nikolai Nikolayevich during King Nikola's funeral in San Remo, Italy.

political map of Europe redrawn thereafter. Kaiser Wilhelm II had gone into exile in Holland and Germany's principalities had fallen in the post-war revolution; it was quelled by mid 1919 and a republic was declared. The Russia revolution had been followed by the chaos of civil war. The Austro-Hungarian Empire had been dissolved and the Ottoman Empire was approaching the same end. Even the victorious Allies were facing up to the huge cost of the war and the consequent political and social upheaval.

Exile, as Queen Milena had observed, represented relatively good fortune. Milica, Stane and their families had narrowly escaped the revolutionary firing squads, as had their niece, Jelena Karadjordjević. Her husband, Ioann Konstantinovich, had been killed by the Bolsheviks in Alapayevsk, along with Tsarina Alexandra's sister 'Ella'. Ana and Franz Josef had fled from the turmoil in defeated Germany and, apart from the unfortunate Mirko, who had died from tuberculosis in 1918, the other family members had survived the war. There was, however, little expectation that they would be able to return home.

Nikola and Milena were struggling financially and had scaled down their lifestyle. *Villa Lisserons* was a modest house by the standards of wealthy *Cap d'Antibes* and the local residents were surprised to find the ex-King of Montenegro living among them in such modesty, without even a carriage or car at his disposal.

(Right and insets below right) Princess Ksenija's correspondence in exile with former Montenegrin Foreign Minister, Pero Šoć. After World War Two Yugoslavia's new rulers stopped the incomes that had been given to the surviving members of the Royal Family. From 1945 until her death in May of 1960, Ksenija had a long and unsuccessful struggle with the Yugoslav Government, in which Pero Šoć tried to mediate. Ksenija refused to accept the Government's offer of monthly payments because she had been forced to borrow from friends and wished to pay them back. In July of 1958 she wrote: *"I would like to clarify that all the money due should be given in one payment and without any further commitment from the Government in the future. A monthly payment would not do me any good; I could not live in tranquillity as all the people who have helped me in these last few years would never receive back what they gave me . . . I would rather suffer and be without anything than fail my word."* Ksenija was as good as her word, but the matter was not resolved and in August of the following year she wrote: *"My long wait (August 1945-August 1959) of fourteen years has put my body to the test . . . my situation has deteriorated considerably and I will have to take a decision to start looking for work (seventy-nine years-old) to support myself . . . Work is always honourable and I do not retreat in the face of any obstacle so long as I have my health . . ."* In the harsh winter of 1960, in January, she prepared to move from *Bort l'Etang* to Paris: *"I am gathering all my papers to burn, some old clothes to give to the poor and generally to put my affairs in order. A wave of terrible cold has broken out . . . I cannot live in my room as the heating does not work anymore. The temperature in my room is slightly less cold than the third floor where I keep my belongings and some pieces of furniture that will be put on sale here. The amount they will be sold for is insignificant, but these things are very precious to me because of the memories they hold; so many things that belonged to my mother; they have no value to anyone except myself! One can see that life has trouble in store for us, great or small, that we do not expect . . . I should have been in Paris by January 15 but the roads are all blocked by snow . . . My destiny is to wait for always and everywhere. Again, happy 1960 and my very best wishes."* A few months later Ksenija died in Paris aged seventy-nine. Ksenija's life was not a happy one, but her determination remained undimmed, as did her patriotism and nostalgia for her homeland. In 1956 she wrote to Pero Šoć: *"Last night I heard on Radio Paris the declaration of Ambassador Bebler. What an excellent speech, it came from the heart . . . Talking of the Great War and the glorious victims who fell for their country, he spoke of the Serbian and Montenegrin army. It was so wonderful to hear that as from the previous regime I never even heard these two countries mentioned . . ."* (Below) Princess Ksenija during her French exile. Ksenija's misfortune was to be born with intelligence and strength of character but to expend much of it in the defence of lost causes. She died in Paris on March 9, 1960. On May 27 Princess Natalia Obolensky, Ksenija's companion during her last years, informed Pero Šoć: *"The remains of the late Princess Ksenija of Montenegro were buried in the Russian Orthodox church in Cannes, next to her two sisters, Grand Duchesses Milica and Anastazija, and their husbands, Grand Dukes Nikolai and Peter. A very festive church ceremony was performed on April 29, 1960, in the greatest privacy and in the presence of HM the King of Italy, Princess Jelena of Serbia, Prince Roman of Russia and his wife, the Princess of Savoy, Jolanda Duchess Calvi di Bergolo and her husband, Princess Maria and her husband Louis Bourbon-Parma, Russia's Princess Marina Galicin with her husband, and my three children, because I was too sad and tired to travel."*

There had been warnings as early as 1917 that age and the stress of exile were becoming too much for Nikola's health. The pleurisy he caught at the end of the year was so severe that he had redrafted his Last Will and Testament. Recovery came, it was noted, as the fortunes of war turned in the Triple Entente's favour and a return to Montenegro seemed imminent.

For the last year Nikola's health had held up and he had continued working with some of his old idiosyncratic energy: bed at 10pm, waking around 3am, when he would make himself a Turkish coffee in his room so as not to disturb the servants, work and cigarettes until 6am, then a short nap. Waking again in time to read the morning newspapers he would then take a walk; refreshed, he would work for another hour. On days when he felt depressed he would play the *gusle* and sing.

But now Nikola's strength was clearly failing and the family hoped that seeing his servant and friend would provide a tonic. Ilija Jovanović-Bjeloš travelled down from Paris by train, arriving at *Villa Lisseron* on the evening of December 16. Nikola greeted him in a depressed mood. *"And how do you find me?"* he asked. Jovanović tried to raise his morale, *"Not as poorly as I had been told, Master.*

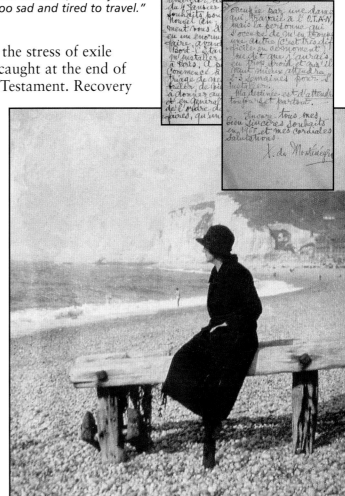

1989: the return of King Nikola and Queen Milena to Cetinje. (Top) The funeral cortège makes it way through the streets of the former capital. (Above) The religious ceremonies were conducted in the Orthodox tradition.
Facing page: (Top) Nicolas Petrović-Njegoš with his wife, Francine, and their two children, Boris and Altinai, during the ceremony. King Nikola's great-grandson from Prince Mirko's marriage to Natalija Konstantinović, Nicolas Petrović is by lineage the heir to the throne. He lives and works in Paris, France. Also visible to the right are representatives from the House of Savoy: Prince Vittorio Emanuele, Princess Maria Gabriella and Princess Maria Beatrice. Behind on the far right is Prince Dimitri Romanov, grandson of Grand Duchess Milica and Grand Duke Peter Nikolayevich. (Centre) Representatives from the Karadjordjević family. From left to right: Princess Katarina, daughter of King Aleksandar's son Prince Tomislav, Princess Elizabeth, daughter of Regent Pavle, and Princess Linda, Prince Tomislav's second wife. (Bottom) Cetinje Monastery.

You have been more ill and recovered, that can happen again." "Oh no my eagle, I am finished"[1] was the melancholy response.

Ilija Jovanović and Queen Milena decided that the frugal diet the doctors had prescribed was doing more harm than good. The return to a more varied and enjoyable diet saw Nikola regain some of his zest and strength. He was soon active and walking again, there were even trips to see Danilo at *Cap Martines* and to Cannes, Monaco and Nice.

The rejuvenation was brief, lasting only until January 20, 1921. In the afternoon Ilija Jovanović heard the King ring his bell. He found Nikola sitting on his bed unable to speak and the doctor was called. Blood was drawn from Nikola's left arm, after which he recovered. He managed a joke: *"Were you scared when I was unable to talk to you my eagle?"*

Nikola was growing weaker, too weak to even join the family at the dining table, and Milena asked that Ilija Jovanović supervise his meals. Despite his deteriorating condition, Nikola's positive nature energised him to use his remaining days creatively. He continued to work on his biography of the sons of Ali Pasha Rizvanbegović of Mostar.

He wanted it to be his literary legacy in exile.

However, the final blows from the political defeat were still raining down. When the inevitable news finally came, via a letter from Pero Šoć, now Minister of Justice in Jovan Plamenac's cabinet, that France would no longer recognise Montenegrin political institutions, it was a crushing blow to Nikola's spirits. The remote possibility of returning home was gone. The timing was a consequence of the Treaty of Rapallo which had settled the delimitation of the Italian-Yugoslav border, providing the French with an appropriate opportunity to cut their remaining ties with the King.

The Government was called to discuss its response. What was left of it was a shadowy affair in which Jovan Plamenac stirred the émigré community to sporadic activity while drifting ever further from the Yugoslav camp. Nikola's direct involvement in politics was by now minimal and his main concern was to resolve whether or not Crown Prince Danilo would carry on the struggle after his death.

On February 20 at *Cap d'Antibes*, the Government, the King and the Crown Prince met. Nikola told his son: *"As I am unwell and I believe that I have not long to live, I recommend Montenegro to you. Rule and take care of the people and you will be able to achieve much with them. If you do not wish to rule, I recommend your nephew, Mihailo* [Prince Mirko's eldest son]*, and ask you to advise and help him to rule."* Danilo, struggling with his emotions, could only offer his father one last disappointment: *"Father, parting from you is very hard for me and even more so for the Montenegrin people. As for my rule, you already know my feelings."*[2] Danilo had nothing to offer his father or Montenegro and had no illusions as to the possibility of a restoration. The Government returned to Paris, Danilo to his residence in *Cap Martines* and Nikola was left to the care of the family. He had only days to live.

On the evening of March 1, Nikola was unable to eat and the family gathered around anticipating the worst. Almost all were present: Milena, Milica and Stane with their husbands Peter and Nikolai, Ana and Franz Josef, Petar, Ksenija and Vjera.

Ilija Jovanović tried to feed Nikola some stewed prunes; he managed only one, after which he dropped the spoon, his head fell forward and, barely conscious, he rested while the family stayed to comfort him.

At around 10pm Milica brought the token from Carev Laz, a piece of earth which Nikola had taken with him when he fled the Austro-Hungarian advance in January 1916. She placed it in her father's hand, symbolically reuniting

him with the homeland. The end was close and many present, both family and servants, were already crying.

At around 11pm Ilija Jovanović went to the salon and found Milena and the family still watching over Nikola. Jovanović helped the King up and, as he did so, Nikola took his wife's hand. *"Goodbye Milena"* he told her. She went to her room upstairs to let him rest while Nikola, helped by Jovanović and a servant, went to his room on the ground floor.

As the servant was helping him undress, Nikola suddenly screamed. They helped him into bed and called for Ksenija, who ran to the bedroom to find her father paralysed on the right side of his body. She implored him *"Father, look at me."* Nikola turned toward her and smiled but could not speak.

Ilija Jovanović telephoned the doctor who rushed over. After examining the King he said there was nothing more that could be done, he might survive another forty-eight hours at most. It proved to be much less than that as he passed away a short while later, the mercy being that it was a peaceful and painless end. The time of death was recorded as 11.15pm on the evening of March 1, 1921; the cause of death a cerebral haemorrhage. The King was seventy-nine years old.

Milena and the family were at his bedside. She had been a model of composure throughout and now kissed her late husband's hand, after which the family left to allow the body to be prepared for the funeral.

The King's body was dressed in his national costume which he had brought with him into exile, and the golden sable given by Tsar Alexander II was placed at his side. The family was called in to view the body as, at the same moment, Danilo arrived. He ran over to the table where his father's body had been placed, broke down and wept. Milena took him to her room to comfort him.

Danilo's first duties as head of the family were to contact Queen Elena in Italy and the French authorities. Condolences flooded in and President Millerand ordered that the King be buried with full honours. However, after so many French betrayals, it was hardly surprising that the funeral did not take place in France, but in San Remo, Italy.

On the morning of March 5 the King's coffin was taken from *Villa Lisseron* to *Port d'Antibes*, where Italian warships were waiting as an honourary escort for the sea journey. Salvoes rang out from the French warships which accompanied the Italians out of French waters. It was a moment of supremely bitter irony: the King's protectors had proven to be his captors; his political demise and, the émigrés concluded, his too early death had been brought about in no small measure by French duplicity.

At 11am King Vittorio Emanuele (Queen Elena was unable to come as she was unwell) offered his condolences to Milena and the family as they disembarked ship in San Remo. Together they escorted the hearse the few hundred metres from the docks to the Russian Orthodox Church. The streets were lined with a military escort, behind which the people jostled to gain a view of the funeral procession. Half an hour later the coffin lay in the chapel and the funeral service was performed. The King lay in the chapel for two days to allow the people to pay their respects, after which he was buried in the crypt that had been hastily prepared. It would later be turned into a small chapel for the Royal Family.

With King Nikola's death the royal era in Montenegrin history was over, but the final act in the drama of defeat was left to the reluctant Danilo. Seeking the quickest way to discard his burden, he decided to announce his abdication in favour of his nephew, Prince Mihailo. Representatives of the émigré community were invited to San Remo's *Hotel Reale* to be informed of the Crown Prince's decision.

Characteristically Danilo stayed away and Jovan Plamenac was left to give the news to his anxious countrymen, among them forty army officers from Gaeta who had come to lay a wreath at the King's grave. They were shocked and refused to accept the abdication: *"Long live Danilo King of Montenegro. Let us go to the front of the hotel and call him to tell him that we do not want any other as king."* Fetched by Ilija Jovanović, Danilo returned and did himself one more discredit: he pretended to change his mind, telling the crowd from the hotel balcony: *"Brother Montenegrins, I would like to tell you that I accept the duty of being King of Montenegro."*[3] Having pacified the situation, he instructed Jovan Plamenac to make sure the officers train fares back to Gaeta were paid for. Danilo then went onto Milan, from where he reconfirmed his abdication a few days later.

The émigrés' desperation was understandable. After Danilo's renunciation of his rights the Italians decided to withdraw their support and, by July, the Montenegrins were told to evacuate Gaeta. Unable to return home most became permanent exiles, dispersing mainly to France, Russia, Greece and Turkey.

The Petrović-Njegoš dynasty and the independent state of Montenegro, the two having become synonymous with one another, had fallen together. Montenegro had been singularly unfortunate in that it was the only allied nation not to be restored after the war. William Gladstone's son, Viscount Herbert, was a suitable marker for that twist of fate: "*What worse could have befallen Montenegro if, instead of being our ally from the very first, it had fought against us in the enemy camp.*"[4]

King Petar Karadjordjević died a few months after King Nikola, in August of 1921, and his son Aleksandar took on the task of building Yugoslavia. Its internal complications were considered very much its own problem and Europe's political leaders did not want to deal with, or even acknowledge, there was still a 'Montenegrin question'. Resistance to the centralised Yugoslav state was left to those prepared to become fugitives in their own country. However, many soon reconciled themselves with the new polity; even Jovan Plamenac returned in 1925 to resume his political career in Belgrade.

King Aleksandar had set about building the new state with a determination his grandfather would have been proud of but, having played such a large part in his downfall, it was only human that Aleksandar felt regret that they had not been able to reconcile before Nikola's death.

In 1925 Ilija Jovanović-Bjeloš had an audience with Aleksandar in Belgrade and they talked about old times. Aleksandar remembered it all, from his happy childhood days in Cetinje to his last meeting with Nikola in *San Giovanni di Medua*, and he asked: " *'Ilija, tell me about my grandfather, about his illness, was he in pain before he died?' When I told him about the suffering and pain of his grandfather his eyes filled with tears as did mine. The King said this to me: 'Let us hope that those who prevented my grandfather returning to his fatherland pay for it to God, because everything was arranged, if he had only received me in Paris when I asked for an audience to see him.'* "[5] What else could Aleksandar say? Perhaps he really believed that the aborted meeting with his grandfather would have made the difference.

The dynastic rivalry had precluded that possibility and, from the longer perspective, it is clear that the Serbian and Montenegrin dynasties were always likely to come to blows: the antagonisms between them had been evident for the best part of a century. That the Karadjordjevići had finally

Prince Danilo, second from the left, on the French Riviera. On the far left is Lady-in-waiting Miss Daubne. After his father's death, Danilo abdicated in favour of his nephew Mihailo.

(Above) Nikola and Milena in Nice, France. Both died in exile at *Cap d'Antibes* on the French Riviera: Nikola on March 1, 1921, and Milena on March 16, 1923.
(Facing page) One of the last photographs of Milena, with her daughters Elena and Milica.

triumphed was as much due to timing as anything else. If the South Slavs had managed to emulate the Italians and Germans by uniting in the 1860's or 1870's, the Obrenovići or the Petrovići would have claimed the glory; if it had come about between 1878 and 1903, King Nikola would have undoubtedly been the leading candidate for a united throne.

Having been for so long the doyen of Balkan monarchs and having come so close to being the dynastic unifier, Nikola's refusal to play second fiddle to his Serbian counterparts is readily understandable. Ultimately, Nikola's failure to unite the competing families to his advantage, and the mutual hostility between the Petrovići, Obrenovići and the Karadjordjevići, which increased as the possibility of unification grew closer, meant that the Petrović-Njegoš dynasty came to view Serbia as a threat to its existence.

At the same time 'Old Montenegro' was clearly not a viable project for the twentieth century and Nikola's conservatism was too gradualist to placate the clamour for reform. Despite his achievements, the weaknesses in patriarchal rule had been apparent for some two decades before his deposition in 1918.

A German newspaper reporting on the historic visit to Belgrade of June 1896 praised the ruler's *"firm hand and rare wisdom"*, but also prophesied his downfall: *"Prince Nikola, despite being politically active, does not neglect his nation. However, if certain signs do not deceive us, the nation has begun to oppose autocratic rule. The signs of dissatisfaction are the increasing emigration of Montenegrin people and the exile of respected vojvodas, who dared to call for the reform of patriarchal-autocratic rule, which demands obedience from the people without allowing them political rights. The Prince will manage for a long, long time to suppress these hostile ambitions . . . Once, when culture is extended and entrenched, these mountain falcons, imbued with heroism, intelligence and pride will, like the Serbians and Bulgarians, become modern citizens and demand their human rights. The heroic epoch of Montenegro will end. Nikola I will be its most magnificent but final standard bearer."*[6]

It was a good analysis of the flaws of patriarchal rule but, unfortunately, it was not progress that did away with 'Old Montenegro'. Indeed, a modest dose of peace and prosperity might have allowed the monarchy to survive as a reminder of past glories.

Instead, the final and least attractive decade of Nikola's reign was concerned with the battle for dynastic survival and domestic issues were overshadowed by political machinations, leaving little opportunity for economic improvement or successful political reform. The romantic era had passed and many Montenegrins looked to a unified South Slav state for a better future, but for the greater part of his reign Nikola's talents had served the nation well and his political gymnastics, which he faced so much criticism for after his fall, had been a vital asset, particularly at times of crisis.

It is to his detriment that he was not prepared to stand aside and sacrifice his throne to that nebulous virtue the 'greater good', but who among Europe's leaders could claim they had done so either in the build up to war or in its aftermath? The Great War was followed by yet another botched and venal peace treaty which sowed the seeds of even greater tragedies. The new and better world so desperately hoped for was crippled before it had begun to walk and ominous portents were all around.

During his brief period of exile there was very little for Nikola to take solace in. As part of the post-war flotsam he was consigned to the dustbin of history with the vindictiveness that contemporary politics required and propaganda facilitated. At the least he had avoided ending his days, as he feared he might, a street beggar, but only barely. He had been forced to sell much of his remaining personal property and was reduced to asking the Crown Prince for funds. It is striking that in his Will he expressed relief at leaving his children with only small debts. In his latter years he had been accused of harbouring excessive ambition and delusions of grandeur; the reality was that his aims were no greater, and in many cases more modest, than those of his contemporaries.

After Nikola's death the royalist movement quickly collapsed under the weight of its own divisions. Milena's brief regency on behalf of her grandson, Prince Mihailo, is noteworthy as she came into conflict with Jovan Plamenac, who had resigned after the King's funeral. In September 1922 the nominal Prime Minister, Milutin Vućinić, died and Plamenac saw an opportunity to retake power and make another attempt to return to Montenegro. Milena was in San Remo taking advice on appointing a new premier when Plamenac proclaimed himself Regent, Prime and Foreign Minister. Milena refused to confirm it and stood by her choice of General Ante Gvozdenović. Plamenac responded by declaring the regency unlawful and accused Milena of negotiating with Belgrade to give up Montenegro's rights. The exiles split into two camps, both without influence or power.

Milena passed away a few months later, on March 16, 1923. Queen Elena had been informed of her mother's poor health and had spent a few days with her in *Cap d'Antibes*. She was on her way back to Italy when Milena died and returned immediately to organise the funeral. Milena was buried in San Remo alongside Nikola.

At the time Nikšić's *Slobodna Misao* reported that Milena and King Aleksandar had reached agreement for the family's return to Yugoslavia, where she would have lived at the royal court in Belgrade. Without that reconciliation Nikola and Milena's children and grandchildren became permanent exiles. They were at least given incomes from the Yugoslav state until World War Two brought the Karadjordjević era to an end.

The interwar years were too turbulent for Yugoslavia to honour King Nikola's wish that his remains be taken back to Montenegro; although, in the 1930's, Prime Minister Milan Stojadinović had met with Queen Elena in Rome and told her that, with the support of the Patriarch of Serbia, he planned to build a new church in Cetinje for the King and Queen's final resting place. The post-war Communist government led by Marshall Tito hardly had much time for the country's royal past, but it was a relatively moderate regime which claimed to have no official objections to the King's return. When Tito visited Cetinje in 1968 the local authorities were able to raise the matter. They explained their wish to bring the King's remains home and the country's new master was apparently about to give his consent but the meeting was interrupted.

Another two decades passed before the King and Queen finally returned to Montenegro. The political obstacles and delays were finally gone and, after the consent of the family was gained, Nikola and Milena were brought home. In October 1989, in the presence of representatives from the Petrović-Njegoš, Karadjordjević, Romanov and Savoy families, the Republic of Montenegro celebrated the return of the Royal Family.

Notes

Chapter I: Duklja, Zeta, Crna Gora.

1 Njegoš. The Mountain Wreath (translated by James W Wiles). George Allen & Unwin Ltd: London, 1930.
2 Ivan Crnojević's 'Charter' translated from Milutinović, Sarajlija Simeon. Istorija Crne Gore. Belgrade, 1835.
3 Denton, William. Montenegro: its people and their history. Dalby, Isbister: London, 1877.
4 Paolo Giovio: 1486-1552.
5 Vladika Petar I (1784-1830).
6 Goodwin, Jason. Lords of the Horizons: a history of the Ottoman Empire. Vintage (Random House): London, 1999.
7 Vladika Rade (1830-1851): February 19, 1843.
8 Medaković, Vojvoda Milorad G. Život i Običaj Crnogorca. Novi Sad, 1860.
9 Djilas, Milovan. Njegoš, Poet, Prince, Bishop. Translated by Michael B Petrovich. Harcourt, Brace & World Inc: New York 1966.

Chapter II: Rule of the Vladikas, 1696-1830.

1 Vladika Petar I (1784-1830). Qouted in Djilas, Milovan. Njegoš, Poet, Prince, Bishop. Translated by Michael B Petrovich. Harcourt, Brace & World Inc: New York 1966.
2 Vladika Rade (1830-1851). Quoted in Wyon, R & Prance, G. The Land of the Black Mountain. Methuen and Co: London, 1905.
3 Vladika Danilo I (1696-1735).
4 Medaković, Vojvoda Milorad G. Vladika Danilo. Belgrade, 1896.
5 Vladika Danilo I (1696-1735).
6 Milutinović, Sarajlija Simeon. Istorija Crne Gore. Belgrade, 1835.
7 Vladika Petar I (1784-1830): February 1786.
8 Vladika Petar I (1784-1830): Quoted in Wyon, R & Prance, G. The Land of the Black Mountain. Methuen and Co: London, 1905.
9 Vladika Petar I (1784-1830): Encyclicals
10 Vladika Petar I (1784-1830): October 1825.
11 Vladika Petar I (1784-1830): December 1827.

Chapter III: Vladika Rade, 1830-1851.

1 Vladika Rade (1830-1851) to Osman Pasha: October 1847.
2 Vladika Rade (1830-1851) to Jeremija Gagić: August 12, 1843.
3- 4 Medaković, Vojvoda Milorad G. P. P. Njegoš, Vladika Crnogorski. Belgrade, 1882.
5 Vladika Rade (1830-1851) to Dr P. Marinković August 10, 1850
6-7 Medaković, Vojvoda Milorad G. P. P. Njegoš, Vladika Crnogorski. Belgrade, 1882.
8 Vladika Rade (1830-1851) to Ilija Garašanin: April 12, 1844.
9 Vladika Rade (1830-1851) to Jeremija Gagić: June 3, 1838.
10 Vladika Rade (1830-1851) to Jeremija Gagić: October 4, 1840.
11 Vladika Rade (1830-1851) to Jeremija Gagić: December 30, 1844.
12 Vladika Rade (1830-1851) to Jeremija Gagić: March 26, 1846.
13 Vladika Rade (1830-1851): October 18, 1850.
14-16 Medaković, Vojvoda Milorad G. P. P. Njegoš, Vladika Crnogorski. Belgrade, 1882.
17 Vladika Rade (1830-1851) to an unknown correspondent in Trieste: November 20, 1848.
18 Vladika Rade (1830-1851) to Jeremija Gagić: March 24, 1851.
19 Popović, Vuk. Kotorska Pisma. Editor Golub Dobrašinović. Belgrade, 1964.
20 Popović, Vuk. Kotorska Pisma. Editor Golub Dobrašinović. Belgrade, 1964.
21 Medaković, Vojvoda Milorad G. P. P. Njegoš, Vladika Crnogorski. Belgrade, 1882.

Chapter IV: Prince Danilo, 1851-1860.

1 Dr Lazar Tomanović. Vladika Rade at the End of his Life. Published in Zetski Glasnik. Cetinje: May 27, 1934.
2-3 Petrović-Njegoš, Nikola I. Memoari. Cetinje, 1969. First edition 1937 (editor Dušan Vuksan).
4 Vuk Stefanović Karadžić: 1852
5 Quoted in Jovićević, Milan. The Montenegrin Royal Marriages. Narodni Muzej Crne Gore: Cetinje, 1988.
6 Popović, Vuk. Kotorska Pisma (editor Golub Dobrašinović). Belgrade, 1964.
7-9 Petrović-Njegoš, Nikola I. Memoari. Cetinje, 1969. First edition 1937: editor Dušan Vuksan.
10 Medaković, Vojvoda Milorad G. Vladika Danilo. Belgrade, 1896.
11-12 Petrović-Njegoš, Nikola I. Memoari. Cetinje, 1969. First edition 1937 (editor Dušan Vuksan).
13-15 Popović, Vuk. Kotorska Pisma (editor Golub Dobrašinović). Belgrade, 1964.

Chapter V: Nikola Mirkov, 1841-1860.

1 Petrović-Njegoš, Nikola I. Memoari. Cetinje, 1969. First edition 1937 (editor Dušan Vuksan).
2 Popović, Vojvoda Simo. Memoari. Cetinje-Podgorica, 1995.
3-22 Petrović-Njegoš, Nikola I. Memoari. Cetinje, 1969. First edition 1937 (editor Dušan Vuksan).
23 Popović, Vuk. Kotorska Pisma. (editor Golub Dobrašinović). Belgrade, 1964.
24-29 Petrović-Njegoš, Nikola I. Memoari. Cetinje, 1969. First edition 1937 (editor Dušan Vuksan).

Chapter VI: The Young Ruler, 1860-1874.

1 Petrović-Njegoš, Nikola I. Memoari. Cetinje, 1969. First edition 1937 (editor Dušan Vuksan).
2 Strangford, Viscountess. The Eastern Shores of the Adriatic in 1863: with a visit to Montenegro. Richard Bentley: London, 1864.
3-4 Petrović-Njegoš, Nikola I. Memoari. Cetinje, 1969. First edition 1937 (editor Dušan Vuksan).
5 Strangford, Viscountess. The Eastern Shores of the Adriatic in 1863: with a visit to Montenegro. Richard Bentley: London, 1864.
6 Petrović-Njegoš, Nikola I. Memoari. Cetinje, 1969. First edition 1937 (editor Dušan Vuksan).
7 Strangford, Viscountess. The Eastern Shores of the Adriatic in 1863: with a visit to Montenegro. Richard Bentley: London, 1864.
8-9 Petrović-Njegoš, Nikola I. Memoari. Cetinje, 1969. First edition 1937 (editor Dušan Vuksan).
10 Gordon, Winifred. A Woman in the Balkans. Hutchinson: London, 1916.
11 Strangford, Viscountess. The Eastern Shores of the Adriatic in 1863: with a visit to Montenegro. Richard Bentley: London, 1864.
12-14 Petrović-Njegoš, Nikola I. Memoari. Cetinje, 1969. First edition 1937 (editor Dušan Vuksan).
15 Prince Petar Karadjordjević quoted in Vuković, Vojvoda Gavro. Memoari. Cetinje, 1996.
16 Prince Nikola to Ilija Garašanin 1866. Petrović-Njegoš, Nikola I. Pisma. Cetinje 1969. First edition 1937 (editor Dušan Vuksan).
17 Prince Nikola to Prince Mihailo Obrenović January 28, 1867. Petrović-Njegoš, Nikola I. Pisma. Cetinje 1969. First edition 1937 (editor Dušan Vuksan).
18-21 Petrović-Njegoš, Nikola I. Pisma. Cetinje 1969. First edition 1937 (editor Dušan Vuksan).

Chapter VII: War and Recognition, 1875-1878.

1-2 Stillman, W.J. Herzegovina and the Late Uprising. Longmans, Green and Co: 1877.
3 Seton-Watson, R.W. Disraeli, Gladstone and the Eastern Question. London: Frank Cass and Co Ltd, 1971.
4 Stillman, W.J. Herzegovina and the Late Uprising. Longmans, Green and Co: 1877.
5-6 Petrović-Njegoš, Nikola I. Pisma. Cetinje 1969. First edition 1937 (editor Dušan Vuksan).
7 Stillman, W.J. Herzegovina and the Late Uprising. Longmans, Green and Co: 1877.
8 The Daily News: August, 1876.
9 Petrović-Njegoš, Nikola I. Memoari. Cetinje, 1969. First edition 1937 (editor Dušan Vuksan).
10-11 Petrović-Njegoš, Nikola I. Pisma. Cetinje 1969. First edition 1937 (editor Dušan Vuksan).
12 Petrović-Njegoš, Nikola I. Memoari. Cetinje, 1969. First edition 1937 (editor Dušan Vuksan).
13 Petrović-Njegoš, Nikola I. Pisma. Cetinje 1969. First edition 1937 (editor Dušan Vuksan).
14 Quoted in Mackenzie, David. The Serbs and Russian Pan-Slavism 1875-1878. Cornell University Press: New York, 1967.
15 Prince Nikola had banned headhunting during the 1876 conflicts.
16 Petrović-Njegoš, Nikola I. Pisma. Cetinje 1969. First edition 1937 (editor Dušan Vuksan).
17 Quoted in Mackenzie, David. The Serbs and Russian Pan-Slavism 1875-1878. Cornell University Press: New York, 1967.

Chapter VIII: The Patriarchal Ruler.

1 Karadjordjević, Djordje. Istina o mome životu. Belgrade, 1998.
2 Vuković, Vojvoda Gavro. Memoari. Cetinje, 1996.
3 Marie, Queen of Romania. Ordeal: the story of my life. Charles Scribners Sons: New York, 1935.
4 Mijatović, Čedo. Servia of the Servians. Isaac Pitman: London, 1911.
5 Denton, William. Montenegro: its people and their history. Dalby, Isbister: London, 1877.
6 Matavulj, Simo. Bilješke jednog pisca. Belgrade, 1939.
7 Mijatović, Čedo. The Memoirs of a Balkan Diplomatist. Cassell and Company Ltd: London, New York, Toronto and Melbourne, 1917.
8 Wyon, R and Prance, G. The Land of the Black Mountain. Methuen and Co: London, 1905.
9 Ellison, Grace. A New Country and its People. John Lane: London, 1933.
10 Anonymous. The Near East Illustrated. Doubleday Page & Co: New York, 1907.
11 Vuković, Vojvoda Gavro. Memoari. Cetinje, 1996.
12 Karadjordjević, Djordje. Istina o mome životu. Belgrade, 1998.
13-19 Jovićević, Milan. Tako je sudio gospodar. Nikšić, 1998.

20 Popović, Vojvoda Simo. Memoari. Cetinje-Podgorica, 1995.
21-23 Wyon, R & Prance, G. The Land of the Black Mountain. Methuen and Co: London, 1905.
24 Miller, William. Travels and Politics in the Near East. T. Fisher Unwin: London, 1896.
25-29 Matavulj, Simo. Bilješke jednog pisca. Belgrade, 1939.
30 Petrović-Njegoš, Nikola I. St. Petersburg Diary, 1908.
31 Petrović-Njegoš, Nikola I. Pisma. Cetinje 1969. First edition 1937 (editor Dušan Vuksan).
32 Mijatović, Čedo. The Memoirs of a Balkan Diplomatist. Cassell and Company Ltd: London, New York, Toronto and Melbourne, 1917.
33 Petrović-Njegoš, Nikola I. Memoari. Cetinje, 1969. First edition 1937 (editor Dušan Vuksan).
34 Djilas, Milovan. Njegoš, Poet, Prince, Bishop. Translated by Michael B Petrovich. Harcourt, Brace & World Inc: New York, 1966.
35-36 Vuković, Vojvoda Gavro. Memoari. Cetinje, 1996.
37 Wyon, R & Prance, G. The Land of the Black Mountain. Methuen and Co: London, 1905.

Chapter IX: Petar and Zorka.

1 Popović, Vojvoda Simo. Memoari. Cetinje-Podgorica, 1995.
2-4 Vuković, Vojvoda Gavro. Memoari. Cetinje, 1996.
5 Karadjordjević, Djordje. Istina o mome životu. Belgrade, 1998.

Chapter X: Elena and Vittorio Emanuele

1.Karadjordjević, Djordje. Istina o mome životu. Belgrade, 1998.
2.Vuković, Vojvoda Gavro. Memoari. Cetinje, 1996.
3. Marie, Queen of Romania. Ordeal: the Story of my life. Charles Scribners Sons: New York, 1935.
4 Vuković, Vojvoda Gavro. Memoari. Cetinje, 1996.
5 Queen Elena to Sophia Bisi Albini.

Chapter XI: Princess Ksenija and the Obrenović Connection.

1-5 Vuković, Vojvoda Gavro. Memoari. Cetinje, 1996.
6 Leipziger Illustr. Zeitung: July, 11, 1896.
7-9 Vuković, Vojvoda Gavro. Memoari. Cetinje, 1996.

Chapter XII: The Happy Marriage of Princess Ana and Franz Josef of Battenberg.

1 Marie, Princess of Battenberg. Reminiscenses. George Allen & Unwin Ltd: London, 1925.

Chapter XIII: The Unfulfilled Promise of the Reluctant Crown Prince.

1-3 Matavulj, Simo. Bilješke jednog pisca. Belgrade, 1939.
4 Dr Eismenger. Quoted in Dedijer, Vladimir. The Road to Sarajevo. MacGibbon & Kee Ltd: London, 1967.

Chapter XIV: Mirko and Natalija.

1 Popović, Vojvoda Simo. Memoari. Cetinje-Podgorica, 1995.
2-3 Vuković, Vojvoda Gavro. Memoari. Cetinje, 1996.
4 Petrović-Njegoš, Mihailo. Memoari. Glas Kanadskih Srba. Toronto (Ontario), 1961.

Chapter XV: Patriarchy in Decline, 1903-1909.

1 King Aleksandar Obrenović to his ministers, 1896. Quoted in Petrovich, Michael Boro. A History of Modern Serbia 1804-1918. Harcourt Brace Jovanovich: London, 1976.
2-5 Mijatović, Čedo. A Royal Tragedy: being the story of the assassination of King Alexander and Queen Draga of Servia. Everleigh Nash: London, 1906.
6 Vuković, Vojvoda Gavro. Memoari. Cetinje, 1996.
7 Durham, M. Edith. Twenty Years of Balkan Tangle. George Allen & Unwin Ltd: London, 1920.
8 The Literary Digest. New York: June 20, 1903
9 The London Standard. Quoted in The Literary Digest. New York: July 4, 1903.
10-11 Anonymous. The Near East Illustrated. Doubleday Page & Co: New York, 1907.
12 Prince Nikola to Queen Margherita of Italy March 25, 1899. Petrović-Njegoš, Nikola I. Pisma. Cetinje 1969. First edition 1937 (editor Dušan Vuksan).
13 Sloane, William M. The Balkans: A Laboratory of History. Eaton and Mains: New York, 1914.
14-15 Anonymous. The Near East From Within. Cassell: London, 1915.
16-21 Popović, Vojvoda Simo. Memoari. Cetinje-Podgorica, 1995.
22 Anonymous. The Near East From Within. Cassell: London, 1915.

Chapter XVI: The Zenith of Royal Montenegro.

1 Durham, M. Edith. The Struggle for Scutari. Edward Arnold: London, 1914.
2 Prince Nikola to King Ferdinand of Bulgaria, September 7, 1896. Petrović-Njegoš, Nikola I. Pisma. Cetinje 1969. First edition 1937 (editor Dušan Vuksan).
3-4 Quoted in Treadway, John D. The Falcon and the Eagle: Montenegro and Austria-Hungary 1908-1914. Purdue University Press: West Lafayette, Indiana, 1998.
5-7 Durham, M. Edith. The Struggle for Scutari. Edward Arnold: London, 1914.
8 The Morning Post: July, 1911.
9-10 Durham, M. Edith. The Struggle for Scutari. Edward Arnold: London, 1914.
11 Seton-Watson, R.W. The Balkans, Italy and the Adriatic. Nisbet & Co Ltd: London, 1916.
12-14 Durham, M. Edith. The Struggle for Scutari. Edward Arnold: London, 1914.
15 Rankin, Reginald. The Inner History of the Balkan War. John Lane the Bodley Head Ltd: London, 1914.
16 John Prioleau in the Daily Mail: October 29, 1912. Quoted in Rankin, Reginald. The Inner History of the Balkan War. John Lane the Bodley Head Ltd: London, 1914.
17 Berri, Gino. L'Assedio di Scutari: sei mesi dentro la città accerchiata. Fratelli Treves: Milan, 1913.
18 Rankin, Reginald. The Inner History of the Balkan War. John Lane the Bodley Head Ltd: London, 1914.
19 Durham, M. Edith. The Struggle for Scutari. Edward Arnold: London, 1914.
20 The Daily Telegraph: November 26, 1912.
21 Leon Trotsky in Kievskaya Mysl: December 21, 1912. Quoted in Trotsky, Leon. The War Correspondence of Leon Trotsky (translated by Brina Pearce). Monad Press: New York, 1980.
22 Durham, M. Edith. The Struggle for Scutari. Edward Arnold: London, 1914.
23 The Daily Telegraph: January 9, 1913.
24 The Danish origins of the Greek Royal Family were a source of some resentment amongst their subjects.
25 The London Times. Quoted in Rankin, Reginald. The Inner History of the Balkan War. John Lane the Bodley Head Ltd: London, 1914.
26-28 Durham, M. Edith. The Struggle for Scutari. Edward Arnold: London, 1914.
29 M Popović. Quoted in Rankin, Reginald. The Inner History of the Balkan War. John Lane the Bodley Head Ltd: London, 1914.
30-31 Quoted in Rankin, Reginald. The Inner History of the Balkan War. John Lane the Bodley Head Ltd: London, 1914.
32 King Nikola to Count John De Salis: May 4, 1913.
33 King Nikola quoted in Neues Wiener Tagblatt.
34 Durham, M. Edith. The Struggle for Scutari. Edward Arnold: London, 1914.

Chapter XVII: Opening the Floodgates of History.

1 Wyon, R & Prance, G. The Land of the Black Mountain. Methuen and Co: London, 1905.
2 Jovanović, Ilija Bjeloš. Na dvoru kralja Nikole. Cetinje, 1988.
3 Quoted in Treadway, John D. The Falcon and the Eagle: Montenegro and Austria-Hungary 1908-1914. Purdue University Press: West Lafayette (Indiana), 1998.
4 Jones, Fortier. With Serbia into Exile: an American's adventures with the army that cannot die. Andrew Melrose: London, 1916.
5-8 Jovanović, Ilija Bjeloš. Na dvoru kralja Nikole. Cetinje, 1988.

Chapter XVIII: The Final Struggle.

1-3 Devine, Alex. The Mystery of Montenegro. Richard Clay & Sons Ltd: London, 1920.
4 Bonsal, Stephen. Suitors and Supplicants: the little nations at Versailles. Reissued by Kennikat Press: New York, 1969.
5-9 Hajduković, Niko. Memoari. Podgorica, 2000.
10 Vossiche Zeitung: February 2, 1916. Quoted in Devine, Alex. The Mystery of Montenegro. Richard Clay & Sons Ltd: London, 1920.
11 Hajduković, Niko. Memoari. Podgorica, 2000.
12 Radović, A, Bošković R & Vukotić, I. The Question of Montenegro. Paris, 1919.
13-14 Hajduković, Niko. Memoari. Podgorica, 2000.
15 Bonsal, Stephen. Suitors and Supplicants: the little nations at Versailles. Reissued by Kennikat Press: New York, 1969.
16 Hajduković, Niko. Memoari. Podgorica, 2000.
17 Bonsal, Stephen. Suitors and Supplicants: the Little Nations at Versailles. Reissued by Kennikat Press: New York, 1969.

Chapter XIX: The End of an Epoch.

1-3 Jovanović-Bjeloš, Ilija. Na dvoru kralja Nikole. Cetinje, 1988.
4 Lord Gladstone: March 11, 1920. Quoted in Some Pages from the Bloody Album of the Karageorgevitch. Typography of the State of Montenegro: Rome, 1920.
5 Jovanović-Bjeloš, Ilija. Na dvoru kralja Nikole. Cetinje, 1988.
6 Leipziger Illustr. Zeitung: July, 11, 1896.

Select Bibliography

Anonymous. The Near East From Within. Cassell: London, 1915.

Anonymous. The Near East Illustrated. Doubleday Page & Co: New York, 1907. Also published as An Observer in the Near East. Le Queux, William. E. Nash: London, 1907.

Backović, Marko. Montenegro at the End of the Nineteenth Century. Belgrade, 1895.

Bakić, Mitar. Montenegro. Belgrade.

Barneschi, Renato. Frau von Weber: vita e morte di Mafalda di Savoia a Buchenwald. Rusconi libri: Milan, 1982

Berri, Gino. L'Assedio di Scutari: sei mesi dentro la cittá accerchiata. Fratelli Treves: Milan, 1913.

Boehm, Christopher. Blood Revenge. University Press of Kansas: Kansas, 1984.

Boehm, Christopher. Montenegrin Social Organisation and Values. AMS Press: New York, 1983.

Bokhanov, A. The Romanovs: love, power & tragedy. Leppi Publications, 1993.

Bonsal, Stephen. Suitors and Supplicants: the little nations at Versailles. Reissued by Kennikat Press: New York, 1969.

Brajović, Toman. Crna Gora u delima likovnih umetnika drugih krajeva i naroc. Cetinje: 1967.

Brockett, Dr. L.P. Porter & C. Bliss. The Conquest of Turkey: or the decline and fall of the Ottoman Empire 1877-78. Hubbard Bros: Philadelphia, 1878.

Cesarini, Paolo. Elena: la moglie del re. La Voce: Firenze, 1953.

Criscuolo, Luigi. Montenegro's Betrayal. Reprinted from The Forum. New York, 1922.

Cvijić, Jovan. Studies in Jugoslav Psychology. London, 1930.

Cvijić, Jovan. The Zones of Civilization of the Balkan Peninsula. Geographical Review: New York, 1918.

Dedijer, Vladimir. The Road to Sarajevo. MacGibbon & Kee Ltd: London, 1967.

Denton, William. Montenegro: its People and their history. Dalby, Isbister: London, 1877.

Devine, Alex. The Mystery of Montenegro. Richard Clay & Sons Ltd: London, 1920.

Devine, Alex. Montenegro in History Politics and War. T. Fisher Unwin Ltd: London, 1918.

Djilas, Milovan. Land Without Justice: an autobiography of his youth. Methuen: London, 1958.

Djilas, Milovan. Njegoš: Poet, Prince, Bishop (translated by Michael B Petrovich). Harcourt, Brace & World Inc: New York, 1966.

Djonović, Svetozar. Crnogirci - Srpsko Pleme. Belgrade, 1999.

Drašković, Aleksandar. Mojkovačka bitka. Podgorica, 1989.

Dujovič, Jovan. Sukob Knjaza Nikole sa crnogorskim vojskovodama. Belgrade, 1987.

Durham, M. Edith. The Burden of the Balkans. Thomas Nelson & Sons: London, 1905.

Durham, M. Edith. The Struggle for Scutari. Edward Arnold: London, 1914.

Durham, M. Edith. Twenty Years of Balkan Tangle. George Allen & Unwin Ltd: London, 1920.

Dvorsky, Viktor. Černohorskoturecka Hranice od usti Bojany k Tare. Prague, 1909.

Ellison, Grace. A New Country and its People. John Lane: London, 1933.

Glas Naroda (The Voice of the People). Ex-King Nicholas of Montenegro and His Court: the epilogue to an unworthy reign. Sarajevo, 1919.

Glasnik skopskog naučnog društva. Njegoš u Dubrovniku 1833. Skopje, 1940.

Goodwin, Jason. Lords of the Horizons: a history of the Ottoman Empire. Vintage (Random House): London, 1999.

Gordon, Winifred. A Woman in the Balkans. Hutchinson: London, 1916.

Helmreich, Ernest Christian. Diplomacy of the Balkan Wars 1912-1913. Harvard Historical Studies (Russell and Russell): New York, 1969.

Hajduković, Niko. Memoari. Podgorica, 2000.

Jones, Fortier. With Serbia into Exile: an American's adventures with the army that cannot die. Andrew Melrose: London, 1916.

Jovanovič-Bjeloš, Ilija. Na dvoru kralja Nikole. Cetinje, 1988.

Jovičević, Milan. Tako je sudio gospodar. Nikšić, 1998.

Jovičević, Milan. The Montenegrin Royal Marriages. Narodni Muzej Crne Gore: Cetinje, 1988.

Jovičević, Milan. The Court of King Nikola. Narodni Muzej Crne Gore: Cetinje, 1999.

Jovičić, Lena A. The Biography of a Servian Diplomat. The Epworth Press: London, 1939.

Kapičić, Andje. Umjetnička zb`irka Državnog muzeja na Cetinje. Cetinje, 1999.

Kapičić-Dragičević, Andje. Kralj Nikola u djelima likovnih umjetnika. Cetinje-Belgrade, 1991.

Kapidžić, Hamdija. Omer Paša Latas u Bosni. Sarajevo, 1938.

Karadjordjević, Djordje. Istina o mome životu. Belgrade, 1998.

Karadžić, Vuk Stefanović. Izabrani istorijski spisi. Belgrade, 1956.

Katz, Robert. The Fall of the House of Savoy. George Allen & Unwin Ltd: London, 1972.

Kennedy, R.J. Cettinje to Windsor: being an account of the visit of the Prince of Montenegro to Her Majesty the Queen: May, 1898.

Knodt. Ernst Ludwig: Grossherzog von Hessen und bei Rhein. Darmstadt, 1978.

Koch, A. Prince Alexander of Battenberg. Whitaker & Co: London, 1887.

Le rôle de la France dans l'annexion forcée du Montenegro: documents officiels publiés par le Ministère des affaires étrangères du Montenegro. A Manuce: Rome, 1921.

Lederer, Ivo J. Yugoslavia at the Paris Peace Conference: a study in frontier making. Yale University Press: London, 1963.

The Literary Digest. New York: June 20, 1903.

Ljušić, Radoš. Ljubavi srpskih vladara i političara. Niš, 2000.

Ljušić, Radoš. Karadjordjevići. Belgrade, 2001.

Ljušić, Radoš. The Obrenovićs and their Genealogy. Gornji Milanovac, 1998.

Ljušić, Radoš and Veselinović, Andrija. Rodoslovi srpskih dinastija. Belgrade, 2002.

Lumbroso, Alberto. Elena di Montenegro, Regina di Italia. 1934.

Mackenzie, David. The Serbs and Russian Pan-Slavism 1875-1878. Cornell University Press: New York, 1967.

Marcotti, Giuseppe. Il Montenegrin e le sue donne. Milan, 1896.

Marge, Pierre. Voyage en Dalmatie, Bosnie-Herzegovine et Montenegro. Paris, 1912.

Maria Gabriella di Savoia. Casa Savoia: diario di una monarchia. Arnoldo Mondadori Editore: Milano, 1996.

Marie, Princess of Battenberg. Reminiscenses. George Allen & Unwin Ltd: London, 1925.

Marie, Queen of Romania. Ordeal: the story of my life. Charles Scribners Sons: New York, 1935.

Markus, Jovan. Povratak Kralja Nikola I u otadjbina. Cetinje, 2001.

Marmier, X. Lettres sur l'Adriatique et le Montenegro. Paris, 1854.

Martinović, Dušan i Uroš. Cetinje Spomenici arhitekture. Obod.

Martinović, Savo Matov. Memoari. Podgorica, 1996.

Matavulj, Simo. Bilješke jednog pisca. Belgrade, 1939.

Medaković, Vojvoda Milorad G. Cetinje, Crnogorska prestonica. Novi Sad, 1894.

Medaković, Vojvoda Milorad G. P. P. Njegoš, Vladika Crnogorski. Belgrade, 1882.

Medaković, Vojvoda Milorad G. Povjesnica Crne Gore od najstarijeg vremena do 1830. Zemun, 1850.

Medaković, Vojvoda Milorad G. Život i Običaj Crnogorca. Novi Sad, 1860.

Medaković, Vojvoda Milorad G. Vladika Danilo. Beograd, 1896.

Mijatović, Čedo. A Royal Tragedy: being the story of the assassination of King Alexander and Queen Draga of Servia. Everleigh Nash: London, 1906.

Mijatović, Čedo. Servia of the Servians. Isaac Pitman: London, 1911.

Mijatović, Čedo. The Memoirs of a Balkan Diplomatist. Cassell and Company Ltd: London, New York, Toronto and Melbourne, 1917.

Milaković, Dimitrije. Istorija Crne Gore. Pančevo.

Miller, William. Travels and Politics in the Near East. T. Fisher Unwin: London, 1896.

Milutinović, Sarajlija Simeon. Istorija Crne Gore. Belgrade, 1835.

Moka. Il Re in un angolo, colloqui a Cascais. Rizzoli: Milano, 1950.

Montenegro: Handbooks prepared under the direction of the historical section of the Foreign Office. H.M. Stationery Office: London, 1920.

Njegoš. The Mountain Wreath (translated by James W Wiles). George Allen & Unwin Ltd: London, 1930.

Osio, Mario Bondioli. La giovinezza di Vittorio Emanuele III. Simonelli Editore: Milano, 1998.

Palairet, Michael. The Balkan Economies c1800-1914. Cambridge University Press: 1997.

Pavlowitch, Stevan K. A History of the Balkans 1804-1945. Addison Wesley Longman: New York, 1999.

Perazić, Prof, Dr. Gavro i Mr. Radoslav Raspopović. Medjunarodni ugovori Crne Gore 1878-1918. Podgorica, 1992.

Petrović-Njegoš, Mihailo. Memoari. Glas Kanadskih Srba: Toronto (Ontario), 1961.

Petrović-Njegoš, Nikola I. Autobiografija, Cetinje 1969. First edition 1937 (editor Dušan Vuksan).

Petrović-Njegoš, Nikola I. Govori. Cetinje, 1969. First edition 1937 (editor Dušan Vuksan).

Petrović-Njegoš, Nikola I. Memoari. Cetinje, 1969. First edition 1937 (editor Dušan Vuksan).

Petrović-Njegoš, Nikola I. Pisma. Cetinje 1969. First edition 1937 (editor Dušan Vuksan).

Petrović-Njegoš, Nikola I. Putopisi. Cetinje, 1969. First edition 1937 (editor Dušan Vuksan).

Petrović-Njegoš, Vladika Petar I. Kratka istorija Crne Gore.

Petrović-Njegoš, Vladika Vasilije. Istorija o Crnoj Gori. Moscow, 1754.

Petrovich, Michael Boro. A History of Modern Serbia 1804-1918. Harcourt Brace Jovanovich: London, 1976.

Poincaré, Raymond. The Memoirs of Raymond Poincaré (translated by Sir George Arthur). William Heinemann Ltd: London, 1929.

Popović, Djordje. Istorija Crne Gore. Belgrade, 1896.

Popović, Vojvoda Simo. Memoari. Cetinje-Podgorica, 1995.

Popović, Vuk. Kotorska Pisma (editor Golub Dobrašinović). Belgrade, 1964.

Prpic, George. South Slavic Immigration in America. Twayne Publishers: Boston, 1978.

Radović, A, Bošković R & Vukotić, I. The Question of Montenegro. Paris, 1919.

Rajković, Nikola. Isprave crnogorskih sudova. Podgorica, 1998.

Rankin, Reginald. The Inner History of the Balkan War. John Lane the Bodley Head Ltd: London, 1914.

Romanoff, Dimitri (Prince). The Orders, Medals and History of Montenegro. Balkan Heritage: Denmark, 1988.

Ruvarac, Ilarion. Montenegrina, Prilošci istoriji Crne Gore. Zemun, 1899.

Šćepanović, Milovan-Mušo. Organizacija i rad sudova u Crnoj Gori do 1918. Podgorica, 1999.

Sementery, Michel. La descendance de Nicolas I, Roi du Montenegro. Editions Christian: Paris, 1982.

Seton-Watson, R. W. The Southern Slav Question and the Hapsburg Monarchy. Constable: London, 1911.

Seton-Watson, R.W. The Balkans, Italy and the Adriatic. Nisbet & Co Ltd: London, 1916.

Seton-Watson, R.W. Disraeli, Gladstone and the Eastern Question. London: Frank Cass and Co Ltd, 1971.

Sforza, Count Carlo. Fifty Years of War and Diplomacy in the Balkans. Columbia University Press: New York, 1940.

Siccardi, Cristina. Elena: la regina mai dimenticata. Paoline Editoriale Libri: 1996.

Simonović, Budo. Zeko Mali. Belgrade, 2000.

Sloane, William M. The Balkans: a laboratory of history. Eaton and Mains: New York, 1914.

Some Pages from the Bloody Album of the Karageorgevitch. Typography of the State of Montenegro: Rome, 1920.

Spinosa, Antonio. Vittorio Emanuele III: l'astuzia di un re. Arnoldo Mondadori: Milano, 1990.

Stillman, W.J. Herzegovina and the Late Uprising. Longmans, Green and Co: 1877.

Strangford, Viscountess Emily. The Eastern Shores of the Adriatic in 1863: with a visit to Montenegro. Richard Bentley: London, 1864.

Taylor, Edmond. The Fall of the Dynasties. Doubleday & Company Inc: New York, 1963.

Tomanović, Lazar. Vladika Rade at the End of his Life. Published in Zetski Glasnik. Cetinje: May 27, 1934.

Tomović, Slobodan. Crnogorske vojvode Marko Miljanov i Miljan Vukov. Cetinje, 1979.

Tošković, Janko. Memoari, Bilješka ka iz ustavne vladavine Kralja Nikole i njenog tragičnog svršetka od 1905-1918. Cetinje, 1974.

Treadway, John D. The Falcon and the Eagle: Montenegro and Austria-Hungary 1908-1914. Purdue University Press: West Lafayette, Indiana, 1998.

Trotsky, Leon. The War Correspondence of Leon Trotsky (translated by Brina Pearce). Monad Press: New York, 1980.

Vojinović, Dragoljub. Italija i Crna Gora 1914-1925: Studija o izneverenom savezništvu. Belgrade, 1998.

Vuković, Vojvoda Gavro. Memoari. Cetinje, 1996.

Vuksan, Dušan. Petar I Petrović-Njegoš i njegovo doba.

Vuksan, Dušan. Zapisi, Glasnik cetinjeskog istorijskog društva. 1936.

Warren, Whitney. Montenegro: the crime of the Peace Conference. Brentanos: New York, 1922. Reprinted Podgorica, 2000.

Wheatcroft, Andrew. The Ottomans: dissolving images. Penguin Books: London, 1995.

Wyon, R & Prance, G. The Land of the Black Mountain. Methuen and Co: London, 1905.

Živković, Miloš. Pad Crne Gore. Podgorica, 2000.

Index